The Germanic Invasions

The Germanic Invasions

The Making of Europe AD 400-600

Lucien Musset

Professor of Medieval History
University of Caen

Translated by Edward and Columba James

THE PENNSYLVANIA STATE UNIVERSITY PRESS
University Park, Pennsylvania

Published in the United States of America by
The Pennsylvania State University Press

ISBN 0 271 01198X
LC 75 14261

Printed in Great Britain by Bell and Bain Ltd., Glasgow

Contents

Part Two: Unsolved Problems and Subjects for Further Research

Part Three: Sources and Studies

Maps

Preface

The aim of this account is to give an understanding of the Germanic invasions of western Europe in the fourth, fifth and sixth centuries. I have limited myself to very brief incursions into institutional and political problems, and economic and social questions; literary and artistic matters have also received but scant attention. Whereas in Parts One and Three I have tried not to omit anything of importance, Part Two is the result of a long process of selection, which has on occasion been fairly subjective. I have deliberately tried to deal with a wide variety of problems, in the hope of throwing as much light as possible on the barbarian world. I have emphasized the geographical, linguistic and social aspects of the invasions rather than the problems of source criticism, of chronology or of political interpretation. The formation of a general historical perspective must take precedence over the technical preoccupations appropriate to the work of a medievalist. Finally, although the author of such a work as this is much more the mouth-piece of a whole generation of historians than the advocate of his own theories, I shall not resist the temptation to give a personal opinion from time to time, without always having space to defend it or to base it on a scholarly argument.

As my subject is the study of a continuous uninterrupted process, I have not been able to confine it within precise chronological limits. I have taken up the history of each invading people a little before the moment that it starts on its migration and I have abandoned it as soon as the people settles down, or disappears. Hence my intrusion at the beginning of the period prior to the fatal date of 176, which traditionally marks the limit of competence of the western medievalist. I must beg the indulgence of my readers for this temerity.

LUCIEN MUSSET

A*

CHRONOLOGICAL TABLE

Dates	The Empire		Western Germans	Goths	Steppe peoples and Slavs
	In the East	In the West			
350				341: Ulfila, Bishop of the Goths	
			358: the Salians in Toxandria		
375	364–78: Valens	364–75: Valentinian		375: the Huns destroy the Gothic kingdom of Ermanaric	
		375–92: Valentinian II		376: the Goths enter the Empire	
				378: Battle of Adrianople	
	379–95: Theodosius	392–5: Theodosius		397: the Goths in Illyricum	
	395–408: Arcadius	395–423: Honorius			
400	408–50: Theodosius II		406: the invasion over the Rhine Radagaisus in Italy	410: Alaric at Rome	409: the Alans in Spain
			409: the Vandals in Spain	413: the Visigoths in Aquitaine	
				418: foundation of the kingdom of Toulouse	
425		423–55: Valentinian III	429: the Vandals in Africa		434: Attila, King of the Huns
			436: the destruction of the Burgundian kingdom of the Rhine		
			436: Genseric at Carthage		

x

Year	Eastern emperors	Western emperors	Kingdoms and events	Ostrogoths and Visigoths	Huns
450	450–7: Marcian		443: foundation of the Burgundian kingdom of Geneva		451: Battle of the Catalaunian fields
			449: 'Hengist and Horsa' in Britain		452: Attila in Italy
					453: death of Attila
					454: end of the Hunnic Empire
		455–6: Avitus	455: sack of Rome by Genseric	466–84: reign of Euric	
	457–74: Leo	457–61: Majorian			
		467–72: Anthemius	c.472: the Burgundians at Lyons	473: Theodoric, King of the Ostrogoths	
			476: Odoacer master of Italy	c.470–80: the lawcode of Euric	
475	474–91: Zeno	476: the deposition of Romulus Augustulus			
			c.480–516: Gundobad, King of the Burgundians	484–507: Alaric II, King of the Visigoths	
			481: Clovis comes to power	488: the Ostrogoths leave for Italy	
			486: defeat of Syagrius	493: Theodoric takes Ravenna	
	491–518: Anastasius		c.495: foundation of Wessex		
500			c.501–515: the lawcode of Gundobad	506: the *Breviarium Alarici*	
			c.507–511: the first drawing-up of the *Lex Salica*	507: the defeat of Alaric II at Vouillé	
			511: Death of Clovis		
	518–27: Justin			524: the execution of Boethius	

CHRONOLOGICAL TABLE (Continued)

Dates	Eastern Empire	Western Germans	Goths	Steppe peoples and Slavs
525	527–65: Justinian		526: the death of Theodoric	
		c.530: Frankish protectorate over Thuringia	531: disappearance of the traditional royal dynasty of the Visigoths	
		533–4: the Byzantine reconquest of North Africa		
		534: the conquest of the Burgundian kingdom by the Franks	536: the beginning of the Byzantine reconquest of Italy	
550		c.536: Frankish protectorate over Alamannia	552: the death of Teia, the last Ostrogothic king	
			554: the capital of the Visigothic kingdom fixed at Toledo	
		c.555: Frankish protectorate over Bavaria	561: last rising of the Ostrogoths	
	565–78: Justin II	568: the Lombards enter Italy	568–86: Leovigild, King of the Visigoths	570: the Avars enter Pannonia
575		572: the Lombards take Pavia		
		574–84: interregnum among the Lombards	585: the Suevian kingdom annexed by the Visigoths	582: the Avars take Sirmium
			587: the conversion of the Visigoths to Catholicism under King Reccared	
600		590–616: Agilulf, King of the Lombards		
		597: the beginning of the conversion of England		c.602: the Slavs before Salona

	607: the Lombard King Agilulf converted to Catholicism	612–621: Sisebut, King of the Visigoths	617: the Slavs before Constantinople
			c.625: Samo, King of the Slavs in Bohemia
625	c.626: the Lombard capital fixed at Pavia		626: the Avars before Constantinople
	628–52: Rothari, King of the Lombards	636: death of Isidore of Seville	
	c.640: the Lombards take Genoa		
	643: the Edict of Rothari		
650		654: King Recceswinth promulgates the *Liber Judiciorum*	
	c.662: the last Arian reaction among the Lombards (Grimoald)		
	671: the final abandonment of Arianism	672: the first known royal anointing (Wamba)	
675			c.680: the Bulgars south of the Danube
700		711: the Muslims enter Spain; end of the Visigothic kingdom	705: the Bulgar Khan Tervel recognized as Caesar

Part One
The Facts

Introduction : The Age of Invasions

Stability of population in western and southern Europe, which we take so much for granted, is a relatively recent phenomenon and indeed one which eastern Europe has not yet achieved. According to the traditional view, the period of the 'great invasions' is a time of turmoil sandwiched between two eras of stability and normality: that of the Roman Empire and our own. It would be wiser to adopt the opposite attitude and consider the Roman period the exception, a temporary lull in a whirlwind of invasions.

It is not, however, wrong to isolate the invasions that came after the disruption of Roman unity. There is a considerable difference between the last invasions of proto-history and those which we are about to study. The migrations which preceded the Roman conquest started from central Europe and radiated in all directions; there was at least one movement from west to east. The Celts migrated towards the west to Gaul and Britain, towards the south to Italy, where they took Rome in 391 BC, towards the south-east to Greece, where they took Delphi in 278, and towards Asia, where the Celtic Galatians settled around 275 to 270 BC. From the middle of the third century BC and more particularly from the second century BC onwards, the great migrations moved from east to west or from north-east to south west. The Roman conquest, followed by the construction of the *limes* along the Rhine and the Danube, for a time interrupted the progress of migrations in this direction, but they form a point of departure for our investigation and mark the beginning of a period of crisis whose end is very difficult to date.

Looking at events on a European scale one cannot stop at the period when the power of the Franks had become accepted in Gaul. There was still another extremely important wave of invasions to come towards the end of the sixth century, marked by the Lombard invasion of Italy, the arrival of the Avars in the Pannonian basin and the Slav advance across the Danube. One can hardly ignore the effects of the Muslim conquests of the seventh and eighth centuries in Africa and later in Spain and Gaul, nor the various piratical enterprises which prolonged the crisis to beyond the eleventh century in the Mediterranean world; and once the Muslim expansion had got under way two other movements followed almost immediately, that of the Vikings, which really started about 790 and continued without any evident

3

interruption until at least 1066, and that of the Hungarians, which covered roughly the period from 875 to 955. It would even be possible to consider the Mongol invasion of the thirteenth century, which reached Russia in 1237 and Hungary in 1241, as the last wave of the great invasions. But this volume will only be concerned with the earliest invasions, which set up Germanic kingdoms within the former Roman Empire.

This turmoil, which lasted for seven or eight centuries, carried along with it many extremely varied peoples. The interactions between them are so complex that it is rarely possible to say who was responsible for initiating each movement. The fourth- to fifth-century wave primarily involved the Germans, but a Turkish people (the Huns) played a decisive role in setting it in motion, and an Iranian people (the Alans) and a Celtic one (the Irish) were equally involved. The sixth century wave pushed westwards a Germanic people (the Lombards), Asians (the Avars) and a mass of Slavs. The wave of invasions in the ninth century involved Scandinavians, Arabs, Berbers, Finno-Ugrians and Turks, although admittedly usually in different areas. This study has therefore had to follow the general chronological sequence rather than the history of each ethnic group.

A movement so prolonged and so composite must have had complex causes. Certain common factors can be distinguished in each great wave. The weakness of the Later Roman Empire in the fifth century, the incomplete nature of Justinian's reconquest at the end of the sixth century, and the decadence of the Carolingian Empire at the end of the ninth century are the most obvious ones. But one cannot really be satisfied with an explanation of the invasions which only takes account of conditions among the invaded, and not among the invaders themselves. Moreover it is impossible, even with a people as self-contained as the Huns, to attribute their migration to a single cause. The Huns may have been forced to go westwards by Chinese policies in the Far East, or attracted by the greater wealth of the western steppes— the 'black land'—or impelled by the threat of other mounted nomads advancing to their rear, or simply motivated by the lure of plunder; more probably it was a combination of all of these factors. We have thought it wiser to reject from the start all global explanations, like the simplistic one so dear to the scholars of the Middle Ages who attributed everything to polygamy (mistakenly considered to be a cause of demographic expansion) and a hatred of Christianity, or the more modern theories that all the migrations were caused by climatic variations, or resulted from the relations between the Chinese world and its neighbours.

It is very difficult to assemble sufficient trustworthy information about any invasion. General disruption does not encourage the compilation of historical information; troubled times frequently lead to the destruction of documents; disasters are overestimated and the vanquished have a natural tendency to explain the success of an enemy by its irresistible superiority of numbers; in a situation of panic the most extraordinary stories, especially rumours of treason, are readily believed. Moreover during the early Middle Ages, immediately after the adoption of Christianity, the most profound thinkers were inclined to see historical events as merely a comparatively unimportant reflection of the mysterious plans of God, which alone deserved attention. Then again, as they had inherited from the classical world a complete indifference to concepts which we take for granted—such as the language or the exact 'nationality' of the barbarians—one can appreciate that the information transmitted by classical historians is often misleading. Finally we must remember that all our texts after the fifth century come from ecclesiastical sources. Consciously or unconsciously all facts were seen through the eyes of the Church and the clerics: thus the Arian barbarians were systematically disparaged while the Catholic Franks were loudly praised.

It would be well to bear in mind these narrow and often frustrating limitations to our knowledge. Resorting to ancillary disciplines, even on a large scale, very rarely allows one to compensate for them. To many questions, therefore, there can be no definite answer.

1 The Whirlwind of Invasions

THE BARBARIANS

The Germanic World

Towards the beginning of the Augustan era the Romans became aware of the size and relative unity of the Germanic world for the first time, and needed a term with which to define it. The word *Germani* was probably introduced into literary language by the Greek historian Poseidonios in the first century BC, and was certainly popularized by the *Commentaries* of Caesar. At first this name seems to have been applied to the largely Celticized tribes on the left bank of the Rhine, the *Germani Cisrhenani*. The word might legitimately be supposed, therefore, to be of Celtic origin, like *Cenomani* or *Paemani*. A hypothesis currently entertained is that the word is an Illyrian term, which is a convenient theory, in view of our total ignorance of this language.[1] At any rate the Germans never applied any generic name to themselves; it was only those who stayed on the continent after the Anglo-Saxon migration that invented, possibly in the eighth century, the rather uninformative name of *Deutsche*, literally 'men of the people', which was used at first mainly to underline the difference between Germanic and Romance elements within the Carolingian Empire. The Scandinavians had no generic name except those later invented by scholars: *Nordboer* and *Skandinaver*.

Classical Antiquity first discovered the Germanic world by sea, as we know from the account of Pytheas of Marseilles of the fourth century BC.[2] Then came scattered contacts with the forerunners of the first migrations: Bastarnae and Skirians on the Black Sea at the end of the third century BC, and Cimbri and Teutones in Noricum, Gaul, Spain and Italy between 113 and 101 BC. But it was the campaigns of Caesar and Augustus that made possible the first comprehensive view of the Germanic world. After a century of wars and commercial contacts the Romans had reached the stage of attempting syntheses: we have those of the geographer Strabo, writing about AD 18, of Pliny the Elder before AD 79, of Tacitus in his unfortunately over-literary *Germania* of AD 98, and finally of Ptolemy, writing about AD 150.

The Latin authors proposed several different systems of classification for the Germans. Pliny's was topographical, and distinguished five groups: Vandals (comprising Burgundians, Varini, Charini and Gutones), Ingvaeones (comprising Cimbri, Teutones and Chauci), Isthaeones (a single people with a mangled name, probably the Sicambri), Herminones (comprising Suebi, Hermunduri, Chatti and Cherusci), and finally Peucini or Bastarnae. Tacitus's system takes the form of the mythical genealogy so dear to ancient historiography. He has the Germans springing from a common ancestor, *Mannus* (man), and his three sons, progenitors of the Ingvaeones near the ocean, the Herminones and the Istaevones. But since the only true Germanic unity is linguistic in nature, it is to the linguists that we must turn for the basis of a rational classification of present-day or vanished Germanic peoples.

Since the birth of comparative philology at the beginning of the nineteenth century, the prevailing classification has had three categories:

North Germanic dialects: Old Norse and modern languages derived from it

East Germanic dialects: Gothic, and probably Burgundian, Vandal, Rugian, Bastarnean etc., all extinct

West Germanic dialects: The other dialects, including those of the Franks, Alamans, Bavarians, Lombards, Angles, Saxons, and Frisians, and also modern German, Dutch and English

Provided it is remembered that this scheme has only a relative value, which is more geographical than historical or genealogical, it can still be used to locate approximately the different peoples that took part in the invasions. But linguists today tend to distrust it, preferring to emphasize the relative similarity between North Germanic and Gothic, and the links between North Germanic and the dialects of the interior of *Germania*. The leading exponent of this modified view, E. Schwarz,[3] proposes for the period of the invasions a new classification, also under three headings: at the two opposite poles he has Continental Germanic (the dialects of the Franks, Alamans, Bavarians, Lombards and others) and Gotho-Scandinavian (the North Germanic and East Germanic dialects of the traditional classification); in between he sets a North Sea Germanic (*Nordseegermanisch*), the foundation of Anglo-Saxon and Frisian, and, more tentatively, an Elbe Germanic (*Elbgermanisch*).

Historians and linguists usually turn to the archaeologists when attempting to identify the original homeland of the Germans—the most hazardous task of all, for it is unrealistic to believe that a proto-historic people can be assigned to any particular linguistic group on the basis of archaeological material alone. However, the primitive

Germanic culture can easily be identified with a Late Bronze Age civilization which sprang from a centre in southern Scandinavia (where the linguists have never been able to find a pre-Germanic substratum) and began to spread over the coastal region between the Oder and the Weser. We can follow the expansion of this civilization across the great European plain: by about 1000 BC it stretched from the Ems to central Pomerania; by about 800 it had reached Westphalia in the west and the Vistula in the east; by about 500 it had reached the lower Rhine, Thuringia and lower Silesia.

All this must be treated with caution, but it is certain that from the fifth to the second century BC, during the La Tène period, the Germanic advance southwards was slowed down by the Celtic expansion. The Celts, who had been masters of central Europe for some time, enjoyed such prestige that their institutions were imitated by Germans as far away as Scandinavia. This Celtic obstacle disintegrated during the course of the last few centuries BC, probably because the Celts had spread too fast and too far to occupy the territory to any great depth. The first Germans to come in contact with Mediterranean peoples were the Bastarnae in the east, followed by the Cimbri and the Teutones in the west, and lastly by those peoples in the region in between. The Roman conquest soon set limits to their expansion, at first in the west with the conquest of Gaul between 58 and 51 BC, and then to the south with the organization of the provinces of Raetia and Noricum in the year 16–15 BC; it was only in the east that the Germans were able to continue expanding for some time, across the ill-defined territories between the Baltic and the Black Sea.

From the third century BC onwards, and perhaps even earlier, the Germanic world was continually affected by migratory impulses, desultory at first, but gathering momentum as time went on. Contemporary historians were aware of this, as witness the concise formula of the Goth Jordanes: *Scandza insula, quasi officina gentium aut certe velut vagina nationum* (the island of Scandza, which was like a hive of peoples, or indeed like a womb of nations. *Getica*, IV, 25). As always in such a situation, it is impossible to attribute the phenomenon to simple causes. The climate probably deteriorated towards the middle of the first millennium BC in Scandinavia and the Baltic regions, but this does not seem to have been serious enough to make migration necessary. There is no indication of overpopulation; on the contrary, the last few centuries BC in Denmark are among the poorest in archaeological finds. It is possible that there are sociological explanations (we know that the Germans had the custom of the *ver sacrum*, which obliged all the young men of one generation to go abroad and seek their fortune by force of arms). Perhaps it was merely a matter of a general thirst for adventure and booty. We shall probably never know.

The first impulse affected little-known peoples who had not broken away from Celtic influences to any great degree, and who moved extraordinarily freely across Europe, which appears to have been only thinly populated at the time. About 230 BC the Greek colonists of Olbia (now Nikolaiev), near the mouth of the Dnieper, witnessed the arrival from the steppe lands—until then the territory of Iranian nomads, the Scythians and Sarmatians—of a new and frightening people, the Galatians, or Gauls, and with them two Germanic tribes, the Bastarnae and the Skirians. The Dacians of the lower Danube, and later the kings of Macedonia, had to fight against these trouble-some neighbours, whose centre of gravity appears to have been in the eastern Carpathians. It is thought that they came from the north via the Baltic/Black Sea isthmus. The Romans defeated them in 29 BC, but the Bastarnae remained peacefully in this region until the third century AD. The Skirians were caught up again in the migration of the Goths; their independence lasted until 469, and it was from their ranks that Odoacer emerged to put an end to the Western Empire in 476. Few Germanic peoples had such a long career.

There is no need here to give more than a brief summary of the dramatic but short-lived enterprise of the Cimbri, the Teutones and the Ambroni. After leaving Jutland they crossed central Europe, clashed with the Celtic Boii of Bohemia, and in 113 BC arrived in front of the Roman fort of Noreia in Carinthia. Having defeated four consuls one after the other they proceeded to follow an illogical route through Bavaria, eastern Gaul, the Rhône valley and Catalonia. Marius annihilated first the Teutones at Aix-en-Provence in the autumn of 102, and then the Cimbri at Vercelli in Piedmont in the summer of 101.

The Cimbri have given their name to the Himmerland, to the south of Aalborg; the Teutones may also have given theirs to the Ty penin-sula, on which Thisted stands, and the Ambroni to the island of Amrum. It is unfortunate that some hypercritical scholars, like the Swede L. Weibull, misled by an error of Strabo's, should have located the source of the migration on the banks of the lower Elbe.

The migration of the Bastarnae and the beginning of the Cimbric venture illustrate the first direction taken by the Germanic expansion, namely the slow advance towards the south-east, from Scandinavia to the southern coast of the Baltic and thence towards the Ukraine and the steppes. At a later period the Goths were to follow step by step the route taken by the Bastarnae; and later still the Vandals and the Burgundians in their turn followed it for part of the way.

The end of the Cimbric expedition saw a move in another direction, towards the south-west, of which the best-known episode is the invasion led by Ariovistus in 58 BC. His objective was to conquer the territory in the hands of the Celts of central Europe, whose power had drastically declined, and if possible the lands occupied by the Celts in Gaul, who were protected by their submission to Rome. (An advance party which ventured west of the Rhine, composed of the Germani Cisrhenani, was cut off by the conquest of Gaul and underwent intense Romanization.) The southernmost limit of the Germanic settlement around the time of Augustus ran along the entire course of the Danube down as far as the Pannonian basin.

The following period, up to the reign of Marcus Aurelius, is characterized by relative stability. It was not that the Germans had ceased to move around: there are signs of constant shifting, especially in the east, as the enemies of Rome fighting the legions all along the *limes* withdrew exhausted and were replaced by others. But the barrier was sufficiently strong and the counter-attacks sufficiently frequent to ensure that the Germans gained no new ground. Encouraged by this stabilization, Roman influences penetrated the Germanic world. A number of Germans, such as the Batavian Civilis and the Cheruscian Arminius, served as auxiliaries in the Roman armies and thus became Romanized to some extent; even Scandinavians were affected. Commercial contacts were established. Archaeological finds indicate the important trade routes: one of them went from Aquileia to the Baltic, crossing the *limes* at Carnuntum, up-stream from Bratislava; another went via Westphalia from Gaul to the coast of western Jutland, rich in amber.[4] The wealthiest Germans adopted certain features of Roman luxury. A form of alphabetic writing of Mediterranean origin—runes—was developed, probably in Denmark in the second century.

The origin of the runic alphabet (called *futhark* because of the order of the first six characters) has been the subject of violent argument. It is agreed at present (although one wonders how long such agreement will last) that the alphabet can be traced back to north Italian inscriptions in the form in which they were on the eve of the Roman conquest. The first, very brief, texts are inscribed on weapons and jewellery of the third century.[5] Although it never contributed very much to intellectual life, this alphabet lasted on the continent until the seventh century, in England until the ninth century, and in Scandinavia until the fifteenth century. The invention of runes shows a certain desire to raise German civilization to the level of that of the Mediterranean world.

This period of relative calm came to an end in the second half of the second century AD, perhaps owing to a weakening of the Roman defences, perhaps because the population of what is now central Germany had grown, thus increasing the pressure on the *limes*, but most probably thanks to a chain reaction started by the migration of the Goths at the eastern end of the Germanic world. The storm broke in 166: a twofold breakthrough brought the Quadi and the Marcomanni into Venetia, and the Costobocci and the Bastarnae into Achaea and Asia. Their enterprise was shortlived, but it took relentless fighting to close the breaches they had made in the *limes*.

The middle of the third century brought a new crisis. The *limes* of upper Germany fell in 254, there was a strong barbarian thrust into Belgium about 259, and between 268 and 278 the whole of the interior of Gaul was ravaged; bands of barbarians even penetrated as far as Spain. Some cities succumbed, but others surrounded themselves with walls enclosing a much smaller area than the original town and often built with rubble from the ruins of the *suburbium*. Hundreds of villae were burned to the ground. It was the worst catastrophe in the history of Gaul, and it brought about a dislocation which was probably more profound than that caused by the so-called 'great' invasions of the fifth century.[6] The Alamans invaded Italy in 260 and 270, and from 258 to 269 the Goths raided Thrace, Greece and Asia Minor by land and sea. Aurelian managed to re-establish the *limes* along its former lines except in Dacia, which was abandoned to the Goths, and in Gaul, where the task was not carried out until 278, when it was finally accomplished by Probus. There was yet another catastrophic breakthrough in Gaul under Maximian.[7] In the end the brutal energy of Diocletian succeeded, after a generation of disasters, in keeping the Germans out of the Empire. But they had weighed up both its wealth and its weakness, and were not to forget either.

Our knowledge of the crises of the third century comes almost entirely from archaeology and numismatics. Thus as far as Gaul is concerned it is almost impossible to tell whether particular cases of destruction were the result of invasions by land or by sea. The barbarians' only preoccupation seems to have been to plunder and to live off enemy territory. There is no indication that they ever intended to set up kingdoms there; they did not do so even in Dacia, where they remained in control of the territory. The Roman world, therefore, gained a great deal by not being overwhelmed until a century or a century and a half later; in the meantime the Germans were able to devise less rudimentary plans, and Rome, for her part, had time to perfect her mechanisms for assimilation.

The third century is characterized by the failure of the Germans to follow up their continual breaches of the *limes*, and also by the reorganization of the Germanic world. The confederations that Pliny and Tacitus mention, which were based more on community of worship than on political convenience, broke up, and new formations of a more military nature came into being from the end of the second century onwards. The inhabitants of the North Sea coastal region renounced the name of Chauci and began calling themselves Saxons. At the beginning of the third century the peoples of what is now central Germany regrouped themselves under the name of Alamans, and the tribes just beyond the *limes* of the lower Rhine combined to form the people known as the Franks. In the fourth century the Thuringians took over from the Hermunduri. This evolution continued until the fifth century when the last of these regroupings came into being—that of the Bavarians. Simultaneously, confused movements reshaped southern Scandinavia: the former tribes of Jutland—the Cimbri, Teutones and Charudes—disappeared, the Heruls of the Danish islands emigrated, and in their place the Jutes and the Danes appeared. Finally, the North Sea Germans discovered their vocation for the sea, and from roughly 285 onwards all the coasts of Gaul, Britain and even northern Spain were infested with pirates from the regions of present-day Germany and Denmark. In this way the Germanic world acquired the features it was to have at the time of the great migrations.

From now on the civilization of the Germans is complex and varied. The Germans of the steppes (the Goths and their neighbours), those of the forests (most of those living in what is now Germany) and those of the sea (Saxons, Frisians and Danes) led very different lives. We shall therefore confine ourselves to the most general characteristics, which were sometimes common to the Germans and the peoples associated with them in their career, like the Alans.

By the fifth century the Germanic languages were already sufficiently different to render communication between the various peoples impossible. Only two began to crystallize within a written tradition. Norse was written in runes, on a limited scale (the continental Germans did not adopt runes until the sixth century, and then not to any great extent). And thanks to the initiative of one extraordinary man, the Arian bishop Ulfila (c.311 to c.383), Gothic suddenly became a fully-fledged literary language, applied first to a translation of the New Testament. (For this reason West Germanic dialects owe part of their Christian vocabulary to Gothic: whether or not they also borrowed political terms is a much discussed question.) Equipped with an alphabet inspired by the Greek one, Gothic proved itself the equal of the other great literary languages, only to perish without direct descendants towards the end of the sixth century. After a long evolution some other dialects were to achieve the status of a literary language, but their progress was slow and many others disappeared.

There was, then, no linguistic cohesion among the Germans. It is almost impossible to know whether there was at that time any religious unity. We know nothing about the form of worship of certain crucial peoples, like the Goths, and there are practically no sources between Tacitus and the era of the Christian missions. There is a hint of a common pantheon, made up of several different chronological layers; as for mythology, the only one known is the Scandinavian one, set down in writing in the thirteenth century in the verse Edda, and expanded in the prose Edda of the Icelandic scholar Snorri Sturluson. The great divinities are *Wôthanaz (Germ. *Wotan*, Old Norse *Óðinn*), god of magic and victory; *Tiuz (*Ziu, Týr*), god of law and assemblies; *Thunraz (*Donar, Thôrr*), god of thunder; and the gods of war and fertility, *Njördhr* (Norse form), who was a goddess (Nerthus) according to Tacitus, and *Freyr* with his feminine counterpart *Freyja*. The only clear indication of the significance of these gods to the Germans at the time of their invasions of the Roman Empire is the incorporation of their names into those of the days of the week. Only a few features of worship and ritual are known: mass sacrifice by drowning of prisoners with their weapons after a victory, attested in the history of the Cimbri and confirmed by Danish archaeology, processions with sacred wagons, and some rites of divination or propitiation. On the eve of the invasions the paganism of the southern Germans seems to have been weak, if not deliquescent; it offered no resistance to Christianity except in the debased form of popular superstitions. However, paganism continued to flourish among the Saxons, the Swedes, and perhaps also the Danes, for among all of them a national cult with central sanctuaries is evident from the eighth century onwards, although this phenomenon probably originated much earlier: there is at least one indication that from the fifth century onwards Saxon paganism was comparatively strong—the fact that it was brought to Britain.

It would be even more dangerous to treat the Germans as a unit from an anthropological point of view. We are all familiar with the western barbarian as represented by the Graeco-Roman authors and sculptors: tall, fair-haired, strong-featured, with a fierce expression, a picture passed down from century to century, applied in turn to the Galatians in Asia, the Celts in Gaul, and finally to the Germans. In a famous passage which should teach us to be on our guard Strabo acknowledged only minor differences between the Celts and the Germans: 'The Germans live beyond the Rhine to the east of the Celts; they are very similar to the Celtic people, except that they are taller, fiercer and more blond. Apart from that they are very similar as regards their physical appearance, their customs and their way of life.'[8] The skeletons show a comparative, but never exclusive, consistency of the dolichocephalic type in Scandinavia, more variety of type in the south of Germania and an increasing tendency towards dolichocephaly and greater height in the areas conquered by the Germans at the time of the invasions. There is little else that can be added, except to say that certain East Germanic peoples, mainly the Burgundians, show strong signs of cross-breeding with Mongoloid elements. The very extensive practice of cremation in the first centuries AD deprives us of material for the earliest periods.

Economic life showed many variations. All the Germans practised sedentary agriculture, but the Saxons and Frisians, whose houses were perched on the hillocks of the *geest* in the middle of a moist plain, concentrated on raising cattle. The Germans of the forest grew crops in areas intermittently cleared for cultivation by burning; this cultivation was probably organized on a collective basis. Although they had villages and practised arable farming to some extent, the Germans of the steppe lands devoted much of their energies to stock-rearing, especially of horses. Pottery, and to a lesser extent textiles, were still of poor quality, but the Germans became capable of producing real masterpieces of metallurgy and goldwork (see pp. 201–4). It is significant that many terms relating to trade, transport and measurements have been borrowed from the Latin of the garrisons (Germ. *kaufen*; Dan. *købe*; O.E. *cēap* [a bargain or agreement—it survives in the word Cheapside] all from Latin *caupo*; Germ. *pferd* < Lat. *paraveredus*; Dan. *øre* < Lat. *aureus* etc.). An enormous number of Roman coins came into Germania and Scandinavia, but these were never used as currency, and the standard of value continued to be cattle, or bars and rings of precious metal. The Germans continued to be unwilling to accept urban life. Because of the gulf that existed between the two economic systems on either side of the German *limes*, speculators were able to make fat profits.

We know only the broad outlines of the social structure of the Germans before the great invasions. Several important points are unresolved, in particular whether or not a nobility existed outside the royal family among many of the peoples. The basis of society was formed by the free men, warriors whose murder required the payment of the highest compensation. Below the free men, who may not have constituted a majority everywhere, there was a large class of semi-free men—an arguable term—who were probably originally conquered peoples. Lastly there were the slaves, assigned either to domestic or to agricultural work; these were often captives. In the fourth century transplanted Roman subjects (like the Cappadocian ancestors of Ulfila, the apostle of the Goths) played a role of considerable importance among some Germanic peoples. Whether the people had a monarchical or a 'republican' system of government, the basic aims of the state were of a military nature, and the only solid subdivisions were those of the army. What held the social hierarchy together was an essentially martial institution, the brotherhood of warriors (Lat. *comitatus*, Germ. *Gefolgschaft*), which bound together by oath the leaders and their groups of young warriors of known loyalty. [9]

In times of peace the authority of the leaders depended entirely on their social influence and on the number of their faithful followers; kings had religious prestige in addition to these factors, but true power was in the hands of the local assemblies of free men (O.Germ. *mahal*, Lat. *mallus*, Scand. *thing*) which were held periodically in the open air. In times of war, on the other hand, hereditary chiefs or elected leaders (Lat. *duces*) enjoyed almost absolute power, provided they respected certain basic rights, such as the soldiers' right of plunder. The Scandinavian world, Saxony, and to some extent the Anglo-Saxon kingdoms, belonged to the first type, that of a peace-time society. Most of the states set up on Roman territory were the result of conquest, and for this reason resembled rather the structure of a people at war. The Merovingian kingdom, in which the *mallus* played an important part but in which the authority of the king was also considerable, lay midway between these two types.

Our last task is to describe the picturesque figure of the Germanic warrior at the time of the invasions, as portrayed, for example, by Sidonius Apollinaris. His clothes were fitted and sewn, not merely draped like those of the citizens of ancient Rome, although by the fourth century the toga was merely a ceremonial garment. His most characteristic item of dress was trousers (which were referred to as breeches, the Celtic word for them, Latinized as *braca*). He wore his hair long—in the case of the Sueves long enough to wear in a bun, the so-called 'Swabian knot'—and he smeared it with grease; sometimes he wore a beard. The Romans were horrified that the Germans cooked with lard, although the latter quite quickly adopted Mediterranean recipes (a Greek doctor was later to compose a culinary treatise for Theuderic I). Worse still, they had neither public baths nor gymnasia.

There was an obvious gulf between the Germanic world and Roman society: the former inspired by an extraordinary dynamism but completely rural, almost illiterate, without any real political organization; the latter somewhat decaying, based on towns and written laws, and since the time of Diocletian subject to the crushing authority of a totalitarian bureaucracy.

The Germans in the fifth century represented the continuation of a type of society which the Romans had encountered and destroyed about the beginning of the Christian era in Gaul, Britain and the Danubian regions, a much more archaic and rudimentary institution than the advanced systems which Rome had inherited from the Graeco-oriental world. Thus the Germans' military revenge on Rome meant a retrograde step, a return to a past which men had believed to be over and done with. In particular, the contact between two such very different civilizations inevitably brought about a general rearrangement of the whole social framework. It was from this crucial process that the European Middle Ages emerged.

The Asiatic Background and the World of the Steppes

To the north-east of the Mediterranean world lay an immense area of steppe land, stretching from the Carpathians to the Amur with an annexe in the Pannonian basin. It was the territory of shifting and unstable nomadic communities, in contact along their southern borders with widely differing settled civilizations whose various influences they received, blended together and propagated. In spite of their ethnic and linguistic differences the peoples of the steppes had similar social and cultural characteristics which allow them to be considered as a homogeneous whole.

Until the second century AD the peoples of this region had not behaved as a unit, however. Those of the western area were relatively independent; of course they did not deny themselves the pleasure of raiding their settled neighbours, but they did so only in limited expeditions which usually involved only one people and hardly ever affected the stability of Europe. This situation changed abruptly with the appearance of the Huns, the first non-Indo-European people to come from the heart of Asia. Soon the whole of the steppe from the Pacific to the middle reaches of the Danube was unified; the migratory whirlwind sucked in more and more peoples from the periphery who were strangers to the nomadic way of life.

The western steppes had at first been the domain of Iranian peoples— the Scythians and, later, from the fourth century BC, the Sarmatians; in the second century BC the Roxolani occupied the land between the Don and the Dnieper, and thrust a related people, the Iazyges, towards the Pannonian basin. From the first century to the fourth century AD Iranians faced the Romans across the *limes* of the Danube along its whole length downstream from Aquincum (Budapest). But these Iranians wore themselves out in the constant struggle to maintain their position, and were taken in the rear by newcomers, principally Germans. Many of them begged asylum from the Emperors, and even got as far as Gaul (hence the incidence of place-names like Sermaize). However, those who remained beyond the *limes* were reinvigorated by the arrival of the Alans, an Iranian tribe which had left modern Turkestan in the first century AD. At first the Alans directed their energies towards the south across the Caucasus, against the Parthian Empire. The replacement of the weak Parthian state by the Sassanian Empire in 226 induced them to turn again towards the west. They formed a loosely-knit state between the Urals, the Caucasus and the Don. Propelled by the invasion of the Huns, they and the Goths swept across Europe at the end of the fourth century, except for a remnant which managed to survive on the northern slopes of the Caucasus and still lives there today as the Ossetes.

From the third century BC there were Germans—the Bastarnae—living among the Sarmatians of the lower Danube. In the second century AD these were reinforced by newcomers belonging to an East Germanic group, the Costobocci, and then by the Goths and their dependents. These Germans lived in harmony with the Iranians; numerous texts from the first century onwards attest the contact between the Bastarnae on the one hand and the Sarmatians and Roxolani on the other, and in the fourth century there is evidence of intermarriage between the Alans and the Goths. The Iranians, who had an advanced civilization, and one which was, moreover, better adapted to an environment unfamiliar to the Germans, passed on to the latter numerous cultural features, such as mounted combat, items of dress (the fur robes of the Gothic kings seem to be of an Iranian type), and most notably the famous 'art of the steppes', whose origins were Sarmatian and Sassanian.

This coexistence seems to have been fairly stable when the equilibrium of the world of the steppes was upset by the arrival of a new group of nomads, who were to continue to flow westwards for seven or eight centuries—the Turks and their satellites, whose advance party was represented by the Huns.

The first reference to the Huns is in the *Geography* of Ptolemy, completed in AD 172; he mentions the presence of Χοῦνοι in the steppes to the north of the Caucasus not far from the Roxolani and the Bastarnae, probably between the Manych and the Kuban. Nothing further is heard of them until their unexpected victory in 374–5 over the Alans and the Goths, the report of which fell like a thunderbolt on the Roman world: Ammianus Marcellinus refers to the *Hunnorum gens, monumentis veteribus leviter nota* (the people of the Huns, hardly known in ancient writings)[10] and then to a *repentinus impetus, subita procella* (sudden attack and unexpected turmoil). From 378 they were in contact with the Roman armies in Thrace. At the same time tribes of the same name, and probably identical to them, attacked northern and eastern Iran: the White Huns (Hephthalites) were mentioned for the first time around 390. They settled down in Bactria and Sogdia in the fifth century, then conquered the north-east of India, where their kingdom lasted until about AD 650.

The Huns are usually said to be of Turkish origin, but the arguments are not absolutely conclusive. The origin of the Huns is an exceptionally complex problem. Repeated efforts since the eighteenth century (De Guignes, 1756) to reconcile Chinese and Western sources seem on the whole to have failed, with the result that any overall picture of the development of the Hunnic migration is today regarded as illusory by the majority of orientalists, such as Haussig, Moor, Altheim and Hambis. The following account confines itself to the few established facts. It rejects hypotheses based on the alleged identity of the Chinese *Hsiung-Nu* with the Greek *Khounoi*. This cuts the history of the Huns off from all the Far Eastern prehistory to which it has traditionally been attached. Whatever the origins of the Huns, it is clear that we are dealing with a people of distinctive characteristics and unusual customs. They shaved, practised deformation of the skull, killed off their old people and cremated their dead. They appeared to Mediterranean eyes to be the very incarnation of ugliness and barbarity. It is possible that they had a Mongoloid cast of features, but this is not certain. Had they any form of art? The answer is yes if we attribute to them the bronzes of the Ordos and the burials of Minoussinsk and Pazyryk at the foot of the Altai mountains, prototypes of the 'art of the steppes'; no if we attribute these to the Hsiung-Nu, a Caucasoid people which conquered part of northern China in the last centuries BC. In any case the Huns participated in the civilization of the steppes, and played a major part in its diffusion towards the west.

Their European career began with a master-stroke. In 374–5 the king of the Huns fell on the Goths in the Ukraine, led by King Ermanaric, who was defeated and committed suicide. It was twenty years before the Huns exploited their victory to the full. By around 396 they had occupied the plains of present-day Rumania, and had spilled into the Pannonian basin; some years later the power of the Huns stretched from the eastern Alps to the Black Sea, and a state more or less worthy of the name was formed under Kings Uldin and Mundiuch.

In the wake of the Hunnish advance only secondary peoples of Turkish origin appeared at first: the Sabiri, who came from Siberia to the north of the Caucasus at the end of the fifth century and fought until the end of the sixth century against the Byzantine Empire east of the Black Sea; the Uguri, who moved from the steppe lands of the River Ural, under pressure from the Sabiri, into those of the Volga and then, at the end of the sixth century, made several raids into the Balkans, before contributing to the formation of the Bulgarian people in the seventh century and the Hungarian people in the eighth century; and finally the Old Turks who, without crossing the Volga, were in continual contact with Byzantium during the sixth century. None of these peoples played a particularly important part in European history, but on their heels, about 461, the first Avars appeared on the horizon of the historiographers of Constantinople. They were to loom large in the foreground for about three centuries. Their origin is hardly less controversial than that of the Huns. Since the eighteenth century they have generally been identified with a branch of the Tungus people, the Jouan-Jouan, quoted by Chinese sources as being the founders of a short-lived empire between Korea and Turkestan. In 552 these Jouan-Jouan, whom a Byzantine text calls also 'Abaroi', were wiped out by the Turks. It would seem that this people had nothing to do with the Abaroi mentioned by Priskos in 461 as being nomads in Kazakhstan; at most, one tribe had merely adopted the name of the other. We have no means of knowing whether the Avars who appear in European history were Turks, as the title of their leader—*khagan*—would seem to indicate, or eastern Iranians, as Haussig claims. It is certain that their civilization showed a strong Turkish influence.

The role of the Avars in Europe began in 558. Pushed westwards by the Turks, they asked Justinian to give them land, but he refused. By 561–2 they had reached the Danube; in 567 they began to settle in the Pannonian basin, which had been unoccupied since the dissolution of the Hunnic empire, meanwhile also making sorties into the Balkan interior and threatening Byzantium itself on occasion. After a century of struggling against the Eastern Empire they turned their attention towards the west, in the middle of the seventh century; their wars with the Franks lasted until the time of Charlemagne. The Avar state, which was better organized and more soundly based than that of the Huns, had considerable influence on European history. This is seen especially in the disruption of the great trade route from the Adriatic to the middle Danube and the Baltic, one of the axes of Europe in Antiquity.

Behind the Avars came compact groups of Turks. There were the Bulgars, mentioned for the first time in 482, at which point they were in the Ukraine, but who really only burst upon the scene in 680 when, led by the khagan Asparuch, they crossed the Danube and occupied Moesia. A section of this people did not take part in the migration, but remained on the middle Volga until the twelfth century, though they were gradually driven back into the forests by more fortunate tribes. In the course of their migrations the Bulgars absorbed the remnants of several peoples who had preceded them, notably the Uguri.

Then there were the Khazars, first mentioned in about 626, when they were living to the north of Iran. They settled soon afterwards between the Caucasus, the Azov Sea, the Don and the middle Volga, and the River Ural, where they remained until their disappearance at the end of the tenth century under the assaults of the Russians and the Petchenegs. During this wave of Turkish invaders the Magyars, mostly Finno-Ugrians, were advancing, from the eighth to the tenth century. Then came more Turks: the Petchenegs from the ninth century to the eleventh century, followed by the Cumans from the eleventh to the thirteenth century. The onslaught of the Mongols in the thirteenth century is in a sense still part of the same movement, whose last spasm was to be the arrival of the Kalmuks in the steppes to the west of the lower Volga in the seventeenth century.

During a millennium and a half, therefore, the steppes witnessed a series of migratory waves from the east, monotonously following the same formula. A people would appear, coming from some unknown area in the grasslands of the east. Although at first small in numbers they would quickly snowball and sweep towards the west. If they could not manage to conquer some well-defined area of the plain that was in contact with settled communities they could exploit, their career would be very short-lived. If they could, it would last for three, five or even ten generations. A more or less solid political organization would be formed, and a certain level of prosperity attained which would give rise to envy among other peoples who had stayed behind in the east; a fresh wave of migration would start as these peoples in their turn swept westwards, destroying everything in their path, and the peoples who had been so powerful before their arrival would vanish almost overnight. Only the Magyars succeeded in breaking out of this vicious circle.

How can we explain this recurrence, these sudden births and deaths? First of all, it must be remembered that our sources give the history of ethnic names rather than of individuals. Successful peoples swelled in numbers as scattered groups flocked from far and wide to join them, causing apparently spontaneous generation; but even the name of a defeated people would be abandoned. The name of a successful people had such prestige that it was often improperly borrowed by others: this is doubtless what happened with the name of the Avars, and, according to some, with that of the Huns also. Very often the survivors of a defeated people stayed in the same area waiting for their luck to change, and soon joined a new group. Several empires could be built up in this way, one after the other, made of the same materials, though appearing to us to be very different in composition because we only hear about the ruling clans, which did change. Too much reliance should not be placed on linguistic labels: many of these ephemeral confederations were multi-lingual, like the states founded by Genghis Khan and his successors in the thirteenth century, and the name of the people often survives after its whole composition, including even its language, has changed. This is what happened to the Bulgars, a Turkish people who later became Slavs.

Yet the real importance and scope of the migrations cannot be denied. They appear to have been linked with a revival of nomadism, which between the fifth and the eleventh centuries affected not only the cold steppes but also the subtropical deserts of the Mediterranean world, as may be seen in the Arab and Seljuk expansions and the rebirth of Berber nomadism in North Africa. It may be simply a question of climatic change, and this hypothesis is certainly attractive, but historical climatology is still in its infancy. As regards climatic change in Africa, historians are still sceptical, but Russian and Hungarian scholars believe it may explain the movements of the Avars and Magyars. At any rate the halt in the migrations to the west was due, generally speaking, to a process of settling down in semi-humid country. As it takes ten times as much land to support a horseman in the steppes as it takes to support a peasant in his field, wave after wave of migration was able to arrive in the Pannonian plain and settle there without causing overpopulation.

The contribution of the steppe peoples to the formation of Europe is not comparable to that of the Germans, but it was important in the short term. They brought to the West objects of domestic use and weapons and jewellery produced by oriental artisans, and hence to an arguable extent caused an aesthetic and technical revolution (see p. 201). We can mention a few of these imports here. A fifth-century medallion with a Pahlevi text was found at Wolfsheim in Rhenish Hesse. The tombs of the chiefs of Wolfsheim, Hochfelden and Mundolsheim (near Strasbourg) are of the same type as those of Pannonia, the Ukraine or western Siberia. At Airan (Calvados) a hoard of Pontic jewellery of the fifth century was found in 1876. The tomb of Pouan (Aube), possibly that of the Visigothic king Theodoric I who was killed in 451, contained two weapons from southern Russia.

The prestige of the Huns made such a deep impression that Attila became one of the central characters in German epics, and certain Germans, particularly Burgundians, began to imitate the strange practice of cranial deformation. The tactics of the nomadic horsemen led to the transformation of warfare in Byzantium and Persia, which gave increasing prominence to mounted archers. Some authors have even believed that the Huns influenced institutions, although this is wholly conjectural.[11]

The world of the nomads seems to have been attracted more towards China than towards the West, and the European side of its history is certainly less important than the Asian side. The two aspects are, however, curiously symmetrical: in the evolutionary stages, when the nomads came in contact with settled communities, the diplomatic reactions of the old-established empires in both the Byzantine and Chinese capitals were more or less the same.[12] In both cases the settled community always tried to contain the barbarians by calling in other barbarians from even further away, and sought to sow dissension among the nomads rather than confront them directly.

THE ROMANS

There is no need to reconstruct here a picture of the Later Roman Empire at the end of its decline, nor to recall the destruction of this totalitarian state, which was almost constantly in a state of siege, using savage means in its attempt to ensure the survival of a limited ruling class made up of learned senators and uncouth military officers. The Catholic Church won a dominant place for itself by conforming to the framework laid down for it by the civil power, and economic life declined in the West, while the East remained prosperous.[13] It is only necessary here to recall the fates of two institutions, the army and the Empire, in order to show how their disintegration paved the way for the triumph of the barbarians.

Roman Methods of Resistance

Attacked on every one of its frontiers, the Roman world had had to resign itself to military reforms which we know very little about. Our basic source, the *Notitia dignitatum*, written between 428 and 430, is a collection of miscellaneous documents, probably dealing with the army of Diocletian as far as the East is concerned, that of Constantine for the greater part of the West, and perhaps that of Julian for the Rhine frontier.[14] This work shows that in the fourth century, instead of having a line of defence along the banks of the Rhine and the Danube, it was becoming increasingly the custom to use field armies under the immediate command of the prince or the *magistri militum*, armies which were capable of bringing rapid aid to threatened points. The government probably never made a conscious choice between frontier forces and field armies, but circumstances did favour the latter. If large detachments were kept immobilized for a long time guarding the *limes* or its coastal equivalent, the *litus saxonicum* of Gaul and Britain, it would appear that these were troops of secondary importance only. In fact, in the fifth century not a single decisive battle was fought on the frontier itself or on the coast. Those regions which had only *ripenses* or *limitanei* were sacrificed, like Britain after 407 or Noricum.

The only attempt at efficient and energetic defence was made by the field armies, the *comitatus*. However, they were certainly a heavy burden on the provinces where they were used: they usually waited until the enemy had penetrated deep into Roman territory before attacking, so that the devastation was considerable; and as they were often composed of the most savage barbarians—Aetius, for example, liked to use Alans and Huns—their presence in the neighbourhood was not necessarily reassuring. But their military and political value was unquestionable. They sometimes achieved resounding successes, for example against Attila in 451, and they never betrayed Rome. Most of them outlived the Empire itself.

One of the most important of these field armies was stationed in the north of Gaul; it was commanded successively by Aetius, Count Paul, Aegidius and Syagrius. After the death of Majorian in 461 it was left to its own devices and held out independently for twenty-five years until defeated by Clovis in 486. Its headquarters were then at Soissons. Another army was in northern Italy, between Milan and Ravenna and on the Isonzo; it was commanded by Ricimer until 472, then by Orestes and finally by Odoacer, and was not really disbanded until Theodoric took Ravenna in 493. A third and less important one, a remnant of the army of the Danube, withdrew to Dalmatia; from 454 to 481 its independence was virtually absolute under Marcellinus and his nephew Julius Nepos, Emperor from 474 to 475; afterwards its loyalty was divided between Odoacer and the Eastern Empire. Britain had lost its small field army in 407, when the usurper Constantine III brought it over to the continent. The African army seems to have lost its fighting corps before the end of the fourth century. Spain never had one. The presence of these armies in certain areas explains the survival of some shreds of Roman civilization, notably in Dalmatia and in the north of Gaul. The fact that from the start the Merovingian kingdom incorporated one of the last and most solid bastions of the Roman defence was of fundamental importance, and decisively influenced its orientation. The German way of life made no lasting conquests except outside the radius of action of these armies.

The fate of the armies defending the frontiers had been sealed much earlier. Lack of manpower made it impossible to maintain the innumerable garrisons on the *limes* simultaneously. Whole sections of the *limes* were abandoned without a fight. The soldiers who were lost defending Hadrian's Wall in Britain at the time of the breach of 367 were never replaced, and it appears to have been deserted after 388 except for some troops recruited locally. From then on the system of defence was based on individual town walls, and the battles against the Picts in the fifth century took place deep in Roman territory. In Gaul it would seem that the lower part of the Rhineland *limes* downstream from Xanten was not re-established after the invasions of the third century. A fortified line which may have replaced it, along the road from Cologne to Boulogne via Tongres and Bavai (see p. 225), ceased to be properly defended in the time of Gratian. The organization of the rest of the Rhine defences broke down completely after 406; there was nothing left but *castella* and fortified towns lost in the middle of undefended countryside. In what is now Switzerland the *limes* seems to have been abandoned shortly after 401; after that all that remained was a scattering of hastily fortified refuges. The Danube frontier was stripped of its garrisons by Stilicho between 395 and 398, as the troops were needed to swell the field armies in Gaul and Italy; most of the *castella*, however, held out for another generation. The inhabitants withdrew to the towns, which were defended until about 440 in Pannonia and about 475 in Noricum, pending the general evacuation in 488.

Theoretically these were doubtless the only possible tactics, in view of the lack of funds and of trustworthy men, but in practice they proved disastrous. Roman civilization was based on the complementary qualities of the towns and the country, and on the security and rapidity of communications. The intervening zones of countryside—which were more or less deliberately abandoned—were just as necessary to Rome's prosperity as the administrative and commercial centres, which were defended to the bitter end. By the time effective imperial authority had become confined to four or five regions which had great difficulty in communicating with each other, say from the years 405–10 onwards, the Empire was nearing its end. For a good part of the fifth century Roman public opinion failed to foresee the logical outcome of imperial defence tactics; however, it was obvious that the armies were undefeated and that the countryside was nevertheless being devastated, and consequently officers of barbarian origin or upbringing were accused of treason. Nothing was further from the truth: almost all remained faithful to the end to the Roman ideal (although not necessarily to every short-lived Emperor) and it was precisely the barbarians who fought in the Roman armies who were most receptive to Roman influence.

The Decline of the Empire in the West : Odoacer

The fate of the Empire was sealed from the moment when the barbarians succeeded in settling down in the stretches of countryside between the centres of resistance—without at the same time participating in the Roman way of life.

During the whole of the Later Roman Empire barbarians continued to flood into Roman territory. Some entered by force, although until 378 all those who tried to do so failed and their adventure ended in death, capture or expulsion. Others entered peacefully as slaves sold by merchants, as peasants in search of land, or as soldiers seeking their fortune. The last were often successful, sometimes holding the highest positions near the Emperor himself, although for that they had to embrace Roman civilization.

This state of affairs changed when whole peoples who thought of themselves as foreigners, and behaved as such, penetrated collectively into the Empire and managed to stay there by force of arms. Rome refused to accept this situation and hoped to regain the upper hand in the end, as it had done after the crisis of the third century. But later the barbarian occupation was legalized. The *foedus*, that political contract which was at first offered to peoples living near the frontier who had to be made to fit in with the objectives of the Roman government, was now offered to barbarians who had taken root in the very heart of imperial territory. By a legal fiction two authorities were superimposed on the same piece of land, that of the barbarian chieftain who continued to be the absolute master of his troops, on condition that in principle he would not use them except in the service of Rome, and that of the Roman civil government which theoretically remained intact on condition that it provided the barbarians with food and shelter. Naturally the first of these two authorities, being armed, had an enormous advantage over the second which, being outside the zone of action of the Roman armies, had nothing to back it up but its moral authority and the resources of an irregularly filled treasury. From the moment this régime became widespread, the Empire was heading, step by step, for disintegration.

The Visigoths were the first German people to succeed in entering the Empire, peacefully at first in 376, then by force after their victory at Adrianople, after which they spent twenty-three years wandering round the Balkans, without anyone managing to drive them out. They were also the first to enjoy on a large scale the benefits of the *foedus* inside the Empire, from 418 on. A second wave of Germans penetrated into the Empire by breaking through the Rhine *limes* in 406; its principal elements were the Vandals, Alans, Sueves and Burgundians. The Romans were not able to expel them either. Later the *foedus* was offered to most of them—to the Vandals in 435 and to the Burgundians in 443. Finally the Ostrogoths, after having enjoyed a more or less recognized status in the Balkans for about twenty years, became exemplary federates in 480. The whole of the fifth century up to the time of Clovis, therefore, is dominated by this system, which sooner or later granted the invader a legal right to occupy the land. Since the Empire did not survive in the West the system was not used in the sixth century, but the formulae for coexistence which were set up in the course of this long transition period affected even those peoples who had not themselves lived through it.

Even after its territory was split up the Empire continued to exist. There is no need to retrace here the history of its disappearance in the West, but it is relevant to recall some dates and facts. Legally the Empire did not disappear. When the 'Roman' army in Italy under the leadership of Odoacer rebelled, demanding to be given land, and when the last Emperor, the child Romulus Augustulus, was deposed on 4 September 476, in theory the whole Empire was again under the authority of one man, the Emperor Zeno in Constantinople. In the eyes of the Romans Odoacer was just one more patrician, like Ricimer and Orestes. (Considered in greater detail, the situation is more complicated: the Eastern Empire, watchdog of all legitimacy, did not recognize the Western Emperors Glycerius (473–4) and Romulus (475–6); its own candidate was Julius Nepos, the commander of the army in Dalmatia, who died on 9 May 480. It was only then that Zeno resigned himself to the proposals of Odoacer.) Theodoric, the enemy and successor of Odoacer, respected the fiction of imperial authority in Italy. As the authority of an Emperor like Glycerius or Romulus was already fictitious, the exchange of one fiction for another probably went unnoticed.[15]

What did this ghost of an Empire consist of at the moment of its disintegration? To answer this question we must look at each province separately. Britain was totally lost, preserving no contacts with Rome, although certain Celtic chieftains still appealed to Rome from time to time. In northern Gaul a Roman power still existed—the army of Syagrius, which had not, however, recognized any Emperor since 461. Aquitaine, which had in effect been taken over by the Visigoths, was in law subject to a *foedus* renewed in 453 or 454, but in this province hardly any heed was paid to imperial prerogatives. The lands of the Rhône which had been taken over by the Burgundians showed more respect for these prerogatives: from 472 onwards King Gundobad held the title of 'patrician'. South-east Gaul, on the other hand, remained truly Roman, centred on the praetorian prefect at Arles and on numerous aristocrats who had fled to the region from elsewhere. But this small oasis quickly became even more reduced in size: the Auvergne, its bastion, capitulated to the Visigoths at the end of 475; Lyons, its largest town, was occupied by the Burgundians from about 472 onwards. Only Provence remained, until Odoacer abandoned that too to the Visigoths in 477. (The façade of a Roman province, with its prefecture at Arles, was re-established there in 508–9, to suit Theodoric's political needs. It lasted until 537).

In Spain the only legal title held by the Visigoths was the *foedus* of 453–4 which obliged them to hunt down the Bacaudae—peasant rebels—in Tarraconensis. It was confirmed in 475 and 477 by Odoacer in the name of the Emperors, but the Visigoths occupied the other provinces without any legal title whatsoever. In Africa treaties of 435 and 442 had regularized the position of the Vandals; Mauretania and Tripolitania were included in 455. In Dalmatia, Rome held on to her full rights until the death of Nepos in 480; after that the status of the country was aligned with that of Italy. Raetia, Noricum and Pannonia, or at least those parts of them which were still organized, shared the fate of Italy after 476.

Thus four Roman strongholds had held out until the end: the three areas controlled by the field armies, and the civilian stronghold of the south-east of Gaul. In the course of the previous century there had been countless *coups d'état* on the pretext of putting one claimant or another on the imperial throne, but in reality trying to ensure the temporary success of some faction, usually backed up by a barbarian people. It was to one of these *coups d'état*, achieved in a barefaced manner without any imperial pretext, that Romulus Augustulus succumbed in 476. The Empire was overthrown from within, not overwhelmed by an invasion.

The person who benefited from the manoeuvre this time was a barbarian. His rise to power represents a transition between the Roman government and the Germanic kingdoms, to which he passed on some of the solutions he had put into operation. Odoacer, or Odovacar, was most probably a Skirian, although certain texts would have it that he was a Herul and some have inappropriately suggested that he was a Hun. The Skirians lived on the middle Danube; they were an East Germanic people who were associated with the Bastarnae for a long time and the last remnants of them seem to have ended up in Bavaria. Odoacer's father, Edica, had belonged to the entourage of Attila and had been killed in 469 by Theudemir, the father of Theodoric; his elder brother, Hunwulf, had had a brilliant career in the Eastern Empire. He himself had come to Italy with other Skirian refugees on the death of his father, and had joined the bodyguard of Anthemius. It is not known exactly why the troops decided to elect him king at Pavia on 23 August 476.

The régime which he set up, and which his hereditary enemy Theodoric was to imitate very closely, was based on a curious dualism. On the one hand Odoacer was king by virtue of his princely lineage, and on the other by the election of his soldiers; he was called simply *Odoacrius rex*, without further qualifications, because his troops were of very mixed origins (the majority were Heruls, but there was also an admixture of Skirians, Rugians and Turcilingui, the latter so obscure that there is no other mention of them). He was king of an army, not of a Germanic people. He stationed his troops in northern Italy, with their headquarters at Ravenna, Verona and Milan, and divided them up among the large estates according to the already familiar system of *hospitalitas*. The presence of the barbarians was thus hardly more conspicuous than it had been before 476. He wielded direct authority over these troops. But Odoacer was also a Roman patrician who adopted the imperial *nomen gentilicium* of Flavius towards the end of

B*

his administration, and governed in the same way as the last of the
Western Emperors, through the administration at Ravenna and through
the Roman Senate. The members of the aristocracy, who valued the
aulic and bureaucratic tradition more than the person of the Emperor
himself, showed themselves consistently loyal and satisfied: this is true
even of the ex-Emperor Romulus, who lived on as a rich landowner
in the south until about 510.

The sovereign alone controlled military appointments; he surrounded himself with Germanic personal attendants and continued to
be an Arian, but he respected the Roman civil government and
maintained a satisfactory relationship with the Catholic Church. The
régime set up by this 'destroyer of the Empire' was therefore a compromise which upheld Roman interests better than a powerless and
despised Emperor would have done. He brought peace inside and
outside the country, and promised to drive out of Italy the great
barbarian peoples, who were infinitely more voracious than the modest
tribes which made up Odoacer's army. This was accomplished at the
cost of abandoning several regions: Provence was ceded to the Goths
in 477, and Noricum was evacuated in 488; but Italian opinion hardly
raised an eyebrow.

Odoacer did not allow himself to break these prudent rules he had
laid down for himself until the very end of his reign, when Zeno had
unleashed the Ostrogoths against him. Then he had several coins
struck in his name, and later, when he was hard-pressed, he proclaimed
his son Thela Emperor. These acts had no practical consequences,
however. Odoacer was killed on 15 March 493. From beyond the
grave he bequeathed to Italy his own brand of government which
continued until the reconquest of Justinian and served as a model for
the reorganization of Spain after 507. The Heruls, Skirians, Rugians
and Turcilingi in Italy all perished in the same catastrophe as the
sovereign whom they had elected, but the Goths harvested the fruits
of their labours.

2 The Land Invasions:
The First Wave, the Fourth and Fifth Centuries

From the end of the fourth century to the end of the sixth century three great migratory impulses spread across Europe. The first and most important of these affected the whole of Europe from the Caspian Sea to Gibraltar and even beyond, and carried a people which had been formed on the shores of the Baltic as far as Africa. The following waves were weaker and less far-reaching, while the movement of the peoples that brought up the rear, like the Bavarians, can hardly be called invasions at all. But whereas the most permanent of the kingdoms that resulted from the first wave did not survive beyond 711, one modern state, France, owes its origins more or less directly to the succeeding wave.

In about 375 the Huns attacked the Goths in the Pontic steppes; the Roman Empire, which had been reconstructed by Diocletian almost a century before on an apparently firm foundation, was still intact from the lowlands of Scotland to the first cataract of the Nile. In 439 Genseric entered Carthage, and the western half of the Empire was reduced to a few crippled enclaves among which the barbarians circulated freely. In the period between, an unparalleled sequence of disasters highlighted by two events—the battle of Adrianople (modern Edirne) in 378 and the breaching of the Rhine frontier in 406—had brought Roman civilization to the brink of a precipice. However, it was to be defended for a long time yet, and so successfully in the East that in the end the Empire of Constantinople outlived all its enemies. In the West the Roman political structure, mortally wounded, lingered on for some time before eventually disintegrating, but the Roman social structure succeeded in imposing itself from within on the new kingdoms founded by the conquerors. When the first wave had died down, it was found that nowhere on the continent had the Roman way of life entirely disappeared, that some of the victorious peoples were spontaneously preparing to adapt themselves to the civilization of the defeated Romans, and that brute force had not prevailed everywhere. It is doubtful if medieval Europe would really have differed very radically from Roman Europe had it not been for the succeeding waves of invasion.

INVADERS FROM THE EAST

The driving force behind the first wave of migration was a group made up of three very different peoples, Turks, Iranians and East Germans. The lines traced out by their various routes across Europe are long and meandering, constantly coming together and drifting apart. The entire history of Europe during the fourth and fifth centuries has to be seen against this background.

The Huns

In spite of their decisive role in triggering off the great wave of migrations at the end of the fourth century, it would be wrong to believe that the Huns appeared immediately as the inevitable and implacable enemies of Rome. The distant rumble of thunder in 375—the destruction of the Gothic kingdom in the Ukraine—went unheeded. At first the Eastern Empire had a perfectly peaceful relationship with the newcomers, and may have encouraged their settlement in the Pannonian basin in about 390. As long as Alaric's Visigoths represented the principal danger in the Balkans the friendship of the Huns was regarded as a valuable asset. Relations began to sour only after the Goths had left for Italy when, around 408, the Hunnic King Uldin tried to establish himself in Thrace and Moesia. The Western Empire did not consider itself directly threatened, so it was able to have a political understanding with the Huns for nearly half a century. The man chiefly responsible for this was Aetius. This future *magister militum* had spent his youth (probably since 406) as a hostage of the Huns, and he made personal friendships among them and also formed a strong admiration for their military ability. At crucial moments in his career Aetius sought the help of the Huns—against the Visigoths in 427, the Franks in 428 and the Burgundians in 430—and it was among them that he took refuge when he fell from favour in 432–3. In return for this he helped them to establish themselves firmly in Pannonia. The Huns were the friends and allies of Rome, or at least of certain Romans, for a much longer time than they were the 'scourge of God'.

The Huns only began to be a grave danger when, at some point between 425 and 434, they set up a true state in Pannonia, a transformation which seems to have been the work of Kings Mundiuch and Rua, the father and uncle respectively of Attila. There are sufficiently good reasons for believing that their model was the Sassanian state, whose influence on Hunnic art has in fact been established. Rituals practised in the presence of the king, like proskynesis (bowing to the ground) and libation, seem to have been borrowed from Iranian ceremonial, as was the use of the diadem as a sign of sovereignty. Society was reorganized round a hereditary royal family, with the domination of a court nobility replacing the former tribal structure. These nobles, who had grown rich on booty, were not all true Huns, for they included Germans and at least one Roman from Pannonia, Orestes, father of the future Emperor Romulus Augustulus and head of the royal civil service. According to Priskos, the ambassador sent from Constantinople in 449, there was even an attempt under Attila to endow the kingdom with some sort of capital: as well as a mobile camp the king had a palace constructed of wood and stone, built with materials imported from the Empire. This nascent monarchy owed its invincibility to military techniques inherited from the nomadic tribes. In absolute terms the Hunnic cavalry did not, perhaps, equal that of the Alans, the excellence of whose horses was a byword from the third century onwards, but Hunnic horsemen were numerous and indefatigable, and experienced in the tactics of oriental archers. We cannot say for sure whether they also had a heavy armoured cavalry corps like that of the Iranians or the Hephthalites. Their equipment consisted of a reflex bow, arrows with triangular heads, a wooden saddle, a whip, a lasso and a sword with one or two cutting edges. Around the Hunnic core were gathered contingents of vassal peoples of mainly Germanic origin.

It is difficult to assign a definite territory to a nomadic state. Some scholars have envisaged an empire stretching from the Oder to the Irtysh; others have limited the kingdom of Attila to Hungary and Rumania, while expressing some doubts about the region of the lower Danube. The first interpretation is certainly too wide—those who propose it are thinking of an area of civilization and not of political supremacy. The second is acceptable only if the density of settlement is taken into account; only the eastern part of the Puszta was densely occupied by the Huns, but they had pushed forward into the adjacent plains of Serbia, Wallachia, the Ukraine and even Silesia.

During Attila's lifetime the Huns were the dominant power in the barbarian world. More than one Germanic people learned from them and adopted their fashions, the Burgundians in particular. The importance of their role in the epic accounts of the Nibelungs is well known (although it must be added that these accounts confuse the Huns who were auxiliaries of Aetius with the soldiers of Attila). Archaeology confirms one aspect of this prestige: the extraordinary abundance of gold in the possession of the Hunnic aristocracy.

Attila put to the test the power which his predecessors had built up.

He was born in about 395 and came to power in 434, ruling jointly with his brother Bleda until 445. During the first fifteen years of his reign all his enterprises were conducted in the East. The West, ruled at that time by Aetius, was friendly enough to hand western Pannonia over to the Huns in 439. Each year the Huns and their satellites— Ostrogoths, Gepids, Rugians, Heruls and Skirians—made raids into the Balkans; in 447 they swept through Macedonia as far as Thermopylae. Almost all the larger towns were devastated: Naissus, Viminacum, Singidunum and Sirmium. In 449 Attila, then at the height of his power in the East, received the ambassador sent by Theodosius II in his camp, probably in Wallachia: Priskos's account of this embassy is our main source of information on the Hunnic state.

In the following year Attila abruptly changed his policy. For several years a number of earnest requests had been attracting his attention towards the West. In 449 he had welcomed Eudoxius, the leader of the Bacaudae of Gaul, who had doubtless informed him of the weakness of the Roman government. A Frankish clan had appealed to him to help them put their candidate on the throne. The Vandals may have made overtures to him with a view to forming an alliance against the Goths. Last, but not least, Honoria, the sister of Valentinian III, incensed with her brother for having killed her lover, offered Attila her hand in marriage. It seems evident that Attila's about-face was not the thoughtless whim of a barbarian, but rather the result of a remarkably informed and carefully prepared diplomatic policy. Moreover, his aim was still the same as in the expeditions in the East: not to conquer territory but to collect as much booty as possible with the least risk.

A preliminary raiding party set off, at the beginning of 451, up the left bank of the Danube and then towards the Rhine, which was crossed in the region of Mainz; Belgium was devastated, and Metz burned on 7 April. At the end of May the Huns arrived at Orleans. Aetius came to the rescue from Italy, but not quickly enough (he was probably waiting for Gothic auxiliaries). Orleans was being defended by the Alan king, Sangiban. Whether the city was actually besieged, as described in the famous traditional account of Sidonius Apollinaris and in the life of St. Anianus, has recently been called into question, though not very convincingly.[1] Attila next turned back, hotly pursued by the 'Romans' (in fact an extraordinary collection of barbarians, from Franks to Burgundians, with a few Gauls from Armorica thrown in), and by the army of the Visigothic king, Theodoric. His pursuers caught up with him in Champagne on 20 June, 451, and after a bloody free-for-all (called the battle of the Catalaunian fields, or the *campus Mauriacus*) Attila was defeated, though not seriously. He was able to return to Pannonia without further opposition.

In the spring of 452 he set out once again, this time towards Italy, broke through the defences of Friuli, and took Aquileia, Padua, Mantua, Vicenza, Verona, Brescia and Bergamo in turn. He may have been considering a march on Rome (Ravenna was unassailable behind its marshes). It was at this point that he had an interview with Pope Leo on the Mincio, an interview which is as famous as it is difficult to assess. Attila was offered the hand of Honoria and some tribute, but we do not know whether this is what sent him hurrying back to the East or whether it was the fact that the Emperor was attacking on the Danube. Shortly after his return, in 453, he died.

His sons Ellac and Ernac then disputed the succession, and the satellite Germans took advantage of this to re-establish their independence. Ellac attacked the rebels, but was defeated and killed at the River Nedao in Pannonia in 454. This was the end of the Hunnic supremacy. Stripped of their prestige, the Huns who survived were just another small and insignificant people. Several groups took service with the Eastern Empire and were stationed south of the Danube; others remained as tributaries of Rome; some managed to return to the Ukrainian steppes. A war between the last two sons of Attila, Ernac and Dengizech, completed the downfall of the Huns. Their name is mentioned from time to time thereafter until the reign of Zeno (474–91), but after that nothing more is heard of them. The name of the Huns continued to be notorious, however, thanks to Attila's reputation. Many historians applied it to other peoples of the steppes, including Avars and Magyars. Conversely, several tribes claimed to be their heirs, particularly the Bulgars and the Siculi (Hungarian mountain-dwellers from Transylvania). In spite of the political talents of their leaders, the Huns had only a negative impact on history, magnified to some extent by literature. They were never great in any real sense except at the head of a coalition in which the Germans were probably the dominant element. When luck turned against them their satellites regained their liberty, and within a generation the Huns had disappeared from the map.

The Alans

The history of the Alans in Europe begins at the same point in time as that of the Huns, in 375, when the latter wiped out the empire of the Alans in the area of the Caspian Sea. After this catastrophe the Alans never again managed to form a political unit. Bands of Alans wandered aimlessly across the whole of western Europe and North Africa in the fifth century, and then, in spite of very different ethnic origins, merged with the mass of the German conquerors. Their historic role is of only secondary importance. Virtually nothing is known of the migration of the Alans from east to west between 375 and 406.[2] However the Alan resistance to the Huns, which was of great importance in the events of 451 in Gaul, becomes more comprehensible if the Alans of Orleans were the descendants of those defeated in 375.

From 406 onwards the Alans split up into bands lacking any kind of common interest. They all took part in the crossing of the Rhine, but soon afterwards one group under King Goar took service with the Romans, first in the Rhineland and then in central Gaul. Another group, under King Respendial, made common cause with the Vandals and, following in their wake, burst into Spain in 409. Others besieged Bazas around AD 414. Others again, about thirty years later, are mentioned as being in the Rhône district, near Valence, ruled by a King Sambida.

Most of the Alans in Gaul ended up by allying themselves with Rome. They were taken in hand by Aetius and quartered on the middle reaches of the Loire, at first in order to hold back the Visigoths, and later to bar the way to the Huns. Although his loyalty was rather unreliable, the Alan King Sangiban played a decisive part in the defeat of Attila at Orleans. Shortly afterwards the Alans surrendered to the Visigoths. Aetius must have considered settling Alan federates in Armorica; it is probably from them that place-names such as Allaines (Eure-et-Loir, Somme) are derived. Several archaeological finds (such as the bronzes from the region of Vendôme) are also attributed to them, but with rather less justification.

The Alans who entered Spain in 409 received Lusitania and Carthaginiensis for their portion, a considerable stretch of territory which they were not numerous enough to hold properly; as early as 418 their independence was destroyed by Visigoths sent from Rome. The remainder of the Alans formed an alliance with the Asding Vandals and followed them into Galicia, Andalusia, and later Africa. The Vandal kings always bore the title *rex Vandalorum et Alanorum* thereafter, but in fact the Alans were assimilated fairly quickly, and made no lasting impression on the Vandals.

The Goths

The Goths were of much greater importance, the only people to travel across the Empire from one end to the other, the first to found lasting kingdoms and to be successful in creating a synthesis of Germanic and Roman elements, and finally the only people to enjoy an independent intellectual culture. Until the time of Justinian the Goths assumed the leadership of the barbarian world, and their ensuing prestige among other Germans was expressed in the epic tradition for over a thousand years.

The question of the origin of the Goths is a difficult one, and the best approach is to go back to the traditions which Cassiodorus and Jordanes collected in the sixth century among the Ostrogoths in Italy.[3] According to them the Goths came from 'the island of Scandza', crossed the sea to 'the shores of the Hither Ocean', took the land of the 'Ulmerugians' and defeated the Vandals. In our terms this means that having left Scandinavia, they settled on the southern shore of the Baltic Sea, somewhere near the present-day Polish coast. (The name of Scandza is the same as that of Scania, and hence of Scandinavia; the Ulmerugians seem to be the 'Rugians of the Islands'—probably the islands at the mouth of the Oder.) Although spiced with legendary details, this version of the facts seems to be quite credible. It gives a fairly plausible account of the merging of a group of peoples who had had close connections for a long time—Goths, Rugians, Vandals and soon Heruls and Skirians. It would then date from the time that they all lived along the shores of the Baltic Sea.

Although thanks to Ulfila the Gothic language is well known to us, the study of linguistics cannot enlighten us very much as to the origin of the Goths: it only indicates that we must not seek it too far from the Nordic context. But the limits of the latter on the eve of the first century AD are not known. Two Scandinavian peoples in the Middle Ages have names which resemble that of the Goths—the *Gutar* of the island of Gotland, and the *Götar* of Götaland (the southern half of medieval Sweden). There is no convincing argument which allows us to decide between these putative cousins. Most historians favour Götaland simply because its greater surface area seems more appropriate for the homeland of a great people. The dialects of both regions are North Germanic, however, and have nothing to do with Gothic, which is the best-known of the East Germanic dialects.

Archaeology, too, can only provide us with contradictory information. From the time of their stay in Pomerania onwards the Goths had a very distinctive funerary custom, which differed from that of all the other Germanic peoples: they did not leave weapons in the graves of their men. Now this omission is also found, just before the first century AD, in the western part of Götaland (Västergötland), a region which seems to have been depopulated at the very time when the Roman sources attest the settling of the Goths on the southern shores of the Baltic.[4] On the other hand, almost all of the Goths of the Vistula seem to have practised inhumation, while only cremation was practised in Scandinavia. Archaeologists can therefore neither seriously contest nor definitely confirm the thesis of Jordanes.

The real history of the Goths begins with Pliny, who mentions

Gutones about AD 75, and with Tacitus, who has heard of some *Gothones* in about AD 98. At that time they were in the north-east of Germany, and soon Ptolemy locates them more precisely on the right bank of the lower Vistula. The area under their dominion probably extended towards the north, for it is thought that there are numerous borrowings from Gothic in the Baltic languages. A little before the year 150 King Filimer decided on a migration towards the south-east, across the Pripet marshes in the direction of the Pontic steppes. About 230 the Goths are found to have settled to the north-west of the Black Sea. Between the Carpathians, the Don, the Vistula and the Sea of Azov they set up a state with fluctuating borders which seems to have centred on the lower Dnieper valley. They assimilated the survivors of the Bastarnae and the Skirians, and were strongly influenced by the former Iranian inhabitants of the country. The Goths became semi-nomadic horsemen, took to wearing coats of mail and, in the case of the kings at least, Iranian costume, to such an extent that the Graeco-Roman authors frequently confused them with the Scythians, or took the Alans to be a branch of the Goths. The real Goths probably formed only a part of the population of this vast area, where the ancestors of the Slavs had already settled.

It is at this point that the Goths split into two groups, a division which was to last throughout their history. At first these two groups were called the *Tervingi* and the *Greutingi*, names which were soon replaced by those of Visigoths and Ostrogoths. There has been much debate about these names, which appear in a corrupt form in the *Historia Augusta* in connection with the events of 269. It is generally accepted that *Tervingi* means 'forest people' (of the Russian taiga, or perhaps the Carpathian forest) and that *Greutingi* means 'shore people'. The second pair of names, *Ostrogoti* and *Vesi* (later *Visigoti*), was at first interpreted as 'Eastern Goths' and 'Western Goths'; this inter-pretation, which has been regarded with complete disfavour for the last thirty years (Splendid Goths and Wise Goths being proposed instead) is starting to gain ground again, because it is supported by Jordanes. At any rate neither unity of language nor feeling of kinship, which remained very strong, was affected by the split. Groups and individuals passed from one people to the other without any trouble. But there were probably two separate monarchies, that of the Ostro-goths enjoying a certain primacy. Two satellite peoples, the Gepids and the Taifals, kept their autonomy.

The first contact between the Goths and the Empire took place in Dacia under Gordian III; as early as 238 a raid into Thrace is recorded. Then the Goths discovered the sea—as the Slavs and the Varangians were to do later, in the same part of the world. Together with the Heruls, the Goths raided the shores of the Black Sea and forced their way through the Bosporus, first in 257–8, and then five or six more times before the year 276, when they got as far as Cilicia. After this brief blaze of glory they concentrated again on campaigns by land, which proved to be extremely profitable: in 271 Aurelian had to abandon Dacia to them. The only lasting effect of the maritime phase was to install among the Goths a large group of Cappadocian captives, who were the mediators between Greek culture and the Germanic world. Seventy years later one of the descendants of these Cappadocians, Ulfila, became the apostle of the Goths (see below). For a century the territory under Gothic domination bordered that of the Romans all along the course of the Danube from the Pannonian basin to the delta. No memorable incident occurred between the two powers. Like all the neighbours of the Empire the Goths provided recruits for the imperial armies and collected tribute from the Romans. After a Roman victory in 332 a *foedus* was concluded with the Visigoths: it was respected for thirty-five years and allowed remarkable cultural exchanges, notably the penetration of Christianity among the Goths.

The mission to the Goths started at the beginning of the fourth century (a Gothic bishop sat at the council of Nicaea). Arianism had its most remarkable success among the Goths, after a Visigoth of Anatolian descent, Ulfila, was consecrated bishop in 341. Ulfila had truly remarkable intellectual qualities. he invented a script and a literary language for the Goths so that he could translate the New Testament. He brought Christianity out of the narrow circle of the descendants of prisoners, so effectively that in 348 and 369 the Gothic rulers began to persecute Christians. The apostle of the Goths died in exile in Constantinople, probably in 383. His faith was not adopted by the aristocracy until after the Goths had entered the Empire. Thus the Gothic people became the crucible of an intellectual and religious experience unique among those who were involved in the invasions.

All this was happening among the Visigoths. We know practically nothing about the Ostrogoths before 375. At that time Athanaric was the leader of the Visigoths (with the title of 'judge'), and Ermanaric, a vigorous warrior, reigned over the Ostrogoths. Gothic society, which had seemed to be set on a course of rapid stabilization, suffered a severe setback when the Huns attacked in 375. The Ostrogoths who had settled on the lower Don were seized with panic; Ermanaric committed suicide, and his successor was killed in battle. Two leaders, the Goth Alatheus and the Alan Safrac, took the people westwards, beyond the Dnieper and then beyond the Danube. The Visigoths followed them, as did Alans, Rugians, Skirians, Taifals and Heruls. At least, this is the account of the only reliable source, Ammianus Marcellinus. Jordanes gives a totally different picture: according to him the Goths submitted to the Huns. Although many of the details may have been invented, this tradition does contain a grain of truth: a party of Goths did stay in the Ukraine under Hunnic suzerainty, while some took refuge in the mountains of the Crimea (see p. 223).

In the autumn of 376 the Goths demanded asylum in the Empire. Most of them, led by the Visigoth Fritigern, were welcomed and settled in Thrace, where the Roman merchants took full advantage of their plight, selling them food at extortionate prices. The rest went up the left bank of the Danube and, under Athanaric, settled in the Carpathians and in Moldavia, under the protection of the Huns. These Goths are credited with the construction of the *vallum* of Moldavia from the Seret to the Danube, which was intended to separate the Gothic settlements of upper Moldavia from the steppes of the south which had been left to the Huns.[5] There were both Ostrogoths and Visigoths in these two groups, but the majority of the former stayed to the north of the Danube while almost all the latter entered the Empire. Until about 470 it was only the Visigoths who caused the Romans any concern.

In 377 the Visigoths revolted against the conditions in which they were living in Thrace. Valens wanted to wipe them out, but it was he who died in the battle of Adrianople, on 9 August 378, and the Goths advanced to blockade the capital of his Empire. However Theodosius, Valens' successor, quickly made them loosen their grip. A barrier was then set up again all along the Danube. But Fritigern and his Goths stayed within the Empire and wandered about the Balkan peninsula, only accepting the *foedus* at the end of 382, probably in return for lands in Moesia, a province which had been totally disorganized by the invasions. This truce lasted no more than eight or nine years. In 392 Stilicho managed to impose a renewal of the *foedus* on the new Visigothic leader Alaric, but it was again broken in 395 and again the Goths prepared to besiege Constantinople. The eastern part of the Balkans was soon so devastated that Alaric set out towards Illyricum, ravaging Greece on the way. In 397 the Empire had to resign itself to abandoning Epirus to him, and to appointing him *magister militum* in Illyricum, which gave him complete military power in the western half of the peninsula. Meanwhile other Goths, led by Gainas, an officer who had been in the service of Rome for a long time, rose in rebellion near Constantinople in 400: it proved necessary to call in the Huns to help defeat him. It seemed as if the *pars orientis* was about to fall into the hands of the Goths, but by this time it was probably too devastated to satisfy their craving for plunder. In 401 Alaric abruptly decided to lead his people into Italy.

During their stay in the Balkans the Roman policy had been to try to divide the Goths, by encouraging a pro-Roman faction under Fravittas and especially under Gainas. Gothic officers obtained high-ranking positions in the Roman army. But the majority of the Gothic people remained hostile. During the whole of his career Alaric seems to have vacillated between two possible courses of action: making a personal niche for himself within the Empire or ensuring a definitive settlement for his people. It was almost certainly during these years in the Balkans that the conversion of the Visigoths to Arianism was completed. All this has been brought to light in a remarkable way by E. A. Thompson [no. 172].

Thus a Balkan phase of twenty-five years in the history of the Goths was succeeded by an Italian phase of eleven years. This brought no significant changes in their aims or way of life. They were still an army wandering from place to place, exhausting one after another their sources of food supplies. Almost without a blow being struck, Alaric installed his army in Venetia in the winter of 401–2, then marched on Milan. Honorius was in residence there, but he managed to take refuge in Ravenna, which was inaccessible behind its marshes. The following years were spent in countering Stilicho's delaying tactics the length and breadth of northern Italy. A treaty sent the Goths back into Dalmatia for a short time, then into Noricum, and it was during this intermission that the invaders under Radagaisus poured into Italy, bringing other Gothic elements in their wake. Then the treaty was broken and in 408 Alaric again arrived in the Po valley, demanding the enormous sum of 4,000 pounds of gold. This was the moment that Honorius chose to have Stilicho assassinated. In October 408 Alaric arrived unresisted at the gates of Rome. He demanded a huge tribute, obtained part of it and withdrew to Tuscany; he carried on interminable negotiations, then lost his temper and forced the senate to proclaim a usurper, Attalus, as Emperor before going off to blockade Ravenna. (Attalus was deposed even before the sack of Rome, but remained a faithful adviser of the Visigoths, with whom he identified to the point of renouncing his pagan religion and having himself baptised into the Arian faith.) The impossibility of reaching an agreement with Honorius exasperated Alaric who, to avenge himself, decided to sack Rome, which no one attempted to defend and which a revolt in Africa had reduced to a state of famine anyway. On 24 August 410 the Gothic leader entered Rome, probably thanks to treason, and the Eternal City was looted, save for a few sanctuaries. This event seemed to be not only a terrible catastrophe, but also a great scandal, rocking the faith of some in the Fortune of Rome and of others in Divine Providence itself. The moral shock was worse than the material damage and the loss of life, considerable though these were.[6] A good part of the population fled, never to return. The whole episode, however, lasted for only three days. On 27 August the Goths left Rome, taking Galla Placidia, the sister of the Emperor, with them as hostage.

Their intention was to go to Africa and look for another likely place to plunder, but lack of ships prevented them from crossing to Sicily. Alaric died in Calabria very shortly after this set-back, at the end of 410.

Athaulf, his brother-in-law, led the Visigoths back towards the north. After a year and a half of indecision, he crossed into Gaul by the Mont-Genèvre pass in the spring of 412. Gaul at that time was in the hands of a short-lived usurper, Jovinus. Athaulf offered to overthrow him in the name of Honorius, but as the promised food supplies failed to arrive the king took Narbonne, Toulouse and Bordeaux, the last in 413. This was the end of the long march of the Goths. They remained in Aquitaine for three generations and at Narbonne for three centuries.

In order to pave the way for a definitive reconciliation between the Goths and the Romans, Athaulf married his hostage Galla Placidia, the daughter of Theodosius, at Narbonne in January of 414 in a completely Roman ceremony. We shall look at the political implications of this later. Then he set up a rudimentary government at Bordeaux, led by Aquitanian aristocrats, including Paulinus of Pella. Nevertheless the king continued to wage war against Ravenna, but having crossed into Spain to obtain provisions was assassinated at Barcelona in August 415.

This murder revealed an internal tension within the Gothic people, among whom only the aristocracy had grasped and supported Athaulf's policy of settling conquered territory. The new king, Wallia, found that pressure was being put on him to start another migration; like Alaric he wanted to cross to Africa (via Gibraltar), but did not succeed in doing so. At this point a very able leader, the patrician Constantius, managed to recruit him for the service of the Empire in 416, after taking various military measures, including a blockade. Wallia left Spain and negotiated a settlement in Aquitaine, but died just when this agreement was about to come into force. It gave birth to the first barbarian state to be established firmly on imperial soil, the state traditionally known as 'the kingdom of Toulouse', although its capital alternated for a long time between Bordeaux and Toulouse (and was sometimes, under Euric, at Arles). The details of the *foedus* of 418 are unknown to us. We do not know why Constantius recalled the Goths from Spain to Gaul, or what provinces were given to them. But two facts are established: the concession was made according to the system of *hospitalitas*, and it gave back to Rome the province of Narbonensis I, the bridge between what was left of Roman Gaul and Spain.[7]

The region where the Visigoths carried out their political experiment was one of the richest in Gaul, one of the least affected by previous invasions, and probably also one of the least war-like (in contrast to the Auvergne). The concession of this region satisfied the scruples even of those Goths who were most opposed to Rome. Theodoric I (418–51) was able to respect the *foedus*, give military assistance to the Empire three or four times, and die fighting Attila, while at the same time looking after the interests of the Gothic leaders, who henceforth became a landed aristocracy. His son Theodoric II (453–66) could read Virgil, it is said, and knew a little about Roman law; the mildness of his régime earned him the praises of Salvian. After renewing the *foedus* he put himself at the service of Rome to put down the Bacaudae in Spain, and then to eliminate the Suevian threat. But his great ambition was to place his protegé Avitus, the father-in-law of Sidonius Apollinaris, on the imperial throne. The attempt to do so cost him dear, and eventually failed. Majorian later forced him to give back the gains he had made in Gaul and Spain during Avitus' brief spell as Emperor. Once Majorian was dead, however, he made good his loss by occupying Novempopulana and Septimania in 462.

Theodoric II was assassinated in 466, and his brother Euric (466–84) brought the kingdom of Toulouse to the height of its power. Taking advantage of the decline of the Empire, he pursued a double policy: his aims were to enlarge his dominion in Gaul (which he did by defeating the Bretons in Berry in 469, by occupying Aquitania I, by temporarily occupying Arles, Avignon and Valence in 470–1, and by conquering the Auvergne in 474–5), and, from 468 onwards, to consolidate his protectorate in Spain. It is not even sure whether his brutal seizure of two of the strongholds of Roman civilization, the Auvergne and Tarraconensis, caused the renunciation of the *foedus*. At any rate Euric had no difficulty in having his conquests legalized— of the Auvergne in 475 by Nepos, and of Tarraconensis, together with Provence, in 477 by Odoacer and Zeno. Relatively mild measures— like the exile of Sidonius to Bordeaux and Llivia—were sufficient to break down local resistance.

Euric was a law-giver, who apparently appreciated Latin literature. His court at Bordeaux attracted all sorts of barbarians, including Ostrogoths and even Saxons, and foreshadowed that of Theodoric the Great at Ravenna. His minister Leo was a forerunner of Cassiodorus. Euric respected the Roman administrative hierarchy, and raised both Goths and Romans indiscriminately to the rank of count and duke. While continuing to wear the costume of a Gothic king, he himself voluntarily assumed the minor titles of imperial protocol (*clementia vestra, mansuetudo vestra*); but he showed his independence by rejecting consular dates in favour of reckoning by his own regnal years.

The Gothic people probably stayed on in the regions where they first settled and around strategic points like the valley of the Garonne, the area around Bazas, Bas-Quercy and Montagne Noire. No place-names can be attributed to them with any certainty except those among the numerous toponyms ending in *-ens* which have a Gothic personal name as their first part, because place-names ending in *-ens* seem to have been abundant even after the Frankish conquest. Reliable archaeological evidence is lacking, except within Septimania.

Alaric II (484–507), the son of Euric, seems to have been of mediocre ability, and to have occupied himself chiefly in enjoying what had been amassed by his father. However he did consolidate Gothic domination in Spain by initiating a system of civil colonization on top of the military occupation: the Chronicle of Saragossa for the years 494–7 mentions 'the entry of the Goths into Spain', and then a 'settling of Goths'. Various small pockets of resistance were brutally eliminated. There is no clear proof that this first plantation, like the succeeding one, took place in Old Castile. But the greatest problem of this reign was to prevent the Franks from advancing south of the Loire; as early as 498 Clovis's troops had reached Bordeaux. We know very little about the chronology of this series of battles (see p. 229), but it ended in catastrophe: Alaric was defeated and slain at Vouillé in 507, and Catholic Aquitaine found no difficulty in rallying to the victor.

The Visigothic people was saved by the intervention of the Ostrogoths in the name of the solidarity which united the two branches; for a whole generation Theodoric and his deputies took the destiny of the conquered people in hand. But this rescue operation was successful only at the cost of a radical transformation: the kingdom of Toulouse, which had been outward-looking and essentially Gallic in character, became the kingdom of Toledo, almost entirely Spanish and jealously inward-looking. However, its fundamental institutions— Arianism, the *modus vivendi* with the Romans, and the structure of government—were preserved. Theodoric seems to have wanted to extend to Spain the dualist régime which he practised in Italy.[8] But the customs of the kingdom of Toulouse gained the upper hand after 531, when the kingdom resigned itself to being Spanish alone.

Helped by these structural reforms the Visigothic people moved in a mass exodus from Aquitaine to Old Castile, motivated no doubt principally by the decision made by a Gallic council in 511 to close the Arian churches. The main body must have crossed the Pyrenees at Roncesvalles or the Somport, but a small handful of Goths stayed on in Septimania.

The Ostrogothic interlude came to a head with another drama. Amalaric, having attained his majority, wanted to interfere in the disputes of the sons of Clovis, his brothers-in-law. He was defeated in 531 and killed near Barcelona. That was the end of the dynasty of the Balts. The former Ostrogothic governor Theudis then took the throne and established his court at Barcelona. He conciliated the

Romans by encouraging the convocation of Catholic councils and by marrying a Roman woman. His cautious foreign policy was largely successful: he repulsed a Frankish invasion in 541, discouraged the Byzantines, who had held Ceuta since the fall of the Vandals, from crossing the Straits of Gibraltar, and above all made sure that Spain was spared the consequences of Justinian's victories over the Ostrogoths. When he was assassinated in 548—an occupational hazard for rulers of the Visigoths—another Ostrogothic general, Theudisclus, replaced him and was assassinated in his turn at Seville in 549. A Visigoth of unknown origin, Agila, came to power this time. Faced with the threat of a Byzantine invasion in 551 he moved his court to Mérida. But his Arian intolerance of Catholicism did not go down well in the completely Roman south of Spain. He was assassinated in 554. Seeing the progress the Byzantines were making under the direction of one of Theodoric's former ministers, the patrician Liberius, Agila's successor Athanagild withdrew to the heart of the meseta and established his capital at Toledo, at the very edge of the territory colonized by the Visigoths.

This event marks the end of the migration of the Visigothic people. The kingdom of Toledo stood firmly on these foundations until the Islamic invasion of 711. The Byzantine danger which had looked so menacing in the middle of the sixth century came to nothing in the end, for the armies of Justinian were exhausted by the interminable struggle in Italy and were never able to make a serious attempt to reconquer Spain. A coastal strip from Denia to Cadiz was all that they managed to reoccupy, with the naval base of Cartagena as its centre. The Byzantine province survived until some time between 620 and 630, although very little is known about it. The sympathy which Byzantium could have found among the Spanish Catholics was never exploited to the full.

The Visigoths enthusiastically set about forming a united Spain around their court at Toledo. The first problem was to bring about religious unity. From 570 to 580 Leovigild attempted to unite the population in the bosom of Arianism, but without success. Reccared triumphantly achieved religious unity by himself converting to Catholicism in 587. As a result, the unique institution of the councils of Toledo was created: these assemblies, which were both political and ecclesiastical, put their talents at the service of the monarchy until the end. The next problem was to achieve political unity. The Suevian kingdom in Galicia was wiped out by Leovigild in 585, the Byzantine enclave was conquered by Sisebut (612–21), and Basque separatism was dealt with more or less effectively. Leaving aside the Jews, who were numerous in the Mediterranean areas and were widely persecuted, spiritual unity grew rapidly with the sharing of a common faith, a common culture (noted for the renaissance which spread from Baetica at the time of Isidore of Seville) and the same legal system (unified at the latest in 654 by Recceswinth, see p. 211).

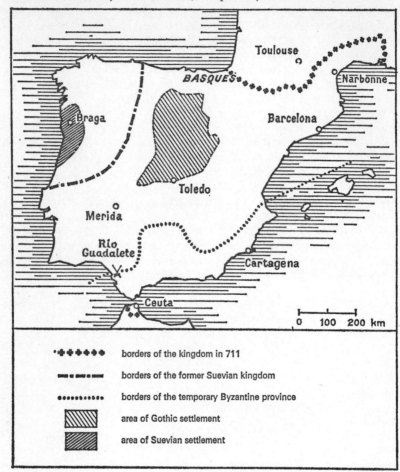

Fig. 1 Visigothic Spain

In spite of its weaknesses—its policy concerning the Jews was a conspicuous blunder, creating allies for Islam even before the conquest—and its chronic political instability (which the Goths fomented with a truly Spanish passion), the monarchy of Toledo is worthy of an eminent place in the history of the barbarian kingdoms. It was the only one, after the death of Theodoric the Great, to favour intellectual life. Above all it left to Europe a legacy of some of the most characteristic institutions of medieval kingship: the coronation oath (recorded for the first time in 638) and the rite of anointing with holy oil (which is first known to have been used in 672 at the coronation of King Wamba). Thus it deserved to inspire the posthumous and almost fanatical attachment of the first generations of Spaniards of the Reconquest (a ridiculous and excessive attachment according to certain modern Spanish scholars who deny the 'Spanishness' of Visigothic history, very wrongly in our opinion). The Chronicle of Albelda shows Alfonso II (791–842) at Oviedo reinstating *omnem Gotorum ordinem sicut Toleto fuerat* (the whole organization of the Goths just as it was at Toledo).

What, in sum, was the Gothic contribution to Spain? Firstly a rich store of personal names, which were sufficiently vigorous to survive the crises of the eighth century (for example Adefonsus, Alvarus, Fredenandus and Rodericus); a much more limited number of place-names (especially in the provinces of Burgos and Segovia); some legal customs and a few items of administrative vocabulary; and finally some funerary and sartorial fashions. (The Gothic language, which was already moribund, died out with the abandonment of Arianism.) But, most important, a national spirit was born, the most powerful that the barbarian West ever produced, which was capable of winning over Romans as steadfast as Isidore of Seville.

The career of the Ostrogoths was shorter than that of the Visigoths, but more brilliant. At the time of the battle of Adrianople they were divided into two groups: one lived on in Pannonia as a satellite of the Huns on what had formerly been Roman territory, but was now so devastated that they were barely able to scratch out a meagre living for themselves; the other, which had taken service with the Empire, was billeted in the Balkan peninsula. This second group, which was clearly smaller in numbers and without any political independence, was an intermediary between the civilization of Constantinople and the Ostrogoths when the survivors rejoined Theodoric the Great's Ostrogoths around 482.

The Goths in Pannonia, led by Valamir, a descendant of a brother of Ermanaric, showed themselves to be faithful vassals of Attila, whom they accompanied into Gaul and Italy; but they did not feel themselves to be so bound to his sons, and remained neutral when the Hunnic empire collapsed in 454. In the turmoil which followed Valamir made his peace with the Empire. A *foedus* in about 455 ceded to him the region of Lake Balaton. It was about this time that Theodemir, the brother of the king, had a son by a Catholic concubine, who was to become Theodoric the Great. From time to time, when the Eastern Empire was backward about paying the tribute, Valamir would raid Illyria, and then the agreement would be renewed. At

the time of the *foedus* of 461 the young Theodoric was sent to Constantinople as a hostage, an event which was to have important
consequences. In the capital Theodoric was placed under the tutelage
of the Emperor-maker Flavius Ardabur Aspar, an Alan with Gothic
blood in his veins, who was to Leo I what Ricimer was to the sovereigns
of Ravenna. For nine years—the years when a man's character is
moulded, between the ages of eight and seventeen—Theodoric was
able to observe both the grandeur of the Empire and the means of
harnessing it to the advantage of the barbarians. Theodoric regained
his freedom in 470, a year before Leo had his troublesome protector
assassinated. The lesson had taken effect.

Meanwhile Valamir had been killed by the Skirians. Theodemir had
succeeded him and had defeated his worst enemy, the Skirian Edica
(the father of Odoacer), in the battle of Bolia in 470, and later the
Sarmatian King Babai too. When the murder of Aspar relieved them
of all allegiance to Rome both father and son were encouraged by
these successes to try their luck in Illyricum. The Ostrogoths advanced
along the Morava-Vardar corridor, threatening Salonica and then
Adrianople. In 473 Leo made a treaty with Theodoric, who had succeeded to the throne on the death of his father. The Goths were to
become federates billeted in Macedonia and were to receive a tribute;
their king became *magister militum praesentalis*. After a century of
waiting at the borders of the Empire the Ostrogoths had finally
obtained a legal status similar to that accorded to the Visigoths in
418. However even this did not persuade them to settle down: in 475
they crossed into Moesia, and they turned up again in Macedonia in
479, in Epirus in 480 and in ripuarian Dacia in 483. Theodoric was
sometimes at loggerheads with the new Emperor Zeno and sometimes
allied with him. He reaped some substantial benefits from this: the
imperial *nomen gentilicium* of Flavius, the ordinary consulate in 484 and
the triumph in 485 after a brief campaign against a usurper in Asia
Minor. On the other hand he was not above military action against the
Emperor when the occasion arose: in 488 he blockaded Constantinople
on both shores of the Bosporus. Meanwhile he gathered up the various
Gothic bands who were living in the Balkans, in particular the one
commanded by his namesake, Theodoric Strabo.

In the end Zeno realized that the only way he could be rid of the
Goths was to send them further away. For a long time he had dreamt
of driving Odoacer out of Italy, and he saw Theodoric as the perfect
tool. An agreement was reached between them in 488, all the more
easily as a sort of family feud already existed between Odoacer and the
Ostrogothic king. Theodoric concentrated all his volunteers at Novae
(Sistova in Bulgaria). It was almost as motley a collection as that of
Radagaisus, in which the real Ostrogoths can have formed only a

minority. All kinds of other Goths were represented in it, as well as a 'Roman' battalion under a relative of Zeno, and also the remains of the Rugians. (The last-mentioned wanted to avenge a defeat which Odoacer had inflicted on them near Vienna at the end of 487. The Rugians preserved a certain autonomy within the Gothic army, even after the conquest of Italy: they did not intermarry with the Goths, and they kept their own administrators. In 541 at the time of the destruction of the Gothic state they elected a king of their own called Eraric, who reigned for five months. This did not prevent their disappearance in the same catastrophe as the Ostrogoths.) The army moved off in the autumn, wintered in Croatia, and presented itself on the borders of Italy in the spring of 489. Odoacer had had time to organize his defences on the Isonzo, but Theodoric's army burst through these on 28 August 489; Odoacer then fell back on the Adige and was defeated there on 30 September, near Verona. Many of his soldiers defected, and the rest shut themselves up in Ravenna. Theodoric was able to occupy the countryside of Upper Italy without a fight, and even Milan and Pavia too. But it was four more years before he was able to inflict a final defeat on Odoacer, in 493.

The vicissitudes of this campaign are not particularly important. Sometimes Theodoric was besieging Odoacer in Ravenna, and sometimes he was himself being besieged in Pavia. Odoacer vainly tried to awaken Roman patriotism by re-establishing the imperial dignity for the benefit of his son Thela. After a ruthless blockade of Ravenna, in which Theodoric used a fleet based at Rimini, Odoacer capitulated on 25 February 493, on condition that he and Theodoric would be co-regents of Italy. But when Theodoric entered the capital of the Western Empire on 5 March he organized the assassination of Odoacer together with his family and lieutenants—an atrocious beginning to a reign which, surprisingly enough, turned out to be quite reasonable and humane. This was Theodoric's last gesture towards a purely 'barbaric' policy.

The experience which Theodoric had built up as a hostage in Constantinople, as head of the federates in the Balkans, and then during the years of conflict in Italy, was to enable him to carry out a project very different from that which the past history of his people, on whom so little civilization had rubbed off, would lead one to expect. But this project, even more than that of the Visigothic kings, had the weakness that its success depended solely on the person of the king. All went well while the king was still alive, but it took less than a generation after his death for his achievements to be completely obliterated. Theodoric's fundamental idea was to organize Italy on a dualist basis—Goths and Romans were to live there under parallel administrations whose only link would be the person of the prince and a few government offices. This delicate system was built up with real mastery, the two communities complementing one another. The material strength came from the Gothic army, but Theodoric realized that Roman civilization was the only foundation on which to build a state capable of assuring the Ostrogoths lasting supremacy among the barbarians.

As far as his army was concerned Theodoric lived and thought like a Germanic king. Like Odoacer, he took the title of king—*Flavius Theodericus rex*, and not *rex Gothorum*. It must always be remembered that his army was multinational and that all the free Germans, the *capillati*, were equal in Italy. With the other barbarian princes Theodoric pursued a policy of family alliances. He married a sister of Clovis, married off one of his daughters to the Burgundian Sigismund and another to the Visigoth Alaric II, and finally married his sister to the Vandal Thrasamund. He assured all Germans who were in difficulties of his concern, and to the petty kings of Thuringia who were threatened by the Franks his minister Cassiodorus sent letters which conformed to the best canons of Latin rhetoric. He took under his protection the Heruls of Pannonia, the Varini of the Rhine, the Alamans who had been conquered by Clovis and the last survivors of the Gepids. All able-bodied warriors were welcomed, and he paid such good wages that they came to him from as far away as Scandinavia. In short, the Ostrogothic king was the protector, and the good angel, of the barbarians of the West.

Even taking into account the fact that thanks to the correspondence of Cassiodorus we are much more informed about his policies than about those of his contemporaries, Theodoric still appears to have had a breadth of vision denied to the other barbarian kings, who were never able to look beyond their own personal problems, or at most their tribal or dynastic ones. He had a powerful sense of the solidarity necessary among the Germans, and he was able to carry on diplomacy on a European scale, thanks in part to the exceptional peace which the Goths enjoyed at that time. No one was pressing on their borders, and the peoples of the steppes had faded out of the picture for the moment. Perhaps it is a question of whether the Ostrogothic people measured up to the ambitions that Theodoric had for them.

Theodoric was more acceptable to the Romans in Italy than many other barbarian patricians. He showed a demonstrative attachment to Roman traditions and institutions, and he was almost sincere when he called the former Emperors *majores nostri*, and when he proclaimed himself *bono reipublicae natus*. His journey to Rome for his enthronement in 500 was the occasion of a speech in which he set out his plans for the future of Italy, a speech which must have pleased even the most conservative Roman. 'We rejoice in living under Roman law, which we hope to defend by force of arms. What good does it do to drive out barbarian disorder if we do not take our rule of life from the laws? Our ambition, with God's help, is to reap such victories that our subjects will regret not having placed themselves under our sovereignty sooner.'[9] But mindful of his barbarian descent Theodoric prudently stopped short of expressly claiming the Empire for himself; he always respected the formal prerogatives of the Eastern Emperor.

It is not absolutely certain what sort of powers Theodoric exercised in Italy in the name of Zeno. The most probable answer is that suggested by E. Stein.[10] According to him Theodoric must have been *magister militum per Italiam*, and therefore theoretically a colleague of the Burgundian King Gundobad, who was *magister militum per Gallias*: but Theodoric interpreted his functions as a general delegation of imperial rights. The inscription in Terracina gives evidence of a cunning moderation: *Augustus* is there but not *Caesar*, *triumphator* but not *imperator*.[11] The king took the risk of having a gold coin struck (which was an imperial prerogative) on which he is represented in imperial dress, but so discreetly did he do so that only one example of it has survived! At his court he retained certain elements of imperial protocol, such as the adoration of the purple.[12]

Inspired by this dual ideology, Theodoric governed the Goths by means of *comites Gothorum*, who were both civil and military officials whose orders were given to them directly by special agents called *saiones* (and not by the *cursus publicus*). His German generals, like Ibbas or Tuluin, were the most trustworthy executors of his policies. For the Romans he preserved the traditional hierarchy of the courtly and senatorial functions, which he caused to work with exemplary regularity. His 'political testament' ordained that the Goths should 'love the senate and people of Rome, and do their best to keep the good will of the Eastern Emperor'.[13] But the king interfered in appointments, almost systematically preferring the provincial aristocracy to the leaders of the senate.[14] It was from among the former that he chose his principal adviser and spokesman to the Romans, Cassiodorus, a Calabrian whose father had been a high-ranking civil servant under Odoacer. He was appointed governor of Lucania, and made consul in 514, then *magister officiorum* and finally praetorian prefect from 534 to 536, but he left his mark above all on the post of *quaestor palatii*, which he occupied from 507 to 534. His literary reputation was such that five hundred items of his administrative correspondence have been preserved for us, under the name of *Variae*.

The Gothic military administration and the offices of the Sacred Palace at Ravenna coexisted without friction. The king had rather less success with the two parallel churches, the Arian and the Catholic, but managed to avoid overt conflict. His method was a rigorous separation of the duties and the functions of the two peoples, which went as far as real social segregation. The Romans were forbidden to bear arms and the Arian Goths were forbidden to proselytize.

The prefect Liberius billeted Theodoric's army, under the rules of the system of *hospitalitas*, in the same places where Odoacer's troops had been concentrated, especially in the valley of the Po and around Ravenna, and also in Tuscany, Picenum and Samnium, with a few more isolated garrisons in Campania and Dalmatia. Because of the superimposed Lombard traces the toponymic contribution of the Goths in these areas is difficult to assess; it consists mainly of some of the names ending in -*engo* in modern Lombardy, as for example Gottolengo, Marengo and Offanengo. Their linguistic contribution appears to have been slight; Gamillscheg probably overestimates it when he puts it at seventy words, mainly practical terms used in everyday life. The maintenance of these colonies did not pose too many problems, for the Goths were mostly stationed in *Italia annonaria*, which had been organized since the beginning of the fourth century with a view to supplying vast quantities of cereals and wine.

Theodoric applied a similar, though simplified, system of government to the dependencies of Italy, that is Raetia (of which the northern part was only a protectorate), northern Illyricum, Dalmatia and a small part of Pannonia, where the king was represented by a half-breed Hun-Gepid called Mundo. Except for eastern Sicily the Italian islands were abandoned to the Vandals. After the battle of Vouillé Theodoric took over the running of Provence, without formally annexing it, and set up an embryonic autonomous government there, under a prefect with his headquarters at Arles.

At the heart of this vast state was the court at Ravenna. Theodoric was the only barbarian king to grasp the Roman concept of a capital. He loved Ravenna and embellished it, carrying on the work of Galla Placidia and of Valentinian III. He erected many buildings—palaces, churches and a baptistery—and even set up an equestrian statue of himself, pending the construction of his mausoleum. In Rome he was almost as energetic, although he did more restoration than construction. His buildings were of a high standard, as good as those of Justinian, who took over where he left off. But it was in the intellectual sphere that the reign was really outstanding. It is dominated by three names: Ennodius, the future bishop of Pavia, noted for his formal literary style; Cassiodorus, who was a statesman before he created his repository of culture in the monastery at Vivarium; and, most important, Boethius, the last truly original mind produced by Antiquity, like Cassiodorus an administrator, but first and foremost a philosopher and mathematician imbued with Greek culture. The hopes which the king entertained for the birth of a truly Gothic culture were not realized.

The reign was exceptionally long and prosperous: thirty-six years, for thirty-three of which there was absolute peace in Italy. But the last years are full of indications of the difficulties that were to beset everything that he had created as soon as the king died. Firstly, Theodoric lived to see the start of a dispute on the question of the succession: he wished to leave Italy to his son-in-law Eutharic, and had obtained the consent of the Emperor Justin, but Eutharic died and only a small child of seven years was left—Athalaric, the grandson of the old king. Then he had to acknowledge the failure of his policy of barbarian solidarity: his allies among the Burgundians and the Vandals were eliminated. Last, but by no means least, his collaboration with the Roman aristocracy and with the Catholic church was seriously jeopardized in 523–5: Boethius was executed for treason, accused of conspiring with the Eastern Empire, and Pope John was thrown into prison, where he later died, for having failed to defend the religious policy of the king at Constantinople, a policy which demanded liberty of worship for the Arians in the East.

Theodoric died on 30 August 526. The transfer of power was accomplished smoothly as Athalaric reigned under the regency of his mother Amalasuntha. Until 534 it seemed that nothing had changed, except that Spain had recovered its freedom. But elsewhere events took a dangerous turn: the Burgundians were conquered by the Franks, the Byzantine army began the reconquest of Africa and the kingdom was left with only one official ally—Justinian. Then in 534 Athalaric died without an heir. In order not to lose her power the regent went into partnership with her cousin Theodahad, but shortly afterwards he rid himself of her in a sordid drama which disgusted public opinion. Justinian was just waiting for this opportunity to interfere: he presented himself as the avenger of Amalasuntha and sent Belisarius with an army into Italy. The first landings took place in July 536, in the south, and had one immediate effect: Theodahad was deposed, assassinated and replaced by a worthy general, Witigis, who tried to ally himself with the Amal dynasty by forcing Athalaric's sister to marry him against her will. Witigis's forces were concentrated in the north, so they could not prevent Belisarius from entering Rome on 10 December 536 and starting energetically to restore the imperial unity.

The Romano-Gothic state collapsed; but a Gothic army remained, fighting under elected leaders against another army which, although fighting under Roman standards, was scarcely less barbarian in composition.[15] On both sides the interests of Italy and of the civilian population were cold-bloodedly sacrificed. The only prospect facing them was the exchange of one set of barbarians, who had been tamed by long contact with them, for another set who were demonstrably more rapacious. Besides, the imperial forces were so few in number

c

that they could not carry out more than one operation at a time. The war dragged on interminably, punctuated by atrocities throughout its twenty-five years, and in the end effected not the liberation of Italy but its total destruction.

The reserve with which the Romans greeted the imperial forces is understandable, for they could not identify themselves in the slightest with the soldiers of Belisarius. Only the south of Italy, where there were hardly any battles and where the links with the East were still strong, gave the imperial forces a fairly warm welcome. Elsewhere the dominant attitude was one of despairing neutrality. A few Romans espoused the cause of the Goths. But the officials at Ravenna were discouraged by the progressive 'rebarbarization' of Witigis's army, and Cassiodorus, who had remained at his post as long as there was any hope of a negotiated solution, retired when he realized that this was a war of extermination. The Goths were dubious about the loyalty of the Romans, and took hostages from the senatorial class—three hundred young people, who were put to death in the final catastrophe of 552. The survivors were removed from positions of command in the reconquered areas and replaced by civil servants from Constantinople. Finally, many were completely ruined: in 546 Rusticiana, the daughter of Symmachus and widow of Boethius, was reduced to beggary. The senatorial aristocracy never recovered from these blows, and its disintegration marked a turning point in Italian history, for it was this class—active, competent and well-educated— which had ensured the continuity of Roman Italy through the successive régimes of puppet Emperors and barbarian kings.

Faced with destruction the Ostrogoths showed a sense of solidarity and a determination much stronger than that shown by the Vandals when faced with the same enemy in 534, or by the Visigoths towards the Arabs in 711. For almost a whole generation the Ostrogoths courageously held their own. When their first leader Witigis, despairing of the state of Italy, capitulated in 540, allowing Belisarius to enter Ravenna, they replaced him with a man called Hildebald and then with his nephew Totila, who held out for eleven years with considerable inventive genius (at one stage he may even have tried to bring the war onto the social front by rallying slaves to his side). When Totila was slain in battle in 552 he was replaced by Teias, who died in a last battle at the foot of Vesuvius on 1 October 552. Detachments of Goths held out in several places until 555, and a rising even broke out in Brescia and Verona as late as 561.

Confronted with such relentless tenacity Justinian decided to wipe out the Ostrogothic people. At the time of his earlier victories, when he optimistically foresaw a rapid and easy conquest, he had considered clemency. In 540 the Ostrogothic army had simply been sent back to its own territory, and in 550 Justinian again sent to Italy two men who were bent on reconciliation. But by 552, when Narses again took command, clemency was out of the question. Even Persians were sent as reinforcements to Italy, and the Lombards of King Audoin. All captured Goths were deported to the East. A few who had changed sides fairly early on were able to salvage their personal position and small groups of Goths survived at the foot of the Alps: others are mentioned in the papyri of Ravenna as slaves in the city which had been their metropolis.[16] But as a positive historic force the Ostrogoths ceased to exist. Their only consolation was that in their downfall the last shreds of Roman Antiquity disappeared as well.

The fate of two of the capitals can be taken as symbolic of what was happening. Milan, which had declared itself in favour of the imperial forces in 538, was destroyed by Witigis in 539 and was eclipsed in importance by Pavia for the next four centuries. In 537 Rome suffered its first siege, which lasted a year. Belisarius was shut up in the town and to force him to submit Witigis cut off fourteen aqueducts, which were never repaired. In order to survive Belisarius expelled all the 'useless mouths', who never returned. A second siege, directed by Totila, lasted for two years, from 544 to 546, and resulted in the partial dismantling of Rome and the destruction of the Trastevere. A third siege lasted from the spring of 547 until January 550, making a total of six years of siege out of thirteen. It was only thanks to its religious function that Rome managed to survive at all. Ravenna alone remained relatively intact. The Lombards unconsciously avenged the Ostrogoths less than twenty years after the death of Teias, but that did not bring Italy back to life again.

INVADERS IN THE WEST

The mass influx of the Ostrogoths into the Empire marked the final stage in the series of migrations which emerged from eastern Europe due to pressure from the Hunnic expansion. After this the Empire enjoyed relative security on this front until about the middle of the sixth century: the Danubian *limes* held firm until the Avaro-Slav migration. But the Western *limes*, which had remained more or less inviolate in spite of short-lived breaches all through the fourth century, was swept away in the first decade of the fifth century by a tidal wave of invaders which eventually flooded the whole of the Western Empire. Most of the peoples who made up this wave crossed the Rhine frontier after the memorable breakthrough of 31 December 406.[17] Others led by Radagaisus had tried a more direct route towards Italy in 405, but their fate was much less fortunate: their enterprise was crushed by

Stilicho at Fiesole in August 406 while members of the first group pursued a successful career even in Africa. Not very much is known about the so-called expedition of Radagaisus. A composite group of peoples entered Italy from the north-east and managed to reach Tuscany, but a single battle sufficed to defeat them. The 'Roman' army at Fiesole had much the same ethnic composition as that of the invader: under the command of a leader of Vandal stock called Stilicho and a Visigoth called Sarus, it consisted largely of Alans and Huns.

It is useless to try to establish too clear a demarcation line between the eastern and the western branches of the Germanic invasions. Peoples of the same groups are found in both halves of the Empire. Their attacks on the Roman defences were more or less simultaneous; their ventures were complementary—without Radagaisus it is difficult to explain Alaric—and as early as 412 both groups were to be found together in Gaul. There is no doubt that a liaison must have existed between the two movements: the repercussions of the great advance of the peoples of the steppes were felt even in western Germany, since both the Alans and the Huns themselves ended by crossing not the lower Danube but the Rhine. In spite of their lack of a general view of the barbarian world, contemporary writers seem to have been clearly aware of these connections, at least in so far as they led from the Pontic steppes to Illyricum. [18]

Those who benefited from the breakthrough of 406 did not play a role comparable to that of the Goths or of the great peoples of the second wave of invasions. Many of them did not succeed in founding a state of their own. Among those who were successful, two had only an ephemeral existence—the Spanish kingdoms of the Siling Vandals and of the Alans. Only three managed to survive for more than a few years, although their careers did not last very long either: the Vandal and the Burgundian kingdoms were both destroyed in 534, and the Suevian kingdom disappeared in 585. The Burgundian kingdom alone managed to achieve a fairly stable synthesis between the barbarians and the Romans. The history of the Vandals is only a curious parenthesis in the history of North Africa, and the Sueves hardly have a history of their own at all: the sources are completely silent about them for almost a century, from 469 to 558.

The Vandals

Accounts of the early history of the Vandals draw on unreliable information mixed with Gothic, Lombard and English traditions, and on some onomastic and archaeological evidence. Most of this data points to Scandinavia as the land of their origin and to a context very similar to that in which the Goths originated. The Vandals may have left their name to the tiny region of Vendsyssel (whose inhabitants still call themselves *Vendel-boer*) in the extreme north of Jutland, beyond Limfjord, although the same root is also found elsewhere in Scandinavia. Their language seems to have been an East Germanic dialect similar to Gothic. And finally, archaeology indicates similarities between the material found in Vendsyssel and that found in Silesia, the first attested settlement of the Vandals at the end of the first century BC. It is possible therefore that the Vandals followed a route parallel to those of the Cimbri and the Goths.

History caught up with the Vandals for the first time in the first century AD, on the southern shores of the Baltic. At that time the name *Vandali* or *Vandili* referred to a vast group of peoples, among whom Pliny mentions the Burgundians and the Varini; it has been suggested that their settlements may have been in Pomerania or the region of Poznan. Later the name was restricted to two peoples, the Silings, who according to Ptolemy inhabited modern Silesia, and the Asdings, who are first mentioned in the third century by Dio Cassius and probably inhabited the area between the upper Vistula and the upper Dniester. (The Silings have bequeathed their name to Silesia; the name 'Asdings' strictly speaking seems to have been applied only to the royal family.) From the third century to the fifth century the two tribes led parallel, but separate, existences.

The inclination to move towards the Empire was first noticed among the Asdings, in 171: they tried in vain to penetrate Dacia, swept along by the same current as that which had brought the Goths towards the Black Sea. In the middle of the third century the two peoples moved swiftly towards the south-west; the Asdings are found in the Pannonian plain from 248 on, the Silings on the upper Main from 277. They remained in these regions for a century and a half, until the arrival of the Huns. Due to prolonged contact with the *limes* the eastern group had developed quite rapidly, but it is not certain that they were already Arians at this point. Their conversion probably did not take place until after they had gone to Spain.

Shortly before 400 the Asdings, who were probably being harassed by the Huns, set off towards the west along the left bank of the Danube. On the way they met the Silings, and the two groups seem to have re-established their alliance. About 401 they were just across the Danube from Raetia, and around 405 they were at the Rhine, in the midst of the peoples who were trying to break through the *limes*. The Asding King Godegisel was defeated and slain during the breakthrough but the two peoples, led by his son, managed to cross *en masse* into Gaul. They were probably heading towards the Mediterranean, but the threat of a double counter-attack by the Romans, with troops brought from Britain and Italy, persuaded them to look for another area to plunder. It is impossible to reconstruct the exact itinerary of the Vandals in Gaul; because of their unfortunate reputation they were blamed for many disasters which had nothing to do with them. During the whole of this expedition they were accompanied by some of the Alans and probably by the Sueves as well.

When the Vandals invaded Spain in the autumn of 409 it was not only defenceless, but divided by a civil war. The result was total disaster: only a few towns were defended. In 411 or 412 the barbarians shared the country out among themselves like so much booty. The Asdings and the Silings had separate portions, the former receiving the north-west of Galicia, the latter the rich province of Baetica. The arrival of the Visigoths in Gaul removed any inclination they may have had to return, and soon concerned them even more directly: Wallia was charged by Rome with restoring Spain to the Empire, and acted with great brutality. The king of the Silings was captured and sent off to Ravenna, and by 419 his people had been crushed and were no longer able to lead an independent existence. The numbers of the Asdings, who had been spared, were swelled by the survivors of the Alans, who had likewise been defeated by Wallia, and all that was left of the Siling Vandals also rallied to the Asdings. Dissatisfied with inhospitable Galicia and with the vicinity of the Sueves, they then moved to Baetica in 419 or 420 and the Empire was unable to stop them.

Not much is known about the Vandal state in Spain. (The similarity between the name of the Vandals and that of Andalusia is purely coincidental.) It was probably never more than simply an army billeted in enemy territory. But in spite of the law which forbade on pain of death the initiation of barbarians into the art of ship-building, the Vandals took to the sea and became formidable pirates. As early as 426 they attacked the Balearic Islands and Mauretania, and in 428 they took the naval base of Cartagena. For twenty years they seem to have lived solely by plunder; under this régime Spain's resources were rapidly exhausted. At this point King Genseric (or Gaiseric) formed the plan, which he had unconsciously inherited from Alaric, of exploiting the only Western province left intact—Africa, whose defences at that time were paralysed by a civil war.

It was a risky and complicated undertaking. Only one detail of the expedition is known: the concentration of all the participants— Asdings, Silings, Alans and a few Hispano-Romans—at Tarifa in May 429. They probably landed near Tangier and followed a land route through the gap of Taza.[19] The army drew up in front of Hippo in Numidia (the modern town of Bône) in May or June of 430, having covered almost 2,000 kilometres of hostile territory in one year. In spite of this period of grace the count of Africa was unable to put up any effective show of resistance; he shut himself up in Hippo, which held out for a year. (It was during this siege that St. Augustine died.) Probably some of the Vandal vanguard had already reached Africa Proconsularis.

Finding themselves unable to repulse the Vandals, the Romans offered them a *foedus*; Genseric, fearing that he might not be able to take any other fortified towns, accepted it at Hippo on 11 February 435. The territory conceded to him probably covered the north of Numidia, the western part of Proconsularis (with Hippo and Guelma) and almost the whole of Mauretania Sitifensis, the easternmost of the three Mauretanias. The regions further to the west were probably not included in the agreement. Genseric was not content with this for long: on 19 October 439 he attacked Carthage, which he managed to occupy almost without a blow being struck. The town was systematically looted, and some of its buildings were set on fire or demolished. [20] Then all the rest of the province of Africa as far as Tripolitana was invaded. Genseric next threatened to take Italy in the rear, from the south: the Vandals landed in Sicily in 440. In order to stop them Valentinian III offered them a new *foedus* in 442 which established them in Proconsularis, Byzacena and part of Tripolitana and Numidia. This was how the shape of the Vandal kingdom was fixed for the years to come.

Theoretically Rome still kept the three Mauretanias, the west of Numidia and the eastern part of Tripolitana. These were the poorest regions and those in which Berber resurgence was most marked: the Empire did not regain control of them for a long time. There are no more traces of imperial intervention in Latin Africa after 455. A good part of the western regions fell into the hands of Berber tribes; some coastal towns, like Tipasa, received a Vandal garrison at an unknown date, and there were Vandal influences—direct or otherwise—as far west as Oran, perhaps even as far west as Tangier. Strictly speaking the Vandal kingdom did not extend further west than the meridian of the town of Constantine in Numidia.

Most of the Vandals were billeted in Proconsularis, especially around Carthage, although a few small groups settled in the north of Byzacena and on the coast of the Mauretanias, at Tipasa and Cherchel. Arian bishops were installed in the principal communities. The common language from the start was Latin—nothing has survived of the Vandal language apart from a few proper names. In the third generation King Thrasamund showed a definite taste for Latin literature, even theological literature, and had his court poets, although these were not very talented.

In order to build up his army Genseric made extensive confiscations, instead of adopting the principle of sharing according to the rules of *hospitalitas* like the other barbarian kings. Some of the lands he seized went to make up the lots (*sortes*) of the Vandals, and the rest reverted to the Crown. Many Roman landowners still remained, and the Vandals began to imitate their way of life. There is nothing to indicate that they farmed with their own hands. They adopted the tastes of those they had supplanted, including even such pleasures as the baths and the circus. The former owners of the confiscated lands were sent to Italy or to the East; their descendants sometimes managed to recover a little of their property,[21] but Genseric's high-handed behaviour created a gulf of hatred between the Vandals and the Romans which Arianism made even wider. Until the end the Vandal kings had to rely on force to maintain their position.

Their institutions bear witness to this. The Vandal people, like an army, continued to be divided up into groups of 1,000 men. Just before his death Genseric made arrangements for perpetuating unity of command at the expense of the tradition which decreed that the kingdom should be partitioned among the royal sons. The head of the administration had the title, borrowed from military vocabulary, of *praepositus regni*. At first no important posts were entrusted to Romans, and the provincial officials disappeared. A handful of *notarii* sufficed for the essential needs of the kingdom, above all for a new assessment of the land tax, which was levied from the Romans alone. In all it was an improvised government which did not trouble itself about traditions and which functioned blatantly and shamelessly for the exclusive benefit of the conquerors.

This picture is drawn from terse and hostile sources and is incomplete and probably biased; but the texts at our disposal do not authorize any other interpretation. The only documents relating to the practical side of life—the famous Albertini Tablets [no. 13] and the *ostraka* of the region of Khenchela [no. 12 *bis*]—show that the ordinary people were governed by purely Roman institutions. In spite of their ruthlessness the Vandals continued to respect some imperial prerogatives, such as the minting of gold coins and the payment of tribute. Nevertheless royal documents were dated by regnal years.

The first-generation Vandals in Africa seem to have had only one political ambition: continued expansion and the finding of fresh regions to plunder. They settled down in the province of Africa, perhaps simply because they did not dare to brave the Libyan desert, and soon they began making periodic raids throughout the whole Mediterranean world. This is all that the so-called 'Vandal Empire' really amounted to. Genseric applied all his cunning to this end: a fleet based at Carthage allowed him to get a foothold in Sicily as early as 440, although the true conquest of Sicily did not take place until

468. The island served above all as a diplomatic pawn, for Rome was dependent on Sicilian grain. Odoacer obtained the island in 476 in return for the payment of a tribute; in 491 Theodoric occupied it, but in 500 he gave the western part back to the Vandals as his sister's dowry, and it continued to be shared until the time of Justinian's reconquest. About 455 Genseric seized Corsica and Sardinia, and probably also the Balearic Islands; these were only colonies to be exploited, and places of exile for political or religious undesirables. The coasts of Spain, Greece and Italy were likewise raided, culminating in the sack of Rome in 455. The Vandals did not abandon this aggressive policy until the death of Genseric in 477, after a generation of peaceful enjoyment of the wealth of Carthage. It is only at this point, after three-quarters of a century, that the history of their migration comes to a close.

One has only to look at the succession of kings to see how swiftly the process of Romanization advanced. But the religious gulfs prevented this progress from bearing fruit, for the Roman influence only succeeded in blunting the harshness of Vandal might. Huneric (477–84), who had been a hostage at Constantinople, married the daughter of Valentinian III by force, and tried in vain to introduce a system of hereditary succession on the Roman model. Practically nothing is known about Gunthamund (484–96). Thrasamund (496–523) was, *mutatis mutandis*, the Theodoric of the Vandals. Not only did he marry the sister of the Gothic king but, like him, he realized that the German minority could only survive by adapting itself to the Roman way of life. He loved poetry and architecture, and was interested in theology, but unlike his brother-in-law he found no sympathy in the only class capable of providing officials, the senatorial aristocracy. Hilderic (523–30) was by blood and by inclination more than half-Roman but was, unfortunately, an inept ruler. Gelimer's reign, from 530 to 533, was too short to make any lasting impression.

The fragility of the Vandal achievement is demonstrated by the swiftness of its disappearance. The kingdom collapsed like a house of cards when attacked by Justinian. Belisarius landed on 30 August 533; by 15 September he had reached Carthage; two battles effectively delivered the whole of the province of Africa into his hands. In March 534 Gelimer, who had taken refuge in the west, surrendered and was deported to Asia. His people followed him as slaves, either deported or press-ganged into the Byzantine army. Some very small groups hid among the Moors, but perished in a second round-up in 539–40. The Vandals who were sent to the East disappeared into the ethnic chaos of the Byzantine army engaged in the war against Persia. 'The history of the Vandals ends in a void', as Courtois puts it. The Germans made no lasting impression on North Africa, and the events of 534

contributed just as much as the Islamic conquest to orientating it in
a different direction from the rest of the Western Empire. The principal
contribution of the Vandals was a negative one; after a century under
a savage régime Roman Africa lost most of its spiritual strength and the
flower of its ruling class, as well as a good part of its peripheral
territories.

The Sueves in Spain

The name of the Sueves, like that of the Vandals, had an illustrious
reputation which was far superior to their actual importance in 406.
At first the word 'Suevi' was used to describe a vast sub-group of the
Herminones, and at the same time referred to a more restricted
nucleus which made its début in history about 72 BC, led by Ariovistus.
At that time the Sueves lived on the middle reaches of the Rhine.
Later they were to be found somewhere around modern Moravia,
either bearing the same name or occasionally being called Quadi. It
is fairly difficult to reconcile these facts with the name of *Suebicum mare*
which Tacitus gives to the Baltic Sea and with the mention of *Suebi
Nicretes* on the Neckar. Probably the Suevian people was split up
into several different branches which pursued different policies in their
dealings with Rome. At the time of the invasions the Sueves were to
be found in the background more or less everywhere—in Swabia (to
which they gave their name), in Venetia, in Flanders, in Britain and
finally in Spain.

Only the group in Spain was of any real importance. It is fairly
certain that they crossed the Rhine in 406–7; in 409 they entered the
Iberian peninsula. (For a discussion of their itinerary, see p. 223.)
The partition of 411 gave them the southern part of Galicia, a portion
which they doubled by acquiring the northern part in 419 when the
Asdings left. The departure of the Vandals for Africa and the temporary
retreat of the Visigoths allowed the Suevian King Hermeric to set up
a true state around Braga (which was his capital) and Lugo. The
Hispano-Romans wanted Aetius to come and destroy the Sueves, and
sent as their envoy the Galician bishop Hydatius, who is our only
source for these events. Aetius, however, was preoccupied with Gaul
and refused to intervene, so the local authorities concluded a sort of
foedus with their troublesome guests (agreements are known to have
been made in 433, 437 and 438).

Nevertheless the Sueves continued to expand within the political
vacuum of the Iberian peninsula. In 439 they took Mérida, then
Seville in 441 and even part of Carthaginiensis. It looked as if the whole
of Spain was going to fall into the hands of King Rechiarius, but the

Sueves had neither the stature nor the numbers to occupy Spain or to govern it. An expedition undertaken by the Visigothic King Theodoric in 456 in the name of the Emperor Avitus dashed all their hopes. Rechiarius was overwhelmed on 5 October in front of Astorga on the River Orbigo; two weeks later the Visigoths entered Braga and sacked the town, slaughtering both Sueves and Romans indiscriminately. They caught up with Rechiarius on the coast near Oporto; he was put to death and his dynasty ended with him. But as soon as the Visigoths had returned to Gaul the Sueves made another bid for independence. About 464 Remismundus managed to obtain official recognition from the court at Toulouse, after which the kingdom—like Galicia itself—disappeared from historiography for nearly a century.

The Suevian kingdom, like that of the Vandals, seems to have been marked by instability, brutality, and even a policy of enslaving the Hispano-Roman inhabitants. The extensive damage done to the towns of the north-west of Spain is confirmed by the texts and by archaeology; at least three Roman cities and two indigenous towns are known never to have recovered.[22] All that we know about the internal history of the kingdom concerns its religious vacillation, which is a reflection of its external weakness: King Rechila, who died in 448, was a pagan; his son Rechiarius (448–56) became a Catholic in order to curry favour with the Empire and prevent Visigothic intervention; but about 465 a bishop called Ajax, who had been sent from Visigothic Gaul, persuaded the Sueves to return to Arianism. Then about the middle of the sixth century King Chararic seems to have become a Catholic temporarily in order to obtain the intercession of St. Martin of Tours, and possibly also to achieve a Frankish alliance. Arianism once again got the upper hand, but it was undermined by the mission of another Martin, this time Martin of Braga. Then in about 561 King Theudemir became a Catholic. This was seen as a challenge to the kingdom of Toledo, which was still Arian. Leovigild attacked King Miro in 576. In 585 the last Suevian king, Andeca, was captured and his kingdom annexed—a year before the Visigoths embraced Catholicism. There were two more Suevian rebellions in the following year before the Sueves were finally assimilated by the Visigoths.

The Sueves have left a few slight onomastic and archaeological traces in Galicia, along the coast above and below Braga. Practically nothing of their language has passed into Portuguese—five or six words at most—but Galicia probably owes some of its originality, particularly in ecclesiastical matters, to them. Nothing is known about their institutions except that they minted coins on the imperial model before 456. There was no Suevian culture as such, apart from the writings of

Martin of Braga—and even he owes very little to local traditions, having been steeped in Greek culture during a long stay in Palestine.[23] Galician art is only a local variant of Hispano-Gothic art. In historical terms nothing very important would have been changed had the Sueves of Spain never existed.

The Burgundians

The Burgundians[24] appeared in the first century AD in the Baltic region, within the group of the Vindili, before settling in the interior on the middle Vistula. But their language and their traditions indicate that they probably came from Scandinavia: their East Germanic dialect was similar to Gothic and their traditions, written down long afterwards, lead back to the 'island called *Scandinavia*'.[25] In fact, several places in Scandinavia have names analagous to theirs: the district of Borgund on the Sognefjord in Norway, and especially the Baltic island of Bornholm, which was called *Borgundarholm* in the thirteenth century.

During the course of the third century the Burgundians left their Polish settlement and began to move westwards. After 260 they were supporting the Alamans in their attempts to break through the *limes* of the *Agri Decumates*, but they did not manage to settle in Roman territory. They became so well established in the area between the Rhône and central Swabia that in 359 there is a mention of boundary-stones on the frontier between the territory of the Romans and that of the Burgundians.[26] For a hundred and forty years their contact with the Empire allowed the development of a certain amount of economic activity. They were drawn towards the West, probably against their will, in the upheavals which heralded the breakthrough of 406. The latter brought them west of the Rhine into Germania II, that is to the region downstream from Koblenz. As early as 411 these Burgundians took service with a Roman faction led by the usurper Jovinus. In 413 they concluded a *foedus* with the legitimate Emperor which gave them 'that part of Gaul nearest to the Rhine'. A persistent historiographical tradition has tried to deny that the kingdom was below Koblenz in Germania II, as we are told in a fragment of Olympiodorus, and to locate it in Germania I around Worms, on the sole authority of the *Nibelungenlied*, in which Worms is the capital of King Gunther. A healthy reaction has set in recently, and scholars have now begun to call it 'the Rhenish kingdom of the Burgundians' instead of 'the kingdom of Worms'.[27] This Rhenish kingdom lasted for about thirty years. The attempts of the Burgundians to expand into Belgium earned them the hostility of Aetius: in 436 he unleashed his friends the Huns

against them. King Gundahar was killed, the royal family was liqui-
dated, and the Burgundians were compelled to migrate: the whole
people set off for the south.

This catastrophe had great repercussions in epic tradition, as
witnessed by the *Waltharius* in the ninth century and by the *Nibelungenlied* (which wrongly has Attila as one of the protagonists). Gundahar
became famous throughout the whole Germanic world as Guðhere in
the Anglo-Saxon *Widsith* and as Gunnarr in the *Edda.*

The Rhenish episode in the history of the Burgundians is connected
with the very obscure question of their conversion. Orosius asserts that
they became Catholics in 417,[28] but most authors believe that they
converted directly from paganism to Arianism at some unknown date
between 413 and 436. Only Coville adopts the view of Orosius.[29] It
is curious that the sixth-century apostles of the Burgundians never
refer to a Catholic interlude.

Aetius did not intend to destroy the Burgundians, since they were
able to provide him with good soldiers, but contented himself with
keeping them away from northern Gaul. He had decided that their
future lay in eastern Gaul, fighting other, more dangerous, Germans—
the Alamans, who were their traditional enemies. In 443 the Burgundians concluded another more satisfactory *foedus* which settled them in
Sapaudia, that is to say probably in the French-speaking part of modern
Switzerland and in the south of the French Jura around Geneva. (This
is the fairly convincing interpretation of this rather problematic name
given by Duparc in *La Sapaudia* [no. 225]. In any case it was not
exactly present-day Savoy.) There they behaved like model federates,
ready to undertake any task in the service of Rome; they fought
against Attila in 451 and against the Sueves of Spain in 456. On their
return from Spain in 457 they took payment in kind by seizing a good
part of Lugdunensis I and of Viennensis. Majorian hurriedly brought
an army to recover these territories, and the Burgundians withdrew.
As soon as he had left, however, they came back in force, occupied
Lyons (at an uncertain date—in 461 according to Coville, or possibly
not until 470–4), and then spread out over the Rhône region towards
the south, taking Die in about 463 and Vaison some time before
474, and towards the north, where they took Langres before 485.
About 495 their kingdom stretched from southern Champagne to the
Durance and the Alpes Maritimes.

The Burgundian kingdom had two capitals; the king resided in
Lyons, and his heir in Geneva. It was also composed of two nations,
for the status of the Romans in it was almost equal to that of the
Burgundians. The latter had taken possession of the Rhône area more
or less peacefully; a seventh-century tradition has it that the Burgundians came 'at the invitation of both the Romans and the Gauls'.

The aristocracy had seen in this small people, who were faithful to the spirit, if not always to the letter, of the *foedus*, the lesser of two evils, and almost a guarantee of security. All the Burgundian kings about whom we know anything at all, other than just their names, showed themselves worthy of this trust. Although Hilperic I, the founder of the kingdom of Lyons, was an Arian, he had married a Catholic; he protected the monks of the Jura and was a friend of Patiens, the bishop of Lyons. Gundobad, his nephew, who reigned from about 480 to 516, was almost a Roman himself, being a high-ranking officer in the army in Italy and faithful second-in-command to, and later heir of, the patrician Ricimer, the Emperor-maker. Gundobad had also put two Emperors on the throne—Olybrius in 472 and Glycerius in 473— although he himself probably did not aspire to any title higher than that of patrician, which he obtained from the first of these puppet-Emperors. The arrival of Nepos in 474 had forced him to return to his own people, although he briefly succumbed to his Italian ambitions again in 490 when he went to support Odoacer against Theodoric. Gregory of Tours, who had no love for the Arians, credits him with having enacted legislation protecting the Romans;[30] and until the conversion of Clovis, St. Avitus, the moral head of the Catholic episcopate in Gundobad's kingdom, had a very cordial relationship with the king. The law of the Burgundians (called *la loi Gombette* in French, after Gundobad) is one of the most Roman of the barbarian law codes, and explicitly lays down the effective equality of the Romans and the Burgundians. It even assures to the Romans a *wergeld*, allows them to do military service, and authorizes mixed marriages. The Burgundians reserved only an honorary pre-eminence for themselves.

The distribution of population operated within the framework of the rules of *hospitalitas* which had been imposed for the former kingdom of Geneva by the *foedus* of 443 and renewed for the new Rhône kingdom in 456 with the consent of the Roman senators. The Burgundian settlements, which are mainly betrayed by the place-names ending in *-ingōs* (French *-ans* or *-ens*), are concentrated in the French-speaking part of modern Switzerland, the Jura and the plain of the Saône; they are rarer in Savoy and Burgundy, and almost non-existent south of the River Isère. The archaeological finds of Burgundian type for the period before 534 have a more or less similar distribution pattern. The language was to survive until the seventh century (the runic texts of Arguel (Doubs) and Charnay (Saône-et-Loire) are the only ones which have been found on Gallic soil), and national sentiment remained strong until the ninth century. Burgundian law was one of the last barbarian law codes to yield to Frankish law.

To what extent the Burgundian kingdom was Germanic in character and composition is a complex question. Anthropologists have established—and this is one of their most remarkable contributions to the history of the invasions—that the Burgundians had been 'contaminated, culturally and racially, by the Huns',[31] as is indicated by the practice of cranial deformation. It has been conjectured that the name of King Gundiocus, the brother and predecessor of Hilperic, owed its second part to Hunnic influence. Some Alamans were billeted several times in the Swiss plain and the northern Jura. An appendix to the law of the Burgundians (XXXI, 2) of 524 (?) alludes to some Burgundian refugees, who may have been forced to leave the south of France by the Gothic conquest of 523, and lays down that all assimilable elements, Visigoths and even runaway slaves, should be accepted into the community. An inscription of 527 from Saint-Offange, near Évian, emphasizes the damage done by Frankish raids. It would appear that at this critical moment the Burgundian people thought they were threatened with extinction. True stability was not achieved until the Merovingian period.

The Burgundian institutions are a fine example of dualism. The king had two sets of titles: for the Romans he was *vir inluster, magister militum*, or *Galliae patricius*; for the Germans he was *dominus noster rex*. Until the end respect for the prerogatives of the Emperors permeates the official texts and legal documents, for example the use of consular dates. If the army was still organized with raids and pillage in mind,[32] the administration was closely modelled on that of the palace of Ravenna, and continued to be directed by senators: Syagrius under Hilperic, Laconius under Gundobad, Pantagathus and St. Avitus under Sigismund. And finally, each *pagus* had its Burgundian count who judged the Germans, side by side with its Roman count who judged the Romans.

The Burgundian kingdom was one of those which adapted itself best to urban life, as archaeology has proved at Geneva. The texts confirm the survival of curias, *defensores* and *gesta municipalia*. Nothing is known of the culture of the Genevan period, but that of the kingdom of Lyons was of a reasonably high standard, and wholly Latin. Gundobad corresponded with Theodoric to ask him to send him a water clock and a sundial, and he seems to have had an official poet called Heraclianus. Avitus of Vienne, who was an accomplished man of letters like his relative Sidonius Apollinaris, was influential at the court. Schools of rhetoric were still functioning at the beginning of the sixth century at Lyons and probably also at Vienne, and Latin epigraphy continued to flourish.

In spite of this internal harmony, however, the Burgundian kingdom was scarcely viable. Situated as it was in a region of considerable strategic and economic importance, its ethnic foundation was too slight to withstand its Frankish and Gothic rivals. The situation became untenable when the royal family split up and the Franks were able to make use of their Catholicism to win the sympathy of the Romans.

As early as 500, taking advantage of the quarrel between Gundobad and his brother Godegisel, Clovis managed to penetrate as far as Vienne. The conversion to Catholicism of Sigismund, the son of Gundobad, was the signal for the Goths to attack from the other end of the kingdom, amid atrocious strife. The Burgundians lost the area south of the Drôme, and possibly even that south of the Isère, in 523. The Franks profited by this: Chlodomer captured Sigismund and had him assassinated. Godomar, the brother of Sigismund, took the throne, defeated the Franks at Vézeronce in June 524 and kept going with difficulty until 533–4, when he disappeared in obscure circumstances. The Merovingians occupied the whole kingdom, but respected the Burgundian institutions and nationality within a sort of personal union. Until the eleventh century some individuals appealed to Burgundian law from time to time, but the conversion to Catholicism, which had taken place well before 533, had made assimilation easy. It was within the framework of Merovingian Gaul that the Burgundian heritage blossomed.

3 The Land Invasions :
The Second and Third Waves, Fifth
Century to Seventh Century

THE SECOND WAVE OF INVASIONS: THE FIFTH CENTURY TO THE SIXTH CENTURY

Behind the first wave of invasions which had swept right across Europe came a group of more obscure peoples that had come together later and were less adventurous. They advanced only one step at a time, taking care never to lose contact with their bases beyond the *limes*. There is not a single spectacular raid in their history. They fought very few great battles, and sacked only a handful of large Roman towns. On the other hand, this group was much more homogeneous than those which came before and after it; it was made up entirely of Germans who spoke a West Germanic language and had lived just beyond the Roman *limes* for a long time. They may have been more numerous than their predecessors; at any rate, instead of bands of warriors indulging in colourful exploits, the dominant impression is of masses of farmers managing to colonize vast regions in a lasting way. Although the first wave of invasions had been disastrous for Rome, it had not conquered a single region in the West for the Germanic language. It was the second wave which imposed on the linguistic frontier its only appreciable changes. The states born of the first wave, which had been occasionally brilliant but short-lived, were now faced with the Frankish monarchy, which lasted for over a thousand years, and with the firmly-rooted Alamannic and Bavarian populations around the Rhine and the upper Danube.

Because of the slow and often local nature of its progress, it is difficult to give precise dates for the beginning and end of this wave. The advance of the Franks, the controlling element, did not start to attract the attention of contemporaries until about 440, and the submission of Burgundy in 534 can be considered as the culmination of their migration. The absence of texts for the Alamannic and Bavarian expansion prevents us from setting any limits to it, even approximate ones. We can only say that it came later and lasted longer—at least until the beginning of the seventh century. We could even say that in the Alpine region it was continuous throughout the Middle Ages, although it ceased to have the character of a political conquest.

The Franks

The Franks were one of the last of the Germanic peoples to arrive on the scene, and are among those whose origins are most obscure; yet they were to be the principal beneficiaries of the migrations, and the only ones whose achievement, sustained throughout the early Middle Ages, was to have a deep and lasting influence on the history of the West. This apparent paradox explains the appearance very early on of legends about the origins of the Franks and their dynasty. It was difficult for the master-race of the West to be satisfied with the casual, but just, assertion of Gregory of Tours (*Hist. Franc.* II, 8) that *de Francorum vero regibus, quis fuit primus, a multis ignoratur* (it is unknown to many people who was the first king of the Franks). Already the same Gregory is referring to a legend that the Franks came from Pannonia. Soon that was no longer sufficient: the Merovingian period elaborated a complicated mythology whereby the Franks were descended from the Trojans, like the Romans, which made them their equals.

The name 'Franks' actually appears for the first time in a marching song of the Roman army reported in the *Historia Augusta*—an unreliable source—in relation to the events of 241, and then in a more trustworthy context in the accounts of the great invasion of Gaul in the reign of Gallienus, probably in 257; a band of Franks may even have reached Spain. Shortly afterwards an extraordinary account of the time of Probus (276–82) tells of a party of Franks who arrived, no one knows how, at the Black Sea and returned to their homeland via Gibraltar. Finally we hear that in about 286 Carausius was put in charge of defending the coasts of the Straits of Dover against the Saxon and Frankish pirates. So the first Franks appeared in the guise of a people who were dangerous both by land and by sea, and were probably based somewhere on the middle or lower reaches of the Rhine.

Where did they come from? Their name tells us almost nothing, for it seems to derive from a root meaning 'bold, courageous' (like Old Norse *frekkr*). This was the interpretation of Isidore of Seville in the seventh century: . . . *a feritate morum nuncupatos* (they are called after the fierceness of their customs), and of Ermold the Black in the ninth century: *Francus habet nomen de feritate sua* (the Frank gets his name from his fierceness). The link with the word *frakka* in Old Norse, meaning a hunting-spear or lance, is most probably the reverse of that assumed by certain etymologists: it is the weapon which took its name from the people and not vice versa. The adjective *francus* meaning

'free' has also taken its name from the people. The Frankish language—
from which Dutch and the dialects of north-western Germany are
derived—also tells us very little about the origins of the people. In
spite of the fact that there is not a single ancient or medieval text to
support their argument most historians since the seventeenth century
have agreed that the Franks were the product of a regrouping of several
different peoples that had formerly been known to live by the lower
Rhine. Among the probable components of this merger mention must
be made of the Chamavi, the Bructeri, the Amsivarians, the Chattuarii,
the Chatti, probably the Sicambri, and less probably the Tencteres,
the Usipeti, the Tubanti and possibly even some of the Batavi as well.

These ancestors of the Franks were small peoples with obscure
histories and most of them are not mentioned between the end of the
first century AD and the middle or even the end of the third century—
sometimes not until the fourth century. Unlike the great peoples who
disappeared then—the Quadi, the Marcomanni and so on—they
cannot have taken part in continual attacks on the *limes*, thus, as it
were, conserving their strength. Most of them lived for a long time in
territory immediately adjoining that of the Romans, near commercial
centres like Cologne and Xanten; it was inevitable that this close
contact should influence them profoundly. Of all the Germans they
were perhaps the most ready to understand the Roman way of life.

We do not know what led these peoples to merge in the third century.
Perhaps they wished to offer a stronger resistance both to the Romans
and to pressures from the interior of Germany, such as those exerted
by the Alamans. In any case this fusion continued to be fairly superficial. Apart from the Chamavi, the Bructeri and the Hessians, who
continued to be separate groups until the end, there were always
several fairly autonomous subgroups within the Franks.

The first to be mentioned, and the most important, is that of the
Sallans who first appear, alongside the Chamavi, in an oration
delivered by Julian to the Athenians. Their name figures next in the
list of different auxiliary corps in the *Notitia dignitatum*. It is thought
that they were the spearhead of the Frankish advance into Belgium.
By the Merovingian era their name is no longer any more than a legal
term; they do not appear in the literary or documentary sources, but
they have their own law—the *Lex Salica*—which originally bound
all the Franks between the *Silva Carbonaria* and the Loire (but not the
Rhineland Franks, the Chamavi and other small tribes).

The second group—that of the Rhineland Franks—is less coherent
and had no name in Antiquity. The name 'Ripuarians', which is
current in modern historiography, is improper. But the Cosmographer
of Ravenna, a compiler who was working in 475–80, had heard of a
Francia Rinensis, which took in the banks of the Rhine from Mainz to

Nijmegen, the valley of the Moselle from Toul to Koblenz, the valley of the lower Meuse, and so on.

Before Clovis's time these two unstable groups only constituted political units for brief periods. Historiography has supplied a sufficient number of royal names for the earliest period to prove that at that time there was not a monarchy as such, but several tribal kingdoms which coexisted. The first known king is Gennobaudes, who concluded a *foedus* with Rome in 287–8; he may have belonged to the Chamavi. The fourth-century sources mention seven other names, all unknown to Merovingian tradition. (Gregory of Tours knew some of them, but through the lost work of a Latin historian, Sulpicius Alexander.) It seems fairly evident that these tribal kings are not the ancestors of Clovis.

Where, then, are the latter to be sought? It seems that between the fourth and fifth centuries the Frankish confederation changed its structure, and that some sort of pre-eminence was attained by the Salian chiefs. Already by the time of Gregory of Tours events had become blurred; Gregory mentions, more or less at random, a King Theudomer of whom nothing is known beyond his name. When this passage was re-written in the eighth century in the *Liber Historiae Francorum* Faramund, son of Marcomer, was inserted as the first king. The name 'Marcomer' is connected with the events of 388, but the origin of the name 'Faramund' is not known. The first Merovingian about whom anything tangible is known is Clodio, or Chlogio, whom Gregory credits with the capture of Cambrai and the advance to the Somme in the middle of the fifth century. In spite of the genealogies which were later invented it is not at all certain that he was the grandfather of Clovis: he is more likely to have been the ancestor of three petty kings mentioned at the end of the fifth century, Ragnachar of Cambrai and his brothers Ricchar and Rignomer, who were some sort of cousins to Clovis. As for Merovech, he is the eponymous but mythical founder of the dynasty rather than a historical figure. The continuous history of the dynasty begins effectively with Childeric, the father of Clovis, who appears about 457 as the leader of a body of auxiliaries helping the *magister militum* Aegidius against the Visigoths in the region of the Loire.

Archaeology can do very little to fill out this vague picture. It has not managed either to distinguish the material belonging to each of the different peoples that fused to form the Franks, or to recognize a characteristic Frankish type for the earliest period after the crossing of the Rhine. There is no essential difference between what archaeology describes as Frankish—small rectangular or square half-timbered houses daubed with clay and with a central hearth, coarse rouletted or stamped pottery, often in the form of two cones joined at the base—

and the material found in neighbouring areas, for example among the Frisians. Frankish cemeteries, weapons and jewellery did not become distinctive until the beginning of the Merovingian era, when a new civilization sprang from the soil of conquered Gaul.

Frankish progress within the Empire developed in two distinct ways. The Franks were infiltrating the Roman world from the fourth century, thanks to the increase in the number of Frankish corps within the army and in the number of Frankish leaders in positions of command. This is clearly shown in the texts but was essentially of little importance for the future of the Franks as a people. Then there was the slow process of colonization along the almost abandoned borders of the Empire in regions about which our sources have never at any time had anything much to say and at a social level which did not interest classical historiographers. Although almost unknown this aspect is nevertheless extremely important, for its consequences have lasted to the present day. Fortunately other disciplines can come to our aid here, namely linguistics, the study of place-names and archaeology.

The presence of Franks in the army in Gaul dates from the end of the third century, perhaps from the time of Postumus. Their numbers increased enormously under the Tetrarchy, and the German campaigns of Maximian and Constantius Chlorus were carried out partly with Frankish auxiliaries. It is under Constantine that the first high-ranking Frankish officer, Bonitus, is found in 324. From roughly 370 to 390 a group of Frankish officers dominated the Empire. Three Franks reached the rank of ordinary consul: Merobaudes (377 and 383), Richomer (384) and Bauto (385). Many of these leaders appear to have been of princely family and they were certainly very capable: Ammianus Marcellinus hated barbarians, but made an exception in the case of several Franks. Their loyalty to the Roman way of life seems to have been quite sincere. For a long time the Frank Silvanus, the son of Bonitus (note the Roman names), directed the troops of Constantius with complete loyalty against the Franks of the Rhine. When he became a usurper against his will in 355 he acted in a typically Roman context. Throughout his long career Arbogast, a nephew of the consul Richomer, either lived in the shadow of Frankish protectors like Bauto or was favoured by other Franks like Carietto. But when he came to power in 392 he did not take the Empire from the Romans and hand it over to the Franks: he crowned as Emperor one of the 'last Romans', the rhetor Eugenius, the agent of a typically Roman pagan reaction, and energetically defended the Rhine against the Franks. These men can hardly be called the precursors of Clovis.

At a lower social level Rome brought in numerous Frankish prisoners to repopulate the countryside. A clause to this effect figures in the

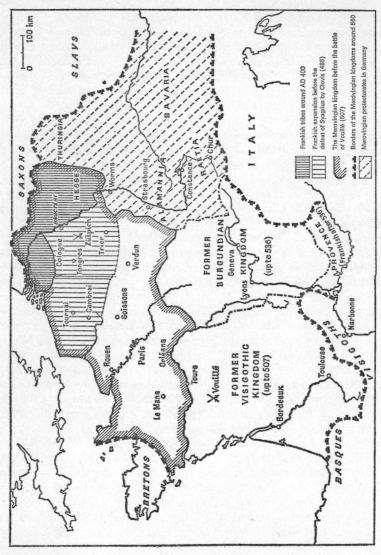

Fig. 2 Frankish Expansion

foedus of 287–8 with Gennobaudes, and Constantine settled some of them in Belgium. Several of these colonies may correspond to the cemeteries of Germanic type which are attributed to the *laeti* (see p. 122). They were able to pave the way for the development of a new Romano-Germanic culture.[1]

Essentially, however, Frankish expansion was made independently of Rome. The first stages seem to be linked with a modification of the Roman defences after the disasters of 268 to 277. Below Xanten the banks of the Rhine were abandoned and the linear *limes* was replaced by scattered *castella*, some near the river but most of them in the interior, protecting the Cologne-Tongres-Bavai-Boulogne road. There are no more Roman remains from the fourth century between the Rhine and this strategic highway. This lack of Roman remains, however, is not as valid an argument as it appears at first sight, for Flanders is a country with very little stone and so there are few recognizable traces of Roman settlements anyway. It may not prove that there was an evacuation, but it does at least indicate an impoverishment and an increasing loss of contact with civilization.

The texts are brief and disappointing. One can start with the account of Ammianus Marcellinus: in 358 Julian was going to attack the Salian Franks who had had the audacity to settle in Roman territory *apud Toxandriam locum*, but he made peace with them at Tongres and agreed to make over the land to them. Where is this *Toxandria locus?* Like the *Texandria* of the ninth century it was probably to the north-east of Antwerp, or else in the region to the west of the Scheldt, where the existence of some Texuandri is mentioned by Pliny.[2] It appears therefore that Dutch Brabant had been colonized by Salian Franks by the middle of the fourth century at least. Then comes the chronicle of St. Jerome, which mentions a Saxon defeat at *Deusone in regione Francorum*, but this place-name cannot be identified with any certainty (although the most likely site is in Guelders, to the north of the Rhine). Finally, in 388, Sulpicius Alexander (as quoted by Gregory of Tours) locates a battle against the Franks, who had crossed the Rhine near Cologne, at a place *apud Carbonariam*, which is equally unidentifiable. The context implies that Francia, and therefore the majority of the Frankish people, was still to the east of the Rhine.

After that there is total silence until the beginning of the fifth century, which seems to indicate that the pressure was lifted. There was probably a peaceful occupation of territories in which Rome had lost interest. The only clear fact is that from 358 onwards the Salians were legally installed to the west of the Rhine, on ground which had once been Roman territory, with a legal status (probably that of federates) which distinguished them from the barbarian enemies of the

Empire. Other Frankish groups like the Chamavi or the Bructeri continued to be troublesome and hostile.

The Franks did not participate in the onslaught of 406, except that some of them in the Roman army opposed the barbarians' attempt to cross the Rhine. The Franks were in no way responsible for the enormous disaster which followed. For them the event had only indirect consequences, in that it weakened Roman authority and defences in northern Gaul. Nevertheless certain groups, doubtless those who had not concluded a *foedus*, could not resist the temptation to join in the scramble for spoils for very long. They are known to have taken Trier twice before 411; in 428 some Franks occupied part of the Rhineland until Aetius drove them out of it; and a rather vague text suggests fresh clashes in 432. Finally, in a text written between 440 and 450, Salvian briefly describes the fate of the towns on the Rhine: Mainz was sacked and demolished, Cologne was 'full of enemies' (and thus surely occupied), Trier was pillaged four times (that is twice more since 411; the final occupation appears not to have taken place before 475).

Verlinden [no. 285] contrasts the 'impetuosity' of the Rhineland Franks with 'Salian immobility'. The fact is that almost nothing is known of what was happening in the north. The only event which definitely occurred, and which was known to Sidonius Apollinaris (he mentions it in the Panegyric on Majorian), is an encounter between Aetius and a band of Franks in a place called *vicus Helena*. The site (probably Hélesmes, canton of Denain, Nord), the date (probably around 440), and the significance of the episode have all been disputed. Sidonius describes it as the breaking up of a Frankish wedding—but would Aetius have bothered about such a trivial affair? All we know for certain is that at that time some Franks had settled peacefully near the modern Franco-Belgian border, with Clodio, a Merovingian, as their leader. Gregory of Tours says that he occupied Cambrai and the territory up to the Somme, but gives no date.

The Roman system of defence may have been re-established in the middle of the fifth century; according to a panegyrist of 446 the Rhine frontier had been taken in hand again. It was a short-lived reconstruction, for in 451 it was once more breached by the invasion of the Huns, in which the Chatti participated. Most of the Franks did not take part, but the *limes* was definitively abandoned. Roman authority in the north of Gaul was reduced to the presence of a field army established in the Paris basin, entrusted in 456 or 457 to the new *magister militum* Aegidius and to a handful of more or less non-existent territorial authorities: the duchy of Belgium in the coastal regions to the north of the Somme, the Tractus Armoricanus from the Loire to the Somme, and possibly also a command organized by Aetius on the Loire, around Orleans. The Frankish kings manoeuvred among these defensive bases. Childeric placed himself at the service of Aegidius who used him in 463 against the Visigoths at Orleans; Paul, the successor of Aegidius, employed him against the Saxons in the region of Angers. What his subjects in the north of Gaul were doing in the meantime is not known, but they were probably pursuing their slow advance southwards.[3]

The best attested fact about the history of Childeric is his death in approximately 481 at Tournai, where his tomb was discovered in 1653 in the middle of a Roman cemetery; this in itself shows a certain continuity in the history of the town. But Childeric was not the only Frankish king: others are recorded just after his death as reigning at Cambrai and at Cologne, not to mention two whose seats of government are unknown. (Rignomer was killed at Le Mans by Clovis, but there is no proof that he was king there; like Childeric before him at Angers he was probably there in the service of the Romans and far from his own people.) Until roughly 508 the Franks were ruled not by one sovereign but by a group of kings related by blood. It is not known exactly who led the advance towards the south-east. There are signs that the Franks must have occupied Mainz in about 459 and Trier, Metz and Toul in about 475. Three more or less secure strongholds checked the Frankish advance at about the time that Clovis came to the throne: Soissons, which is explicitly known still to have been the capital of Syagrius, the son of Aegidius, in the fifth year of Clovis's reign; Verdun, which the *Vita* of St. Maximinus, abbot of Micy (St. Mesmin d'Orléans), claims was conquered by Clovis; and Worms, which the Cosmographer of Ravenna places in Alamannic territory.

It is probable that through the settlements of *laeti* and *coloni*, and through their own campaigns, the Frankish kings had dealings with territory stretching as far as the Loire. That would explain why almost nothing is heard of Clovis's occupation of the regions between the Somme and the Loire during the following period: it was not a real conquest but simply the return of the Franks to areas where they had frequently been seen before. All they had to do was eliminate certain Roman centres like Soissons or Paris; there was no need for them methodically to conquer the whole country. The Frankish advance does not bear the slightest resemblance to the conquest of Italy and Spain by the Goths, or of Africa by the Vandals, for no precise dates can be assigned to it and the itinerary of the conquerors cannot be traced on a map.

The Franks had kept very much in the background until this point but now, led by Clovis, they pushed themselves into the front rank of peoples. But the historical character of this conqueror is very difficult to establish.[4] We cannot date the most decisive episodes in his career to within ten years; we do not know very clearly what his titles signified; and of course we know nothing at all of his political thought. The only relatively coherent account of his reign is that of Gregory of Tours, written after 575 and therefore after a lapse of three-quarters of a century. Moreover, this account appears to be a fairly hypothetical reconstruction, put together by Gregory on the basis of some extremely meagre annals and a few oral traditions. Furthermore, Gregory's intentions were not purely historical, particularly where Clovis was concerned, for the Frankish king, having assured the triumph of the Catholic Church, was bound to appear to Gregory as an instrument of Divine Providence. Yet we cannot do without Gregory: apart from his text we have no more than a handful of letters and saints' lives which only mention the king in relation to certain individual events.

The name 'Clovis' is not strictly accurate: in fact *Chlodovechus* is identical with *Hludovicus* and therefore corresponds to the French name 'Louis'. At any rate, whatever his name, the future unifier of Gaul must have been born in about the year 465, the son of Childeric and the Thuringian princess Basina (which explains why he conducted one of his earliest campaigns in Thuringia). Nothing else is known of him until he came to the throne, probably in 481. In 486, in the fifth year of his reign, with his kinsman Ragnachar, king of Cambrai, he attacked Syagrius, the son of Aegidius, the 'king of the Romans', whose seat was at Soissons. After his defeat Syagrius took refuge at Toulouse with Alaric II, king of the Visigoths; the latter handed him over to Clovis, who had him assassinated. This success probably gave Clovis the whole country as far as the Loire; in any case in the fifteenth year of his reign Amboise was on the borders of his kingdom. Afterwards, it is not known exactly when, Clovis got rid of his colleague Ragnachar and became the sole master of the conquered territory.

That is all that is known about this crucial episode in the Frankish conquest. Even legend has nothing to add. However F. Lot [no. 264] suggested a fruitful line of conjecture. Noticing that, on the one hand, not a single text refers to a direct Frankish conquest in the west of Gaul and that, on the other, Maine and its surrounding regions enjoyed a rather peculiar status within the Merovingian kingdom (with regard to taxation in particular), he believed that the former *Tractus Armoricanus*—which is known to have been making a bid for autonomy in the fifth century—must have negotiated with the Franks on its own initiative, without waiting to be invaded, possibly through fear of the Visigoths or of the Bretons.

After the defeat of Syagrius the chronology of the reign poses extremely difficult problems, which gave rise to a lot of infighting among scholars between 1935 and 1938. We do not propose to go into the intricacies of this controversy here (see p. 229), but we shall give two dates for several of the episodes, the first according to the 'short' chronology of Lot, which is the more acceptable in our opinion, and the second following the 'long' chronology of Van de Vyver. Without following Clovis step by step, we shall trace the major stages of his campaigns. Some were directed towards the east, against the Thuringians (491), then against the Alamans (in 495, or perhaps in 505–6), marked by victories whose full significance we do not know: it seems that they paved the way for the Frankish protectorate in the west of Germany which was to be set up under Clovis's sons. Most were directed towards the south, against the Burgundians (or rather against the faction of Gundobad) in 500–1, with a somewhat inglorious result, and in particular against the Visigoths of Alaric II, until the decisive victory at Vouillé in 507. Then, on the occasion of a campaign against the Alamans, Clovis, who had married a Burgundian Catholic called Clotilde, undertook to turn from paganism and become a Catholic himself. He was baptised by Bishop Remigius, probably at Rheims, on Christmas Day, in 496 or 498 or possibly even in 506. Gradually his people followed his example and found themselves sharing the faith and form of worship of the conquered Romans, the first among the barbarian conquerors to do so.

We must emphasize the importance of the defeat of the Visigoths and the Frankish annexation of the south-west quarter of Gaul. The Goths had ruled Aquitaine for three generations and were in a strong position there, especially as they could count on the help of the Ostrogoths of Italy, via Provence. But they were Arians and Clovis was a Catholic, having been one either for ten years or for just a few months, depending on our interpretation of the sources. Several bishops in the kingdom of Alaric II, such as the African Quintianus, bishop of Rodez, and the bishops of Tours, Volusianus and Verus, had been intriguing with the Franks for some time. Moreover the Emperor Anastasius, who was jealous of Theodoric, was supporting any enterprise which could discomfit the Goths: he probably encouraged Clovis, while Theodoric vainly tried to intercede between the Franks and the Visigoths. The Burgundians, possibly in obedience to advice sent from Constantinople, also supported the policy of Clovis, in spite of the recent war between him and Gundobad.[5]

After an interview with Clovis at Amboise, Alaric II recognized the danger. In 506 he made many conciliatory gestures towards the Catholics: he recalled exiled bishops, authorized the holding of a council at Agde and probably also promulgated the *Breviarium Alarici* on 2 February 506 (see p. 211). He was effectively supported by a group of Romans from the Auvergne, under Apollinaris, the son of the famous Sidonius. But that was not enough. Exactly how things developed is not clear. Clovis, supported by the king of Cologne, his kinsman, advanced along the road from Tours to Poitiers. The battle took place at some distance from Poitiers at a place called Vouillé. Alaric II was slain and Clovis lost no time in occupying his two capitals, Bordeaux and Toulouse, and seizing his treasure, while the Burgundians advanced as far as the region of Limoges and even up to the gates of Toulouse. Clovis contented himself with occupying the north and west of the former Gothic kingdom: the state of his forces probably did not allow him to do anything more ambitious, and prudence advised him not to provoke Theodoric by advancing as far as the Mediterranean. The Franks opposed neither the emigration of the Visigoths to Spain nor the continued existence of the bridge between the Gothic states via Septimania and Provence. It is doubtful whether they occupied Gascony, to the south of the Garonne, in the time of Clovis; however they were determined to stamp out Arianism in those regions which they had decided to annex.

On his return from the Vouillé expedition, which had doubled his kingdom and given him some of the most Romanized regions of the West, Clovis took part in an enigmatic ceremony at Tours. All that we know about it is contained in eight lines of Gregory of Tours: Clovis received from the Emperor Anastasius some 'consular tablets', donned the purple tunic and the diadem in the basilica of St. Martin, and went through the town distributing gold and silver, in consideration of which he was called *consul aut Augustus*. The various possible interpretations will be discussed later. The episode had no practical consequences and the Frankish kings never bore the title of consul or of Augustus. Nevertheless it symbolically consecrated, with the blessing of the Empire, the union between the conqueror-king and the southern part of Roman Gaul which was to provide Clovis's successors with an appreciable number of royal officials.

We know only two facts about the last years of Clovis's reign, but both are of considerable importance. Firstly, he had all the Frankish petty kings (who were his cousins), including Sigibert of Cologne, hunted down and killed, in order to establish the monopoly of his own line within a royal family which had hitherto been very extensive. Secondly, he established his residence at Paris, at a great distance from the region whence he had set out on his conquests, and in an almost completely Gallo-Roman setting. These gestures reveal that Clovis wanted to found his state on a very different basis from that of his predecessors: from then on the Merovingian kingdom was to be a creative synthesis of Roman and Germanic elements.

Clovis died in Paris on 27 November 511, but the Frankish advance continued for another generation, in the form of political expansion rather than as a popular migration. The second generation of Merovingians advanced westwards until they came into contact with the Bretons a little beyond the Rennes-Vannes line. To the south-west Gascony was occupied as far as the Pyrenees. More important, to the south-east the Burgundian kingdom was conquered, annexed and partitioned in 533–4, and then in 537 Provence was occupied with the agreement both of the hard-pressed Ostrogoths and of their enemy Justinian. And so, except for western Brittany and Septimania, the whole of Gaul was united under the authority of the Franks.

The second generation of Merovingians added to Gaul the greater part of Germania, up to the middle Danube, the mountains of Bohemia and a line running approximately from Halle to Duisburg. This conquest was superficial and insecure, and it is not very well documented, but in neglecting it we should be throwing away the chance of understanding a whole facet of the Merovingian achievement. The enterprise was undertaken by the sons and grandsons of Clovis—the kings of Rheims and Metz, Theuderic (511–34) and Theudebert (534–48), in particular—who knew how to turn the waning of Ostrogothic influence north of the Alps to their advantage.

Their policy seems to have been inspired and carried out by a Roman statesman, the patrician Parthenius, a descendant of the Emperor Avitus and a Provençal who had passed from the service of Theodoric to that of the Franks. His great ambition was to recreate for the Merovingian kings the policy that Cassiodorus had created for Theodoric. It was probably he who gave to the laws of southern Germany (Alamannia and Bavaria) their Gothic characteristics. In order to finance this ambitious policy he wanted to reinstitute in Gaul the regular levying of the land tax—which earned him a stoning by the mob on the death of Theudebert. In spite of this personal set-back his policies were fairly successful; they set in motion the slow evolution which finally brought Germany closer to the former imperial territories.[6]

Thuringia, which had been conquered by Theuderic and Chlotar in about 530, became a protectorate under the supervision of Frankish dukes, but continued to be pagan. Then Theuderic, and later Chlotar, attacked Saxony, which at first gave way and paid tribute, but in about 555 revolted and regained its liberty. With regard to the Alamans, Clovis's dealings had been more direct than with other peoples: he destroyed their royal family and annexed their Rhenish territory as a protectorate. The rest of Alamannia was conquered by Theudebert after 536. The west (Alsace and the Palatinate) was closely associated with the kingdom of Austrasia, taken over by the bishops of Strasbourg and Basle, and converted during the course of the seventh century. Alamannia beyond the Rhine, on the contrary, continued to be very independent, under its own national dukes, and was pagan until about 750. In Bavaria and Pannonia the Franks fell heir to the

former protectorates of the Ostrogoths. In about 555 Chlotar imposed
his suzerainty on the Bavarian dukes; for a short time his influence
extended to the Lombards. This expansion, which culminated in
about 560, was followed by a distinct recession in the seventh century.
It was only in very rare instances accompanied by a process of civilization and assimilation, as in Alsace. Nevertheless, it was one of the
great events in European history. For the first time Germany was
subject to a power whose seat of government was west of the Rhine,
and thereby the process of tribal disintegration and regrouping came
to an end. Between the Alps and the North Sea only the Frisians and
the Saxons kept their independence intact.

The establishment of this new stability was made easier by the new
threat offered by the Slavs and Avars in the east. There is no doubt
that the Frankish kings, with Theudebert at their head, felt that they
had a sort of imperial, or imperialist, vocation to organize the Germans,
as is proved by a letter to Justinian written in about 539:[7] 'You have
deigned to concern yourself with the question of who we were and in
what provinces we lived .... By the grace of God we have conquered
the Thuringians, acquired their territory and destroyed their royal
family; the Swabians [which means Alamans here] are now subject
to our majesty; the Saxons and the Eucii [not yet identified] have
placed themselves voluntarily in our hands; our domain stretches as far
as the Danube, the borders of Pannonia, and the ocean.'

Thus it was that inside three generations a small people, whose
petty kings had been quarrelling bitterly over a few cantons on the
Rhine and in Belgium about the year 470, became masters of an area
stretching from the Pyrenees to the Saale and from the English Channel
to the middle Danube. Even more astonishing is the fact that this
state, so rapidly constructed, should have proved the most long-lived
of all the barbarian states in the West. This was probably the result of
the relative equilibrium which existed between the Roman and
Germanic elements of the population.

The Alamans

Like the Franks, the Alamans appear to have sprung from an amalga-
mation of scattered tribes, worn out by prolonged contact with the
Romans of the *Agri Decumates* between the upper Danube and the
middle Rhine. They are mentioned for the first time in 213, but the
start of their career was much more brilliant than that of the Franks:
almost immediately they represented a grave threat to the *limes*. In
260 a successful breakthrough carried them across the Alps and down
to Milan, and they repeated this feat several times in the course of the

next fifteen years. A great victory by Probus in 277 interrupted their explosive career, but they ended up by being masters of the region of the Neckar, occasionally pushing westwards as far as the Alsatian part of the Rhine, to Lake Constance and the Iller. Throughout the fourth century they made frequent attempts to gain a foothold on the left bank of the Rhine; each time they were repulsed (by Constantius in about 350, by Julian near Strasbourg in 357, and by Gratian in Alsace again in 378), in spite of their having penetrated quite far beyond the *limes* several times, as for example in the time of Constantius Chlorus, when they managed to reach Langres.

The very name 'Alamanni' (all men) seems to indicate that they were of composite origin. What were the various components of this people? Since the home of the Alamans eventually became known as Swabia, the Sueves are an obvious possibility; however, at least one important branch of the Sueves did not change its name. The Quadi, the Teutones from the Neckar, the Charudes and the Eudusii (all very obscure peoples) have also been suggested. The history of the *Stammesbildung* of the Alamannic people is an almost insoluble problem. From the sixth century onwards the name of Alamans was used particularly by outsiders (until in French it widened its scope to include all the continental Germans), while internal usage preferred to revive the old name of Swabians.

Straddling the former *limes* of the *Agri Decumates* and with their centre of gravity clearly inside former Roman territory, the Alamans constituted a fairly powerful political unit in the fourth and fifth centuries. They are known to have had a dynasty which lasted until the time of Clovis. Their strength consisted in a powerful cavalry, whose favourite weapon was a long double-edged sword. They seem to have wiped out any Roman organization north of the Danube and reduced some of its inhabitants to slavery—for a long time the capture of human 'livestock' was the only apparent aim of their raids.

The Alamans played a role of considerable importance in the breakthrough of 406. Their first settlements in Alsace and the Palatinate probably date from that time, though these were not consolidated until after an offensive by Aetius shortly before 455. Part of the population managed to survive, preserving some of its former place-names, such as *Tabernae* (Saverne). From this base they first pushed towards the north and north-west, going down the Rhine. They had several clashes with the Frankish kings of Cologne, who stopped them at the famous battle of Tolbiacum (Zülpich, to the west of Bonn). When Clovis took over from these petty kings this direction was firmly barred to them. A vigorous Frankish counter-attack ended in the overthrow of the dynasty and the flight of many of the Alamans towards areas that were Gothic protectorates (especially Raetia). The north-west of the Alamannic territory (the Palatinate, Rhineland Hesse and the region of the Main) was rapidly taken over by the Franks. Alsace, on the other hand, kept its Alamannic character intact, even after it had passed more or less directly under Frankish protection.

The Alamans then turned their attention towards the south and south-east. At first their advance in this direction was nothing more than a disconnected series of raids for plunder. In 457 they once more penetrated into northern Italy, and then between 470 and 480 they again started raiding deep into enemy territory in various directions, from Maxima Sequanorum (Franche-Comté) to Noricum. True colonization did not begin in what is now Switzerland until the last years of the fifth century, after initial setbacks at the hands of the Franks. It is only after 500 that barbarian cemeteries are found south of the Rhine. The advance towards the Swiss plain, which had been checked for a short time by the Burgundian kings, began again once the latters' kingdom had broken up; the Alamans surrounded and took over those towns that were still in existence, such as Augst (near Basle) or Windisch (to the west of Zürich). At the beginning of the seventh century the Alamans reached the region of Avenches, defeating two Frankish counts at Wangen in 610, and occupying the area. At the same time detachments were trying to penetrate into Franche-Comté through the Porte de Bourgogne or the passes of the Jura; the tribe of the Varasqui settled around Besançon, and another has left its name to the country near Ecuens (*pagus Scotingus*). The majority, however, hardly got past the eastern foothills of the Jura.[8] In the whole of this area a considerable proportion of the inhabitants must have stayed put, in spite of the massacres which according to Fredegar followed the battle of Wangen, for nearly all the important places have kept their Roman names (for example *Turicum* > Zürich, *Salodurum* > Soleure or Solothora, *Augusta* > Augst, and so on). One gets the impression that the Alamans only agreed to colonize the Swiss plain because no better alternative presented itself. Their great ambition was still to settle in northern Italy, which they had glimpsed at the end of the third century, and again in the middle of the fifth century. An army of Alamans formed the main body of the troops which the Frankish king Theudebert placed at the service of Witigis in Italy.

Further east the Alamans were peaceably welcomed in the plains of Raetia by order of Theodoric, the Roman inhabitants falling back on the area to the south of Lake Constance and on the Alps. For a long time the two populations remained in close proximity, and a little semi-autonomous Latin state grew up centred on Chur. Later, when the whole region had passed under the direct authority of the Frankish kings, this little enclave was left untouched.

The mediocrity of the political organization of the Alamans after the time of Clovis presents a startling contrast to the dynamism of their colonizing expansion, and is a major difference between them and the Franks. Around 536 Alamannia was placed under the control of a duke nominated by the king of Austrasia; as yet he only rarely had the whole of the country under his authority (from the seventh century onwards Alsace very frequently escaped his control). His power centred on the Hegau and the region to the west of Constance, but there is nothing to indicate even the crude beginnings of the development of state institutions. The people continued to be pagan for a long time yet, in spite of the survival of Christianity in certain places which had originally been Roman: conversion did not begin until the end of the sixth century with the foundation of a diocese at Constance in about 590, and its definite progress only dates from the mission of Columbanus and his disciples. Certain Alamannic leaders may have felt tempted to become Arians when the prestige of the Goths was at its height, notably King Gibvult, but nothing lasting came of this. Alamannic law was only codified under Austrasian influence.

This political backwardness lasted until the dissolution of the Merovingian empire in Germany. At the end of the seventh century the Alamannic dukes regained complete freedom of action, and the Pippinid mayors of the palace had difficulty in trying to restrain them. Charles Martel finally put an end to their independence between 709 and 712. At the beginning of the ninth century the Raetia of Chur yielded in its turn and was put under the authority of Frankish counts. The history of the Alamans merges at this point with that of the German people as a whole.

The Bavarians

The origin of the Bavarians is even more obscure, and their emergence even more belated, than in the case of the Alamans. They are the only group in the history of the invasions to be mentioned for the first time *after* they had crossed the *limes* (in 551, by Jordanes). From then on they occupied the territory still called Bavaria, which they have never left. Linguists and archaeologists have not yet managed to establish a firm ancestry for them.

The circumstances of the Bavarian settlement to the south of the *limes* are no less obscure. It is thought that their arrival took place before the establishment of a Frankish protectorate (although the letter from Theudebert to Justinian written in about 539 does not mention them) and after the period described in the life of St. Severinus, whose biographer was so well informed about the movements of the barba-

D

rians [no. 15]. Their migration would therefore fall between 488 and 539, probably at the same time as the Lombards were leaving Lower Austria for Pannonia. Up to the eighth century there was often close collaboration between the Bavarians and the Lombards: Bavarians took part in the Lombard conquest of Italy (cf. p. 88) and the last dynasty of Lombard Italy was partly Bavarian. Other Bavarians ended up in Burgundy, giving rise to the place-names Beyvière and Beyvier in the north-west of the *département* of Ain.

At first the Bavarians, like the Alamans, only occupied low-lying regions, and thus allowed some important groups of Romans to survive in the Alps and on the plateau, where the population was sparse and scattered. Their advance towards the south took as long as that of the Alamans; in the eighth century they passed the crest of the Alps and spilled into the Alto Adige. But the Bavarians were different from the Alamans in that they rapidly formed a political unit around the Agilolfing dukes, the first of whom, Garibald, came to power in the middle of the sixth century. It is not known whether these dukes were imposed by the Frankish protectors or were of local origin, but what is certain is that the Bavarians rallied to them. At the end of the seventh century they achieved complete autonomy, undertook the conversion of their subjects with the help of missionaries from all over Europe, and by the eighth century had become a centre of attraction for those Germans who wished to escape Frankish supremacy. Charlemagne refused to tolerate this situation and incorporated Bavaria once more (unconditionally, this time) into the Frankish kingdom in 788, when Duke Tassilo III had shown signs of coming to an understanding with the Avars.

To attempt to define precisely the limits of Bavarian territory is a rather delicate task. It is agreed that at the beginning of the sixth century their area of settlement lay along the Danube from Ingolstadt to Straubing. By 565 the valley of the Lech was already in Bavarian territory, according to Fortunatus; the western frontier was soon pushed over as far as the Iller, bordering Alamannic territory. Towards the east they reached the Enns before 600 and about 610 an advance party came in contact with the Slavs in Carinthia. It is not known when the Oberpfalz, which was Thuringian territory in the fifth century, became Bavarian.

The relative meekness with which the Bavarians accepted Merovingian protection in the sixth century is explained by the Avaro-Slav threat. They hastened to reject it, however, when the consolidated Lombard kingdom offered them better security. And it is the renewal of the Avar threat at the end of the eighth century which accounts for their final submission to Charlemagne.

THE THIRD WAVE OF INVASIONS: THE SIXTH AND SEVENTH CENTURIES

With the triumph of Clovis the western barbarians seem to have found, if not stability, at least a certain equilibrium. Each of the broad geographical divisions of the *pars Occidentis* was dominated by a people which was starting to put down roots there: the Anglo-Saxons in Britain, the Franks in Gaul, the Visigoths in Spain, the Ostrogoths in Italy and the Vandals in Africa. Two secondary peoples, the Burgundians in eastern Gaul and the Sueves in northern Spain, still maintained a precarious independence, but already there were signs of their forthcoming absorption by more powerful neighbours. Some regions were still contested (Septimania, Provence and Sicily), but that did not alter the essential picture. The pockets of Celts in Armorica and Basques in Gascony were of no political significance. The process of consolidation was under way in all of the various kingdoms.

Then an unforeseen event occurred whose after-effects brought about the return of instability to the central part of the Mediterranean basin, an instability which was to last for several centuries. This was the reconquest undertaken by Justinian. A swift and lucky start in Africa in the years 532 to 534 encouraged him to carry his enterprise into Italy and Spain. But it took a whole generation of bitter fighting, from 535 to 562, to destroy the power of the Ostrogoths, and the elimination of a people which had succeeded remarkably well in Italy entailed the total destruction of that country. Spain was only saved from a similar fate by the fact that it was further away and that Byzantium had few forces at its disposal: Justinian managed to reoccupy no more than the south-east of the country (after 552).

Justinian's reconquest, which came to an end in about 560, left a blank square on the chess-board of the land ceded to the barbarians: Italy. This vacuum immediately attracted the Lombards, who left Pannonia to occupy Italy in 568. Consequently Pannonia fell vacant and attracted the Avars, who arrived from the Pontic steppes. In order to maintain the tremendous twofold effort of the struggle against the Persians and the reconquest of the West for such a long time, Justinian had stripped the Danubian frontier of troops: the Balkan peninsula was once more open to the barbarians, as it had been in the fourth century. The Avars rushed in without settling there, but the Bulgars and Slavs who followed established themselves there for good. In the world of the steppes this twofold thrust towards the west and the south created a new void which the Khazars, in their turn, came to fill.[9]

This third wave lasted for approximately a century and a half, from Alboin's crossing into Italy until the consolidation of the Bulgar khanate. It was composed of many elements, involving as it did Germans (Lombards), steppe peoples (Avars, Bulgars and Khazars) and Slavs. But it undeniably represents an interconnected series of events within the general movement.

The Lombards

The people who took part in the Lombard invasion, which was the last and possibly the most devastating of the Germanic invasions, had remained in the background until the middle of the sixth century and had given no sign that they were destined to play a role any more important than that of the Gepids, or the Heruls of the Danube. The destruction of the Ostrogothic kingdom by Justinian suddenly opened up unexpected opportunities for them. Thanks in large part to their king Alboin's remarkable capacity for decision, they were the only people to escape from Pannonia before that region became once and for all the territory of invaders from the steppes.

There are two traditions about the origins of the Lombards. Their own national tradition has a mythical quality, and was recorded after the conquest of Italy.[10] It is of the same type as the Gothic traditions: the Lombards said they came from Scandinavia (*Scadanan*) and went from there into *Golaida* or *Scoringa* (possibly on the southern shores of the Baltic), where for a time they bore the name of *Winniles*, and ended up in *Mauringa* (perhaps on the Elbe). Classical historiography is both more laconic and more trustworthy: in 5 BC the Lombards were defeated by Tiberius on the lower Elbe; Velleius Paterculus describes them as 'the most ferocious Germanic people on account of their savagery'; in the time of Tacitus they were still on the Elbe. Then they moved south: in AD 167 they were in contact with Roman Pannonia. Nothing further is heard of them until 489, when they reappeared as the invaders of the territory of the Rugians (Lower Austria) which had been left vacant by the victory of Odoacer.

It is not impossible that they were of Scandinavian origin. The Lombards did speak a West Germanic dialect—*Elbgermanisch*, to be exact—but then before the Christian era Nordic was not the only dialect spoken in Scandinavia. Lombard law seems to present analogies with Scandinavian law. Archaeology is no help, and the Lombards are not known to history before the beginning of their stay on the Elbe. This stay was fairly long, and gave rise to contacts between the Lombards and the Chauci (the ancestors of the Saxons), which accounts for the participation of Saxons in Lombard expeditions between 568 and 573. The name of the Lombards—*Langobardi*—seems to mean 'long beards'. Anglo-Saxon tradition (*Widsith*) has a variant *Headhobeardan*, which means '*Bardi* of battle'; in Norse mythology *Langbardhr* is an epithet applied to Odin. No firm conclusions about the origins of the Lombards can be drawn from this.

The migration of the Lombards towards the south, parallel with the migration of a whole group of small peoples (Rugians, Heruls and so on), stretches over a long period. At the end of it, in 489, the Lombards occupied part of what is now Lower Austria, where they stayed for a time (fifteen years or possibly fifty-seven) as clients of the Heruls. During that period they were a people of only secondary importance.

At the beginning of the sixth century all this changed. Rallying the remnants of several peoples, the Lombards crossed into Pannonia and there became semi-nomadic horsemen. From this central position they made raids into Dalmatia. Their king, Wacho, who reigned roughly from 510 to 540, was a figure of international stature. He married his daughters to the Merovingian kings Theudebert, Theudebald and Chlotar, kept on good terms with Byzantium, and remained neutral in 539 when Witigis begged his help against Justinian. This Pannonian kingdom prospered thanks to the great trade route from Aquileia to the Baltic; it became civilized, and probably converted to Arianism about this time. (The only source which mentions this conversion is a late text which states that they became converted in *Rugiland*, and thus about 489–505; it could have been the work of Rugian missionaries. We cannot say with any certainty whether or not it was preceded by a period of Catholicism.) Many Lombards served in the imperial army and borrowed from the Romans the framework for an efficient military organization (including the ranks of duke, count, centurion and *decanus*).

Audoin, the brother-in-law and successor of Wacho, concluded a *foedus* with Justinian just after 540, whereby his people were to be quartered in Pannonia and Noricum and were to receive subsidies. Justinian was thinking of using them against both the Franks, who had just occupied Noricum, and the Goths, to threaten their rearguard and prevent help from flooding in from the north. The Lombards even co-operated in Narses's final campaign in Italy in 562: several dukes took the field on the plain of the Po with 2,500 warriors and 3,000 auxiliaries. As things turned out it was foolish of Narses to have used them, for it gave them an idea both of their own capabilities and of the wealth of Italy.

Alboin, the son of Audoin, was disposed to profit from this realization as soon as possible, for he was having difficulty both with Byzantium and with the nomadic people that had now arrived on the scene, the Avars. At first the Lombards and the Avars had fought together against the Gepids: the latter were crushed in 567 and Alboin had killed their king with his own hand. But Byzantium protested against this violation of its protection, and when it came to dividing the conquered territory the Avar khagan Baian was dangerously demanding.

Alboin then made an extremely daring decision: to leave Pannonia and conquer Italy. A treaty which he made with the Avars ceded Pannonia to them with the reservation that the Lombards should have the right to return at any time within a period of two hundred years. The whole population then headed westwards. All sorts of incongruous elements joined in this trek—'Gepids, Bulgars, Sarmatians, Pannonians, Sueves, and Noricans', according to Paul the Deacon. Presumably in this very literary text the term Pannonians is used to describe the former Romanized provincial population; the term Noricans is either used in the same way or refers to Bavarians or Bulgars.[11] To those explicitly mentioned by Paul the Deacon must be added Thuringians, Bavarians, Saxons and Taifals. They were not even obliged to renounce their independence: for a long time after the conquest the Bulgars, Sarmatians and Saxons formed separate bands. The exodus took place in April 568. The Avars slowly occupied the vacated country, encroaching on Byzantine territory to the south of the Save whenever the opportunity presented itself.

This evacuation of Pannonia is an event of cardinal importance in the history of the European continent. The route from the Adriatic to the Baltic was permanently severed and for a long time an impenetrable barrier of barbarians flanked the northern side of the Empire, encouraging the Bulgars and Slavs to invade the Balkans. The repercussions of this can clearly be seen as far away as the Scandinavian world, where the influx of Mediterranean and oriental gold dried up until the time of the Vikings.

In order to conquer Italy Alboin had to break through the *limes* of Friuli, which had been disorganized by the wars between Justinian and the Goths. It gave way almost immediately, on 20 May 568. Aquileia was taken directly afterwards, its patriarch having taken refuge on the coastal island of Grado: this marked the beginning of a general flight of the population to the coast. The Lombards captured the *castella* of Venetia one after another, sending their scouts far ahead of them. The following year Alboin occupied almost the whole of the Po valley and took Milan on 3 September. The former capital was in a sorry state, but its importance was still such that Alboin had the years of his reign as *dominus Italiae* counted from the date of Milan's capture. However, the success of the Lombards was not yet complete: the Byzantines still held on to some enclaves, small forts which controlled the Alpine passes (Aosta, which fell in 575, Susa, which fell in 576,

Chiavenna and the Isola Comacina which held out until 588, and in particular Oderzo in upper Venetia, which resisted until about 650) or fortified towns on the plain: Padua, Mantua, Cremona and, most

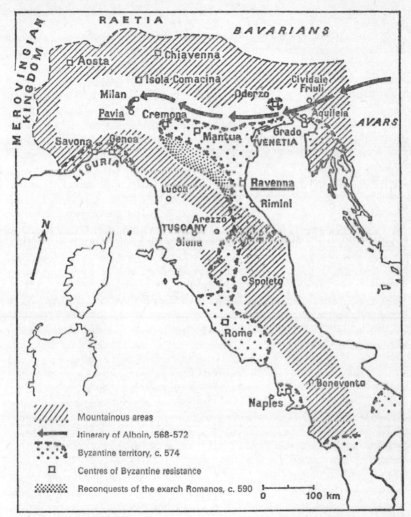

Fig 3. Lombard Italy at the End of the Sixth Century

important of all, Pavia. It was around Pavia that the decisive battle was fought: Alboin took three years—from 569 to 572—to capture it. There is scarcely any doubt that Alboin's first intention was to take the place of the Ostrogoths in Italy and consequently to establish himself at Ravenna. It was only for want of any better alternative that he set up his headquarters at Verona. His successors made Verona, Pavia and Milan their capital in turn. The capital was finally established at Pavia—which had been a secondary residence of Theodoric and a stronghold of Arianism—only in about 626.[12]

During the siege of Pavia the Lombard dukes and their troops spread out in all directions. To the west, across the southern Alps, they penetrated Gaul three times between 569 and 576. To the south they rapidly crossed the central Apennines and invaded Tuscany and Latium; Rome was blockaded by land from 575 onwards. To the south-east other detachments followed the Via Aemilia and the Via Flaminia, passing to the south of Ravenna, and laid the first foundations of the future duchies of Benevento and Spoleto, probably in 575. As early as 578 mention is made of a troop of Lombards in Campania under the dukes Faroald and Zotto.

Alboin did not have time to profit from these successes, for he was assassinated in 572, and his dynasty died with him. The king elected to succeed him, Cleph, was killed in his turn just two years later, and the Lombards then decided to do without kings. For ten years they were led by thirty-five dukes who were bound in a loose alliance. Thus during the decisive years of the Lombard occupation there was no organization, but merely a number of warrior bands wandering about in search of booty.[13] When the kingdom was re-established in 584 in favour of Authari, the son of Cleph, the foundations of Lombard Italy had been laid. This explains why until the eighth century the Lombard people appeared to be no more than a series of *exercitus* quartered in the various regions.

Except towards the south-east the impetus of the conquest slowed down noticeably from the beginning of the interregnum on, thus giving the Byzantines time to recover. They managed to hold on to Istria, the coast of Venetia, the region of Ravenna and the triangle of territory along the River Po as far as Cremona; the military road from Ravenna to Rimini and Rome, held by a system of fortified posts, and the country around Rome, with the remains of southern Tuscany; the Ligurian coast, with Genoa; the coast of Campania; and Calabria and the region of Otranto. All of this territory was administered by an exarch living in Ravenna. Moreover, the thought of a reconquest was constantly in the minds of the imperial authorities: in 586, for example, the exarch managed to recapture, for ten or fifteen years, Modena, Reggio Emilia, Padua and Piacenza. The archbishop of Milan and the vicar of Upper Italy, who were confined in Genoa, did not accept the new state of affairs until the eve of the occupation of their place of refuge by King Rothari in about 640. The situation did not really achieve any stability until the middle of the seventh century, after a significant Byzantine setback. Meanwhile Byzantine diplomacy tried its favourite method of persuading other barbarians (in this case the Franks and their Alamannic and Bavarian auxiliaries) to attack the Lombards in the rear: this policy did not, however, prove a success.

The first and most obvious result of the Lombard invasion, following hard on the heels of thirty years' bitter strife between the Goths and the Romans, was to plunge Italy into appalling anarchy. The Roman ruling classes had either perished or shut themselves up in places of refuge on the coast, and there was nobody to take their place. The first generation of Lombards established no lasting settlements, Their armies lived on booty and swept along with them some formidable auxiliaries (such as Bulgars in Benevento, and Avars). The defence of the frontiers was abandoned and Italy only narrowly escaped being invaded by the Slavs (as the Balkans had been) via Istria and the Adriatic coast. The Avaro-Slav danger (the Avars being the spearhead, as in the Balkans, and the Slavs the main body of the army) is mentioned for the first time in Istria in 601.[14] In 603 the Lombard King Agilulf led a Slav corps, sent by the Avar khagan, to besiege Cremona.[15] In 611 another Slav invasion took place in Istria. Then the movement ceased, possibly as a consequence of the reconstruction of the *limes*. However, around 700 the Slav people pushed forward as far as the River Natisone, west of Cividale. A Slav landing in about 640 on the Adriatic coast of the duchy of Benevento is mentioned.[16] The re-establishment of the Lombard monarchy in 584 occurred too late to wipe out the traces of the early phase of anarchy in Lombard Italy. Even when it had been put on a firm footing the Lombard state remained incomplete: the Empire still kept its bridgeheads on the coasts and in Rome; the warrior bands, which in the north had been eliminated with the organization of the kingdom of Pavia, survived in the south, where the Lombard principalities continued to promote unbelievable disorder until the eleventh century; the key positions in the Alps remained in the hands of the Franks. These circumstances explain why the Lombards never formed a coherent national state in Italy comparable to those of the Franks in Gaul or the Visigoths in Spain.

The decision of the imperial authorities to organize the withdrawal of their officials to the coast must take a large share of the responsibility for the destruction of Italy. What had been at first only a temporary expedient became, in the end, a permanent state of affairs. It was in Venetia that this policy had its most marked effect. Aquileia, an ecclesiastical and economic metropolis, was abandoned in favour of Grado on the coastal archipelago. The bishops of Concordia and Oderzo took refuge at the mouths of the Livenza and the Piave. The fugitives transformed fishing villages into full-scale towns, especially at Rialto, which formed the nucleus of the future Venice. This 'new

D*

Venetia' on the coast, which was loyal to Byzantium, was forced to be outward-looking and dependent on the sea; the results of this are well known. A parallel phenomenon, though on a smaller scale, affected Liguria: Milanese refugees here contributed to the development of Genoa. It is difficult to assess the fate of the towns of the interior, which is only known to us through lacunae in the episcopal lists. Were these lacunae the result of the Gothic wars, the Lombard wars, or simply of Arian intolerance? The situation did not begin to return to normal until the middle of the seventh century: a large number of sees reappeared on the occasion of the Lateran Council in 649.

The Lombard kingdom essentially dates from the time of Authari's son Agilulf (590–616). In his reign the settling of the conquerors in the Italian environment took its final form. His marriage to a Catholic Bavarian princess, Theudelinda, facilitated a *modus vivendi* with the Catholics; the survivors of the ruling classes, who had been allowed to retain a certain intellectual and artistic role, regrouped around the palace of Monza. After the conversion of the king in 607 there was still a good deal of Arian reaction, but the Lombards had set out on the road to conciliation and there was no turning back. The decision to establish the court and the seat of government in a very active town, Pavia, in 626, confirmed this tendency. Anarchy was replaced by law and order.

To a large extent the settlement of the Lombards took the form of military colonization. The basic administrative unit—which replaced the Roman province—was the duchy, the area of competence of an *exercitus* commanded by a duke. In order to maintain the cohesion of the army and accommodate the Arian cult the population was divided into compact groups, which gave rise to local inequalities: thus in Tuscany, Siena had its *exercitus*, while Lucca and Arezzo continued to be governed by their Roman *cives*. The major part of the linguistic contribution of the Lombards comprises either military and administrative terms (such as *arimannus*, soldier; *gastaldus*, administrator of an estate; *sculdahis*, a sort of provost) or social ones (like *adelingus*, noble; *aldio*, half-free), together with the vocabulary of a new legal system. This indicates the far-reaching nature of the social reorganization and forms a striking contrast with the Goths, who respected the Roman institutional legacy to such a large extent.

During the period of the troubles the bulk of the land passed from the hands of the Roman aristocracy into those of the Lombard leaders. Paul the Deacon describes an instance of violent expropriation in the reign of Cleph, accompanied by massacres; the survivors must have been reduced to the status of tenants of the Lombards, handing over to them a third of their harvest.[17] It is certain that the Roman aristocracy, which had already been hard hit by the Gothic wars, was eliminated as a social and political force. It has even been thought (without justification) that Lombard law ignored the free Roman. In fact he continued to live under his own law, though with an inferior political status (for example, the carrying of weapons—the sign of a free man—was forbidden to the free Roman until the eighth century).

The status of the Romans continues to be very obscure, for lack of source material. We know nothing of Lombard law before the edict of Rothari, issued in 643. This was very Germanic in character, and probably only applied to the members of the *exercitus*, in spite of certain declarations of principle in clause 386. The eighth-century laws recognized the peculiar position of the Romans (for example under Liutprand, on the question of inheritance). It would appear that in its final state the law of the kingdom of Pavia combined territorial elements (public law and military institutions) and personal ones (private law). It was only on the eve of the Frankish conquest in 769 that the *professio legis* (the declaration of which form of law one lived by), which was to be so important in Italy until the twelfth century, appeared for the first time. It seems that the Lombards did not fully recognize the legal autonomy of the Roman element of the population until after a long struggle of conscience.[18] The sense of their own superiority persisted to the end: Aistulf still speaks of *traditum nobis a Domino populum romanum* (the Roman people entrusted to us by the Lord).

As Gaul became France, so Italy became known as Longobardia among several of its neighbours, notably the Byzantines and, later, the Varangians; but in the ninth century the older name triumphed once more. On the other hand, from the eighth century onwards the main part of the Exarchate of Ravenna became known in Italy as *Romania* (Romagna).

Despite the lowering of their social status the Romans gave to the civilization of Lombard Italy its most interesting features: its relatively urban character, its high standard of Latinity (Paul the Deacon, a Lombard from Friuli, contributed to the Carolingian Renaissance), its architecture and its sculpture (modelled on those of Byzantium, with oriental elements, particularly in the sixth century). These influences were probably due, not so much to the survivors of the first conquest, as to the administration which was re-established after the victories in the seventh century (in Liguria, Emilia and Venetia) and to the clerics who had returned from Byzantine enclaves when Arianism had lost its virulence. All that was truly Lombardic—especially the law and the army—was partly eliminated or assimilated by the Franks after the destruction of the kingdom by Charlemagne; there was not a great deal of difference between the conquerors and the conquered. It would hardly be an exaggeration to say that the main result of the

Lombard invasion was to pave the way for the entry of northern Italy into Carolingian Europe by bringing it down to the same level of civilization.

The Avars

The Lombard invasion of Italy was the occasion, if not the real cause, of the Avar invasion of central Europe. In the middle of the seventh century this nomadic people lived to the north of the Caspian Sea. Pressure from the Turks obliged them to set off westwards, so their khagan, Baian, led them up to the Danubian frontier of the Empire; Justinian, however, refused to let them cross it. For some years they wandered around Rumania, looking for a place to settle, at the expense of the Gepids (who were in eastern Hungary at that time) and the Lombards, and even of peoples further west. We have already seen how their victory over the Gepids in 567 was followed by the Lombards' departure from Pannonia. As early as 570 the Avars occupied the middle basin of the Danube in force; in 574 Tiberius II gave them the country around Sirmium, and in 582 Baian took the town itself, then the principal centre of communications in Danubian Europe.

Thus the Avar kingdom carved out a territory for itself; but as its main resources consisted of pillage and tribute, almost every year the cavalry, driving before it masses of Slav foot soldiers, raided far afield —to the Black Sea, Constantinople (in 626), Thessalonica, Venetia, Bavaria and Thuringia. It was the ultimate success of the Bulgars, rather than the Greek system of defence, which kept them out of the Balkans. They continued to be a serious threat to Italy until the time of Charlemagne. In the west they hardly got past Upper Austria. According to archaeological evidence Avar territory corresponded more or less to present-day Hungary. The Avars shared this with Turks, Slavs, Bulgars and the remnants of a few tribes of Germanic origin, but the Avars themselves formed the ruling class. The skeletons and skulls are of predominantly Mongoloid type among the men, though not among the women, which would seem to indicate that the Avars practised exogamy.

The activity of the Avars seems to have come to a head twice: once under Baian at the end of the sixth century, and again in the last years of the eighth century; in the interval practically nothing is known of their movements. This lull is also seen in the lack of finds of Byzantine coins, and corresponds to the period of the formation of the Slav kingdom in Bohemia, by Samo.

As far as one can judge the Avar kingdom was a relatively sophisticated one: it had a nomadic capital (probably a town of tents, like those of the Mongols) which Carolingian writers call by the Germanic name of 'ring'. It had a developed diplomacy and from time to time probably minted coins. The Avar settlements were surrounded by protectorates in Slav country as far afield as upper Franconia. Nevertheless economic activity seems to have been fairly limited—such treasure hoards as were found by Charlemagne and again by modern archaeologists are simply the result of the accumulation of plunder. There were no proper towns or cities.

Repercussions of the renewal of attacks on Bavaria and Friuli from 787 onwards resulted in the destruction of the Avar state. The Franks hit back in 791 and again in 795, this time with help from some of the enemy. The surrenders which had begun in 795 grew more and more numerous after the destruction of the 'ring' by Pippin of Italy in 796. The entire people had submitted by 811. Charlemagne had thought of converting the Avars and keeping them where they were in a state of vassalage, but the conquered people broke up before the Frankish missionaries could intervene. There is not a single reference to the Avars after 822.

4 The Maritime Migrations in North-West Europe

At the same time as the great land migrations, lesser-known movements were taking place in the coastal areas of north-west Europe. Most of these originated in southern Scandinavia, coastal Germany and the Low Countries, while others, which were wholly independent at first, came from the north and west of the British Isles. Towards the end of the third century these two currents began to converge, resulting principally in the destruction of Roman authority and civilization in Britain. This migratory activity reached its peak in the fifth and sixth centuries and at that time affected the whole of the coastline of Europe from Galicia to the Norwegian Sea. It gradually died down, but several incidents suggest a continuity between this first onrush of the maritime peoples and that of the Vikings and the Varangians.

THE GERMANIC WAVE: PRE-VIKINGS, ANGLES, SAXONS AND JUTES

The history of the maritime migrations begins with the little-known raids carried out by the Heruls, who probably lived somewhere in eastern Denmark or southern Sweden. In the middle of the third century the Heruls suddenly launched themselves on a maritime career which foreshadowed that of the Vikings and the Varangians, while simultaneously certain elements among them joined land migrations in the direction of the middle Danube. To the east some Heruls reached the Azov Sea in 267; having forced their way through the Bosporus they ravaged the coasts of the Aegean, and in 276 they struck once more, against Asia Minor. Most of them, however, set out for the west; in 287 and in 409 they attacked Gaul; in about 456 a band of Heruls pillaged the Galician and Cantabrian coasts; around 459 they pushed forward as far as Baetica. Realizing that the growing power of the Franks was hampering their expansion they tried to secure an alliance with the Visigoths, but after the beginning of the sixth century nothing further is heard of them.

The movement which occurred next was much more important and of a very different character. Although it too began with piracy, it quickly changed into a process of conquest and colonization. Led by the Angles, Saxons and Jutes, the participants came from the whole of the coastal zone between Jutland and the Rhine and directed their attention particularly towards Britain.

In Roman times the inhabitants of the shores of the western Baltic and of the North Sea to the east of the Weser formed a coherent group, Pliny's *Ingvaeones*, who probably spoke the dialect known to linguists as *Nordseegermanisch*. Among these peoples Tacitus distinguished the Chauci between the Ems and the Elbe, the Anglii at the base of Jutland, and a number of other peoples on the same side of the peninsula, of whom only the Varini were to survive. In the second century Ptolemy is the first to mention a new people in the region, the Saxons, whom he seems to locate in Holstein. These Saxons, who may have been a breakaway branch of the Chauci, rapidly supplanted the latter in their former territory; in the middle of the third century they seem to have been in possession of Lower Saxony from Holstein to as far as the Weser. To the west they managed to make contact with another maritime people, the Frisians, who had been mentioned by classical writers as early as the first century. These three peoples, the Saxons, the Angles and the Frisians, were to lead the Germanic invaders of Britain, together with a fourth group, still shrouded in mystery, the Jutes.

Until the middle of the third century all of these peoples remained in the background. Their first noteworthy appearance was in 286 when the Roman authorities instructed Carausius to sweep the Saxons and the Franks from the seas. This was the start of an expansion which lasted almost four centuries and was primarily maritime, though it later also proceeded by land. What were the reasons for this sudden emergence?

Since the Middle Ages both geological and demographic explanations have been put forward. Recent studies have confirmed that on the North Sea coast of Germany there was a period of relative geological stability which lasted from 300 BC to the beginning of the Christian era. The next six centuries were marked by a rise in sea-level and large-scale submersion of coastal regions, followed by a breathing space from the seventh to the tenth centuries. The most obvious consequence of the submersions was the continuous rise in the level of the coastal settlements (an average of 2.4 metres from the first to the fourth centuries) and hence the formation of settlements on mounds (called *terpen* in Frisia and *wurten* in Lower Saxony). But the submersions cannot wholly account for the migrations, especially when it is considered that the Saxon expansion on the continent, which took up where the maritime expansion left off, reached its peak during a period of relative stability, in the sixth and seventh centuries. Other periods of coastal submersion, such as that which began in the tenth century, did not bring about a single migration. A survey of the cemeteries, on the other hand, does seem to show a certain overpopulation of the coasts of Lower Saxony, principally between the Elbe and the Ems, but this is not true of the whole of the region. The problem remains, as usual, almost insoluble. Opportunity must have played a decisive role, the first successes encouraging others.

We must also remember the progress that was being made in ship construction, even though perfection was very far from having been achieved. The only ship of the period that we know of is the one found in 1864 at Nydam on the Baltic coast of Sønderjylland, which shows a considerable degree of innovation (such as planks joined in clinker fashion with iron nails) but still has some astonishing inadequacies (for example the shallow keel, the absence of a mast, the total dependence on oars and the limited dimensions—23 metres by 3.25 metres). The fourth-century ships, therefore, were not nearly as technically advanced as those of the Vikings. Most voyages from Lower Saxony to Britain must have hugged the coast, stopping on the way in Frisia and probably also in Flanders or in the region of Boulogne, near the Straits of Dover.

The maritime expansion of the secondary peoples—Angles, Frisians and Jutes—seems to have been directed only towards Britain. The Saxons, on the other hand, explored the coastal regions almost all the way from the Firth of Forth to the Gironde. In several places, as in Britain, they attempted colonization, of which traces remain and which frequently foreshadows that of the Vikings. Four regions in particular attracted the Saxons: the shores of the Low Countries, those of the regions of Boulogne and Bayeux, and the Atlantic coast of Gaul. The extent of the anxiety felt all along the English Channel and, to a lesser degree, the Atlantic coasts from the third century onwards is borne out by the extraordinary number of coin hoards buried in the coastal zones and still more by the organization on the continent under the Later Roman Empire of a system of defence called the *litus saxonicum*, the Saxon Shore. This defence system does not seem to have been as solid on the continent as it was in Britain and has not left any definite archaeological traces.

Not much is known about the role of the Frisians in the migration to Britain. Only the Byzantine historian Procopius places them on the same level as the Saxons among the conquerors of the island. Supposed traces of them have been found in various regions of England, notably in East Anglia. Between the fourth and seventh centuries the Anglo-Saxon and Frisian cultures were still very similar, as were the two languages. The Frisian expansion was mainly directed towards the north-east, at first between the Ems and the Weser, possibly during the seventh century, and then between the Elbe and the Eider, perhaps in the ninth century, to occupy the space left by the departure of the Saxons.

The Jutes present us with an insoluble problem. Bede attributes to them the colonization of Kent, the Isle of Wight and part of Hampshire. It is possible that they were Jutes from Jutland, but these seem to have belonged to the group of peoples speaking a North Germanic dialect, and there is no evidence in Kent to suggest that such a linguistic element was ever introduced. The colonists to whom Bede refers may, of course, have been a West Germanic people who merely borrowed the name of the Jutes; but perhaps it would be better to follow a line indicated by the archaeologists and seek a different answer altogether. Grave goods in Kent offer close analogies to those in the Frankish lands on the lower Rhine, and similar analogies have been found among legal institutions, especially agrarian ones. It has been suggested that the name 'Jute' may have been used to describe some sort of hybrid Franco-Saxon culture, yet the distinctive features found in Kent are not found in either of the other 'Jutish' territories, the Isle of Wight and Hampshire. Certain scholars think they can explain everything by distinguishing two stages in the colonization: first a small-scale settlement by North Germanic peoples at the end of the fifth and the beginning of the sixth centuries, and then a period of superimposed Frankish colonization from roughly 525 to 560. If we take Old English texts into consideration it only makes the problem more difficult: *Geatas* play an important part in them, but we have no way of knowing whether these peoples were Jutes, or Götar from southern Sweden.

Fortunately the case of the Angles is much clearer. The majority of them came from the region of Angeln on the east coast of Schleswig, which remained vacant for two centuries after they had emigrated to Britain. Neither their language nor their civilization differed very much from those of the Saxons; like them they must often have stopped over in Frisia. In fact their movements can hardly be distinguished from those of the Saxons and it is no longer thought possible to assign clearly defined areas of colonization to them.

After the emigration of most of the Jutes, those who had stayed behind merged with the Danish people. The Angles seem to have disappeared from the continent altogether, leaving their territory to Danes, Swedes, Frisians and Slavs. The Varini tried to take advantage of the departure of many of the Saxons by carving out a territory for themselves in northern Germany, but they were overwhelmed by the Franks in 594. The Saxons who stayed behind on the continent soon showed considerable dynamism, this time by land. Their migration towards the south-west involved the defeat of the Bructeri between the Lippe and the Ruhr in about 695, the occupation of the whole of Westphalia, and encroachment on Hesse and Thuringia. They continued to advance until checked by Pippin the Short and Charlemagne.

The fundamental problem in Anglo-Saxon history is obviously the conquest of Britain. This had three phases, all of which overlap to some extent: the first raids, the settling of the first small groups, and full-scale colonization. The process was much less sudden and spectacular than that of the barbarian onslaughts on the continent; hence the scarcity of precise information from contemporary sources, since a phenomenon spread over four or five generations may easily go unnoticed by chroniclers. There is no record of a single episode before 449 in English medieval historiography. Only archaeology can help to reconstruct the chronology of the migrations to Britain.[1]

The first warning signs seem to date from the end of the second century: in the reign of Marcus Aurelius (161–80) several coin hoards were buried near the Thames and the Wash, the two principal gateways to England from the east. In the reign of Caracalla coastal fortifications appear in the same areas (at Reculver, in Kent, towards 210–20). At the end of the third century, under the usurper Carausius, defences were co-ordinated to form a sort of *limes*, probably as much for protection against the legitimate Emperor Maximian as against pirates. During the first two-thirds of the fourth century this system, the *litus saxonicum*, seems to have been effective—it was not breached until 364, and was still holding out at the time of the *Notitia Dignitatum* in the early fifth century. It covered the whole of the eastern and southern coastline of the island, with its headquarters at Rutupiae (Richborough) to the south of the Thames estuary.

Following the normal practice of the Later Roman Empire, the soldiers who manned this line of defence were probably former enemies of Rome who had taken service with the Roman army. The first Saxons who settled in Britain must have been *foederati*—mercenaries, not conquerors. Archaeologists believe they have found traces of them as early as the first few years of the fifth century, especially in East Anglia around Caistor-by-Norwich, where the pottery is similar to that of the Angles of Schleswig. The indigenous population probably turned a blind eye to these Saxon settlers, for they must have seen their arrival as counterbalancing the threat of the Picts and the Scots, which was much the more serious problem at that time. In any case there were many other barbarians among the garrisons, particularly Franks (one of whom was *dux Britanniarum* as early as 367) and Alamans (one tribe of whom was settled in Britain by Valentinian I).

In the end it was the permanent state of crisis of the Roman army which was to open up unexpected horizons for the Saxons. Shortly after 395 Stilicho, the *magister militum*, had carried out a general patching up of the defences in Britain; but in 406, when disaster struck the Empire on the continent in the form of the breaching of the Rhineland *limes* and the Alpine defences, the whole system crumbled. Cut off from the Roman government at Ravenna, Britain elected three usurpers in succession, the last of whom, Constantine III, set out to try and save Gaul and landed at Boulogne in 407 with the army of Britain. This force disappeared in the chaos of Gaul. The Saxons learned of the departure of the army from Britain, and took advantage of it: a Gallic chronicle includes the laconic note *Britanniae Saxonum incursione devastatae* (Britain was devastated by a Saxon raid).

However, they waited for a whole generation before undertaking full-scale colonization; according to archaeological evidence there was no regular influx of immigrants until 430–40. It even appears that the main wave did not come until around 500, for none of the Anglo-Saxon dynasties claimed to have taken root before the first quarter of the sixth century. Two factors may help to explain why they took so long: the poor quality of the ships at their disposal and the fact that at first the Saxons dissipated their efforts. Their decision to invade Britain in force was made when they received information that the island was a fruit ripe for plucking, at a time when the consolidation of the Franks had destroyed all hope of expansion into Gaul.

Britain was in a way wide open to the Saxons, as a result of internal disintegration. Everywhere, even in regions where the Saxons never settled, a distinct recession can be seen from the end of the fourth century on. It is likely that other invaders, Picts and Scots, were partly responsible for this, but the reasons for the phenomenon go deeper than that. As in Armorica, but to a much more marked degree, we can see an irreversible decline of urban life and of the large estates, in favour of more primitive indigenous institutions, and a growing refusal to submit to the traditional authorities. In so far as it survived at all, the municipal aristocracy yielded to the temptations of provincial autonomy. Judging by coin finds, trade with the continent almost came to a standstill about 410–20. This picture of decadence is not true of the whole country, however. In the middle of the fourth century the towns and the villae in certain areas enjoyed a sort of renaissance within the shelter of fortifications. After 400 some cities (such as Ilchester, Wroxeter and, in particular, Verulamium/St. Albans) were still functioning, but most of the villae had already been abandoned.

After the departure of Constantine III the Romano-Britons believed for a time that they could manage by themselves. The Greek historian Zosimus writes: 'The Britons, rejecting Roman domination, lived according to their own customs, without obeying Roman laws.' Since what was left of the administration had more or less compromised itself at the time of Constantine's usurpation it was easy to get rid of it in the name of a theoretical loyalty to Honorius. In this way authority passed into the hands of the *civitates*, who retained some contact with the Empire. There were exchanges of correspondence and occasional reinforcements of troops, and it is highly probable that the south-east of the island was taken over by the Roman government again. In the time of Honorius the garrisons seem still to have been regularly provided with money, but not a single coin of his successor has been found among them. But soon the Romans lost the opposite shore in Belgica II, which was overrun by the Franks when they settled in Tournai. The umbilical cord connecting Britain to the Empire had finally been cut.

When St. Germanus of Auxerre came to Britain in 429 to combat Pelagianism he did not find a single official of the Empire left, but he did find some authorities still functioning there, for example at Verulamium where there was a *vir tribuniciae potestatis*. Britain at this time might be described as an autonomous Celto-Roman country, a loose confederation of cities. Most of the towns must have kept their decurions and an even greater number had their own bishop. But this surviving structure was extremely weak and Germanus found the Britons hard put to it to withstand the Saxon, Pictish and Scottish incursions. The saint, who in his youth had been governor of a Gallic province, reorganized the Britons and led them to victory against the barbarian Picts and Saxons on Easter Sunday 429, in the so-called Alleluia victory. When Germanus returned to Britain between 440 and 444 the disintegration was more advanced. It seems that the organization of the cities had gradually been replaced by the authority of the Celtic tribal chieftains, the *tyranni* whom Gildas later denounced, and by a handful of Romans who imitated them. A little is known about some of these leaders, in particular a Celt called Vortigern, pledged to the Pelagian party and therefore hostile to the bishops, and, a little later, a 'Roman' called Ambrosius Aurelianus who was credited with being a member of a consular family and who upheld orthodoxy. Faced with this disorder the aristocracy made repeated appeals to the 'Roman' army in northern Gaul under Aetius. Gildas, writing a century later, assures us that there were three such appeals, one of which in particular is known to us. It was made in 445, and may have been asking for protection against both Vortigern and the barbarians. Aetius was dilatory in replying; he was involved in the struggle against Attila until 451, and was killed in 453 before he could do anything to help the Britons.

It was probably about this period that certain petty kings who were fighting one another had the idea of calling in Saxon auxiliaries. Bede dates the arrival of the chiefs Hengist and Horsa in Kent at the request of Vortigern to 449. The whole episode smacks of legend, but the date and the place appear to have been judiciously chosen (the installation of Saxon garrisons in the forts along the Straits of Dover could provide a defence against a landing by Aetius). It was probably in 455 that these mercenaries revolted, and this event would mark the beginning of the Saxon conquest proper. Many details are still suspect (even the name Vortigern) but scholars have recently been regarding this thesis in a more favourable light than did the historians of the 1930s. At any rate archaeology shows that there was no sudden and general catastrophe, that Anglo-Frisian types of pottery spread gradually, and that the first Saxon settlements were small-scale, almost family, affairs. It would appear that on both sides there was a certain delay in marshalling forces, after a prolonged period of confusion.

The second half of the fifth century is the most obscure period. Advancing from three landing areas (the Thames area and Kent, the Fens, and the Humber estuary) the Saxons rapidly occupied the eastern third of the island. These early colonists seem more or less to have dispensed with political organization. It is only with the new wave of immigrants after 500 that the royal dynasties appear, all claiming divine ancestry. Archaeologists are wondering if this second wave of invasion originated in the same place as the first. Some scholars believe they can see northern elements—possibly from Jutland or Scania—in East Anglia. The royal cemetery of the Wuffingas near their residence at Rendlesham (near Ipswich) offers analogies with contemporary Swedish cemeteries. In Kent it is during this period that Frankish borrowings are most evident (as, for example, in the cemetery at Lyminge). After the success of the first colonists the migration gathered momentum.

In spite of the picture inherited from Bede it is not really possible to assign to each people an area of coherent settlement. The 'kingdoms' of the sixth century seem to have originated in the regrouping of very diverse elements, as is proved by their names: these have either been borrowed from Romano-Celtic place-names (Kent, and perhaps Bernicia) or are of a purely geographical nature ('people of the march', Mercia; 'people from north of the Humber', Northumbria; Wessex; Sussex and so on). In order to find real tribal groups we have to look at a much lower social category, that of the *subreguli*, for example the *Haestingas*, who have bequeathed their name to Hastings in Sussex and who are the 'people of Hasta', their chieftain, and the *Hrodhingas* of Essex.

The newcomers, being less interested in pastoral farming than the Britons, occupied the arable land and proceeded along the valleys, which had not previously been exploited much by the Britons. We do not know the exact date on which any town was taken, since by now the towns had lost all significance. It is through the study of place-names and grave goods that we can define the various stages in the march towards the west and the cores of British resistance. The annals, which were all compiled fairly late, only mention a few violent and memorable incidents, whose location is often difficult to identify.

Within the limits imposed by these means of research, it seems that their progress was neither continuous nor uniform. There were outposts set up by the Saxons very early on in the heart of the country, for example on the upper Thames, and pockets of British survival fairly far to the east, for example near Cambridge. After 500 the Britons succeeded in checking the progress of the Saxons to some extent, and in reorganizing themselves about the middle of the sixth century along a line of resistance stretching roughly from Edinburgh in the north to Portland in the south—half the island had already been lost.

The elimination of the indigenous population poses one of the most perplexing problems in British history. To begin with, some facts are well established: English has borrowed from the language spoken by the Britons no more than fifteen or sixteen words, all of little significance, together with the names of a few large rivers (such as the Thames) and a handful of large towns (such as London, York and Lincoln) which must have been known to the invaders before the fall of Rome. Most of the urban sites were abandoned as unprofitable (an Anglo-Saxon poet considers them to be *eald enta geweorc*—the ancient work of giants) and practically none of the villae was ever reoccupied. Christianity disappeared, save for remote centres betrayed by the place-names Eccles and Eccleston. Arms, dress, jewellery and grave goods (with the sole exception of a handful of Celtic enamelled bowls) owe everything to Germanic tradition. It is highly unlikely that all the Britons had been killed or expelled. Tradition does preserve the memory of several massacres, such as that of Anderida near Pevensey, but as something exceptional. Obviously there must have been a general flight towards the west, but there is no evidence there of the frightful overcrowding which would have been the inevitable result of the withdrawal of the island's entire population to the western part of the country. We are forced to the conclusion that after a more or less prolonged period of bilingualism part of the Romano-British population was completely assimilated by the German invaders. There are traces in Kent of what may have been an intermediate stage: at the end of the sixth century there were some *læt* in existence there, a social class which in the Germanic world was usually made up of members of the conquered population; and at the time of the arrival of the first missionaries in 597 the ecclesiastical character of certain buildings in Canterbury was still remembered.

Examined in detail, this picture reveals all sorts of nuances. Each name of a town must be considered as a special case on its own: some

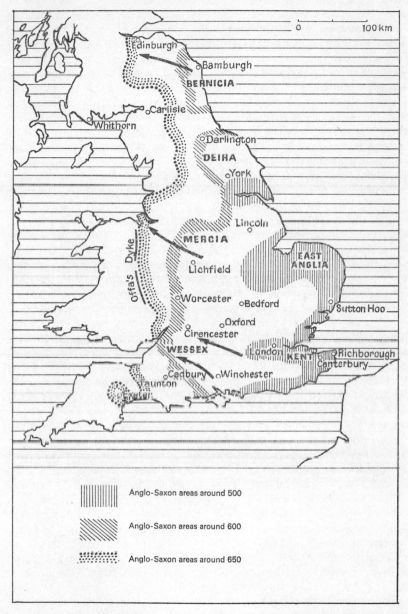

Fig. 4 The Anglo-Saxon Colonization of Britain (after K. Jackson)

names have survived virtually unaltered (for example *Londinium* > London) and some are translations (for example *Durovernum Cantiacorum* = *Cantwaraburh* > Canterbury), but there are many mixtures (such as *Venta* = Winchester) and many more cities dropped their names in favour of some vague general term, for example *Deva* becomes Chester, *Venta Icenorum* becomes Caistor-by-Norwich, and there are many other Chesters, Casters and Caistors. Unlike what happened in Gaul, not a single name of a Romano-British estate has survived in the names of villages, although it is possible that British usage had never adopted them. However, archaeologists have established the continuity of several settlement sites, for example that at Withington in the Cotswolds. Obviously the Saxons did not bother to learn the language of the Britons, and yet a certain number of Old English personal names are either borrowed from British or modelled on it, starting with those of the first English poet, Caedmon, and the great king of Wessex in the seventh century, Caedwalla. (The frequent recurrence of such names in the Wessex dynasty suggests mixed marriages.) Finally, although the grave goods are definitely Germanic, certain types of brooch worn by women owe a lot to British influences. It would be a worthwhile project to draw up a precise map showing these survivals, as Max Förster has done for the names of waterways. Almost all of the main rivers have British names, while the names of those of medium size are Saxon or British in more or less equal proportion, and all, or nearly all, of the streams have Saxon names. Survivals are particularly scarce in the south-east, and especially numerous in the west. The Roman roads have survived, but with Saxon names. There is not a single Saxon find before the seventh century in London, but it seems to have been continuously inhabited because the Roman plan of the city has largely survived, and if the public buildings quickly disappeared, it was because they were being used as a source of building materials, proving that the inhabitants themselves had survived. Certain authors (for example T. C. Lethbridge) have gone so far as to define Anglo-Saxon culture as a mixed culture drawing widely on provincial Roman sources.

The Saxon conquest only got into its stride after the foundation of the principal kingdoms, that is to say from the middle of the sixth century onwards, when arrivals from overseas had practically ceased. Only three kingdoms actively took part in this last phase: Wessex, Mercia and Northumbria.

Tradition dates the origin of the kingdom of Wessex to 495, and the founder is said to have been a chieftain called Cerdic, who appears to have been a legendary figure. Archaeology indicates that the real origin of this conquering kingdom is to be sought in the convergence of two thrusts towards the west, one setting out from the Saxon settlements on the upper Thames, and the other from those on the coast of

Hampshire. Their progress towards the west, which was opposed by the Britons of Dumnonia (Devon and adjoining regions), is punctuated by a whole series of battles which are difficult to locate geographically, from the battle of Mons Badonicus, fought against the 'last of the Romans', the Romano-British chieftain Ambrosius Aurelianus (possibly at Badbury Rings, on the Stour in Dorset), to the battle of Dyrham in 577, in which three British 'kings' were killed. The battle of Dyrham not only gave the Saxons possession of the Roman cities of Cirencester, Gloucester and Bath but also gave them access to the west coast for the first time and cut the Britons of Cornwall off from those of Wales. After a halt in the proceedings at the beginning of the seventh century, probably marked by the construction of an earth rampart, the Wansdyke, the process of expansion began again in about 650. It took two generations to subjugate the Celts of Somerset and Devon, a good number of whom were driven over to Brittany; but the subjugation of Cornwall after 815 was a very different story. This time it was a question of simple political conquest, which left the Celtic population intact. At first the expansion of Wessex seems to have been too rapid for its resources in terms of manpower: hence the numerous set-backs attested by the Anglo-Saxon Chronicle, and a certain slowness in the settlement of central Hampshire and Wiltshire. But in spite of this, Wessex continued to be remarkable for its dynamism right up to the day when its dynasty ruled over the whole of a unified England in the ninth century.

The kingdom of Mercia came into being somewhat later, and its origins are more obscure. This 'march' began with the settlement of colonists in the upper Trent basin around Lichfield; under King Penda they succeeded in annexing the lands of the *Hwicce* on the middle Severn in the second quarter of the seventh century. Their main thrust was directed against the north-east, reaching the Irish Sea near Chester in 604 or 616, thus driving a wedge between the Celts of Wales and those of Strathclyde (in Cumberland and Westmorland) and Elmet (around Leeds). At the end of the eighth century the frontier with the Welsh was to be consolidated by an enormous earth rampart, Offa's Dyke, running from the Severn to the Dee, more or less along the line of the present boundary.

Northumbria contained two kingdoms at first: Deira, between the Humber and the Tees, and Bernicia, between the Tees and the Firth of Forth. The former may have sprung from the settlements of federates in the neighbourhood of York after 450, while the latter seems to have originated in the settlements of pirates along the coast in the sixth century, particularly at Bamburgh, in what was still a very Celtic milieu. (The oldest Bernician institutions present striking similarities to those of Wales.) The two states merged at the beginning of the seventh century and Northumbria rapidly occupied the south-east of Scotland and the whole of the mountainous region as far as the Irish Sea, but without driving out the former inhabitants. Northumbrian culture, vigorous and original up to the time of the Viking onslaughts, owes its highly individual flavour to its readiness to accept Celtic elements, unique in the Anglo-Saxon world. This had consequences of enormous importance, particularly in the ecclesiastical world.

When this process stopped, about the end of the seventh century, the area where medieval England was to emerge had been completely occupied, and almost everywhere the language of the Anglo-Saxons was triumphant, with dialectal variations corresponding to the political groupings which had taken place during the last stage of the conquest. Latin must have died out with the upper classes, as early as the fifth century. The British language had been driven back to the three coastal areas of the west, which were the poorest parts of the island. In each one of these, after the break-up of territorial unity sometime between 580 and 620, it took on an individual colouring. Cornish survived in about fifteen neighbouring parishes of the Land's End peninsula until the beginning of the eighteenth century: the last native speaker of Cornish died in 1777. In Wales and the adjacent county of Monmouth, Welsh still flourishes. The British of the kingdom of Strathclyde probably disappeared about the eleventh century, undermined successively by Norwegian colonists and Norman conquerors.

In the whole of the area within these bounds a homogeneous civilization grew up. In spite of regional variations the language was recognizably one, and all the oldest texts refer to it by the same name, *Englisc*. The same form of paganism, although quite unorganized, except perhaps in Northumbria, had spread all over the country. The multiplicity of kingdoms—of which there were more than a dozen, differing widely in importance—did not prevent political institutions from being virtually identical throughout the country. Archaeological evidence does not show very distinct regional variations—at most it is merely a question of minor differences such as those which result from the different degrees of loyalty to the primitive Saxon rite of cremation, which was quickly abandoned in favour of inhumation, possibly under British influence.

The only exception to this uniformity seems to have been in the matter of agricultural organization. By the end of the sixth century the immigrants had largely lost contact with maritime life. (The royal ship burials in Suffolk are the most important vestiges of their sea-faring past.) They changed remarkably quickly into peasants obsessed with the problems of the land, but these they solved in very different ways. Although almost everywhere the villa or the indigenous types of hamlet which shared the agricultural land[2] had been replaced by the village surrounded by a vast open field, usually on a totally new site, Kent was an exception in that its population lived in hamlets and had a very different conception of community laws. The agricultural organization of East Anglia lay midway between that of Kent and that of the heart of the Saxon lands. The Anglo-Saxon village, as revealed by excavations, is fairly similar to that of Lower Saxony, being made up of rectangular wooden houses, more or less lined up to form a street. Equipment was rudimentary and often lacked even such simple devices as the potter's wheel, but already the legal organization of the village was well developed, with land distribution in standard units called hides, and regular crop rotation.

When they occupied Britain the Saxons brought over with them part of their intellectual heritage, in particular runic writing, which they did not, in fact, use very much. For a long time their literary traditions continued to be similar to those of the continental peoples, and the epic texts, as set down in writing in the Christian period, do not refer to their history in Britain at all, but rather to the heroic deeds of dynasties in Scandinavia (as in *Beowulf*) or on the continent (as in *Widsith*). It was not until the eighth century that England created an autonomous culture, within a framework which had become firmly Christian. At this time ties with the 'Old Saxons' were severed, except for a few nostalgic memories (especially in Bede).

The colonization of England stands out as a special case in the history of the great migrations. It started as a series of maritime raids, which seem *a priori* less favourable than travel by land would have been to mass migrations; moreover, it was effected not by a military élite, as with most of the barbarian kingdoms of the continent, but by whole populations. In the British Isles the effects of the migrations of the fifth, sixth and seventh centuries were at once much more deeply rooted and much more lasting than elsewhere in Europe.

PICTS AND SCOTS

Until the middle of the third century Roman Britain's relations with Ireland had been both peaceful and very limited. Relations with Pictland had been confined, until about 350, to skirmishes along the Wall; to the west and north there was no external danger. All this changed in the fourth century. For three or four generations before the conquest of the Saxons the Picts and the Scotti (from Ireland) came to the fore. It was doubtless they who were responsible for the early and extensive destruction in Britain, and for some of the most violent shocks sustained by the Roman edifice in the island.

The part of modern Scotland to the north of the Clyde and the Firth of Forth was inhabited by obscure peoples whom we call the Picts; they were probably of pre-Celtic origin and had a reputation for extreme barbarity. (To the south some Celtic populations, close neighbours of the Britons, got an equally bad press: St. Jerome accuses the Atecotti of cannibalism.) The first Pictish raid is mentioned in 367, and traces of their passing have been found as far south as East Anglia. It was against them that St. Germanus fought in 429. They wrought havoc everywhere they went, and the memory of this and of the terror with which they were regarded is found in Bede. They did not establish a single settlement south of the Wall, however, and their fighting instincts were soon absorbed in defending their own country against the Scots.

Like the Saxon danger in the east, the danger from the Scots on the west coast began in the middle of the third century. Several hoards were buried at this time, and roads and fortified posts were constructed in Lancashire and Wales, particularly in Pembrokeshire. Shortly before 300 a naval base was set up on the Bristol Channel, a fort was built at Cardiff, and several villae were fortified. The raids got worse after 350. Irish traditions (of fairly late date) claim that Romano-British deserters helped the Scots to become a powerful naval force. The Irish King Niall of the Nine Hostages is said to have organized raids into Britain (probably at the end of the fourth century) and even into Gaul, where his nephew Dathi must have died about 425, possibly as a pirate but perhaps as a Roman mercenary. One of these raids on the west coast of Britain had extremely important consequences for the history of religion. Around 400 the family of the deacon and decurion Calpurnius, a Romano-British dignitary, was carried off from Bannaventa. Two daughters and a son were taken to Ireland as slaves: the son was to become St. Patrick, the apostle of the island.

As in the east, the raids were soon succeeded by colonization: the Irish must have started to infiltrate the western peninsulas (Cornwall, South Wales and North Wales) as early as the fourth century, possibly with the status of federates defending the coast against attackers. These colonists quickly won real independence for themselves. In south-west Wales a little Irish kingdom which survived until the tenth century boasted that it could trace its origins to colonists who arrived in the third century. The Irish settlement in Devon dates back to the fourth and fifth centuries. These Irishmen in the south-west of Britain were the bearers of a distinctive civilization which is attested by the ogam inscriptions, of which there are about fifty, mostly in Pembroke-shire. The immigrants probably continued to speak Irish until the seventh century, but at the same time they managed to acquire a Roman veneer: in forty-four cases the ogam inscription is accompanied by a Latin text in which such typically Roman names as Pompeius, Turpilius, Eternus or Vitalianus are found. The Scots even strove to assimilate the institutions of the Later Roman Empire: a petty king in Wales, who died in about 550 according to Gildas, had a bilingual epitaph engraved for himself: *Memoria Voteporigis protictoris. Protector* had obviously been taken for the title of a Roman dignitary. This is a remarkable case of survival, considering that all imperial authority in Britain had disappeared a century before, and reveals an acceptance of the Roman situation similar to that found in Gaul, very different from the attitude of the Saxons.

Similarly, and with more lasting success, the Scots had undertaken the colonization of Pictish territory. They first appear there as pirates in the middle of the fourth century. In the second half of the fifth century they founded the kingdom of Dalriada, which stretched from the Clyde to the southern Hebrides and was directly dependent on Ulster. At the end of the sixth century King Aedan mac Gabrain extended the perimeter of the land held by the Scots far to the north and east, but he clashed with the Northumbrians in 603 and the conquest was held up until the ninth century. Weakened by the Vikings, the Picts finally yielded to the Scottish king Kenneth mac Alpin in 843. The country was united at first under the name of Alba, but later, adopting the name of its conquerors, it became known as Scotland. It completely accepted the language imported from Ireland, now known as Scots Gaelic (which still survives in the extreme north-west of Scotland), and by the twelfth century Pictish had disappeared. This political expansion benefited from the establishment on the island of Iona in 563 of one of the most vigorous centres of Irish missionary activity.

After her conversion Ireland stopped sending pirates and colonists abroad, but the Irish, particularly the monks, continued to have an extraordinary love of adventure. It was not for nothing that the 'voyages' and the 'exiles' were two of the basic genres of their literature. This adventurousness, together with the ascetic desire to flee the world, drew Irish monks, probably from as early as the seventh century, to the discovery of the islands of the north—the Faroes, the Norwegian coastal islands and soon even Iceland. These voyages are mentioned by the geographer Dicuil, and later by the Scandinavian sagas. The Viking expansion brought them abruptly to an end.

The most extraordinary feature of the Irish migrations is that they were accomplished with an incredibly primitive type of vessel, the *curach* or coracle, a boat made from a wooden framework covered with skins sewn together, incapable of carrying heavy loads and difficult to control, although capable of being propelled by sail as well as by oars.

It is not easy to assess the contribution of each invading people to the destruction of Roman Britain. It was the Anglo-Saxons who played the decisive role, but a closer look at the situation has led to much controversy about the part played by other peoples. One of the most serious disagreements concerns the origins of the great migration of the British to Armorica.

THE BRITISH MIGRATIONS TO THE SOUTH

Abandoned by Rome and hard-pressed by the invasions from the north, east and west, the Britons, lacking political organization, did not know what to do for the best. The last leaders in the Roman style (such as Ambrosius Aurelianus, the ephemeral victor of the battle of Mons Badonicus and one of the prototypes of the legendary King Arthur) disappeared at the beginning of the sixth century. All that remained was a number of tribal petty kings, of whom a few are mentioned in the English chronicles, such as Natanleod in 508, and Conmail, Condidan and Farinmail in 577. For us they are only names. This political incapacity probably explains in large part the departure of some of the Britons for the south; in any case the migration was already well under way before the Saxons had occupied a third of the island.

Britons are mentioned as having been on the continent in various capacities as early as the middle of the fifth century.[3] A British bishop called Mansuetus attended the council of Tours in 461. About 470 the British king Riothamus is said to have taken 12,000 men to fight the Visigoths in Berry on behalf of the Emperor Anthemius, and then to have withdrawn to Burgundy. There is no way of knowing whether he came from Britain itself or from some settlement which had already been founded in Gaul. His troops reappeared before 489 on the Loire, and from the time of Clovis's sons onwards the Franks frequently clashed with compact British settlements in western Armorica. The first embryonic British political structure on the continent (Bro Werec on the south coast of Armorica) belongs to the end of the sixth century. The migration which began about 450 seems to have reached its climax somewhere between 550 and 600, and to have come to an end only at the beginning of the seventh century.

The first waves of emigrants may have left from the south-east of Britain, directly threatened by the Saxons, but the main body came from the south-west, perhaps partly in response to pressure from the Scots. The routes taken by the migration are only known from late, legendary accounts by hagiographers, who have them setting out either from Wales or from Cornwall. These routes followed, though in a reverse direction, trade routes that were quite active at the time. In the Middle Ages the northern coast of western Brittany from Saint-Brieuc to the inlet of Brest was called Dumnonia, a name identical to that of Devon. There is evidence suggesting that a king of the Dumnonii of Devon came to Brittany shortly after 511, and the south-west of Armorica is still called Cornouaille. It is tempting to link this large-scale exodus with the great thrust westwards by the kingdom of Wessex in the sixth century: the end of the migrations would then coincide with the Saxons' pause on the threshold of Cornwall and Wales.

Breton as spoken in the western part of the peninsula must represent the language of the last emigrants, those who came from the south-west of Britain. At all events it is much nearer to Cornish then to Welsh. (Breton and Welsh ceased to be mutually comprehensible in the tenth century, although Breton and Cornish continued to be so until the eighteenth century.) The four dialects of modern Breton, those of the regions of Tréguier, Léon, Cornouaille and Vannes, must have become fixed only after the emigrants had settled finally in Armorica. It is now thought that Gaulish survivals in the interior of the peninsula may have been responsible for several dialectal peculiarities, especially in the Vannes region (see below, p. 237).

Very little is known about how the Britons settled in Armorica. Since positive archaeological evidence is lacking,[4] all that can be said is that there are no objects characteristic of Merovingian civilization in western Brittany, except in the eastern part of the region of Vannes. Only the place-names contribute any solid documentary evidence. The Britons must have arrived in small groups; at first the only organization they had was religious, in the form of parishes founded by Welsh monks. These parishes were very different from the land divisions found in the rest of Gaul, which originated in the Roman system of estates. The Breton *plou*, which was fairly extensive and usually bore the name of a saint (the founder-monk), had nothing to do with any type of estate organization and did not have a true village as its centre. Dioceses were founded in a later period, and like those of the British Isles they preserved a pronounced monastic character. The memory of Roman land divisions may possibly have played some part in defining their boundaries. The population was extremely scattered and completely rural. With the exception of Vannes the towns had been either totally eliminated or reduced to an insignificant status (for example Carhaix, and Locmaria near Quimper).

At first the Breton language probably spread as far east as a line drawn from Dol to Vannes, including the Channel Islands. But the population west of this line was not uniformly Breton-speaking. Throughout eastern Brittany large Gallo-Roman communities survived (notably at Rennes and Vannes), and even in the west we can discern numerous pockets on the coast (such as Morlaix and the peninsula of Taulé-Carantec) and in the interior (around La Feuillée and Quimper) where a form of Latin continued to be spoken. The coast near Vannes seems to have had a mixed population. In the ninth century a vigorous surge forward by the Bretons (as they must now be called) wiped out almost all of these enclaves; moreover, under the leadership of a warlike aristocracy (the *machtierns*), the Bretons pushed the linguistic frontier eastwards as far as a line running from Dol in the north to Donges on the Loire, skirting Rennes to the west. (The political frontier was carried much further east, along the Vire and the Mayenne, at the time of the Breton 'kings'.) The disorganization which followed the Scandinavian invasions from the tenth century onwards caused the language to lose most of the territory it had won so quickly in the ninth century, as well as the Channel Islands. This process of shrinkage, which is still going on today, has been much more marked on the north coast (from Dol to Portrieux) than on the south coast (from Donges to the Rhuys peninsula).

It is difficult to reach an exact assessment of how far east the conquests of the Breton language extended. It probably arrested the normal phonetic development of place-names ending in -*acum* (which throughout a good part of eastern Brittany have come to end in -*ac*, and not in -*é* or -*y* as elsewhere), but it looks as if in many places only the ruling strata were 'Bretonized'. Nevertheless Breton personal names, linked as they undoubtedly were to social prestige, had their enthusiasts quite far towards the east: Judicaels and Riwallons are found in much of Maine and lower Normandy in the eleventh century. Towards the east there must have been a prolonged period of extensive bilingualism, which would explain the number of Romance words which were borrowed by Breton quite early on. However imprecise the linguistic boundary may have been, the political frontier was well defined and much fought over even as early as the sixth century, though the Breton princelings often admitted Frankish suzerainty. The Franks had to organize a system of marches and build a series of fortified posts along it (this may have been the origin of the widespread place-name *La Guerche*).

A thin trickle of British emigrants reached Galicia. As early as 507 a list of the churches in the Suevian kingdom mentions a *sedes Britonorum*, which must be Britoña (near Mondoñedo, in the province of Lugo), whose bishops, bearing Celtic names, are known up until 675. Apart from a few liturgical features nothing is known of the consequences of this British colonization. There was also a small British ecclesiastical colony which settled on the south bank of the Seine estuary in the sixth century. Until 1790 its four parishes formed an enclave of the diocese of Dol within that of Rouen.

The links created by the British migration to Brittany remained unbroken for a long time. Until the tenth or eleventh century Wales, Cornwall and west Brittany constituted a single cultural community whose spiritual leadership was assumed by Cornwall—a community broken up only by the Scandinavian conquests, which denied the Celtic peoples freedom to sail the western seas.

5   The Collision of Civilizations

The principal result of the great invasions was the disintegration of *Romania*, the linguistic, cultural and political unit which the Empire had built up in the West. More or less coherent shreds of *Romanitas* survived in most regions, but differing in vitality and in the extent to which the inhabitants were aware of their status as heirs of Rome. The Germans advanced along the entire length of the former *limes*, occupying the land more or less densely and adopting various compromises, which differed from region to region, with the pre-existing populations. Over extensive areas there was for a very long time uncertainty about which of the two cultures would ultimately triumph over the other. It is impossible, however, to talk of an integral Germanic culture without Roman survivals or influences, just as no Roman culture survived intact without any infiltration of Germanic elements. All the medieval western civilizations are, in different proportions, the heirs both of Rome and of the Germans.

THE CONQUESTS OF *GERMANITAS*: A NEW LINGUISTIC FRONTIER

We can hardly count Britain among the conquests of the German world over the Roman, because there Latin, which was already moribund, seems to have succumbed to a vigorous Celtic revival rather than to have given way before the direct assaults of the Anglo-Saxons. All the phenomena of survival and resistance to the Germanic onslaught—and these are scarce enough—concern the language of the Britons, and not Latin. Some Celtic enclaves survived after the Germans had settled in Britain, but no Roman ones: *Romanitas* in Britain was the victim, not of the invasions themselves, but rather of a social upheaval which the invasions merely assisted.

On the continent it was a different story. There Latin was the sole language of the active elements among the population. Indigenous revivals did not affect the language situation except in the Basque country and possibly in western Brittany. Only the Germanic dialects and civilization seriously affected the area dominated by *Romanitas*, and their gains were exclusively in the regions bordering the former Germanic territories along the Rhine and, more especially, along the

Danube. Gaul, Raetia, Noricum and Pannonia were deeply affected; Italy was barely touched except at the extreme edges; Spain and Africa remained to all intents and purposes intact.

The progress of *Germanitas* has been studied most thoroughly in the Rhine area. Its results are well known: the establishment, well to the west of the river, of a linguistic frontier which has changed very little since the thirteenth century (the earliest time at which it is possible to define it exactly). At that time the frontier began at Boulogne-sur-Mer (although since then Romance has advanced as far as Dunkirk) and ran eastwards in the direction of Lille (leaving Saint-Omer to Germanic) and then north to Tournai; after that it continued parallel to the Sambre and the Meuse, about thirty kilometres to the north of them, crossed the Meuse between Liège and Maastricht, and then ran to the west of Aachen. From there it turned back at a sharp angle towards the south, straight across the Ardennes to the south-west of Arlon (which was Germanic-speaking); then, bending once more, it skirted Metz (obviously a centre of Romance resistance) to the north-east and reached the Donon. Further on in the Vosges it skirted round several high valleys in Alsace which continued to be Romance-speaking. From the Porte de Bourgogne onwards the contact was not with Frankish dialects but with Alamannic, which we shall treat separately, since the advance of the two dialects was affected by very different factors.

Only the study of place-names allows us to go back further than the thirteenth century. Having for a long time made the mistake of looking for all-embracing solutions, this discipline now contents itself with establishing a few firm facts. We know that from as early as the seventh or eighth century the linguistic frontier had settled down in a form very close to that described above, but less linear in appearance, with more salients and enclaves. The main modifications to the thirteenth century picture of which there seem to be clear indications are as follows:[1]

1) In the eighth century Germanic must have been used on the coast approximately up to the mouth of the Canche, probably as far as a line joining Montreuil-sur-Mer to Béthune. The sway of the Frankish language may have been reinforced by the legacy of the Saxon settlements in the district of Boulogne. The great commercial centre of Quentovic may also have been a focus of Germanic culture in the seventh and eighth centuries. The Germanization of the Boulonnais was sufficiently forceful to arrest the normal evolution of place-names ending in *-iacum*, but not to uproot them completely: *Cessiacum* became Quesques there (elsewhere Chessy) and *Gilliacum* became Guelque (elsewhere Gilly). The Romance 'reconquest', which began in the south in the ninth century, halted at the river Aa at the end of the thirteenth century.

2) For a fairly long time Brabant must have been a mixed region. It is possible that there were once pockets of Germanic-speaking peoples to the south-west of Namur and on the Sambre (Lobbes); evidence of the existence of a pocket of Romance around Assche (to the north-west of Brussels) up until the eleventh century is provided by field names, for example *Mutserel* < **macerella* and *Kainoth* < **casnetum*.

3) Romance-speaking enclaves may well have survived for some time, possibly even until the ninth or tenth century, around towns such as Tongres, Maastricht or Aachen.

4) A pocket of Romance continued to exist at least until about 750 in the Eifel, around Prüm, and probably until the thirteenth century there was a large Romance-speaking enclave in the country round Trier; this extended into the valley of the Moselle as a series of disconnected 'islands' as far as the outskirts of Koblenz.[2] Within a radius of approximately thirty kilometres of Trier a rural dialect close to Walloon and the dialect of Lorraine was spoken, as is seen in several place-names (*Tabernae*, which becomes *Zabern* in Germanic areas, hence Saverne, in fact becomes *Tawern* near Trier) and above all in an enormous number of field names (*Longkamp*, in 920, near Bernkastel; *Ruvereit* in 1127 (mod. Rorodt) < **roburetum; Castheneith* in 981 (mod. Kesten) < **castanetum*, etc.).[3]

These slight amendments do not affect the main problem, posed by the establishment early on of a linguistic frontier along a line which neither corresponds with any accident of geography nor conforms to any known political boundary. Why did the tide of Germanic halt there rather than anywhere else? And when did it halt there?

In the past it was believed that physical obstacles which have since disappeared existed along the most arbitrary stretch of the boundary, the part which divides Belgium in two. But the *Silva Carbonaria*, which was said to be one of these obstacles, extended from north to south and not from east to west; and the existence of the *limes belgicus* along the Boulogne-Tongres road is disputed (cf. p. 225), and would not be sufficient to explain anything after the time of Clovis. The 'obstacle' hypothesis has therefore had to be rejected.

Attempting a fresh approach, some scholars have tried to invert the problem: they see the linguistic frontier as marking the limits not of the progress of Germanic, but of a Romance 'reconquest'. According to the supporters of this thesis (Gamillscheg, Petri and von Wartburg) the whole area up to the Loire would have been more or less Germanicized in the sixth century; there would have been extensive bilingualism in this region until the ninth century, followed by the collapse of the Germanic element at the end of the Carolingian period. But this still does not provide a satisfactory explanation for the vagaries of the linguistic frontier.

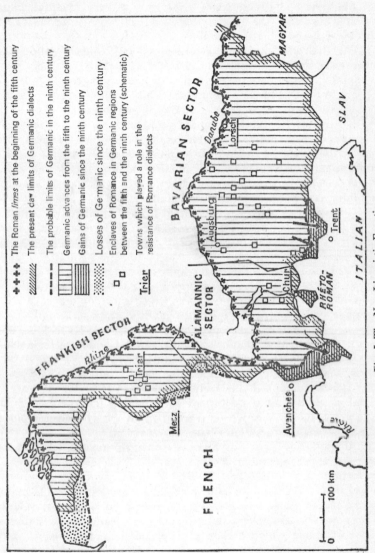

The Roman *limes* at the beginning of the fifth century

The present day limits of Germanic dialects

The probable limits of Germanic in the ninth century

The limits of Germanic from the fifth to the ninth century

Germanic advances from the fifth to the ninth century

Gains of Germanic since the ninth century

Losses of Germanic since the ninth century

Enclaves of Romance in Germanic regions between the fifth and the ninth century (schematic)

Towns which played a role in the resistance of Romance dialects

Trier

FRANKISH SECTOR

ALAMANNIC SECTOR

BAVARIAN SECTOR

Rhine

Trier

Mez

FRENCH

Avanches o

Rhône

0 100 km

Chur

RHÉTO-ROMAN

Augsburg

Danube

Lorsch

o Trent

ITALIAN

SLAV

MAGYAR

Fig. 5 The New Linguistic Frontier

The most typical representative of this school is Petri, who has however rescinded his more extreme views. Nevertheless his thesis [no. 281] rests on an arsenal of arguments of very unequal value. Confining himself to the strictly linguistic evidence, he produces the following to support his arguments:

1) The dialectal area of certain words of Frankish origin (for example *hêtre* (beech) as opposed to *fou* < Lat. *fagus*). This only proves a civilizing influence, not an expansion of the language.

2) The area of toponymic formations which include Frankish words unknown in Romance, whose compounds are formed according to rules peculiar to Germanic languages (for example *baki* (stream) in compounds such as *Marbais* in Hainault = German *Marbach*, 'the stream of the horse'; or *Rebais* in Brie (635 *Resbacis*) = Germ. *Rossbach*, also meaning 'the stream of the horse'). This is more convincing (though the area of place-names ending in *-bais* hardly goes beyond a line joining Abbeville, Versailles and Nancy).

3) The region of place-names formed from the typically Germanic derivative ending *-ing* added to a personal name (for example *Doullens* (Somme), 1147 *Dourleng*, or the fairly widespread name *Hodeng*, *Houdan* or *Houdeng*).

4) The area of certain Germanic habits of articulation, for example the retention of the initial *w-* as opposed to the Romance initial *g-* (for example *warder* instead of *garder*) which more or less covers the *départements* of Nord, Pas-de-Calais and Somme, the whole of Wallonia, the whole of Lorraine, the northern part of the Jura, and the eastern third of Romance-speaking Switzerland (and also Normandy, but probably for different reasons).

Several of these assertions, especially those grouped under 2) and 3), are of real value, but they only establish the sporadic existence of pockets of Franks who continued to use their national language until a fairly late date, for we are dealing on the whole with rare place-names. There is no question of true bilingualism.

Certain scholars have put forward other arguments which have turned out to be untenable. Nothing can be made of the diffusion of place-names ending in *-court*, *-ville*, or *-villiers*, which are purely Romance formations, even when these affixes are joined to Germanic personal names (which were adopted throughout the whole Gallo-Roman population from the sixth century onwards), and are not Latinized versions of names which had originally ended in *-dorf*, *-hofen*, *-heim* and so on. (Place-names from the bilingual zones, such as Thionville/Diedenhofen, are a case apart.) Archaeological and anthropological arguments will be dealt with later.

This dispute has been a fruitful source of ideas. The basic conclusion to be drawn from it is that the intensity of the linguistic influence depended on the density of the Frankish settlements in the course of the first few generations. Wherever the Franks stayed close to their former territory, or wherever the disruption of Roman organization left the way open for direct colonization, the Germanic elements put down roots and sooner or later, exploiting their social and political pre-eminence, eliminated the Romance elements. Further away, where the framework of Roman society held together better, the Frankish peasant-warriors were only able to establish small scattered colonies, which kept going for some time thanks to the cohesion of kinship groups. Some of them penetrated as far as the heart of the Paris basin. The Frankish veneer provided by the existence of aristocratic immigrants all over northern Gaul was not enough to preserve these enclaves from rapid assimilation.

The eventual position of the linguistic frontier would depend, in the last analysis, on two essential factors: distance (the frontier runs very roughly parallel to the *limes* of the fourth century, the point of departure for the conquest, and 100 kilometres to the west of it), and the extent of devastation in the countryside in the fifth century (this is difficult to establish, though it has been shown that in the Moselle valley the persistence of the *villae urbanae* even until well into the sixth century coincides with the late survival of a Romance dialect). This is only one more hypothesis, somewhat more modest than many of its rivals.

Another complementary factor has to be considered: the prior existence of Germanic military or civilian colonies, implanted before the Frankish conquest, could have and must have played an important local role. But scholars cannot agree about the extent and significance of these settlements. The dispute turns on two points in particular: the existence of Germanic speaking groups to the west of the Rhine in the imperial period, and the establishment of *laeti* revealed by archaeological investigation.

There were Germanic elements on the left bank of the Rhine at the time of the Roman conquest of Gaul, notably among the Vangiones, the Nemeti and the Triboci of the Palatinate and Rhenish Hesse, and among the Ubii of the Cologne region. Furthermore the Batavi, a Germanic people, occupied a settlement site straddling the lower reaches of the river. The German character of these tribes is not very obvious in the Roman period—out of approximately 150 attested place-names between the first and the fifth centuries scarcely ten are Germanic—but certain conservative groups must have continued to be aware of their ancestry, for the names of many local divinities, the *Matres*, are Germanic. In general it is thought that the Romanization of the Rhineland was very thorough, and only the smaller rural regions escaped it: Dutch Brabant and Kempen, and the regions of Cologne and Xanten. The towns were all Roman. Thus the Franks were able to take advantage of several Germanic bridgeheads to the west of the Rhine, but only in restricted areas and at social levels without either prestige or influence.

The problem of the so-called *laeti* is a delicate one.[4] The word, the relevance of which is disputed, is used to refer to the barbarian colonists who were tied to the land and settled by the Emperors in the interior of Gaul under military control. The narrative sources refer to their existence from 287–8 onwards, almost all over the north and north-east. They must have formed fairly closed communities, since they were forbidden to marry Roman citizens. These facts are undoubtedly reflected in place-names: a name like *Allemagne* could mean a colony of Alamannic *laeti*. But archaeologists have been a little too casual in claiming to have discovered traces of these colonies whenever they find a synthesis of Germanic and Roman elements in burials. Cemeteries of this type have been found in the region of Namur (Furfooz), in Champagne (Vert-la-Gravelle) and even in the region of Orleans (Cortrat), and have been dated to the end of the fourth century. There is nothing to confirm that these settlements— which were probably civilian ones—enjoyed the legal status of the *laeti*, but there is no doubt that they were pioneers of a Germanic culture. Certain archaeologists, like J. Werner, credit them with having played a decisive part in the development of Merovingian civilization, which is by no means impossible. What is more doubtful is whether they would have had much effect on the linguistic geography.[5]

To the south-east of the Frankish area the situation is very different. The Alamans started pushing across the Rhine about the year 400— that is to say considerably later than the Franks did—but their advance lasted until the thirteenth century. The expansion of the Alamannic dialects therefore lasted for a much longer period than that of Frankish. Although to the west a comparatively simple linguistic frontier with French was finally established (from the Donon to the Great St. Bernard), the position was otherwise in the south and east: in the central Alps the linguistic frontier was not consolidated until modern times, when it settled down along a line which ignores the most obvious geographical features.

In the Vosges the broad outline of the modern language frontier, which tends to run to the east of the peaks, seems to have become fixed since the early Middle Ages, as was the case in Frankish-speaking territory. But beyond the region of Basle this stability disappears: German had been advancing perceptibly since the Carolingian period around Murten and Fribourg, in the Bernese Oberland, and especially in the canton of Valais. About the thirteenth century it crossed the mountain range to encompass Val Gressoney, on the Italian slopes.

Where it comes into contact with Romansh there is a truly chaotic situation; German has taken over all of the towns and several valleys well into Romance territory. This is the only Romance language frontier which is still fluctuating in modern times. Enclaves of Romance also survived for a fairly long time, at least until the eighth century, to the south of Lake Constance in the canton of Saint-Gall and in the Vorarlberg, doubtless with the same associations of social inferiority as still existed in several of the Grisons valleys not so long ago.

This prolonged advance of the Alamannic language took many different forms. It had a military character in the seventh century on the western flank, facing the Burgundians. The territory of the Varasci around Besançon succumbed at the end of the sixth century. In 610 the Alamans defeated two Frankish counts at Wangen near Solothurn, and took advantage of this to destroy the city of Avenches to the north-west of Fribourg, a centre of Romance resistance ever since the middle of the sixth century, when the bishop of Windisch had sought refuge there. Later, from the eighth century onwards, the Alamannic advance towards the south and south-east was more like a process of peaceful colonization, advancing step by step as the high Alpine valleys were gradually brought under cultivation.

Not much is known about how the Alamans Germanized the few towns which survived in their territory. Strasbourg probably continued to have Romance-speaking elements in its population throughout most of the sixth century. Basle was taken over from about 550. At Kaiseraugst (Castrum Rauracense) and at Oberburg (Castrum Vindonissense) Latin lived on at least until the end of the sixth century. Romance held out for longer in only one urban stronghold. This was Chur, the capital of the Kauderwelche (the 'Welsh of Chur', as the Raeto-Romans of today are known in German), under the leadership of the Victorids, a curious dynasty of prince-bishops. Nevertheless, a Germanic minority infiltrated Chur quite early on.

Further east, in the provinces of Raetia II, Noricum and Pannonia, the pattern of development alters yet again. *Romanitas* suffered an almost total collapse in a way which reminds one more of the Balkans than of Gaul. But the real originators of this large-scale withdrawal of *Romanitas*, which was now reduced to tiny disconnected pockets, were not the principal beneficiaries, the Bavarians. This people only took advantage of what had been accomplished by other peoples, Germanic or otherwise, since the beginning of the fifth century, and hence well before the period when the Bavarians crossed the Danube (which was certainly not before the year 500 and possibly not before the second quarter of the sixth century). The first stages in the destruction of Roman institutions are well documented for Noricum, thanks to the life of St. Severinus, written in 511 [no. 15], which gives an exceptionally vivid account of the events which took place between 453 and 488.

The invading tribes of this first wave were not sufficiently numerous to occupy the country in any lasting way. The Germanic language only made decisive progress when the Bavarians arrived. Unfortunately their arrival occurred during a period of total silence in our sources. By the time of Venantius Fortunatus, who is the first to mention Noricum again (in 561), the country seems to have become completely German-speaking.

In reality many Romance-speaking elements lived on, but politically and culturally they had lost all significance. In Bavaria and Upper Austria, Carolingian documents often mention *Romani* (Germ. *Walchen*), and the place-names confirm the importance of these small enclaves. In spite of popular etymology, names like Waldstetten, Wallstadt, Waldsee and Wahlenheim conceal the term *walah-* ('Welsh', or foreigner), and Carolingian texts mention forms such as *vicus Romaniscus*, *Walahsteti*, *Walchsê*, etc. (The attempt by A. Janda [no. 463] to see the descendants of the enslaved Roman populations in the semi-servile class of the *barschalken*, whose existence is attested up to the thirteenth century, seems to have failed.) These descendants of the Romans formed rural communities scattered over the plateau, especially in the valley of the Inn and to the north and west of Salzburg. Except in two Alpine refuges, the Walchengau of the upper Isar and the Vintschgau of the upper Adige, they had lost all cohesion and also all the members of their social élite (except perhaps towards Augsburg, where a bishopric still survived). They spoke Romance at least until the ninth century in Bavaria. In the Alps they merged with the Romansh elements which still survive on the upper reaches of the Inn and the Adige. In spite of the embryonic political organization which had come into existence around Chur not a single linguistic frontier had taken definite shape. But for small exceptions, Germanic made contact with Italian almost everywhere.

The advance of the Bavarians, like that of the Alamans, continued until well beyond the sixth century. Towards the south it was only in the seventh century that it achieved a decisive success at the expense of the Latin-speaking groups of the Tyrol. The Brenner was crossed and the Germanization of the Alto Adige made rapid progress (it is believed to have been complete by the ninth century). Towards the east there were fluctuations; at first the whole of Austria was Germanized, but at the end of the sixth century first the Slavs and then the Avars drove the Bavarians back about as far as Linz; Germanic regained ground in the ninth century, but then lost it in the face of the Hungarian assault. These vicissitudes explain the absence of Roman survivals to the east of the Enns.

In Pannonia *Romanitas* disappeared quite soon, probably as early as the end of the fourth century, but in obscure circumstances. In this case those responsible were the Huns and their allies. Some German peoples (Gepids and, more important, Lombards) profited from it, but without founding anything lasting. The Slavs and the Magyars, after many vicissitudes, finally occupied the country and ensconced themselves between the last survivors of eastern *Romanitas*—the Rumanians —and the Germanic world.

On the whole Germanic penetrated much deeper into the former Roman Empire to the east of Basle than to the west. Why is there this difference? In the west one great wave of invasions had swept over the country after the destruction of the *limes* and had quickly settled down. In the east it was more a question of repeated waves complementing one another over a much longer period. In the west the Merovingian monarchy which had been established in Romance territory undertook to protect *Romanitas* to a greater extent, for example against the Alamans, and to put a stop to the depredations of small groups of fortune-hunters. In the east the only forces capable of supporting *Romanitas* were always based in Italy (under Odoacer, Theodoric and Justinian), and as far as they were concerned the country beyond the Alps was only an outpost of no great interest.

The invasions were only indirectly responsible for the dialectal break-up of *Romania*, for the centrifugal tendencies already existed before the fall of the Empire. They developed freely when there was no longer any common administration or education, that is, when the Roman ruling class had disappeared. As early as the third century epigraphy reveals the progressive differentiation between the Latin of the east, that of Dacia, Moesia, Dalmatia and peninsular Italy, and of the west, that of Pannonia, Noricum, northern Italy, Raetia and Gaul, together with a Hispano-African variety. Apart from contributing a number of loan-words the invasions only had a direct effect in two areas: the isolation of the Balkan Romans from the sixth century onwards meant that Latin there evolved in a very original way; and the Alamans, by cutting off the direct route from Gaul to Raetia, were largely responsible for ensuring that Raeto-Romanic developed independently. [6]

THE RESISTANCE OF THE ROMAN WORLD AT DIFFERENT LEVELS OF SOCIETY

Deprived of central leadership, the Roman world resisted the invasions in many different ways, according to circumstances. It crumbled apart and gave up whole areas of its former prestige, but survived even so and, thanks in large part to the Church, preserved a certain awareness of its unity and its greatness. The invasions overthrew it, but did not wipe it out entirely: afterwards it was often able to recover important areas of influence.

The best way to analyse the resistance put up by a system as hierarchical as the Later Roman Empire is to treat the various social classes separately. We shall take Gaul as our main example.

At the head of the Roman world was a political aristocracy of about 3,000 people,[7] the *ordo senatorius*, made up of families of which at least one member had attained the highest magistrature in Rome or in Constantinople. It was also an aristocracy based on wealth—a magistrate on taking up office was required to provide incredibly expensive circus spectacles. This wealth was founded on the enormous landed fortunes which had been built up since the fourth century on the ruins left by the civil wars. And finally it was a cultured aristocracy, the only one to take full advantage of the provincial schools, like those of Bordeaux or Autun, which added an unexpected lustre to the last generations of the Empire.

This aristocracy enjoyed vast privileges, military, legal and fiscal, which ensured it a prestige out of all proportion to the services it rendered to society. Although it produced several brilliant officials, the majority of its members confined themselves to living the life of great lords, in town or country, and if they devoted themselves to anything at all it was, at most, to the cult of *belles-lettres*. Imperial authority both feared them and made use of them. The Church smiled on them—many bishops were of senatorial rank—but occasionally also deflected them from active life: for one St. Germanus of Auxerre, putting his talents at the service of the defenders of Britain, how many others fled the world!

The triumph of the barbarians and the loss of influence of Rome and the Senate in no way put an end to the career of the senatorial class. In Gaul (where its fate has been studied in greatest detail) it lived on until the seventh century, and in some cases until the eighth century, safeguarding its social position and partly recovering its political influence, thanks to its intellectual superiority. In a moment of crisis it often discreetly faded into the background, but once order was restored it recovered its former position. It was thanks to this aristocracy that whole areas of Roman law, administrative practices and culture were preserved.

The statistics of Stroheker [no. 456] show that the majority of the Gallo-Roman senators had deserted their vulnerable estates in northern Gaul well before the time of Clovis. In the fourth century all the great cities there—Cologne, Mainz, Trier, Rheims, Sens and Tours—had had their senatorial families; the south had far fewer. But the further we advance into the fifth century the more the situation is reversed;

soon there were no more senators north of a line drawn from Soissons to Autun, while there were more and more in the south. The north had been largely evacuated before the fall of Syagrius. The refugees settled down wherever they could, often renouncing temporal ambitions. The former prefect of the Gauls, Dardanus, together with some refugees from Trier, took up residence in a fortified villa in the southern Alps; other refugees played a part in the foundation of the monastery of Lérins. Most of the refugees, however, decided to put their talents at the disposal of the barbarian kings, though laymen who dared to venture among the Franks, as Parthenius did, were rare: only one senatorial dynasty seems to have survived in the heart of the Merovingian kingdom, that of the bishop of Trier, Numerianus. But the senatorial class formed the civilian aristocracy of the Visigothic kingdom of Toulouse and of the Burgundian kingdom; it even provided them with a certain number of officials, not to mention the majority of their bishops. When the Franks took over the south, the senatorial aristocracy continued to hold positions of authority there until the beginning of the Carolingian era. Hence the opposition between the south and the north (the latter dominated by a Frankish aristocracy), which is evident throughout the whole of the early Middle Ages.

The illustrious family of the Syagrii offers the best example of the tenacity of the senatorial order's will to survive. It was descended from Flavius Afranius Syagrius, who was consul in 382, and its members were allied by marriage to Tonantius Ferreolus, prefect of the Gauls in 450. It enjoyed its greatest triumph in the second half of the fifth century, in the persons of Aegidius and Syagrius, the last leaders of Roman resistance in the north. The family survived the catastrophe of 486; in 585 a Count Syagrius, in the service of the Frankish King Guntram, went on a diplomatic mission to Constantinople. Their landed wealth was still enormous at the beginning of the eighth century, for in 739 a certain Syagria was able to give to the monks of Novalesa villae in eight *pagi* scattered from the region of Mâcon to that of Gap. The last known member of the Syagrii was an abbot of Nantua who was mentioned in 757. [8]

One even wonders if the members of this aristocracy—wherever they were fairly numerous—did not see the triumph of the barbarians as an opportunity to blossom forth. The emergence of new political units within the limits of the Empire satisfied their regionalist tendencies, and the multiplicity of the princely courts increased their chances of secular success. In spite of the financial losses and the unpleasantness of having German troops billeted on their land, their way of life was relatively unchanged. It was indeed proto-medieval before the invasions in more than one case: Bourg-sur-Gironde, the *Burgus Pontii Leontii* whose praises were sung by Sidonius Apollinaris (*Carmina XXII*), was already a fortified castle. On the other hand their way of life continued to be very Roman well into the Merovingian era; to convince oneself of this one has only to follow Fortunatus to the houses of his hosts on the banks of the Moselle in 588. In spite of individual incidents this class is the one which emerged from the fifth century most unscathed. Only the Lombard invasion of Italy was able to strike it a blow from which it never recovered, although in Africa the excessive bitterness of the religious quarrels severely limited its role.

The townsmen suffered far more and for much longer, since as early as the third century they were forced to crowd into walled areas of reduced size which permitted neither comfort nor—except in the case of state manufactories—any serious economic activity. But when they did manage to survive the storm they benefited from more than one advantage: the re-establishment of relative peace, the growth of new markets (for example in what had been Free Germany) and the possibility of moving out of their constricting walls again. Moreover they did not have to fear competition: the conquerors for their part were not interested in urban life.

Convincing examples can once more be found in Gaul and in the Rhineland. They confirm the survival along the former *limes* of significant groups of town-dwellers—especially artisans and, of course, clerics—faithful to the Roman way of life and capable of carrying on, if not indeed developing, their traditional activities. The breakdown of the state-controlled economy offered new opportunities to certain merchants—not Latins, admittedly, but Romans all the same, since Syrians, Anatolians and Jews were all Roman subjects.

The case of Trier, the town about which we know most,[9] is rather an exception, in that it suffered just as much from the loss of its status as a capital at the end of the fourth century as from the invasions, eventful though these were. We know from Salvian that by the middle of the fifth century Trier had already been taken four times (probably around 406, 411, 419 and 440); it was probably taken for the fifth and last time between about 475 and 480, but at any rate before 496. Thanks to its status Trier had escaped the worst consequences of the crisis of the third century: in the fifth century it still enclosed within its walls the enormous area of 285 hectares. The aristocracy, which was certainly more numerous in Trier than elsewhere, left *en masse* for the south (Salvian himself reached Marseilles); this migration was encouraged by the transfer of the prefecture of the Gauls to Arles. The imperial buildings, which were by that time in a very dilapidated condition, passed to the Merovingian fisc. The basilica where the Emperor had sat enthroned seems to have been abandoned; the public baths probably became the residence of the Frankish count; the imperial warehouses for the Rhine army were allocated to a monastery in the seventh century. The town walls still stood, but the space that they enclosed was too large, and a good part of it seems to have been uninhabited. However a sufficiently large population remained for the upkeep of an extensive network of streets, keeping to the old grid pattern, and above all for the maintenance of an impressive series of sanctuaries and cemeteries, the latter *extra muros* in accordance with Roman law. The double cathedral bequeathed by Constantine survived. The continued use of the cemeteries is proved by numerous monuments; an unusual abundance of funerary inscriptions[10] shows a strong survival of Roman traditions and even curiously close links with the East, as revealed by stelae of Coptic type and epitaphs of Syrians and Greeks. The inscriptions show all the transitional stages in the general shift from Latin to Germanic personal names: as early as the fourth century soldiers of the guard had Germanic names such as Flavius Gabso and Hariulfus, and until the eighth century a group of Latin names such as Aufidius and Ursianus persists, especially among the clergy. The artisans' workshops, which had been very active in imperial times, had suffered a serious decline by the end of the fifth century as a result of the disappearance of the market for luxury goods, but they revived again in the seventh century.

In the more vulnerable Cologne the scarcity of finds for the period between the fifth century and the ninth century is such that some have believed it to have been completely abandoned. Recently historians have been of an entirely different opinion: although the public baths were abandoned the street grid survived, the temple of the Capitol was turned into a church and the palace (*praetorium*) became the residence of the Frankish counts without any great modifications. The excavations at the cathedral have demonstrated the continuity of its use, notably by the discovery of sixth-century princely burials. There is no denying that Gregory of Tours confirms the existence of a pagan temple in the town around 520, but he also describes, as early as 590, a sumptuous basilica *Ad Sanctos Aureos* (Sankt-Gereon). Thus there was widespread continuity despite the closure of the great glassworks.

There is no point in giving other detailed examples. At Worms the suburban cemeteries continued to be used without a break, the bishopric survived and although the south of the city was half-derelict, the north and the centre continued to be occupied. Strasbourg was destroyed by fire at the beginning of the fifth century, but the population went on living there in makeshift constructions built with the rubble and, in spite of his Germanic name, Arbogast, who was bishop around 550, was sufficiently faithful to Roman tradition to have bricks moulded bearing the words *Arboastis eps ficet*.

It is even more instructive to examine the fate of the *vici* and the *castella*. The best example is the case of Andernach, on the Rhine.[11]

Since about 250 Antunnacum had been a *castellum* on the *limes*, linked with a centre of craftsmanship of almost industrial productivity; its port exported millstones made of basalt from Mayen and Niedermendig (Eifel), and also pottery from the great Mayen workshop. The garrison disappeared at the beginning of the fifth century, but the *castrum* survived so well that the Roman military headquarters became a royal residence in the sixth century. The extra-mural cemeteries confirm almost complete continuity, and their epitaphs bear witness to the late survival of Roman elements there with names like Crescentius, Agriculus and so on, alongside Frankish names like Adelbert and Austroald, themselves inscribed on *tituli* of Roman type. There is every indication that the lava quarries, the potteries and the glassworks carried on their activities without perceptible interruption, and even continued to export their wares to places as distant as Scandinavia. The work of these artisans brought about real prosperity, for the richness of the Andernach tombs contrasts sharply with the poverty of other cemeteries in the region.

Of course, side by side with these cases of continuity there are examples of total and violent destruction, especially in military establishments. Bonn and Neuss each lost its camp with its commercial annex, the *canaba*, but the civilian *vicus* survived to give birth to the medieval town.

What we have just demonstrated with regard to the frontier zone applies still more to the interior of Gaul. Certain towns there disappeared, like Nyon (Civitas Equestrium) on Lake Geneva, but this rarely happened, and usually only with military centres, like Bavai for example. Others moved a short distance away, like the Civitas Vallensium whose inhabitants took refuge in the stronghold of Sion (Valais), or like Lyons, which came down from the Fourvières plateau to the banks of the Saône. But cases of continuity far outnumber these exceptions. H. Pirenne has shown that at Tournai an imperial estate passed directly to the Merovingian fisc and then to the Carolingian one, and this in the very town where Childeric was buried.[12] In Paris the suburbs of the left bank (such as Ste-Geneviève and St-Marcel) recovered rapidly from the disasters of the third century and really flourished in the Merovingian era. It was not until the Normans attacked them in the ninth century that these *suburbia*, which were much more extensive than the city proper, were destroyed.[13]

These archaeological findings, which it would be difficult to refute, correct the widespread view that the invasions of the fifth century were mainly responsible for urban destruction; in fact the real breaks occurred in the third century, and to a lesser degree in the ninth. One can no longer believe that the 'destruction and disappearance of the middle class', essentially the town-dwellers, was directly the result of the invasions. But one fact is certain: at the end of the fifth and during the sixth century part of the economic activity of the towns shifted to country districts. Whereas in the Roman period glassworks and armouries had been urban workshops, in the time of the Franks they were to be found in the country or, to be more exact, in the forests.

It is interesting to note the Germans' reaction to the towns. Sometimes we glimpse a certain distrust of the towns among the Frankish ruling class, but it appears to have arisen late, several generations after the conquest, and may have been due to an anxiety to avoid clashes with the Church (as happened at Trier, when the count left for Bitburg at the end of the sixth century). Often the Franks had to set up garrisons in the former keep: a group of *seniores Franci* is known to have settled down in Rouen.[14] Since both Franks and Romans followed the same form of worship there was no segregation anywhere.

The extent of the survivals and the vigour of certain revivals must on no account be allowed to mask the slow disintegration of urban life, which had begun well before the invasions and was destined to continue for a long time after they had ceased. The large number of new church buildings (often in inferior materials) contrasts with the fact that public works came to a halt almost completely, and the mediocrity of the studies on Merovingian epigraphy cannot entirely account for the overwhelming disproportion between the written testimonies left by the Later Roman Empire and those of the following period. Almost nowhere was the town-dwelling class wiped out, but everywhere it dwindled as a result of an economic evolution which was independent of the history of the invasions.

The fate of the rural populations is the biggest problem, and also the most difficult. The small amount of literary and archaeological evidence which we have turns on three interconnected points: the reorganization of the cultivated lands, the disappearance of the villae, and the rise of the villages. But we are treading on dangerous ground, where there are numerous disputes and where very few facts have been established beyond doubt (see p. 194 ff).

The question of the extent to which the invasions changed the appearance of the land under cultivation has hardly yet started to be asked in concrete archaeological terms. Few cultivated areas seem to have been abandoned completely, and where this happened the events of the third century were more often responsible for it than those of the fifth century. The clearest case is that of the region of the lower Seine, which until the time of Postumus or Constantine had a thick scattering of villae and hamlets, but was later devastated and abandoned to the forest.[15] In the Rhineland, which was more directly exposed, there are hardly any cases of abandonment; on the contrary, the conquest of new soil on the plateaux of the Eifel and the Hunsrück proceeded hand in hand with the almost unchanged exploitation of the valleys and slopes (especially by vinegrowers). The old chess-board field pattern (*centuratio*) survived almost everywhere, especially in northern Italy, where the institution may have been understood until the eighth century, and in Tunisia, but also even in northern Gaul. Unfortunately it was more a question of a fiscal than of an agrarian arrangement, and its significance for the history of the rural population must not be overestimated.

On the other hand there is no obvious sign of importation of new ideas: a healthy scepticism has developed since the time of the pioneers of agrarian history who thought that with the help of a text by Tacitus they could justifiably credit the Germans with the diffusion of triennial crop rotation by collective compulsion (see p. 195).

More is known about the fate of the villae, although one is often misled by the statistics of archaeologists, for the only villae which have been studied in detail are those which were prematurely destroyed and were not replaced by medieval and modern settlements. The *villae urbanae* disappeared in enormous numbers. Many had already been destroyed by the third century, but the Constantinian peace had allowed them to be rebuilt in the wealthy areas—the country around Trier and in southern Auvergne and Aquitaine—sometimes in a more austere fortified form. Even in these cases they rarely survived beyond the fifth century. The only lasting exceptions are a few royal or episcopal 'palaces'; but even these lost the magnificent luxury features, such as baths, and the agricultural equipment, such as reaping machines, with which the best of the old villae had been equipped. There is evident continuity between the great Roman villa and the royal Frankish one, as instanced by the villa at Brinnacus (now Berny-Rivière in the département of Aisne) described by Gregory of Tours. However, such cases of survival or reconstruction are rare, because the great villa was linked with outmoded social conditions.

Generally the villa was just a sort of veneer on the surface of the rural world. It seems likely that the peasant masses had never completely abandoned their Celtic-type hamlets made up of daub and wattle huts, whose only archaeological traces are ill-defined hut floors. In a few rare cases it has been possible to establish continuity between a Celtic settlement and a Merovingian one; in other cases it looks as if the village was built from the ruins of a neighbouring villa. In short, the village was not a new form of settlement, but after the invasions it was very much more vigorous, as is evidenced by the almost infinite multiplication of row-grave cemeteries, reflecting the villagers' passion for collective order even after death.

The springing up of the villages seems to be one of those numerous cases where indigenous practices, revived after the Roman façade had collapsed, coincided with Germanic introductions. The newcomers had never lived in stone-built villae, and even distrusted them, for they often used them as rubbish dumps or for burials instead of patching them up and living in them, whereas the village with its huts was familiar to them. Then again, the village population proved more receptive to barbarian influence than the villa-owning class: the first Germanic influences in Gaul are seen in rural cemeteries.

The transition can take all sorts of widely different forms. The following are the patterns that Böhner [no. 409] has distinguished in the countryside around Trier. Several Gallo-Roman settlements lived on without any obvious Frankish influence, and the villae there were gradually and imperceptibly replaced by villages; the associated cemeteries remained unchanged as to site and appearance, as at Ehrang, at the confluence of the Moselle and the Kyll. More often a Frankish settlement with its own cemetery grew up near the Roman one as, for example, at Wintersdorf on the Sauer. Even more frequently, Franks came to live in the heart of the Roman settlement and respected its church (if it already had one), but buried their dead in the old cemetery whose appearance then changed, as at Pfalzel. Finally there are Frankish villages, especially on the plateaux, which did not supersede any previous settlement, so that the villagers had to create a new cemetery and possibly, later on, build a church, as for example at Wallersheim, near Prüm. The cases of continuity are found especially on the hillsides where the vine, which had been unknown to the Franks, played an important role in the rural economy (as in Alsace).

As far as the interior of Gaul is concerned, the proportions have to be modified, but the general picture is still to all intents and purposes the same.[16] There is one linguistic fact which seems to imply that a gradual transition from villa to village was what most commonly happened: the word villa gradually came to mean 'estate' or 'village'. If discontinuity had been the general rule a completely new word would have been coined.

It is in dealing with the clergy that one finds both the most marked Roman survivals and the most precise information. At the time of the baptism of Clovis the clergy was entirely Roman (though not necessarily indigenous, for it always included oriental elements). In the fifth century its hierarchy continued to be purely Roman, if personal names are any guide, for only two bishops have Germanic names, Chariato of Valence and Arbogast of Chartres. They probably came from Frankish families which had long been in the service of Rome. This bias against barbarians continued for the greater part of the sixth century. Statistics show that out of 477 bishops in Gaul who are known to us only 68, or one-seventh of the total, have Germanic names, although for the laity mentioned in inscriptions the proportion is one-half.[17] There were extremely few bishops with German names in the south—in Narbonensis six out of 153 and in Lugdunensis I only one out of 34, despite the Burgundian settlement in that province. But in the provinces of Rheims and Trier the Germanic names already made up one-third of the total, and in the provinces of Mainz and Cologne, one-half. Nevertheless a fair proportion of the northern episcopate continued to be recruited from the south, even in Trier, at the very heart of Frankish colonization.[18]

Somewhere during the 560s there comes a turning-point. In Trier the first bishop with a Germanic name, Magnericus, appears between 561 and 585. In Bordeaux, after a dynasty of prelates of the senatorial family of the Pontii Leontii had occupied the see for more than half a century, King Guntram appointed his kinsman Bertechramnus bishop shortly before 574. In Le Mans a mayor of Chilperic's palace became the first Germanic bishop, in 581. There are many such examples. Nevertheless it is not until the seventh century that the phenomenon becomes widespread, and not until the eighth century does the fusion appear complete (if we except the Mediterranean region). Such scanty information as we have on the middle or lower clergy points in the same direction—neither flight nor elimination, but compromise and slow fusion.

As long as part of the episcopate to some extent had the feeling that they were not true Franks, there remained a problem of conquest and submission in Gaul. When there was no longer a predominantly Roman ecclesiastical power opposing the German military leaders in the Merovingian kingdom, the fusion could be considered complete.

A NEW CIVILIZATION

The foregoing has sufficiently demonstrated that, among the consequences of the confrontation between the Germans and the Romans, cases of transformation and evolution outnumber those of destruction. The early Middle Ages did not see the substitution of a triumphant German world for a defeated *Romanitas*. Not a single barbarian kingdom, except perhaps that of the Vandals, imposed the dictatorship of a *Herrenvolk* on subjects deprived of all rights. Everywhere there was compromise, a more or less elaborate synthesis of various elements, and the creation of a new civilization distinct both from that of late Antiquity and from that of Free Germany. It can be judged inferior to classical civilization, but its originality cannot be denied, and it cannot be considered simply as an indefinitely prolonged period of 'decadence', or as an appendix to the history of Germanic culture.

Naturally the phenomenon is most obvious in the only two kingdoms which lasted for any length of time: Merovingian Gaul and Visigothic Spain. The Ostrogoths were not able to achieve the predominantly Roman synthesis which Theodoric had envisaged, and the Lombard kingdom began its career too late to benefit directly from the legacy of the Later Roman Empire. In order to catch the essence of this process of gradual change, let us look at some of the problems of archaeology and personal names relating to Gaul.

An examination of burial customs provides us with a good example. Between the end of the Roman period and the triumph of the Merovingians—roughly the beginning of the fifth to the middle of the sixth century—the appearance of the burial-places changed radically. Instead of small, rather untidy and inconspicuous cemeteries with a mixture of inhumations and cremations, we find the spectacular 'row-grave cemeteries' (*Reihengräber*) which quickly became the most common form of cemetery until the Carolingian period. Few changes discovered by the archaeologist are more worthy of the historian's attention.

Row-grave cemeteries are well defined by Werner [no. 311] as having the following characteristics. 1) Alignments of graves in which the body had been laid directly in the earth, or in a coffin made of flat stones or, later, in a trapezoidal monolithic sarcophagus. 2) Fairly frequent occurrence of funerary offerings, often placed inside vessels. 3) The dead buried fully clothed, women with their jewellery and men with their weapons (at least at first). 4) East-west orientation of the body, with the feet to the east. Usually the graves were unmarked; there were a few wooden posts or borders made of planks, but grave-stones are rare, and are usually found in settings which have kept a very strong Roman character. In general, before the seventh century these cemeteries were located in open countryside without any obvious link with a place of worship, and some distance from the nearest village. The number of tombs varies from a couple of dozen to several thousand. When it is a question of cemeteries of sarcophagi, which were expensive, cases of reuse are frequent. Naturally this picture must include perceptible regional variations, depending on the materials available (long cysts of flat stones predominate in the Rhineland, monolithic tombs in limestone areas, and plaster coffins in the Paris region), but they do not alter the impression of a uniform civilization.

This innovation, revealed by archaeologists, cannot be explained merely by the bald fact of the Frankish invasion. No one would dare now to claim that these cemeteries all belong to the invaders. They belong to a whole society which already is no longer German or Roman, but truly Merovingian. In its origins there is nothing essentially Germanic about this type of burial. The Germans did not use it before crossing the Rhine, and one of its most frequent characteristics, the stone sarcophagus, appears to be a Roman feature, for the Germans beyond the Rhine did not work stone and only very exceptionally used coffins of wood, while the Romans had used stone tombs, sporadically throughout their history, and indeed more and more frequently during the Later Roman Empire. Another characteristic, the custom of burying men with their weapons, seems to have been Germanic, though we cannot be sure of this. It is attested by Tacitus as being the custom in Germania, and there are archaeological examples, though they are few, before the fifth century beyond the Rhine; but certain Celts had also practised it since the Hallstatt period, and later as a reaction against Roman influence. One last feature—the orientation of the bodies towards the east—seems to have developed under the influence of oriental religions or of Christianity (though this has been denied[19]).

All these elements can only have come together and fused into a synthesis somewhere to the west of the Rhine, on what had formerly been imperial territory. In general it is assumed, following the lead of J. Werner, that it happened in northern Gaul during the period when *coloni* and German auxiliaries in the service of Rome lived among a population which continued to be Roman, although impoverished and affected by the Celtic revival. Certain fourth-century cemeteries in the Namurois, Artois, Picardy, Champagne, upper Normandy and the region of Orleans seem to represent the transition we are looking for, since they already combine the alignments of row-graves with a mixture of grave goods. After the Merovingian kingdom had been set up this type of cemetery took over throughout the whole of northern Gaul (except for Armorica) and, without the use of sarcophagi, spread throughout the Frankish protectorates beyond the Rhine (Alamannia and Thuringia) and even into some regions that were escaping from Frankish control, like Westphalia. It also spread into southern England. Thus from the Loire to the Elbe a new cultural element emerged which ignored both linguistic boundaries and political frontiers. The invasion was only responsible for it in so far as it brought the populations of the different geographical regions of this area into contact with each other and drew together the various elements of diverse origins which were essential for the synthesis.

From this we can see that the presence of row-graves must not be used as an indication of the presence of Germanic populations. Can we fall back on a few secondary indications? It is probable that the few cases of cremation in row-grave cemeteries must be attributed to authentic Germans—Franks, but perhaps also Saxons; here we are dealing with a non-Christian rite which was abandoned very early on and which can only have been practised by newcomers. But that does not take us very far: four sites in southern Holland, five in the Rhineland, three in Belgium and four in France. The presence of weapons in graves is not conclusive either, at least after 500 (and there may not be even as many as a dozen cases before that date), since the bearing of arms is more a reflection of insecurity or a sign of wealth than an indication of German origin. It was also to quite an extent a question of fashion. Like the use of row-graves, the custom of inhumation with arms became widespread in Germany from the time Merovingian Gaul first came into existence.

What we have said about burials could equally be said of jewellery and pottery, though allowing for a somewhat larger element of indigenous Gaulish traditions. The third century saw a general return to the Celtic past in Gallo-Roman applied art, exemplified in the 'flamboyant' decoration of certain bronze objects, the use of vividly coloured materials, and the stylization of human or animal figures. At the same time throughout the Empire certain articles connected with clothing, such as the fibula which fastened the cloak on the shoulder, or the belt buckle, became highly ornamental, out of all proportion to their utilitarian function.[20] All that Graeco-Roman classicism had held in check now reappeared. The barbarians brought additional elements with them from the Eurasian steppes (which will be dealt with on page 201), but the general tendencies were already there before their conquests.[21]

In the same way the Merovingian period saw the spread of a new type of pottery, much inferior to that of the early Empire, characterized by a fairly coarse black, grey or whitish paste, carinated shapes and roulette decoration in the form of crosses or chevrons grouped within compartments. Its origins are probably to be sought partly in the traditions of Free Germany, but the rustic potteries of Gaul had never completely abandoned this rouletted work since the La Tène period, and from the fourth century onwards it had undergone a brilliant revival in the major factories of Argonne.

In the field of onomastics two processes distinguish the period after the invasions: the almost total changeover from Roman to Germanic personal names, and the less profound, but nevertheless significant, changes in place-names.

The system of personal names of the early Empire, based on the *tria nomina* of the Roman citizen, had died out well before the shock of the invasions. Except among a few aristocratic families, only *cognomina* were used in the fourth century, each man usually having two or three; the etymology of almost all of them was transparent, and they were formed on a Latin or Greek stem with the addition of one of a small number of suffixes, the most frequent being *-ius*, for example Leontius,

Ausonius, and Gregorius. In a very short time—less than a century—
this system had been ousted by another, whereby an individual only
had one name, generally formed, on the model of royal names, from
two Germanic words joined together, although their meaning when
linked was not always very clear (for example *Dagobertus* = shining +
day; *Sigibertus* = shining + victory; *Theudericus* = king + people;
Hariulfus = wolf + army; *Arnulfus* = wolf + eagle etc.). There are no ·
family names, but the hereditary link is often expressed by parents
passing on to their children one of the components of their name (for
example *Chlodovechus* or Clovis called his son *Chlodomeris*). These names,
which were usually long (at least four syllables), were often replaced
in current usage by short forms (hypocoristics), for example *Dado*
instead of *Audoenus*. This system continued to be the basis of personal
names in France until the adoption of surnames between the twelfth
and fourteenth centuries; it still accounts for the majority of surnames and a certain number of Christian names. It was equally
popular in northern Italy and in Spain, but not in Africa.

The diffusion of the new system of personal names is explained by
fashion, by the prestige of the court, and perhaps by a sort of loyalty to
the new régime. Besides, in the fourth century the Germanic names did
not appear out of the blue. The way in which they were formed was
very reminiscent of the old Celtic names, and even the components
sometimes corresponded, for example the Celtic names ending in *-rix*
and the German ones ending in *-reiks*. Moreover it was a long time
since the Germans had shed their native names as soon as they had
crossed the *limes* (like the Batavian Civilis in the first century); there
had even been consuls called Richomer and Merobaudes!

The changes in place-names were less widespread. They hardly
affected a single town, apart from Strasbourg, and they spared most
of the *vici*. But they swept away a large proportion of the names of
rural estates, and in particular they ensured that future names would
be formed in a different way. Perhaps half of the names of communes
in the north of France today would be inexplicable without the
Merovingian era. Many names of areas and medieval administrative
districts, even in the Romance-speaking zones, are Germanic in origin
or in type. But if many towns in Gaul renounced their official Roman
denomination it was only to take up the name of a Gallic tribe (for
example, Tours for Caesarodunum), and it was therefore an effect of
the 'Celtic Renaissance' and not of the invasions.[22]

The survival of Latin names in territory which had become German-
speaking, as well as the appearance of mixed names in territory which
continued to be Romance-speaking, can tell us something about the
genesis of the new civilization. In spite of the destruction of the ruling
class many characteristic names of estates on the old Roman pattern

survived on the left bank of the Rhine. The most typical, which were formed by adding the suffix *-acum* to the name of the proprietor, continued to be numerous in the Moselle, Rhine, Roer and Erft valleys (for example, *Juliacum* (Fr. Juliers, Germ. Jülich); *Tiberiacum* (Germ. Zieverich); *Matriniacum* (Germ. Metternich)), but they practically died out in the Netherlands, probably thanks to an early Roman evacuation. More important than these survivals are the new forms. Once the Germans came into contact with these names of *fundi* and *villae*, they modified their own ways of forming names. Names of villages based on a personal name plus the equivalent of *villa* (*-heim, -dorf, -hof*, etc.) are completely absent from classical sources relating to Germania, but they dominate absolutely, both east and west of the Rhine, from the seventh century onwards. It has been supposed that the Franks forged this type of place-name when they came in contact with the Gallo-Romans as early as the fifth or the sixth century, and then transmitted it to other Germans.[23] Moreover, one of these suffixes, which has become an integral part of German toponymic vocabulary, *-weiler*, is borrowed from the Latin *villare*. In spite of their purely Germanic construction, names ending in *-ing* and *-ingen* could also be modelled on names ending in *acum*, which they sometimes replace. We must therefore reject the hypothesis made fashionable by W. Arnold[24] which attributed the names ending in *-ingen*, for example, to the Alamans, and those ending in *-heim* to the Franks. These types of name were common to several peoples and mingled within the same region. We can distinguish chronological layers thanks to these endings, but not ethnic distribution.

Exactly the same type of name formation spread throughout the north of Gaul in a Romance form between the sixth and the tenth centuries. During the first few generations place-names composed of a Germanic personal name plus the suffix *-acum* continued to be coined, for example *Athanacum* from Athanaric and *Ramnacum* from Chramn; a name formation using the suffix *-iacas* was popular for a short time, for example *Landriciacas*, from Landerich. But these suffixes soon ceased to be used, being rejected in favour of the affixes *ville* and *court*, whose popularity reached a peak in the seventh and eighth centuries, and which are still being used even today. The other part of the word is almost always Germanic, simply because personal names at that time were mostly Germanic. On the margins of the Merovingian kingdom the syntax vacillates between Romance word order (with *ville-* and *court-* at the beginning of a word, for example Villemomble and Courgains) and the Germanic word order (*-ville* and *-court* placed at the end of the place-name) which eventually ousted it.

Thus, superimposed on the linguistic boundary, a sort of toponymic uniformity had grown up, spilling over into what had formerly been

Free Germany as well as into the heart of Roman Gaul. Its roots are neither directly in the Germanic tradition (to which, however, it owes a great deal including, almost everywhere, the syntactical construction of the place-names, as well as the personal names which everywhere form their basis) nor in the Gallo-Roman traditions (which seem to have provided the initial inspiration). The mould within which this uniformity was formed was unquestionably the Merovingian kingdom, together with its protectorates. Within this political structure a creative synthesis came into play, of much greater importance than the phenomenon of invasion and conquest, which was only responsible for the shifting of linguistic boundaries.

A last insight into this new civilization is offered by the linguistic interactions. Those Gallo-Romans who did not adopt the Frankish language nevertheless borrowed important items of vocabulary from it. It would be hazardous to enumerate them, in so far as they are often terms which have fallen into disuse because they relate to ways of life or institutions which died out a long time ago, or are words which are now to be found only in dialects. But the contribution was a considerable one, of the order of at least 500 words.[25] It is certain that the destruction of the educational system on the one hand, and the rapid phonetic development of Vulgar Latin on the other, ensured that the language was in a receptive state during the first few generations after the conquest. The doors seem to have swung shut again before the Carolingian era, but in spite of the centuries which have elapsed since then, French as it is spoken today would be inconceivable without these Frankish contributions.

The borrowings naturally include an extensive vocabulary connected with the new institutions (*sénéchal; maréchal* = marshal, *échanson* = cup-bearer; *chambellan* = chamberlain; *antrustion* = royal follower; *aubain* = non-naturalized foreigner; *rachimbourg* = member of a jury of legal advisers; *échevin* = municipal magistrate; *maimbourg* = legal guardian or executor; *plège* = pledge; *namp* = bail; *essoine* = excuse for absence; *ordalie* = ordeal; *alleu* = allod; *fief; trève* = truce; *arrière-ban* = summons of the royal followers for war, etc.) and with warfare (*garder* = to guard; *guetter* = to lie in wait for; *épier* = to spy; *gonfanon* = banner; *fourreau* = scabbard; *dard* = dart or javelin; *flèche* = arrow; *blason* = blazon or coat of arms; *étrier* = stirrup, etc.). But there are also many terms of greater significance, in view of the extent of their influence: names of parts of the body (such as *hanche* = hip; *échine* = spine; *flanc* = flank or side; *quenotte* = tooth, in nursery language), names of colours (such as *blanc, brun, bleu, gris* and *blafard* = pallid or wan), names of the four points of the compass (although these did not come into general use until after the linguistic reinforcement afforded by the arrival of the Scandinavians in Normandy), names of plants and the like (such as *hêtre* = beech; *troène* = privet; *roseau* = reed; *houblon* = hops; and *haie* = hedge), and finally agricultural terms (like *blé* = corn; *gerbe* = sheaf; *bouc* = he-goat and *fourrage* = fodder, etc.).

In this respect, although the Franks contributed much they took little in return. Not that borrowings from Latin are lacking in the Germanic languages, but most of them go back to before the Merovingian era and are due to the contact between civilians and soldiers all along the *limes*.

An important factor may be overlooked if one concentrates on the vocabulary alone: in many respects it is not fair to compare Latin with Frankish. Latin was a written language with the strength of its literary, epigraphic and religious tradition behind it; Frankish was only a spoken language—there is hardly a single runic text in this dialect—without any special prestige (unlike Gothic), and without religious support. The Frankish aristocracy in Gaul was aware of this situation: it made no effort to write Frankish down or to provide it with a literature of its own. Only brief legal formulae have been recorded in writing; even before the time of Clovis, Frankish kings chose Latin when writing about personal matters, and it was in Latin that Chilperic attempted to appear educated. The idea of hoisting the language of the conquerors up to the level of that of their subjects only took shape under the Carolingians.

AN ATTEMPTED ASSESSMENT: REGIONAL VARIATIONS

The degree of Germanic influence differed widely from one region to another within the former Roman Empire. There is almost none in Africa and the Mediterranean islands, and it is weak in the south of Spain and the region of Rome, but of major importance everywhere else.

Almost nothing is left to indicate that the Vandals ever ruled Tunisia and eastern Algeria, apart from the texts themselves: not a word of their language, and not a single place-name. A very small number of inscriptions, especially funerary ones, has saved a handful of individuals from oblivion, but we have not a single official document or law formulated by the Vandals. Burials and jewellery are remarkably rare. Probably the Islamic conquest was partly responsible for this oblivion; it was able to wipe out all that was perishable in the legacy of the past more thoroughly than any other conquest. However it did not destroy the archaeological remains which are just as abundant for the Byzantine period as for the Roman, both before and after the Vandal occupation. We are forced to the conclusion, therefore, that the Vandals contributed almost nothing to civilization in North Africa. In Sicily, and to a lesser extent in Corsica and Sardinia, Islam has also swept much away: the brief appearances of the Goths and the Vandals on these islands do not seem to have left anything tangible behind.

In the Iberian peninsula the influence of the Visigoths and the Sueves falls into two distinct phases, the watershed being the conversion of Reccared in 587. Until then the presence of Germans had not changed anything essential in the Hispano-Roman way of life; it was only after the conversion that the Visigoths and Sueves were incorporated indissolubly into Spanish historical tradition.

During the first period the presence of the Visigoths and Sueves was primarily a military fact. They were in fairly compact settlements, the Sueves on the Atlantic coast around Braga and the Goths on the northern part of the Meseta, in the present-day *campos góticos;* over the rest of the peninsula they were represented only by a few soldiers and a handful of civil servants. Separated from the Hispano-Roman population by their Arianism, by the prohibition of mixed marriages and probably by having their own legal code, they contented themselves with governing for their own profit a country which does not seem to have been particularly interested in them. The Visigoths may have had their own intellectual culture (although nothing is known of the fate of the language of Ulfila in Spain), and they certainly had their own way of life and distinct style of dress which are confirmed by the burials and jewellery, but the Hispano-Romans refused to be influenced by them. After 554 a community of Romans in the south and south-east was able to escape from Visigothic rule for two generations and, on rejoining the Iberian community, they found their compatriots unchanged. Most of the institutions which were later to underline the individuality of the kingdom of Toledo among the kingdoms which had succeeded to the Western Empire had not yet taken shape.

After 587 the Visigoths are the only Germanic people in Spain who need to be taken into consideration. Their conversion to Catholicism immediately won them favour. Among the Hispano-Roman aristocracy under Reccared and Sisebut there are glimpses of 'the awareness and the willingness necessary for a creative synthesis' which soon resulted in concrete achievements: the intellectual renaissance of the time of Isidore, the drawing up of the seventh-century law-codes, the creation at the very heart of the kingdom of the unique Councils of Toledo, and finally the birth of a new doctrine of kingship, based on royal unction.[26] If the Visigothic kingdom had been destroyed before 587 it would have left nothing to posterity; when the destruction finally came in 711 Visigothic Spain bequeathed to Europe several of the fundamental ideas on which medieval civilization was built. There is no question but that the Romano-Byzantine elements far outnumber the Germanic elements in this synthesis: Leovigild had already symbolically abandoned Gothic costume in favour of that of a Byzantine prince, and the Iberian revivals, especially in the north, played a greater part in the artistic field than the barbarian influences. But Hinojosa and Sánchez-Albornoz have shown the importance of the Germanic elements in institutional development: *gardingi* who formed the royal *comitatus*, *saiones* who ensured that orders were carried out, and finally traditions of private law (but this point is disputed; see p. 209). Until the eleventh century the Spain of the Reconquest fed on memories of the Catholic kingdom of Toledo and reverently gathered up and preserved the shreds of their Germanic inheritance. Although Hispano-Portuguese vocabulary and place-names admitted very few Germanic words—probably less than forty—the peninsula welcomed the new personal names with the same enthusiasm as Gaul. Apart from a few Ibero-Basque names, Germanic names completely dominated medieval Spain.

The cultural synthesis which came about within the kingdom of Toledo was of much greater intrinsic value than that which emerged within the Merovingian kingdom, but the isolationism of Gothic Spain during the last century of its existence, followed by the catastrophe of 711, prevented it from having the same immediate impact. The two kingdoms were engaged in parallel attempts at synthesis quite independently of one another. Moreover the whole of the peninsula did not follow the example of Toledo: whereas former Suevian territory was rapidly won over, the Basque country retreated into complete isolation from which no force of arms could persuade it to emerge; and Baetica, in so far as we can glimpse its own distinct destiny before the Islamic conquest, was always less receptive to Germanic influences than to those which came from the East.

In Italy there were no less than three distinct phases of Germanic influence: firstly in the period of the fifth-century raids and of the domination of barbarian officers in the Roman army, the time of Odoacer; secondly in the period of the Ostrogoths; and finally under the Lombards. In some cases the effect of their influence was cumulative, while in others it cancelled itself out; and the intervening Byzantine phase in the sixth century helped to complicate the problem, for the army of Belisarius was just as barbarian in composition as that of his adversaries.

Of the first of these three phases there are no lasting traces, except for the ruins it left in its wake. The raids of the first few years of the fifth century had disastrously affected the countryside of central and northern Italy, and had encouraged endemic banditry. But many of the towns had escaped, and after a more or less prolonged period of reconstruction most of the others, like Milan (through which Attila had passed), were restored to their former appearance; the city that was damaged most was Rome. The Heruls, Skirians and Turcilingi who made up the people over whom Odoacer ruled were few in number, and their quarters, around Ravenna, Verona and Milan, were no more conspicuous than those of the barbarians in the service of Rome before 476. The events of 489–93 obliterated them completely.

The arrival of the Ostrogoths was far more significant. In the first place it was not a question of a *coup d'état* brought about from within the province, as in 476, but of a conquest. The north-east of Italy suffered grievously and this time immigration was on a much larger scale. Secondly, the personality of Theodoric gave the event a new significance: he wanted to be both the head of a model Romano-Gothic state and the moral leader of the Germans in the West. Of all those who attempted a Romano-barbarian synthesis, Theodoric was without doubt the most fully aware of what he was doing. The weakness of his plan was that it depended too much on a single man, and one with too little time at his disposal. However this did not prevent him from leaving an appreciable heritage in every field.

It was in the intellectual sphere that Theodoric obtained the most remarkable results: he encouraged both the development of a Latin culture loyal to the new order of things, and the birth of the earliest barbarian intellectual culture. Ulfila's Gothic was used by several authors, especially for religious purposes: fragments of a commentary on the gospel according to St. John have come down to us, called the *Skeireins*, some marginal notes and two charters. Almost all that we know about Gothic comes from Italian manuscripts (often palimpsests), though Ulfila's language was also used by the Goths of Egypt and probably by those of Aquitaine and Spain too. But the language soon disappeared, and documents written in Gothic were destroyed as being Arian. Other Goths used Latin, for example the obscure 'philosophers' Athanarit, Hildebald and Marcomir, quoted by the 'Cosmographer of Ravenna', and later the national historian Jordanes, who wrote after the triumph of Justinian but who was brought up within the culture developed under Theodoric. Admittedly these works are not very original: the *Skeireins* may have been a translation from the Greek, and Jordanes merely summarized Cassiodorus. Nevertheless the effort made by these writers is all the more remarkable in that it has the added desire of interesting the Romans in the history of the Goths— Ablabius (of whom we know nothing but the name) and Cassiodorus himself each wrote a *Getica* or History of the Goths.

In the field of politics the Arianism of the Goths and their situation as a minority group obliged them to adopt a policy of segregation. According to the administrative system of the Later Roman Empire, which had been preserved intact just as it had been in Roman times, the Goths were billeted along the north-eastern frontier, around Ravenna, on the plain of the Po and in Tuscany, under the jurisdiction of *comites Gothorum* who were directly answerable to the king. In the towns the Goths had their own separate quarters, around Arian churches. They probably kept their own law—of which not a trace has come down to us—as the Romans continued to have theirs, within the framework laid down by the royal edicts. Only the Goths were permitted to hold certain positions of command, particularly military ones. But what Theodoric proposed to both the Romans and the Goths was a common political ideal, the ideal expressed by his official stamp found on tiles (*Regnante Domino Nostro Theodorico bono Romae . . .*),[27] by his monumental inscriptions, like that on the Via Appia (*. . . rex Theodericus, . . . custos libertatis et propagator Romani nominis . . .*),[28] and by his letters to Cassiodorus, in which 'he prided himself on being the philosopher-king idealized by Plato'.[29] It was a purely Graeco-Roman ideal which he had hoped, over-optimistically as it turned out, the Goths would quickly come to accept.

On the material level Gothic influence continued to be limited. It is doubtful whether the Goths had time to change into an agricultural population. Two hoards of goldwork, those of Desana (Piedmont) and Reggio Emilia, and some pieces of jewellery show the Goths' participation in the broad trends of 'barbarian' art, but Germanic influence had no part in Theodoric's important buildings at Ravenna and Rome.

The linguistic traces of the Goths are slight, and difficult to distinguish from those of the Lombards. They are confined to a handful of place-names with the stem *Gothi*, and probably to some of the place-names in Lombardy which end in *-engo;* those Gothic words which have passed into Italian seem to be connected principally with practical life, and very few have to do with administrative, legal or military affairs, in which Lombard loan-words seem to have obliterated all previous borrowings.

The work of Theodoric was obviously part of the setting for the *captatio benevolentiae* which was directed towards the ruling classes, though it seems likely that he was sincere. His endeavours revived the policies of the fifth-century Gothic leaders—Gainas, Tribigild and Fravittas—who had tried to insinuate themselves into the Roman system in the East. Athaulf's declarations at Narbonne (cf. p. 183) reveal a similar ideal. This sustained effort by the Goths is probably to be explained by the seeds of culture left by the work of Ulfila, and by Gothic pride, whose ambition was to equal Rome.

Theodoric's experiment was not confined to Italy. Before the success of the Merovingians, for a shorter time but with a much greater breadth of vision, he influenced all the Germans in the West. Theodoric was astute enough to exploit the possibilities offered by the great trade route from Aquileia to the Baltic coast via Pannonia. His success may also have had artistic and technical results, for it is believed that Gothic Italy played a considerable part in the development of the ornamental style of sixth-century Scandinavia.

It is not our intention here to study Theodoric's diplomatic attempts to check the Frankish expansion, protect the Visigoths and Burgundians, and restrain the Vandals. He spread his diplomatic network into independent Germany, and took on many secondary peoples as clients: he adopted Rodulf, the petty king of the Heruls of Pannonia, paid the troops of a half-breed Gepid-Hun called Mundo, who was encamped in Moesia, took under his wing what remained of the Alamans of Raetia after their defeat by Clovis, and took Bavarians and the Varini of the lower Rhine under his protection, and even Norwegians also, if Jordanes is to be believed. In all probability if his work had been carried on by others, all of these peoples would have had access to Roman civilization in its purest, Italian, form, whereas what they inherited from the Franks was a much modified version of it. This policy explains Theodoric's subsequent popularity, unequalled by other barbarian kings, with the epic poets and even with Charlemagne, who had the equestrian statue of Theodoric transported from Ravenna to Aachen in 801.

At first the Lombards regarded Italy as a source of booty rather than as a place to set up a state, something which had not even occurred to them at that time. The impact of the first generation of Lombards in Italy was almost entirely negative. Few periods have been as black as the fifty years which separate the landing of Belisarius in 536 and the election of Authari in 584. At the end of it there was little left to salvage.

The settlement of the land really only started after political stability had been achieved. The Lombard armies (*exercitus*) put down roots on the land. Their leaders took the place of the vanished Roman aristocracy and became landowners; they surrounded themselves with free Lombard peasants and set the bulk of the Romans to work to maintain them, in conditions similar to those of the *coloni* of the Later Roman Empire. Very little is known about the details of this operation, but that it was widespread is unquestionable: the Romans lost all influence except inside Byzantine enclaves. Personal names quickly became almost entirely Lombard. Existing place-names were augmented by a flood of new names, especially in the region of Milan, in

Venetia and northern Tuscany, and around Spoleto. Administrative, legal and military terminology acquired new words: Italian still contains more than 300 Lombard words. Finally, in spite of the system of the personality of the laws, more rigorous in Italy than anywhere else, Lombard law rapidly gained the ascendancy in the Po valley and in Tuscany. The Lombard imprint was so strong that until the end of the ninth century northern Italy continued to be the *regnum Langobardorum* (it was not until 817 that a classicizing reaction revived the name of *regnum Italiae*), that southern Italy was called Longobardia right up to the expulsion of the Byzantines in the eleventh century, and that one of the northern provinces of Italy is still called Lombardy today. The Lombard phenomenon in the Po valley is similar to the Frankish phenomenon in northern Gaul, and may even have been more intense. But it was essentially a local phenomenon, and the kingdom of Pavia did not influence any of its neighbours except, briefly, Bavaria. With the Franks ranged against them, the Lombards continued to occupy the position of latecomers, frequently humiliated and constantly threatened.

The extent to which the Lombard kingdom kept its Germanic character poses some complex problems. The Lombard language, of which practically nothing is known except through legal expressions and personal names, must have been spoken until the eighth century, and some knowledge of it survived throughout the Carolingian era. But there were plenty of other Germans in Italy: a ninth-century formulary refers to Goths, Alamans, Bavarians and Burgundians. None of these had a written language, and the ruling class, although proud of its nationality, quickly acquired a veneer of Roman culture. Pavia was the centre: there noblemen and kings in the eighth century had verse epitaphs engraved for themselves which have no equivalent in the other countries of the West at that time.[30] Literary activity revived to a certain extent among the Milanese clergy at the end of the seventh century, and by the eighth century one can even talk of a renaissance. The Germanic character of the nobility, however, was reinforced by Bavarian and Alamannic elements, even after their final conversion to Catholicism in 671.

A famous text of Paul the Deacon describes the massacre of Roman noblemen and the sharing out of the survivors as *hospites* paying tribute to the Lombards (cf. p. 92). Place-names like Fara Vicentina, Fara Novarese and Fara in Sabina show that over a large part of the north and centre of Italy the Lombard settlements were made on the basis of family or military groups called *fara*. There are signs suggesting the existence of colonies of *arimanni* (freemen liable for military service) at strategic points, for example at Friuli and at the entrances to Alpine passes. Archaeological distribution maps show continuous bands of

F

finds of Lombard type right along the foot of the Alps from Trieste to Piedmont, along the Via Emilia and in Umbria, but obviously it is impossible to say whether Romans adopted Lombard styles or not. Artistic influence is confined to a type of cloisonné jewellery with zoomorphic decoration, and is strongly rivalled by oriental influences, particularly Syrian and Coptic ones.

In order to form an unbiased judgment of the attitude of the Lombards to *Romanitas* one must bear in mind their political and military position, which was almost constantly being threatened from Ravenna or from beyond the Alps: treason was always within easy reach of their Roman subjects. Moreover, the Arian problem in Italy was, if not more acute, at any rate more long-lived than elsewhere. The Lombards could only keep themselves in power by behaving more brutally than most other Germanic conquerors. It must not be forgotten, either, that they prevented other still more menacing peoples from having access to Italy. They held the *limes* of the Isonzo against Avars and Slavs, whereas Roman civilization in Illyria, which had been entrusted to Byzantine protection, collapsed.

It is difficult to take in the whole of Merovingian Gaul at a glance, for it was not the creation of the Frankish people alone. In the middle of the sixth century the Merovingians fell heir to the Burgundian kingdom; they managed this inheritance in a very conservative way without diminishing the vigour of Burgundian 'nationality' in the slightest. The Burgundian aristocracy continued to occupy posts of command and even the royal dynasty survived, as one of its members is mentioned in 613. However the Franks badly mismanaged what they inherited from the Visigoths after the battle of Vouillé in 507, for the Visigoths were Arians and continued to be their enemies from outside the Frankish kingdom. The ruling class and most of the defeated people managed to reach Spain; not a single Goth found a place among the Merovingian aristocracy (although after the reconquest of Septimania from the Muslims in the eighth century Goths did join the Frankish ruling class, as in the case of St. Benedict of Aniane). Nevertheless a few Arians stayed on in Aquitaine; although they became nominal Catholics, their loyalty to Catholicism was still a matter of concern in 541. Between 640 and 647 an act of Sigibert III mentions a group of Goths in Rouergue, and the survival of personal names suggests that this group was not unique. Provence continued to be a sort of Roman state in personal union with the Merovingian kingdoms; until the eighth century the Franks allowed it considerable freedom in the running of its own affairs. Alamannia, Thuringia and Bavaria (in the periods when it was subject to the Franks) enjoyed an even greater degree of independence. Even within northern Gaul the former

Tractus Armoricanus was not entirely subject to the political system that had governed the countries first conquered. Finally there were several small groups of Germans who preserved their individuality for quite a long time, such as the Taifals of Poitou, the Saxons of the Bessin and the Sueves of Courtrai.

In spite of all this a common national name, borrowed from the Franks alone, slowly came to be applied to all of these peoples and regions: *Francia*. The authors of late Antiquity used it to mean the region of Germany occupied by the Franks, but from the middle of the sixth century on it was being used to describe the northern part of Gaul, which had effectively been taken over by the Franks, and later, in the writings of certain authors outside Gaul such as Gregory the Great, it meant the whole of the Merovingian kingdom. It was not until the eighth century that this usage was generally accepted and that *Francia* ceased to be used to mean northern Gaul as opposed to *Aquitania*: new terms—*Austrasia* and *Neustria*—had been coined for the regions north of the Loire.[31]

Until roughly the end of the seventh century or the beginning of the eighth, the population of Gaul continued to be very aware that it was composed of two separate entities: the *Romani* and the *barbari* (although the latter term fell into disfavour as early as the time of Dagobert, as it had gradually come to have the meaning of 'pagan'). All the biographies of eminent people take great pains to say exactly to which of these two groups their forebears belonged—even if they themselves were born of mixed marriages—and, should the occasion arise, to which of the 'barbarian' peoples they were attached. Later this awareness declined, or to be more exact the distinction fell within the competence of lawyers, who continued to insist on its importance until the ninth century, at least in Burgundy and in the south. (There are hardly any traces of the *professio legis* in northern Gaul, whereas there *are* traces of it in Septimania, which had been Gothic, right up until the tenth century.) In the seventh and eighth centuries 'ethnic' nationality was replaced by a sense of 'regional' nationality: one was an Austrasian, a Neustrian, a Burgundian or an Aquitanian rather than simply a Frank or a Roman. Probably Germanic elements at the time of the invasions had something to do with the formation of these attitudes; equally, their success is indicative of the successful fusion of the two groups.

Examined in detail, this rather broad and superficial survey has to be modified somewhat. *Romanus* still had an 'ethnic' meaning later on in Raetia and Aquitaine; in the latter area, towards the end of the Merovingian period, it sometimes took on a 'regional' sense, and was used as a synonym for Aquitanian. The Bretons were not involved in the fusion. At the beginning of the eighth century an aggressive but non-German people—the Basques—played an increasingly important part in Aquitaine: many sources call the inhabitants of the country to the south of the Garonne *Vascones*, and the area comes to be known as *Vasconia* or Gascony.[32]

At the level of the ruling classes a real unity, founded on a common way of life and material culture, and sealed by a common faith and numerous cases of intermarriage, came into being from the end of the sixth century on, affecting not only 'Franks' but also 'Burgundians', 'Romans' and other groups that had been allowed some semblance of power, for example some Saxons and Alamans, and a very small number of Thuringians.

At the root of this lay the adoption by the Germanic upper classes of the life-style of the Gallo-Roman landowners. This has been the subject of detailed studies by Bergengruen [no. 393] and Sprandel [no. 415]. The royal fisc, which was extremely rich (apart from the Roman fisc, it had taken over all unoccupied or confiscated lands), distributed hundreds of villae among the Frankish aristocracy in the sixth century, and even more in the seventh century. It seems that under Clovis and his sons the ruling class had been unsettled and mobile, assigned to this or that region according to the needs of the royal service, without any direct links with the Frankish rural colonization which was then developing. (Hence the impossibility of establishing links between the name which forms the first part of the countless place-names ending in *-villa, -curtis, -ingen* or *-heim* and the great families of the Merovingian period mentioned in the texts.) Later the kings made it possible for them to put down roots by conferring on them large estates, thus avoiding the necessity of continuing to pay them. In most of the saints' lives of the seventh and eighth centuries the ancestors of the heroes, who were almost all of noble descent, seem to have settled only relatively recently in their present region. This change in their way of life was undoubtedly prompted by the example of the Gallo-Roman aristocracy. At any rate the new ruling class was not averse to making use of property laws of completely Roman origin. The villae of the Frankish landowners seem to have been organized on the same lines as in the time of the Roman landowners, even though in the north of Gaul there had never been a *foedus* to ensure legal continuity. Lastly, the estates of the Frankish leaders were just as widely scattered as those of the senators had been; the property of an otherwise unknown couple, Vandemir and Ercamberta, which was distributed by them in about 690 in pious gifts, was scattered over thirteen *pagi* from Beauvaisis to Maine and Quercy.

There is small point in giving numerous examples of intermarriage between the two branches of the aristocracy. One will suffice: already by the middle of the fifth century, and hence well before the time of

Clovis, St. Medard was born at Noyon of a Frankish father and a Roman mother.

Not much is known about the various stages in the process of economic and social unification in the lower ranks of society. In the towns where the population was already fairly mixed, containing Syrians and Jews for example, the Frankish element was probably just one more minority group which was quickly assimilated. In the country areas archaeology has only been able to confirm two facts: immediately after the conquest the existence of more than one cemetery in any given place is rare; and in the eighth century the universal grouping of tombs around churches shows that the process of fusion must have been completed a long time before. Whatever their ancestry, all the inhabitants of northern Gaul now thought of themselves as Franks.

Intellectual factors played only a very small part in this fusion. It was within the framework of a general lack of culture, rather than in the bosom of a new culture, that the long-established inhabitants and the newcomers finally came to live in harmony. In this respect the Merovingian kingdom continued to be singularly backward compared with the Gothic kingdoms. The more Romanized south of Gaul kept up a certain level of cultural activity, as witness the continued output of charters and other legal documents and the comparative wealth of inscriptions. Only the south still had schools open to the laity until about the seventh century, and it was the south which produced nearly all the men of letters, a good number of bishops and a fair number of works of art, particularly sarcophagi and capitals. Rather than dwell on the regional variations of the Germano-Roman fusion, we would simply point out that in Provence the Merovingians preserved some of the Ostrogothic administrative machinery; that in Aquitaine in 677-8 Poitiers was the last refuge of municipal life in the Roman manner, and Tours, Bourges, Clermont, Limoges and Bordeaux, together with Poitiers, were the last strongholds of the senatorial aristocracy; and that in Burgundy the ruling class clung to its Roman traditions for a long time, even though the majority of the population had adopted the barbarian way of life. It was precisely the south of Gaul which had escaped direct action on the part of the Franks. In the north things were very different:[33] it is only at the end of the sixth century that one finds here and there a handful of aristocrats who were interested in intellectual matters, and dared to write a few lines of poetry or some stilted letters, following the example of Chilperic, king of Neustria. There is nothing to indicate a desire to preserve and defend the legacy of Antiquity in the manner of Cassiodorus or Isidore of Seville, nor any wish to create a barbarian culture. What we are dealing with is simply a very insipid conformism which never attempts to break out of its narrow confines. In spite of his pure Roman descent, Gregory of Tours had only a superficial knowledge of the liberal arts, and his attempt to compose a national history for the Franks is not at all comparable to that of Jordanes. He says practically nothing about Frankish traditions before their first appearance in classical historiography in the whole of his long book, and he neither quotes nor uses more than four Frankish words (apart from proper names), fewer than Fortunatus, who was brought up at Ravenna!

CONCLUSION

Around 600, just when Christian Europe was getting its breath back, its whole balance was changed. The classical world had centred on the Mediterranean, and until around 550 the first few generations of barbarian kingdoms which resulted from the invasions had not changed this fundamental fact. The West continued to be dominated by the kingdoms created by the Eastern Germans on the shores of the Mediterranean or in their immediate vicinity. What the Anglo-Saxons had achieved in Britain and the Franks had done in northern Gaul was still of little significance, for these were countries which were traditionally of only marginal importance. But in the middle of the sixth century all this was changed. Justinian destroyed the states of Theodoric and Genseric without replacing them with anything of value, while the son and grandson of Clovis more than doubled the extent of his kingdom by incorporating regions whose traditional importance was considerable (one has only to think of the role of Lyons or Arles during the Later Roman Empire). At the same time most of what had formerly been Free Germany, which had hitherto obstinately rejected the attractions of the Mediterranean world, now found itself within the framework of a state whose seat was in former Roman territory. The centre of gravity of the West was transferred to north of the Loire and the Alps, where it was to remain for a very long time. This shift of emphasis in a very real sense marks the watershed between the classical world and the Middle Ages.[1] No doubt the invasions were only partly responsible for it—since at first they had respected the *status quo ante*—but without them the conditions indispensable for this upheaval would never have developed.

Part Two

Unsolved Problems and Subjects for Further Research

Introduction : The Work Still to be Done on the Sources

In spite of the rarity or obscurity of the sources, there is still a considerable amount of work to be done for the fullest use to be made of those that are available. The historian of the invasions has no reference books to help him comparable to those to which the classical historian refers daily: there is no corpus of inscriptions, no *Prosopography*, no *Realenzyklopädie*, nor even an equivalent of the *Thesaurus*. A few works in progress will go some way towards filling in these gaps, like the *Prosopographia imperii christiani*[1] or the *Nouveau Du Cange*. The time is not ripe for broad syntheses; critical reference works, even if incomplete, are what is badly needed.

The most urgent work to be done is in the field of epigraphy. A century ago classical historians learned not to commit themselves without consulting monumental inscriptions; the medieval historian, however, almost always neglects them. This disparity is difficult to condone. It is true that from the fifth century on inscriptions become extremely rare, and in most cases their content is of an exclusively personal nature, but detailed study almost always manages to extract from them some contribution to history in general. An excellent example is afforded by the works of Christian Courtois, whose great synthesis, *Les Vandales et l'Afrique* [no. 233], is based on a critical inventory of African inscriptions (appendix II, pp. 365–8). In another work he has revised a section of Merovingian chronology by using inscriptions from Lyons.[2]

Before epigraphic evidence can be used it must be assembled in critical editions. Scholarship is conspicuously backward in this respect. Nothing serious has been done in France for the last eighty years; other countries, Spain in particular, have done rather better, but one must not be misled by the list of titles given in the general bibliography [nos. 1–12], as nearly all of these works are in need of revision. No doubt the best thing would be to draw up good inventories on a local or regional basis, like that of Gose for Trier [no. 4], before undertaking general corpora. Simultaneously, specialized studies of the formulae and the palaeography of these inscriptions ought to be made.[3] Historians should be encouraged as much as possible to explore the possibilities of this fruitful field of research.

155

F*

The study of archaeological sources is somewhat more advanced, although many inventories were drawn up before archaeology became a science, at a time when knowledge of chronology and typology was still rudimentary and, more important, when the quest for objects to put in one's collection took precedence over the detailed observation of their context, without which a find loses its essential value.[4] The *Manuel des Fouilles* by E. Salin [no. 306] and to a lesser extent his *Civilisation Mérovingienne* [no. 308] warn against such mistakes. One can keep abreast of technical progress by reading the excellent *Revue archéologique de l'Est et du Centre-Est* (Dijon), but it is not within the competence of this book to teach the difficult art of how to direct an excavation.

Even a well-directed and well-published excavation is only the first step. It provides evidence whose true significance is only realized in works of synthesis. These should be of two kinds, of which typological syntheses are unquestionably the more important. The geographical and chronological extent of a given type of object, decorative motif or building plan, and any variations thereof, must be established. Good examples of this kind of research will be found in the works of Denise Fossard.[5] Regional synthesis is a much more delicate task, demanding real skill in the appreciation of complex evidence; it can only be undertaken when general research has reached a fairly advanced state. As an example of regional synthesis we may cite Kurt Böhner's work on the region of Trier [no. 409]. But in the meantime critical catalogues of published finds or those preserved in museums are of inestimable value.[6] In any case, we must insist on the fundamental importance of precise mapping of types and finds. An important mouthpiece of German archaeological research is devoted to this particular facet: *Archaeologia Geographica* (Hamburg, since 1950).

Archaeologists have not developed all the branches of their discipline to the same extent. The sites which have been most exploited have been cemeteries, and they have placed at our service innumerable precedents and tried and tested techniques, but almost everywhere the study of early medieval settlement sites (together with ancillary subjects such as the study of domestic pottery) is still in its infancy.

In Gaul only the Rhineland, in its broad sense, has ceased to be *terra incognita;* England is more advanced, thanks in part to its periodical *Medieval Archaeology*. The monumental archaeology of the barbarian period has just begun to adopt truly scientific methods; in France this is particularly thanks to the influence of the works of Jean Hubert.[7] Only Italy has compiled a systematic regional catalogue of the sculptures of the early Middle Ages.[8] This kind of work should be carried out for the whole of the West. Even without spectacular discoveries— though these are becoming more and more frequent owing to the ever-increasing volume of road building and public works—the historian may expect to enlarge his knowledge very considerably by the rational use of archaeological material.[9]

The literary sources themselves are still in sore need of cataloguing and synthesis. The innovations in the works of Pierre Courcelle[10] are worth studying in this respect. They would be difficult to emulate, but the cataloguing of texts relating to a precise subject still has a great deal to teach us.[11] There are many discoveries to be made in the hagiographical sources,[12] and the study of vocabulary itself can be very informative. Although some research has already been done on the legal side, the field of the history of ideas has only just begun to be explored, particularly under the influence of the Dutch scholar Christine Mohrmann, for the patristic period. It would be worthwhile extending this work. We have given a rough idea in each section of this book of the words which designate the various barbarian peoples. It is incredible that this problem has not yet been the subject of any really serious synthesis. This gives some idea of the immensity of the field still left to be explored.

6 General Problems

THE ORIGINS OF THE 'BARBARISM' OF THE EARLY MIDDLE AGES

'Barbarian Invasions' or *'Migrations of Peoples'?*

Invasions barbares or *Völkerwanderung*: French and German medievalists have always disagreed on this question of terminology. The debate is essentially pointless, but it must be mentioned.

The word 'barbarian' is inherited from the Greek. In the eyes of the Greeks anyone who did not share their language, customs or civilization was a barbarian, even if he belonged to a highly civilized empire like that of Persia. This concept was taken up by the bilingual Empire of the Romans in its turn: now anyone who shared neither Greek nor Roman culture was a barbarian. The term 'barbarians', then, simply means foreigners who have not been assimilated. Certainly the term is not flattering: the Empire thought too highly of itself to have any respect for foreigners. But it is not pejorative, and this is borne out by the fact that the invaders, after having triumphed over Rome, sometimes referred to themselves by this term on their own initiative, for want of a better generic word. Thus, to say that the invasions of the fifth century were 'barbarian' invasions is tautological, the stating of a self-evident fact—that the Empire had been invaded from outside.

The history of the word *barbarus* during the course of the early Middle Ages has still to be written.[1] The term must be studied in relation to its antithesis, *Romanus*, the legal nuances of which have received particular attention; there are also religious nuances, for *Romanus* means 'Catholic' in the Arian kingdoms.[2] Derivatives such as *barbaricum opus* (goldwork), and *barbaricarius* (goldsmith, or weaver who works with gold thread)[3] and composite place-names would also have to be taken into account, as well as synonyms like *gentes*.

We must not overlook the convenience of the concept of 'the barbarian' for historians in Antiquity, for it relieved them of the necessity of pondering on the diversity of their enemies. Nevertheless, in the fourth century the acute mind of Ammianus Marcellinus perceived that the well-organized Sassanian empire resembled the Roman Empire much more than it did the Germanic tribes or the horsemen of the steppes; he therefore refused to treat the Persians as barbarians. Later, after the watershed of the fifth and sixth centuries, we see the word *barbarus* being used in the Germanic kingdoms to denote a foreigner, even if he were another German. Thus for Theodoric *barbari* are people who are neither Romans nor Goths; and the *Lex Salica* uses the term for people who are neither Romans nor Franks. A little later the Franks and Burgundians are referring to themselves as *barbari* and finally, in the seventh century, the meaning of the word shifts towards the religious sense of 'non-Christian German' or 'pagan', or becomes clearly pejorative.[4]

Parallel with the history of the word, the history of the idea has been skilfully described, within a very wide context but with special reference to the Far East, by D. Sinor [no. 545]. There are two predominant concepts: the barbarian is an anarchist, a promoter of disorder, of ἀκοσμία, and he ignores even the common decencies. But 'barbarian' and 'civilized' are complementary ideas: civilization, which is by nature egocentric, cannot be defined without the foil of the barbarian world. These pertinent remarks do not hold good, however, beyond the fifth century: all we know for certain is that Salvian's attempted rehabilitation of the barbarian had hardly any influence.

The period of the early Middle Ages, then, is barbarian precisely to the extent that it is not purely and simply a continuation of the classical world. The object of this section is to throw light on the sources of this 'barbarism'.

The term 'invasions' still remains to be justified. It implies an idea of violence which offends the modern heirs of the Germans, and it obscures the fact that the most widespread intermingling—that which took place outside the *limes*—was often peaceful. It also lays too much stress on an initial stage of the advance at the expense of the permanent settlements which followed it and which were of much greater importance. It would probably be better, therefore, to speak of 'migrations'.

Invasion was only a preliminary aspect of a much more far-reaching phenomenon: the actions and reactions thrown up by the violent clash between radically different societies, the Roman having reached full maturity, even a state of sclerosis, and the barbarian appreciably more primitive, but in the process of evolving with almost explosive rapidity. The invasion itself, which was merely a military event, was confined to a few years, whereas our subject extends over several generations and involves all spheres of social life.

It goes without saying that the social aspects of the barbarian phenomenon are infinitely more important than the ethnic or linguistic aspects, although modern scholars, steeped in concepts which would have been totally alien to the fifth and sixth centuries, have been more interested in the latter. The disparity between the two cultures attracted much attention from contemporaries, whether they were hostile or sympathetic towards the newcomers. In his *De gubernatione Dei* Salvian, as a theorist, dwells on social and moral virtues—justice, humanity and chastity, contrasting the barbarians, whom he praises, with the officials of the Empire, whom he detests. Conversely, in *Carmina XII* Sidonius Apollinaris revenges himself on the Burgundians, whose rule he must endure, by satirizing their dress, their hair-styles and their cuisine. Language as such did not interest the disciples of the classical literary tradition except when it was that of good Greek and Latin authors. If they mention the language of the Germans at all, it is to describe it as raucous, hideous or incomprehensible, or at most to insert some well-chosen Germanic word here and there in their work for the sake of local colour. Not a single contemporary seems to have had any clear idea of the linguistic unity of the Germanic world. The name *Germani* was only applied to the peoples between the linguistic frontier and the Elbe; nobody thought of extending it to the Goths, the Burgundians or the Scandinavians.[5]

Moreover, if the Romans felt very strongly that from the social point of view the barbarian world formed a whole, for their part the barbarians rarely shared this opinion. Theodoric seems to have been almost the only one to think of the idea—which coincided with his most immediate interests—of political solidarity among the Germans in the West, particularly among Arian Germans. The idea of religious unity within Arianism occurred to several writers,[6] but that is all. 'Every man for himself' was the principle which was applied everywhere, and to the eyes of civilized people it was a typically 'barbarian' principle.

Indigenous and Imported Barbarian Culture

A fundamental problem, and one very difficult to solve, is posed by the indigenous revivals—the reappearance of a way of life, with its art, languages and institutions, which had flourished before the Roman conquest and had been temporarily eclipsed by it, but which now re-emerged thanks to the invasions, with the general collapse of the superimposed classical structure. 'Barbarism' did not only come from outside; it could also be the result of conservatism, of deep-rooted continuity with the pre-Roman past. This is being asserted more and more frequently, particularly by archaeologists, but to distinguish between these two converging types of 'barbarism', whose point of fusion is often hidden from us by the superimposed classical or Christian culture, is a very difficult task.

Certain facts are clear, such as the revival of ethnic and political awareness among indigenous elements of the population from Gascony to Cantabria which gave birth to the Basque people. Romanization had not penetrated very far in this area (the inscriptions in the Pyrenees include an abnormal number of indigenous names, both divine and human); what is curious, and even mysterious, is that it should have been totally obliterated during some vague period between the fourth century and the eighth. It has been suggested—probably correctly, though there is no actual proof—that the revolt of the Spanish Bacaudae in Tarazona about 449 was an early manifestation of Basque nationalism.[7] In any case it is quite certain that from the end of the fifth century onwards the Basques zealously and ceaselessly resisted the centralizing efforts of the Visigothic government. Their resistance was continued after the Moorish invasion, and was extended north of the Pyrenees from the eighth century by the chronic bad feeling between the Gascons and the Frankish kingdom. We need not stop to ask here which of the pre-Roman elements of the Iberian peninsula the forebears of the Basques belonged to (although the evidence seems to suggest that they were Iberians). Only the result is important: the lasting obliteration of *Romanitas* achieved without any direct help from the invaders.

The revival of Berber aggression in North Africa can be classed under the same heading.[8] The Vandals failed to control part of Numidia and all of Mauretania, which had been within the *limes* in the fourth century. Although these regions were never occupied by the Vandals, they were prevented from continuing to be truly Roman by their remoteness and by the severing of maritime communications. This abandonment of part of Africa is obviously connected with the advance of the nomads, but it is hard to know which was cause and which effect. The disintegration of the system of policing the desert gave free rein to the nomads, who in their turn made life impossible for settled peoples, whose counter-measures—notably the fortification of farms—proved insufficient and ineffective. The towns could defend themselves, but lost their *raison d'être* once the settled rural life around them had disappeared. We can just refer in passing to two economic questions to which adequate answers have not yet been found. Firstly, to what extent was a deterioration of the climate responsible for the advance of the nomads? Secondly, how much did the increasing use of the camel contribute to the growing aggressiveness of the nomadic tribes? This factor is probably much more important than the first.[9]

We must also mention the vigorous Celtic expansion which took place about the same time in Britain (see Chapter 4) and possibly in Armorica too. In all, this phenomenon probably affected one-fifth of the territory which made up the Western Empire, but as the sources do not mention it we are always tempted to underestimate it, since it is only through its negative consequences that we are aware of it at all.

Moreover, the tendency was much more general than the meagre linguistic evidence would lead us to believe. In spite of the lack of precise studies the similarities between provincial Gallo-Roman art and Romanesque art are often pointed out, particularly with regard to sculpted figures in the round. The hiatus may appear to be over-long, but in Spain Gomez Moreno has established that the horseshoe arch in Visigothic, and later in Mozarabic, churches, and finally in mosques, ultimately goes back to Ibero-Roman art. The roulette decoration on Merovingian pottery carries on Gallo-Belgic traditions inherited from the La Tène period. In Provence the establishment of settlements on hilltops which had been *oppida* in pre-Roman times seems to be part of the same phenomenon, for of the regions of the West, Provence was least affected by the invasions. The general triumph of the village over the Roman villa owes a great deal to the survival of indigenous hamlets of Gallic type despite the redistribution of the land after Julius Caesar. We have dealt elsewhere (p. 135) with those facets of the funerary practices of Merovingian Gaul that seem to be due to indigenous tradition.[10]

This gives some indication of the broad scope of the problem, which is one of the least known, though probably one of the most important, of the early Middle Ages. It crops up again and again, even in political history: the regionalism of north-western Gaul in the fifth century could be to some extent the result of a revival of local feeling, as the return to favour of Armorica, the Celtic name for the region, would seem to imply. It would be unwise to generalize, but in attempting to draw up a balanced account of the invasions one must avoid the pitfalls, on the one hand, of concentrating exclusively on the continuity of typically Roman elements and, on the other, of crediting the immigrant Germans with all aspects of the new civilization which are obviously alien to the Roman world.

Barbarians Within the Roman Empire Before the Invasions

It would be quite incorrect to attribute all the Germanic cultural features in the former Roman Empire to the 'great' invasions (those which came after 406). The progressive 'barbarization' of the Later Roman Empire is well known, but it is necessary to emphasize how deep-seated and far-reaching were its effects.

The army was the most efficient agent in this preliminary infiltration, at both the highest and the lowest levels of society. At the top there were the countless high-ranking barbarian officers, to be found everywhere, especially after the reign of Theodosius.[11] At the bottom, the policy of recruiting barbarian prisoners to repopulate, under the eye of the army, regions which other barbarians had devastated goes back at least as far as the time of Marcus Aurelius, who applied it to the Marcomanni in the Po valley.[12] It was first used in Gaul by Maximian in 287: the *foedus* which he contracted with Gennobaudes provided for the settlement of Frankish *coloni* between the Meuse and the Moselle. Constantine introduced barbarian farmers, among whom were some Chamavi and some Frisians, over the whole of Gaul and Belgica. Thus the problem of the *laeti* which we dealt with above (p. 122) arises again in connection with Gaul. Whatever conclusions may have been reached about its archaeological and legal aspects, the presence of numerous groups of Germans in the rural areas is incontestable.

Place-names can help to identify some of these settlements: *Sermaise* reveals the presence of Sarmatians, *Marmuigne*, *Marmannni*, *Alle- magne*, Alamans, and so on.[13] But settlements of exotic peoples are more likely to have attracted the attention of the local inhabitants than the settlements of familiar peoples like the Franks, and the problem is probably more complex than appears at first sight.[14] Are these names all collective ones? Is it not possible that an isolated individual could have given rise to them?

This practice of reconstructing devastated territories by means of deported prisoners, so alien to our way of thinking since the birth of nationalism, is as old as the world itself. It was common practice in the eastern empires from the Assyrians to the Persians. Its revival in Roman times is known to have set an example for others, including Byzantium, which practised it right up to its collapse.

This infiltration into the Empire, well before its collapse, set fashions whose popularity it would thus be wrong to attribute solely to the pres- tige of the conquerors. Honorius issued three edicts between 397 and 416 forbidding the wearing of barbarian fashions, like fur cloaks and long hair, inside cities; by this date it would probably have been a waste of time to forbid them in the country. Then we know, for example, that St. Genevieve of Paris, although born of Gallo-Roman parents, was given a purely Germanic name—*Genovefa*—well before the middle of the fifth century. These fashions may similarly have influenced more significant spheres of life, such as burial customs or legal practices. In effect the common law may have been partly Germanized before the barbarian conquest. If this were so, it would offer one solution to the dilemma of deciding whether Castilian customs originated in 'Roman vulgar law' or in 'Germanic law' (see p. 209). But the indignant resistance put up by the ruling classes, the only ones who have left us their opinions in writing, will prevent us from ever knowing the exact truth about Germanic infiltration of the Roman Empire.

Social Struggles and the Fight Against the Invader

In any period of invasion the same problem always crops up: to.what extent were external enemies helped from inside, intentionally or otherwise? Did the oppressed social classes take advantage of the situation to have their revenge? Did restless elements exploit the state of confusion for their own profit? And is it not possible that the destruction was caused just as much by outlaws as by the invaders?

The scale of the social movements that affected the Western Roman Empire in the fifth century is impressive.[15] They affected all regions, particularly Britain, western Gaul, the north of Spain and Africa. It is difficult to describe them in any detail, for the sources are both very laconic and lacking in objectivity.

Firstly there was undoubtedly a tremendous amount of banditry, which became more widespread each time the barbarians broke through the *limes*. From the end of the fourth century onwards the legal codes are filled with savage laws against brigands and their accomplices. Although in the Later Roman Empire civilians were normally forbidden to carry arms because of the government's constant dread of revolts, two edicts of 391 and 403 authorized them to take up arms for the purpose of hunting down *latrones publici*. The latter organized themselves into veritable guilds, buying young children to train in their trade (a practice which had to be forbidden in 409 and again in 451) and having their official channels for the disposal of stolen goods. To become a brigand was the most natural resort for anyone who was bankrupt or threatened by the law, or who simply wanted to 'get rich quick'.

At a different level there are those mysterious unsubdued people in Africa, the *circumcelliones*, a word which probably means 'people who prowl around storehouses'. Their motives were complex: rural unemployment and extreme poverty on the one hand, and religious fanaticism inspired by the Donatist heresy on the other, explain the violence of these bands of Berbers who helped to destroy the Roman order in a good part of Numidia after the middle of the fourth century.[16]

In Gaul and in the north of Spain we find a movement which is both social and political, that of the Bacaudae. Both the word and the phenomenon it describes appear to have been deeply rooted in the Celtic world of western Gaul, which was still relatively untouched by Roman influences. The tradition of the Bacaudic revolt went back to the third century, so that when it reappeared following the invasion of 406 it was nothing new, but after several temporary crises it suddenly became much more serious in 435. A certain Tibatto incited the malcontents from practically all over Gaul to an open rebellion which was clearly separatist in intention: *a romana societate discessit* (he left Roman society) as one chronicler puts it. (At this same time St. Germanus of Auxerre was pleading the cause of the Armoricans at Ravenna through legal channels.) When, after a great deal of difficulty, the revolt was put down in the area to the north of the Pyrenees, it immediately sprang up again in the south, in Tarraconensis, and continued until 443. A second phase came in 448: an intellectual, a doctor called Eudoxius, took over the leadership of a band of Bacaudae, was defeated, and took refuge with the Huns; in the following year a member of the Spanish Bacaudae killed the bishop of Tarazona, near Saragossa. It was not until 454 that this final revolt collapsed under the assaults of the Goths sent by Aetius. After that date the Bacaudae seem to have disappeared.[17]

What was the significance of this movement? Its social character is attested by the *Vita Germani* and by Salvian: it was an insurrection by the victims of the totalitarian oppression of the dying Empire, directed against tax officials and judges. There is nothing to indicate that peasants alone were involved. The phenomenon seems to have been very similar to the demonstrations of a desire for autonomy made by the towns of Britain during the same period, under the leadership of their local authorities (see Chapter 4).[18] It would be unwise to go further and see in the Bacaudae tendencies of a Priscillianist nature, or to suggest as some scholars have done that Pelagianism was behind the bid for autonomy in Britain.[19] As for cases of collusion between the Bacaudae and the barbarians, they occurred only incidentally and are offset by the clashes between them, which were at least as frequent.[20] The Bacaudae did however paralyse the forces defending the Empire from the barbarians on more than one occasion. Several factors explain their disappearance after 454, among them the weakening of the State and the slackening of its restraints, and the settling of the barbarians, particularly on the Loire, which dashed all hopes of a successful general rising.

The contribution made by social upheavals towards the destruction of the Roman order is thus firmly established, but it would be unjust to believe that there was conscious collaboration between the enemy within and the barbarians without. It would appear that the barbarians neither sought an alliance with these movements, nor even realized their true significance. The Vandal kings, even while they were locked in mortal combat with the Catholic ruling classes in Africa, did not approach the circumcellions for help. The Goths and the Alans saw in the Bacaudic revolt only an opportunity to hire out soldiers to Rome—

at a high price—for its repression. (Thompson [no. 198] believes that in the early years of their stay in Aquitaine the Visigoths were tempted to make common cause with the rural insurrections; according to him it was the rapid intervention of the patrician Constantius, who granted them the *foedus* in 418, that preserved the social order. This is possible, but the evidence is rather slight.) The only notable exception seems to have been Totila, the penultimate Ostrogothic king of Italy, who, at a time when his people no longer had anything to lose, carried on a 'spartacist' policy of helping slaves against their masters.[21] Totila failed, however, possibly thanks to the strength of the ties of patronage that existed between landowners and peasants. On the whole the Germans were conservative in social matters. The régime of *hospitalitas*, followed by their leaders' acquisition of vast landed properties, inevitably caused them to espouse the interests of the Roman aristocracy.

The fact that the invasions coincided with social upheavals and with several epidemics made a deep impression on contemporary writers, who were prepared by Christianity to look for signs warning of the end of the world. Literary evidence relating to the year 398 (the three hundred and sixty-fifth year after the Passion)[22] and to the sack of Rome in 410[23] has been collected together: the subject deserves to be treated as a whole, for it accounts for much of the defeatism which is so often expressed during the period. A rather exceptional representative of this feeling is Salvian, the priest from Trier who took refuge in Lérins and who castigates Rome and praises the barbarians in such an extraordinary way in his *De gubernatione Dei*.[24] Hidden beneath the often exasperating antitheses of this rhetorician is a mentality which was probably shared only by a minority, but which could explain more than one defection. By the fifth century it is no longer possible to say of the Christian masses that they were unwilling as a matter of principle to take part in the military defence of the Empire, but certain individuals were probably reluctant to commit themselves deeply to an Empire which corresponded so ill to the moral ideals of Christianity, and which seemed to be doomed by fate.

The great crisis of the Empire saw the defection of a large part of the ruling classes. The reasons for this are both numerous and complex. The growing importance in the lives of the aristocracy of service at court and of palace intrigues, at the expense of provincial commands, sapped the energy of local defences. The increasing affection of senators for their native districts came to eclipse the general sense of solidarity with other parts of the Empire. The repugnance felt by the well-born on finding themselves surrounded by the upstarts who officered the army, who were mostly of barbarian stock, also explains a great deal. But the responsibility was not all on one side, for the government, haunted by the fear of conspiracies, did everything possible to keep the aristocracy from active positions in public life. The system of honours in the fourth century caused the magistrates to spend vast sums for ostentatious purposes instead of on useful projects. No doubt the people of Rome benefited by it, but that had very little effect on public affairs, since the seat of power was no longer at Rome. During this period the State had to squeeze every last penny out of the *humiliores* in order to keep going. The family of Melania, the friend of St. Jerome, had an annual income of 12,000 pounds in gold, yet the Emperor did not manage to collect the 4,000 pounds it would have cost to maintain Alaric's army for three years, which would have prevented the sack of Rome. There was even legislation which forced the rich to be useless: there were few people who dared, like the writer Synesios of Cyrene, to break the law which forbade them to take up arms without imperial permission, even in cases of dire necessity.[25]

On the whole the aristocrats did fairly well out of their faintheartedness. Under the barbarian kings they continued to enjoy most of their privileges and a considerable portion of their wealth. It was only in Italy that they lost them, in the second half of the sixth century, as a result of not having preserved the same indifference during the wars among the Goths, Byzantines and Lombards. This attitude, which shocks modern sentiment, at least served to salvage something from the wreckage. Classical literature would doubtless have perished if aristocrats who took no direct part in the action had not exerted themselves to the utmost to preserve it, grouped around a Symmachus or a Macrobius, and had they not later passed on the torch to the monasteries to which they themselves, like Cassiodorus, often retired to forget their disappointments.

A régime of appalling social inequality, a political organization which for the previous two centuries had been based on constraint and suspicion, biased courts and laws of an absurd and ever-increasing savagery (in spite of the triumph of Christianity, atrocious penalties were becoming more and more common)—any of these would be sufficient to explain a deep disaffection even if the system had been efficient, which it was not; during its last years it functioned quite at random and went from disaster to capitulation. Great though the age-old prestige of Rome still was (the famous verses of Rutilius Namatianus show that it had survived the worst catastrophe, that of 410), it could no longer mask this incompetence. It was no longer thought sufficient to find scapegoats like Stilicho and Aetius. The idea of relying solely on oneself, rather than applying for aid through the traditional channels of the Roman world, was gaining ground in many provinces. There had been a foretaste of these regionalist reactions, which were only to be expected at a time of grave crisis, in the third century with the rebellions of Tetricus and Zenobia. In the fifth century they assumed less spectacular forms, and so have attracted hardly any attention from historians.

Regionalist reaction can best be seen in Africa, Gaul and Britain, where it took different forms at the various levels of society. At the top the aristocrats retired to their native districts and placed their affection for that region above their allegiance to Rome. The sentimental and literary aspects of this phenomenon are well known, but it also had political and institutional consequences: only Italians continued to sit in the senate at Rome, and the senatorial career no longer compelled young aristocrats to travel the length and breadth of the Mediterranean world.

The municipal aristocracy was even more receptive of centrifugal tendencies than the senators, and was more interested in local affairs than in what was going on in Rome. This climate of opinion favoured the Armorican and British movements. The Greek historian Zosimus had a very clear perception of what was happening in these regions, and of the connection between the two movements: 'The whole of Armorica and the other provinces of Gaul, in imitation of the British, refused to acknowledge the authority of Rome.' The municipal aristocracies often welcomed ambitious indigenous chieftains—Moorish or British—who offered their services as warriors, and they themselves did not mind vegetating, provided they were beyond the reach of the Roman tax-collector. In under-administrated and under-populated regions, such as the high plateaux of Algeria and the west of Britain, there emerged tribal chieftains who were ready to throw off imperial authority. Some of them were true separatists like the Moor Gildo, whose revolt in Africa lasted from 396 to 398. Most of them, however, were unimaginative, and aspired only to receive or usurp authority of the Roman type, from the *rex gentium Maurorum et Romanorum* of Mauretania to the Welshman who proudly invented the rank of *protector*.

These centrifugal forces were, on the whole, more conservative than revolutionary. It was more a question of an expansion of the idea of self-defence as a form of insurance against the inability of the authorities to protect them from destruction, than of a truly autonomist or 'nationalist' movement. The framework within which lasting institutions crystallized was that of the barbarian kingdoms, not that of autonomous cities or tribes.

Finally, of all the enterprises of the fifth and sixth centuries the most destructive and unwittingly the most revolutionary was Justinian's reconquest. This was the only one which brought about real social upheavals, the obliteration of Rome and the disappearance of the senatorial class over the greater part of Italy. Such were the results of the obstinacy of the Byzantine armies in keeping the field for twenty years without ever being sufficiently strong to effect a real conquest. Whatever escaped the destruction brought about by the strategies of Justinian's generals fell victim to the desperate counter-attacks of the Goths. Numerous texts[26] refer to famine leading to cannibalism, mass suicides, noble ladies reduced to begging for a living, cases of deportation, arrest, and the massacre of hostages, and every other conceivable tragedy—and these were certainly not just literary clichés. In Africa the losses were not so heavy, but in spite of vigorous efforts like those of Solomon, the Byzantine governors could not prevent the situation from deteriorating at the same rate as under the Vandals, if not faster, under pressure from the nomadic Berbers.

Each area should be made the subject of a thorough inquiry, independent of the texts, into the probable agents of destruction, the visible signs of increasing poverty, and the first indications of a return to law and order. A. Audin, for example, has usefully shown that the abandonment of the classical site of Lugdunum on the hill of Fourvières, in favour of the banks of the Saône, was the result not of the assault of the barbarians but of the insecurity caused by the Bacaudic revolt; this had encouraged the anti-social activity of lead thieves (a familiar plague which even today still strikes towns in the wake of a disaster) which had brought about the breakdown of the aqueducts, thereby making it impossible for water to be piped up to the high quarters of the town.[27] The descent of Rome from the Seven Hills to the banks of the Tiber and the Campus Martius was also linked with the destruction of the aqueducts, at the time of the Gothic wars. On the other hand, what better indication can one find of the return to normality than the reconstruction of the arenas at Paris and Soissons by the sons of Clovis, or of the amphitheatre at Pavia by Athalaric?[28]

It should thus be possible to be much more precise about when the upheavals began and ended, and probably also to prove that nine times out of ten they started well before the large-scale breaches of the *limes* by the barbarians, and ended relatively soon after the setting up of the new kingdoms. Clearly some areas were virtually undisturbed, while others suffered enormous disruptions: from the fifth century onwards the social history of the West dissolves into a series of regional histories of widely differing character. The barbarians were not the only ones responsible for this fragmentation.

THE INVADERS

What exactly were the Germanic 'peoples' at the time of the invasions? Some of them give the impression of having been vast confederations, ready at any moment to expand by absorbing others or to dissolve, while others seem to have been small, primitive but very close-knit units; and there are examples of all the intermediate stages. The nature of the evolution of these *Stämme* has been the subject of many studies in Germany.[29]

All sorts of factors were involved in the *Stammesbildung*: some are sociological (such as common ancestry and intermarriage), others religious (such as a common form of worship), legal (such as identical customs and the extent of the king's peace), geographical (such as joint occupation of the same region), or linguistic (such as dialectal peculiarities); the deciding factor, however, was most often political. Almost all the peoples who took part in the scramble for imperial territory had a royal dynasty as their rallying-point. This was probably not a primitive characteristic: Tacitus' Germany, like Caesar's Gaul, contained numerous 'republican' peoples; monarchy only predominated in the east. The conflict with Rome and the sharing out of the spoils favoured monarchies; the only peoples that escaped this tendency were a few who had stayed in the background, like the Saxons (among whom, however, kings appeared soon after they had begun to conquer Britain).

The character of Germanic kingship is twofold, for it is both sacral and military, the relative importance of these aspects varying from people to people. The Gothic and Anglo-Saxon dynasties, like those of Norway and Sweden later on, were reputed to be descended from gods; those of the Franks and the Lombards were of a rather more military nature; but everywhere kingship continued to have a supernatural side, shown for instance in the importance attached to the long hair of the Merovingians.[30]

The cohesion of the *Stämme* also differed to a surprising extent from people to people. Awareness of ethnic unity could survive the most widespread geographical dispersal, as it did among the Heruls. At the beginning of the sixth century they were split into a main group, who stayed on in Denmark, and a branch which settled on the middle Danube. The latter, who were ill-treated by the Lombards in 505, themselves split into two groups: one section settled in the Eastern Empire and the other, led by a royal family, set out to rejoin their compatriots on the shores of the Baltic in about 512. Conversely, great peoples could disappear in a few years almost without trace, as did the Vandals or the Ostrogoths following the reconquests of Justinian or, on a lower level, the Gepids and Skirians, and before them almost all of the peoples mentioned by Tacitus. How can we account for these differences? Firstly, confederations of peoples, especially if spread over a wide area, only survived as long as they were militarily successful: repeated setbacks caused them to break up and their name to disappear, their component peoples regaining their independence or re-forming with other groups. Secondly, the make-up of all the peoples was more or less unstable: a small nucleus clung fiercely to the national name and to the dynasty, while the outer fringes which had been acquired during the historical development of the people were much more loosely attached; because it was so limited numerically the nucleus could be relatively easily destroyed, but as long as it held out 'ethnic' awareness continued to be strong.

This hypothesis, which is ably defended by Wenskus,[31] resolves the apparent contradiction between the tiny extent of the lands of origin assigned to the various Germanic peoples and their numerical importance at the height of their careers. It is impossible that all the Burgundians should have come from Bornholm, or all the Vandals from Vendsyssel. Only the nucleus of each people, the bearers of its traditions, really originated in these places.

For the sake of completeness another type of grouping, which was in fact rather rare, must be mentioned: the warrior bands so dear to Fustel de Coulanges. These were bands of adventurers without a common tradition, held together solely by their hunger for booty.

If the 'constitutional' aspect of the problem is difficult to grasp, we must bravely admit that the numerical aspect is insoluble. For the past sixty years, while classical scholars since Beloch have believed it possible to estimate the size of the population of Athens at the time of Pericles, or of Rome at the time of Augustus, medievalists have wanted to put forward various figures for their own period. None of these figures can be trusted, neither those that have been borrowed from contemporary sources, nor those that have been arrived at on the basis of inconsistent evidence, or rather, on their authors' personal ideas of the phenomena they were studying.

The most coherent attempt was made by Schmidt:[32] he estimates that there were 50,000 Batavi in existence about AD 70; 20,000 Alamans at Strasbourg in 357; 10,000 Gothic soldiers at Adrianople; and so on. Another German historian, W. Reinhart, estimates that 70,000 or 80,000 Visigoths entered Spain. The evidence in Victor Vitensis relating to the Vandals has been the subject of analysis by Courtois:[33] without absolutely rejecting the figure of 80,000 for the Vandals who crossed to Africa he shows that this number had become something of a cliché in the writings of historians of the time.

We shall confine ourselves to saying that the invading armies were certainly not large. Even taking non-combatants and captives into account, they were incapable of overwhelming by mere force of numbers the peoples of the vast areas which they had won for themselves. But we are helpless when it comes to deciding the total numbers of barbarians that settled in the West. Even if we agree that in the case of the Visigoths or the Vandals the total barbarian immigration may have been very close to the numbers involved in the initial invasion, where the other great peoples are concerned we must take into account the strong probability that immigrants, attracted by the success of the invaders, continued to pour in for several generations afterwards. There is no means of assessing these secondary movements, since written sources usually do not mention them.

Similarly, little is known about how the barbarian armies provisioned themselves in the course of their travels across the Empire. Our most reliable evidence concerns the Goths.[34] Throughout the whole of their migration, from Dacia to Aquitaine, the Visigoths depended principally on trade with the Romans and on provisions supplied by them. As early as 369 Valens tried to eliminate the threat of the Goths by closing the markets and organizing a commercial boycott: the Goths had to resort to force of arms. It is clear from Ammianus's account that their own agricultural produce was not sufficient to feed them. Likewise, in 414 Constantius forced them to leave Spain by organizing a naval blockade.[35] In the end a *foedus* was concluded in return for a promise to provide them with 600,000 measures of corn, and subsequently the usual regular supplies as laid down by the system of *hospitalitas*. Admittedly the Visigoths are an extreme case; they were semi-nomads for whom agriculture had never been more than a small part of their livelihood, and they were travelling across the Empire at a time when the *annona* (the imperial corn supply system) and the *cursus publicus* (the imperial system of communications and transport) were still fairly effective, which made it possible for Rome to organize a blockade. Subsequent armies were able to live much more amply off the land: it is likely that as well as pillaging they indulged to some extent in commercial transactions whereby they resold their plunder in return for provisions. The problem of finding food and fodder, therefore, limited the size of the forces which could act in co-ordination in a given area. When the barbarians were advancing rapidly they continually had to split up and re-form according to the resources available. The success of the *foedus* is understandable: it meant that the invaders could return to rural life, their normal mode of existence, and it assured them regular supplies of provisions. It was in the barbarians' own interests not to upset pre-existing conditions too drastically.

Although pitched battles were not very frequent, the history of the invasions is to a large extent military history. We would like to know a lot more about tactics and methods of fighting, but detailed documents are rare.[36] The invasions never brought about a revolution in

Roman tactics. The contacts between the Romans and the barbarians were too close for any change of tactics to have come as a surprise. The Romans were less familiar with the tactics of mounted archers, which were based on mobility. The manuals of tactics from the Later Roman Empire show how manoeuvres could be adapted to cope with different possible enemies, but despite this we know almost nothing about barbarian tactics.[37]

The organization of the barbarian armies was based on the service of all free men who were able to fight and to provide themselves with sufficient arms and provisions, at least for a short campaign. The Burgundians and the Franks extended this system to include their Roman subjects. The organization of military units was probably on a tribal basis at the time of the migrations, but later on it was based on territorial divisions. Military command, which had originally been in the hands of hereditary chieftains or of wealthy men who found themselves in charge of large *comitatus*, by Merovingian times had passed to the local agents of the crown, the counts. The only precise information we have about lesser units relates to the peoples who, over a long period of time, had been in contact with the Roman armies in the East, where organization continued to be strictly maintained, that is to say the Goths and the Lombards.

Thanks to archaeology weapons are what we know most about, at least after the fourth century, when the placing of arms in tombs became common practice. Like so many of the other elements of civilization, they developed enormously between the preparatory stage, that of the *laeti*, and the migratory period of the invasions. For example, among the Franks it was only in the sixth century that the throwing-axe and the sword acquired their definitive shape. Each people had its own characteristic weapons. Later on we shall study the weapons of the Franks, which, like those of the Anglo-Saxons, were mainly the weapons of foot-soldiers. The Alamans, being horsemen, wielded the long sword. Except for the Burgundians none of the western Germans attached any great importance to defensive arms or to the bow. Not much is known about the weapons used by the Goths, as they did not bury them with their dead; the Vandals, the majority of whom were horsemen, used the lance, the long sword and the bow, and often wore a breastplate.

As regards the civil organization of the Germans, one of the most important problems concerns kinship (Germ. *Sippe*), which plays a fundamental part in the interpretations of modern German legal historians, though its details are not very clear to us. In their view the corresponding term is *fara*, a word which is known to have been used by the Franks, as evidenced by place-names such as Fère-Champenoise and La Fère, and by the Lombards, as shown both by place-names and by the historical and legal sources. Apparently members of the *fara* were known as *faramanni*, although this term is known to have been current only among the Burgundians. What exactly did *fara* mean? Paul the Deacon, writing about the Lombards, defines it thus: *fara, hoc est generationes vel lineas* (*fara*, which means descendants or clans).[38] At first sight, then, the *fara* seems to have been a civil institution, a group of people descended from a common ancestor. But Paul the Deacon himself also tells us that it was a basic unit in the army, which is confirmed by the edict of Rothari. The Greek tacticians, moreover, declare that the Lombards fought as families (φῦλαι). In that case what we are dealing with could be either a family group or a unit of self-defence. The Italian expert on the subject, Bognetti, believes that the *fara* took the form of a military association. As for *faramannus*, the Burgundian law (LIV, 2) uses it in the sense of *consors*—'member of an association of Romans and barbarians for the exploitation of an area of land'. Fredegar uses it to refer to the aristocracy, and the term has survived in the dialects of the regions of Forez and Lyons with the meaning of 'vagabond'. All this hardly justifies a comprehensive theory of kinship, and we cannot know for certain whether French and Italian place-names which include the word *fara* indicate colonization by family groups, or military settlement.[39]

Some Suggestions for Further Research

One of the major difficulties confronting the modern historian of the invasions is an attitude of mind inherited from the classical world. When faced with a new ethnic term the classical historiographer was always cautious; if he found in his library of good authors a name which had already been accepted, he preferred to use this instead. Hence the vagueness of many of the texts, and the systematic recourse to out-dated labels which are quite unreliable. This tendency involved the peoples of the steppes in particular: the Goths were christened Geti, the Huns were disguised as Scythians and the Avars became Huns. In this way the Marcomanni, the Quadi and the Sarmatians enjoyed a long posthumous popularity. In hagiographical accounts the Vandals lent their name to a wide variety of invaders of Gaul in a most accommodating way, as did the Alans. 'Sicambri' was a literary term for Franks. The Lombards and the Saxons fortunately escaped these fancy-dress disguises.

A rewarding subject for study would be the iconography of the barbarian conquerors. A considerable amount of documentary information has been assembled on the Goths,[40] for example: both sovereigns and simple soldiers had a recognizable hair-style—long hair covering part of the forehead and forming ringlets below the ears.

For the Vandals Courtois has only found a few texts, one mosaic now lost and another of questionable relevance.[41] Except for the data provided by archaeology from burials no more is known about the other peoples. A parallel study would have to be undertaken of the disappearance from triumphal iconography (which survived in the East for some time after it had vanished from the West) of the classical figure of the barbarian, which was based on Hellenistic depictions of Galatians, in favour of realistic representations like those of the Goths on the obelisk of Theodosius at Constantinople.

The relations between Rome and the barbarians in the fifth century have rarely been looked at from the point of view of diplomatic history, at least in the West. (In the East accounts such as that of Priskos, who was sent as a member of an embassy to Attila, have inevitably attracted attention.[42]) How did the contacts between Rome and the barbarian kings function? Research could be undertaken on the role of the clergy as go-betweens. The interview between Pope Leo and Attila in the presence of high-ranking dignitaries of the state is well known, as are the methods of St. Germanus of Auxerre in dealing with Bacaudae and with British secessionists, and the part played by the bishops as intermediaries between the Gothic kings of Toulouse and the Empire.[43] But we know virtually nothing about the procedure that was used.[44]

What was the significance of the tribute paid by Rome? We would like to know not only how much was paid over, but also what it consisted of (it would appear that the Scandinavians only accepted *aurei*, never *trientes*), how and where payment was arranged, and how effective the tribute really was. The amounts that Alaric, Genseric and Attila extorted from Rome have been estimated, but what were these sums used for? In all probability they were used principally to buy provisions and arms, though they may also have been used to build up hoards of treasure, to send home, and perhaps for religious offerings. It seems that contrary to what took place at the end of the Viking period their contribution to the economy of the barbarian world was negative.

Another, allied subject which merits investigation is the custom of handing over hostages as a pledge that the *foedus* would be kept, which was normal practice throughout the fifth century. In 418 a senator who was a relative of the future Emperor Avitus was sent to Wallia. In his youth Aetius spent some time as a hostage at the court of Alaric, and later at that of the Huns; his son and the son of a senator were handed over to Attila about 448. One feels that these episodes, particularly that involving Aetius, were important in paving the way for an understanding between the barbarian kings and the Roman aristocracy.

It would be helpful if we knew more about the extent to which the Germans were informed, advised, and even guided by Romans in the course of their migrations: the more delicate operations must almost inevitably have involved this sort of collaboration. It is very likely that the five *Hispani* who accompanied Genseric to Africa[45] were the ones who made it possible for him to cross the Straits of Gibraltar in the first place. Having the Roman Artemidorus at his side made it much easier for Theodoric to lead his people from the Balkans into Italy and to break through the *limes* at Friuli, and he rewarded this relative of the Emperor Zeno with the prefecture of the city of Rome. In this way, some time before the conquerors had settled down, the Roman ruling class was already preparing for itself the role it was to play later on at the courts of the kings that ruled within the former Empire. Behind the great ideas of the German kings there often lurks a Roman adviser: Leo of Narbonne was behind the conciliatory policy of Euric in Aquitaine, Cassiodorus behind that of Theodoric in Italy, Parthenius behind the Frankish expansion into southern Germany under Theudebert, and so on.[46] Even Attila may have been inspired by a Roman, his secretary Orestes. It would be interesting to find out where these realists sprang from, and whether they were motivated by financial gain or by ambition alone, or whether their basic motive was simply to serve Rome through the medium of a barbarian king, as was most certainly the case where Cassiodorus, Boethius and Parthenius were concerned.

In conclusion, one must not lose sight of the permanent danger to which the historian is exposed when dealing with those collective abstractions, the 'Goths', the 'Franks' and the 'Vandals'. In the period which we are discussing none of these peoples existed as a simple unit, for all were composite—and sometimes unexpected—combinations of peoples. The Vandals of Africa were made up mainly of Asding Vandals, with some Siling Vandals, some Alans, and a handful of Sueves and Hispano-Romans. There were Asiatic elements among the peoples known as the Visigoths and the Burgundians. The Ostrogoths of Theodoric brought Rugians along with them, and in Italy they absorbed Skirians, Heruls, a few Alamans, and even some Scandinavian adventurers. It is the same story everywhere. This fact alone must have brought about confrontations within each people, causing them to modify their institutions, and thus paving the way for an eventual reconciliation with the Romans.

SYSTEMS OF DEFENCE AND CASUALTIES

Fortifications

There was no need for the towns to surround themselves with hastily-built ramparts with the approach of the barbarians at the beginning of the fifth century; they already had fortifications dating either from the time of the early Empire or from the crisis of the third century, and those that had failed to provide themselves with any had already been destroyed.[47] It was only necessary to restore these fortifications, though restoration was not in fact undertaken on a very large scale and has left hardly any recognizable traces except in Africa, which had been spared by the preceding troubles. In general the barbarians kept the town walls in good repair, so that they survived intact until the Middle Ages. It was only in a few rare cases that they dismantled the fortifications of a town as a gesture of defiance towards a hostile population, as the Vandals did at Tipasa in Mauretania and the Sueves at Conimbriga (near Coimbra) in Lusitania.

In the state of turmoil which prevailed in the fifth century, walls offered the best means of defence, at least on a short-term basis. Most of the time the barbarians, lacking any kind of siege weapons, were unable to take a town by storm. Only by setting up a lengthy blockade and cutting off the town's water supplies could they hope to succeed: this is how the Vandals came to capture Hippo in 431 and the Ostrogoths Ravenna in 493. The campaigns of the Byzantine reconquest of Italy really amount to a series of interminable sieges of Rome. Only large walled enclosures with access to the sea, allowing provisions to be brought in, could put up a prolonged defence; the shrunken and overpopulated towns which were characteristic of Gaul and Spain during the late Empire could only hold out for a few days or weeks. If the blockade showed signs of lasting any longer than this, public opinion—or at least the opinion of the *humiliores*—clamoured for surrender. This is how the siege of Bazas by the Visigoths ended, as described by Paulinus of Pella.[48] Hydatius tells us that nearly all of the towns in Spain taken by the Sueves were occupied *per dolum* or *sub specie pacis*, 'by a trick' or 'under the guise of peace'. As for Britain, it seems that nobody even tried to defend the towns, which had already been abandoned by all their able-bodied inhabitants.

The few towns which had not reduced the size of their walled enclosure in the third century were indefensible by local forces unless they were reinforced by a field army. This doubtless accounts for the ease with which the Franks were able to take Cologne, which had retained an enclosed area of 100 hectares within its Claudian walls, and Trier, which they took four times during the fifth century, as Salvian informs us. (Trier, as the old capital, had the enormous enclosed area of 285 hectares.) On the other hand the Roman defence in the Loire area hinged on Orleans, which had an enclosed area of only 25 hectares, and Syagrius made his stand at Soissons, which had only 12 hectares. The final choice of Toledo as the Visigothic capital may perhaps be explained by the fact that inside this fortified enclosure of only 5 hectares the Visigoths were safe from a repetition of the catastrophe of 507, when Toulouse, with its vast walled enclosure of 90 hectares, proved to be indefensible.

Although the town walls, on the whole, stood the test of the invasions, the fortifications along the land and sea frontiers (that is to say the *limes*, which had already been abandoned before the major onslaught, and the *litus saxonicum* of Gaul and Britain) disappeared for three centuries. Italy alone kept alive the idea of these 'barriers': until the Lombard conquest, fortified lines barred access to the Po valley from the north-east (the Friuli *limes*) and through the Alpine passes, at whose mouths many more forts, called *clusurae*, were built, such as Susa, Aosta and the Isola Comacina.

We do not know enough to be able to form an accurate picture of what in more recent times would be called the Home Guard. As a general rule it seems that the great weakness of the Later Roman Empire was its inability to organize a system of self-defence on a regional basis, even if it had wished to do so. This suicidal failing is accounted for by the totalitarian nature of the State and by its constant and morbid fear of conspiracy and usurpation. However, there are regional variations in the general picture. Private fortifications in the form of villae with towers, or of farms laid out on the plan of *castella*, were quite common along the eastern frontiers. In the West it was only in Africa that they played an important role:[49] excavations in Britain, although meticulous, have revealed the existence of only half a dozen. In Gaul the clearest example is far from the frontiers— Bourg-sur-Gironde, the famous *Burgus* so magniloquently described by Sidonius Apollinaris, the fortified villa of Pontius Leontius.[50]

Since it lacked sufficient military resources to check the advance of the barbarians, it is surprising that the Empire should not have thought of using religion as a means of defence, for the Empire had by now become Christian while in 476 the barbarians were still almost all pagans. Surely converting the barbarians would have made them less dangerous, especially in view of the unanimous contemporary belief in the efficacy of spiritual weapons. Three centuries later this was the reaction of the Carolingian Empire, attacked from the north and from the east. Rome, however, did almost nothing—nothing at all, in fact, before the barbarians crossed the frontier, and very little afterwards. The Catholic Church proved incapable of undertaking what obscure Gothic missionaries from the Arian centres set up by Ulfila accomplished remarkably quickly. Some clerics, such as Niceta of Remesiana, Victricius of Rouen and Amantius of Aquileia, who were in direct contact with the barbarians, were aware of this negligence and sought to remedy it, but they were not heeded.

This lapse is all the more curious in view of the fact that the presence of Christian captives on barbarian soil might well have paved the way for conversion, as it did with the Goths, and that the Eastern Church was indulging in a great deal of missionary activity at the time. The one Western bishop who dared to go among the Germans was an exiled heretic called Audius. The only valid explanation that has been suggested[51] is that in the West it was considered that the most urgent missionary task was to complete the conversion of the inhabitants of the Empire, many of whom were still pagan, whereas the Greeks, who were all Christians by this time, were free to look beyond their frontiers.

Plunder and the Fate of Civilians

There is a very real need for more extensive research into the fate of civilians during the periods of crisis. With very few exceptions[52] this has so far been pursued in a rather abstract manner. In our own times we have had too much direct experience of the problems of invasion to go on looking at them in the same old institutional and legal terms as our forerunners in the nineteenth century. The movements of refugees and the destruction and reconstruction of buildings are more crucial to our understanding of a period than are many legal or linguistic matters.

Because of the nature of the sources, we have more information about the movements of refugees, their complexity, and the resulting mixture of peoples in Italy than elsewhere. The first stage is marked by the arrival of Radagaisus and then of Alaric in Illyricum. A law of 10 December 408 prohibits the enslavement of Illyrian refugees by Italians. In 410 many Italians were forced to flee in their turn by the sack of Rome. The rich scattered in all directions; some of them were to be found in the course of the next few years living on the islands of Tuscany and particularly in Africa (not just in the ports but also in the interior, as far inland as Djemila), in Constantinople and even in Palestine. Sometimes these magnates managed to salvage a considerable portion of their belongings.[53] As in 408, the poor were shamefully treated: Jerome accuses Heraclianus, the count of Africa, of having organized the sale of young refugees to the brothels of the East.[54] This crisis had only just died down when a fresh wave of refugees arrived in Italy, made up of Aquitanians fleeing from Athaulf, who had now crossed into Gaul; Rutilius Namatianus met some of them in Tuscany in 415.

The onslaught of Attila in 452 resulted in the deportation of the inhabitants of Aquileia to Pannonia for six years. The sack of Rome by Genseric in 455 probably provoked a new wave of panic, but this time it resulted most notably in the transportation of an enormous number of captives to Africa. They were kept in two basilicas in Carthage until buyers could be found for them.

Thirty years later Italy welcomed the evacuees from Noricum, who were dispersed all over the country, even as far away as Campania (488). Then a Burgundian expedition crossed the Alps and brought hundreds of slaves back to Lyons; the bishop of Pavia ransomed more than four hundred of them in 495.

The reign of Theodoric provided something of a respite, but the whole process began again in the middle of the sixth century when the Lombard invasion was the signal for wholesale flight towards the coasts of Venetia, Liguria and Tuscany (cf. p. 91), and the whole of Italy became a great slave market. Gregory the Great relates how, when Agilulf's Lombards were besieging Rome in 592, standing on the walls he saw with his own eyes Romans yoked together being led off to be sold in Gaul.[55] In 610 the Avars made widespread raids into Friuli[56] and these continued for some time.

After Italy, Africa is the place about which we have most information. The vicissitudes of life under Vandal domination obliged some senators to make for Italy or Constantinople, and dispersed the Catholic clergy to exile in Spain, Gaul, Macedonia or Greece.[57] The flight continued even after the Byzantine reconquest, which did nothing to allay the general feeling of insecurity.[58] Documentary evidence for Gaul is scarce; the only accounts we have are of the flight of a handful of senators from the north to the south, and of a few Aquitanian aristocrats who left their country just before the arrival of the Goths (such as Paulinus of Pella, who fled to Marseilles), and we cannot paint a picture of mass movements on the basis of this evidence.[59]

Two conclusions are inescapable: the inability of the authorities to provide the poor with even the minimum of aid and, in stark contrast, the propensity of the upper classes for taking refuge as far away as possible. Organized withdrawals were very rare exceptions, the only example in the West being the evacuation of Noricum, and evidence of the rehousing of refugees or the ransoming of captives by the State is almost completely lacking. As regards helping the civilian victims of the various invasions, the only initiative came from the Church, and even that was very limited.

Apart from certain military measures the State was equally un-interested in the work of reconstruction. It confined itself to granting tax relief in the most seriously devastated areas, as in Tuscany and southern Italy in 412. The task of restoring Benevento, which had been burnt by Alaric, was left to a private person of means,[60] and it was Bishop Eusebius who undertook the reconstruction of Milan after Attila had passed through it.[61] In most cases things were left to look after themselves. The barbarian kings were no more interested in reconstruction than the Empire had been, except for Theodoric, who did some rebuilding at Rome—but more for purposes of prestige than out of benevolence. In any case the depleted state of the treasury, hard-pressed by military expenses, would have made effective action impossible, for the taxpayers' resources had already been completely exhausted. One fact corroborates this hypothesis: whereas the third-century invasions, which took the wealthy East by surprise, were marked by the burial of countless hoards, sometimes containing hundreds of pounds of silver, similar hoards dating from the time of the fifth-century invasions are rare.

What became of the spoils of Rome? Probably the major part stayed where it was, only changing hands a few times before returning to the Roman institution which was to hoard a large part of it: the Church. What was formerly independent Germany seems to have kept very little of it. Paradoxically, it is in Scandinavia that the clearest traces of it are found. There the triumph of the Germans led, literally, to an Age of Gold: in the Baltic islands quantities of gold *solidi* were amassed during the fifth and sixth centuries, coins which had not been much in circulation and which came principally from Italy. They were probably the wages which the German soldiers of the last Emperors and of Theodoric brought home with them.[62] This gold was usually melted down and made into jewellery, and ultimately buried in tombs or in votive deposits (one of these contained twelve kilos of pure gold). Since it arrived in the north at a time when the economy was at a pre-monetary stage, this precious metal did not really enrich it at all; by the seventh century it had almost completely dropped out of circulation. One of the most successful raids of the migration period was the sack of Rome by the Vandals in 455. Two notable features of this raid were the methodical discrimination of the Vandals (for example in their choice of statues, proof that they had adopted at least in part the Roman way of looking at things) and the fact that a good part of the booty, including the treasure which Titus had carried off from Jerusalem, was simply transferred from the imperial storehouse to that of Genseric; this meant that the plunder had absolutely no effect on the Vandal economy.[63] All in all, the barbarians did not gain very much from what the Empire had lost.

All these general ideas, still in a tentative state, will only acquire real value when picturesque descriptions give way to critical statistical analysis which could serve as a basis for distribution maps. We await with impatience maps showing the distribution over fourth-, fifth- and sixth-century Europe of forts and walled settlements, treasure hoards of coins and jewellery, and dated cases of destruction and the rare cases of reconstruction. The flight of populations and of individual refugees should also be graphically represented. Probably this would show the predominance of movements from west to east, which made the *pars orientis* the true citadel of *Romanitas*, and secondarily the concentric withdrawals from the fringes of the Empire towards the Mediterranean.

The Fate of the Great Estates

We know what happened to the estates of several senators, estates whose immense size and scattered nature rendered them doubly vulnerable. A famous passage in Olympiodorus allows us to make some calculations: many families had an annual income of 4,000 pounds in gold currency plus a third of that in kind; others had 1,000 to 1,500 pounds; Probus spent 1,200 pounds on celebrations during his praetorship in 424; the orator Symmachus, who was only 'moderately well-off', spent 2,000 pounds on the games which his son, as praetor, had to give, and in similar circumstances Maximus squandered 4,000 pounds on games which lasted for a week.[64] If the wealth and vast size of these estates is impressive, their being so scattered is even more astonishing and is a tangible sign of the unity of the Mediterranean world. At the beginning of the fifth century Melania the Younger and her husband Pinianus had estates in Rome, southern Italy, Sicily, Gaul, Spain, Britain, proconsular Africa, Numidia and Mauretania.[65] Symmachus had property in Rome, Capua, Samnium, Apulia, Sicily and Caesarian Mauretania. Paulinus of Pella, the grandson of Ausonius, had houses at Bordeaux, an estate at Bazas, land at Marseilles and sizeable possessions in Macedonia, around Pella, which he had inherited from his mother.

These large unwieldy estates were hard hit by the invasions: Melania and Paulinus are remembered above all for their losses and misfortunes. Melania left Rome for Sicily as early as 408, and went from there to Africa, where she lived and supported other refugees by selling off her estates. She finally reached the Holy Land via Egypt in 417. Not much of her large inheritance can have been left, but the invasions were not entirely to blame, as it had already been much reduced by her various charities. Paulinus survived the invasion of Aquitaine by the Visigoths unscathed, and even managed to avoid having barbarian troops billeted on his estate near Bordeaux by being of service to Athaulf. But the downfall of the Emperor Attalus, who had made him his *comes largitionis*, or finance minister, forced him to abandon everything he had at Bordeaux. He withdrew to Bazas, but his estate there was ruined by a combination of Bacaudae, Alans and Goths. At this point he wanted to go to Greece, but his wife refused to follow him there as the journey was too dangerous, so he settled at Marseilles where he lived on a small and heavily mortgaged property. Apparently he never managed to touch any of his income from his Greek estates, but by good luck he was able to sell one of his estates in Aquitaine to a Goth. His son returned to Bordeaux to try to salvage some of the family property there, but died without having accomplished anything.[66] After the year 400, family estates which were scattered all over the Roman world had become impossible to administer.

The large estates did not disappear, however, and continued to be just as scattered, but they now had to conform to the new political framework. This was a powerful factor in the crystallization of 'regional nationalities', as it was to be again when the Carolingian Empire was split up, and the phenomenon would merit detailed study.

WERE THE ROMANS AND THE BARBARIANS IDEOLOGICALLY OPPOSED?

Classical historiography represents the barbarians only as a negative factor: they brought disorder and ruin, and were incapable of anything constructive. Was this view confirmed by the events of the fifth and sixth centuries? Were the barbarians motivated solely by a desire to appropriate the wealth of others, to settle on richer soil and in a more pleasant climate than their own, and then to enjoy the fruits of their conquest? Or were they inspired by loftier ideals, for example that of replacing *Romania* with a different political system, and the Catholic Church with a different form of worship?

On the political level this suggestion is hardly defensible. Few of the barbarian kings had a political thought in their heads, and if they had it usually ran on Roman lines, like the 'Platonic' kingdom in which the Amals took such pride. Even Alaric seems to have sought to make a niche for himself within the Empire rather than to set himself up as a replacement for it. The only truly anti-Roman programme is to be found in a famous passage in Orosius,[67] in which Athaulf is supposed to have declared at Narbonne in 414 that he had once wished to substitute an *imperium Gothorum* for the *imperium Romanum*, to transform what had been *Romania* into *Gothia*, and to be for the Goths what Augustus had been for the Romans. But according to Orosius, Athaulf himself acknowledged that this was beyond the capabilities of the Goths, and that the only practical policy was to proceed within the existing Roman political system and to 'increase the glory of Rome by lending her the strength of the Goths'. Whether or not Athaulf did actually arrive at this conclusion, the barbarians were apparently unable to conceive a system capable of replacing the Empire before it had actually disappeared.

The Problem of Arianism

It is only in the field of religion that the question of ideological opposition can properly be raised. When they crossed the *limes* the barbarians did not bring with them any coherent form of religion or any original doctrine. Their paganism was a family affair, unthinking, chthonic, and by no means proselytizing; it seems that they were almost ashamed of it, and their first concern once they were firmly established within the Empire was to shake it off. Only the first generation of Franks and Sueves continued to be faithful to their old religion, and no people remained pagan any longer than that.[68] Not a single contemporary attempted to explain the actions of the barbarians as having been inspired by pagan fanaticism.

There remains, then, the question of German Arianism.[69] It is known that the doctrine originated within the Empire, in typically Hellenistic speculations, and at first had no connection with the barbarians. Two chance circumstances account for its diffusion among the Germans: the arrival of Ulfila, the apostle of the Goths, at Constantinople at a time when the court was Arian, and the Goths' prestige throughout the German world after their victory at Adrianople. There was nothing especially attractive to the barbarians either in the doctrine of Arianism (which they did not study very thoroughly) or in its liturgy (which was chiefly characterized by nocturnal worship). But the use of the vernacular, which is not in itself an Arian trait but an oriental one shared by all the churches founded by the Byzantine mission, did make it more accessible than Catholicism. Moreover, faced with the dominance of the Catholicism of the Romans, the Germans saw in Arianism a way of emphasizing their independence and sense of identity, and a safeguard against too rapid assimilation.

At first, immediately after the consecration of Ulfila in 341, Arianism affected only very limited circles among the Goths—humble people or, like Ulfila himself, the descendants of prisoners. After the crossing of the Danube in 376 the majority of the Goths still continued to be pagan. Their mass conversion to Arianism dates from their stay in Moesia from 382 to 395. Arianism was the official religion of the Visigoths right up to 587, and even after that enjoyed several revivals, the last of which occurred as late as 610: that was the longest career it had anywhere. As early as 400 there were several groups of Christians among the Ostrogoths, but this branch of the Goths did not really abandon paganism until the time of their stay in Pannonia from around

456 to 472, after which they remained Arian until their downfall in the middle of the sixth century. Their example brought two other tribes of the middle Danube into the fold, the Gepids, converted possibly around 472, and the Rugians, converted some time before 482.

The peoples who crossed the Rhine in 406 were all pagans, but they quickly became converted to Arianism as soon as they came in contact with the Visigoths who had reached Gaul. The conversion of the Burgundians probably took place during their stay in Germania I between 413 and 436. That of the Vandals must have occurred after their arrival in Spain, between 409 and 417 (and not during their stay on the Danube, as Courtois believed). The Sueves tried Catholicism for a while under Rechiarius around 450, became Arians in about 465, and reconverted to Catholicism about 570.

The first wave of Arianism had all but died out when the Lombard invasion of 568 reinstated it in Italy. The conversion of the Lombards had probably occurred through contact with the Rugians while they were living on the middle reaches of the Danube, roughly between 488 and 505. They kept their faith intact until 616, and attempts to revive it went on until 662; the ultimate triumph of Catholicism did not come until 671.

The fact that the Germans and the Romans did not share a common faith caused political problems everywhere. Where they settled down in accordance with a treaty, the Arians formed closed, and on the whole inoffensive, communities. But in those regions which had been taken over by force, coexistence was less peaceful. This has given rise to bitter disputes among modern historians about Arian fanaticism, principally with regard to that of the Vandal kingdom in Africa, but also concerned with that of Visigothic Spain and Lombard Italy. Did the Arians in these kingdoms make a stand against the Catholics because of a deep religious hatred, as was believed by all the ecclesiastical authors of the time, and as is still believed by some historians? Or would it be truer to say that religion was just a cloak for a conflict which was fundamentally social or political, as it had been before and has often been since?

It must be acknowledged at once that Arianism did not teach any aggressive doctrine, and that its diffusion among the Germans seems to have been achieved by essentially peaceable means. Several barbarian kingdoms were able to preserve this characteristic, for example those of the Burgundians and the Ostrogoths. Here the Arians asked no more than the full use of a few churches in each area where their communities were large enough to justify it, and this tradition predated the conquest: Ricimer had founded an Arian church in Rome, that of Sant'Agata dei Goti. There was no proselytising even in Ravenna, where the Catholics were to reconcile six Gothic churches in 561.

What one dimly perceives, from scraps of palimpsests, is that the Arian literature of the Goths is purely exegetical, and not at all polemical. Moreover the Gothic sanctuaries are constructed on a plan so similar to that of Catholic sanctuaries that where there are no relevant texts, as at Salona, it is very difficult indeed to determine to which form of worship they belonged.

As for the Visigoths, the same peaceful coexistence characterized the kingdoms of Toulouse and Barcelona, and even the first years of the kingdom of Toledo. Isidore of Seville boasts of the tolerance of King Theudis (531–48), and the Catholic Church seems to have enjoyed complete freedom. There is only one indication to the contrary, and it is a slender one; that is, the efforts made in 465 by an Arian dignitary called Ajax, who was a convert from Catholicism himself, to bring the Sueves back into the Arian fold. Real tension did not in fact creep in until the time of Leovigild (568–86), and it is linked with the Byzantine attempt to reconquer Baetica, the threat of Frankish intervention, and above all, the reaction to the revolt of Hermenegild, whose motives may not have been essentially religious. For the short time that it lasted the persecution was confined to the confiscation of a few churches, the expulsion of some of the Catholic clergy, and the encouragement given to efforts to convert Catholics to Arianism. These are the conclusions reached by the most detailed study of the subject, that of Thompson [no. 199]. We should like to add that the episode is no more than an expression of that Hispanic passion for spiritual unity which was later to take the form of a struggle to eliminate the last surviving Arians after 587 and, immediately afterwards, a persecution of the Jews.

In Italy, even when Theodoric, at the end of his reign, had Boethius executed and threatened to depose Pope John, there are good grounds for doubting whether Arianism was showing any tendencies towards persecution. Boethius and the pope were accused, not of being Catholics, but of being too well-disposed towards Byzantium. It seems that it would never have occurred to an Ostrogoth to convert a Catholic to Arianism, and they appear to have built all their Arian sanctuaries from scratch, without taking over Catholic churches.

It will be seen from this that outside Africa Arianism did not necessarily lead to fanaticism or persecution but rather, sooner or later, to conversion to Catholicism. Why did things develop so differently in the kingdom of Carthage? Were the Vandals solely responsible, or were the circumstances of their conquest to blame? Texts vilifying the religious attitude of the Vandals in the most violent terms are numerous. Even in a secular sense they already had a bad reputation; as early as 406 St. Jerome castigated them with the epithet *ferocissimi*, and their subsequent exploits showed that it was more than justified. Then it was discovered that the numerical value of Genseric's name corresponded to the number of the Beast. But it is in the *Historia persecutionis vandalicae* by Victor Vitensis, written at the end of the fifth century, that the Vandal becomes the archetype of the barbarian persecutor of Catholics. Was this justified or not? It has long been established that the 'vandalism' of this people hardly exceeded that of their contemporaries, but it is much more difficult to make an impartial assessment of the religious problem. The clergy of the time believed that it was a question of pure Arian fanaticism: Courtois suggests that it was the religious offshoot of an essentially social conflict between the Vandal kings and the Roman landed aristocracy. We would prefer to believe that the African Church and Genseric were both trapped in a situation of their own making, the one because of its traditional zeal in taking a stand on politico-religious questions, and the other on account of his brutality and disregard for common decencies.

The origins of the conflict are quite clear: as soon as he had established himself Genseric proceeded to confiscate property on a massive scale, which affected in particular the large landowners, the wealthiest of whom was the Church. Those who had been deprived of their property, among them many bishops, were exiled so as to guarantee security of tenure to the newcomers. In due course their possessions were distributed among the Vandals; the churches were handed over to the Arian clergy, starting with the cathedral at Carthage. The measures taken against the Catholic hierarchy were merely one aspect of the general policy adopted towards the Roman ruling classes, but they were more rigorously carried out and had more repercussions.

Provoked beyond measure, the African Church found ready support both within the province among the landowning class, which had also been hard hit and which had been the Church's ally in the conflict with the Donatists, and externally, from the imperial government, which was by no means reconciled to the loss of Carthage. The resistance of the clergy, therefore, rapidly became tinged with elements of political conspiracy. By 440 the confrontation between the Vandals and the Catholics had already taken the form it was to retain during the course of its whole history. It was a struggle from which any form of compromise was excluded, characterized by the deportation of bishops to the mines of Sardinia or to the Sahara, repeated confiscations (all the Catholic churches were taken over in 484), and edicts ordaining that Catholics were to be converted to Arianism and rebaptized. The real crisis lasted for about forty years. In 495 the churches were given back and the situation calmed down, but until the accession of Hilderic in 523 the episcopate continued to be the victim of restrictive and interfering measures, such as the prohibition of elections.

In short, Arianism was not so much the real cause of the conflict as an occasion for it to break out. It was a conflict in which the violence of the Vandals, which was not religious in origin, came up against the fighting spirit of the African Church, which defended itself against the Vandals with weapons forged during its struggle against the Donatists. Signs of specifically religious intolerance did not appear until the conflict was well under way, and were of comparatively short duration. Only the bishops were consistently persecuted, because they were the effective leaders of Roman society in Africa and represented the main political obstacle to spiritual unity centred on the Vandal king.

There remains the problem of Arianism among the Lombards. In spite of having lagged a century behind its counterpart in Africa, it was closely related to it. Like the Vandals, the Lombards took a strong line as soon as they arrived in Italy, and there was no *foedus* to protect the Romans. As in Africa the Catholic Church closed ranks with the aristocracy, which had been stripped of its possessions; moreover the proximity of Ravenna and Rome, which were still in imperial hands, excited political suspicion among the Lombards. Nevertheless they never went beyond the stage of harrying individuals, possibly thanks to the restraints imposed on them by the Byzantine presence in Italy, and perhaps also because they had inherited something of the tolerance of the Goths. Except in their capital, Pavia, they allowed those Catholic bishops who had stayed behind to remain in office, and there does not appear to have been any large-scale confiscation of churches. It is true that Catholicism in Italy was ill-prepared for conflict; it never presented to its enemies a monolithic front like that of the African Church (for a long time it was split by the quarrel about the Three Chapters, concerned with the refusal of a number of bishops to accept Justinian's condemnation of three writers whose works had apparently been approved by the great Council of Chalcedon) and the policy of evacuation adopted after 569 had led to a severance of contact rather than to open opposition. In our opinion the conclusion to be drawn is that the Arians in the West did not deliberately persecute Catholics. Where the Arians maltreated them it was not a response to the urging of their Church, but merely the inevitable consequence of the general policy of their sovereigns towards the Roman ruling classes: examples of purely religious fanaticism were rare exceptions. The remarkable thing is that Arianism did not exploit more fully the situation which resulted from the barbarian conquest. Mostly it willingly accepted the equal validity of two forms of worship, a concept which Catholicism rejected with horror. Even where its adherents were victorious it was content to remain the humble religion of a minority. The reason for this was probably the intellectual inferiority of the

Arian hierarchy, which was badly equipped for controversy and incapable of contemplating systematic missionary activity. The impetus given by Ulfila may still have inspired some of the clergy of Ostrogothic Italy, but it died out soon afterwards.

Social Segregation

Although they lacked a real ideology to give them a sense of separate identity, the Arian barbarians were able to find among the civil and religious laws of the Empire justification for a form of protective segregation which prevented their small numbers from being immediately swallowed up by *Romanitas*, as had happened to most of the Germanic groups which had been allowed to settle on imperial soil prior to 406.

Since 370 Roman law had prohibited marriage between Romans and barbarians on pain of death. This extreme decree was contrary to ecclesiastical law, but was nevertheless upheld by several barbarian kingdoms, particularly those of the Goths. The Ostrogoths kept it until the end, and the Visigoths only renounced it in the time of Leovigild, when the ideal of Hispanic unity urged them to encourage the fusion of the Goths and the Romans, to the advantage of the Arians. Burgundian law, on the other hand, seems to have removed the prohibition as early as the fifth century.[70] Frankish law never refers to it, doubtless due to the Franks' precocious conversion to Catholicism. The position adopted by the Vandals is not clear.[71]

Custom complemented the law. In Italy—the only country about which anything precise is known—the Roman and barbarian quarters of towns were fairly clearly separated. During both the Gothic and the Lombard periods the Arians grouped themselves around their churches and royal palaces. Gothic Ravenna had its *civitas barbarica* and its six Arian churches (called *ecclesiae legis Gothorum* or *legis sanctae*). Grado and Salona had their two poles of attraction in the Arian and Catholic cathedrals. In Cividale del Friuli, an important garrison town, the Lombard quarter, which included the church of St. John, the *tempietto* famous in the history of art, and the military headquarters, was isolated from the rest of the town within a small walled area between the Roman walls and the River Natisone.[72]

The military profession and the bearing of arms were reserved to the barbarians in several kingdoms such as those of the Ostrogoths and the Lombards, but the Burgundian kings explicitly allowed their Roman subjects to follow a military career, and the Merovingians, without ever proclaiming it publicly, did the same. It depended on whether or not the kingdom had opted for a dualistic state structure.

We shall return later to the doctrine of the personality of the laws, another discriminatory device which helped to preserve the separate identity of the barbarian groups.

A minority readily believes in its own superiority, and a ruling minority never doubts it for a moment. This explains the contempt for the Romans that one glimpses occasionally. Examples of it are rare, however, although it is true that we have very little means of knowing the barbarians' opinions on the subject. There is the prologue to the Salic law, which accuses the Romans of having been merciless masters, and of having put so many martyrs to death (a religious argument which is somewhat out of place in that discussion), the naive declaration in a Bavarian marginal gloss of the eighth century that *stulti sunt Romani, sapienti Paioarii* (the Romans are stupid, the Bavarians are wise), and several other late texts on the same lines, but all this does not amount to much, and does little to counterbalance Theodoric's professions of faith in the Roman way of life. Racial hatred did not really enter into the relationship between the Romans and the barbarians.

PROBLEMS OF BARBARIAN SETTLEMENT

The Limitations of Linguistic and Archaeological Research

Archaeology and the study of place-names unquestionably offer the best approach for an assessment of the intensity of barbarian settlement, but it is essential never to lose sight of their limitations. A strong warning issued by F. Lot thirty years ago is still fundamentally valid. There are the initial difficulties inherent in the study of place-names: the necessity of finding the earliest possible form of the name, which must be meticulously established and dated and then compared with series of parallel cases; and the traps laid by bad writing and false etymology, both popular and learned, and by transfers of names. We shall deal largely with the problems that arise in attempting to interpret onomastic material for historical purposes, with some examples taken from Gaul.

Lot[73] stressed the absolute necessity first of taking into account the importance of the place that the name refers to—the name of a parish being more significant than the name of a hamlet or field—and secondly of placing the evidence in a statistical context, for one cannot consider a region 'Germanized' unless a high proportion of its place-names confirm Germanic influence. But it is not wise to carry this prudence too far: the proportions should be calculated not on the basis of present-day place-names, but on the basis of attested place-names in a period as close as possible to that of the phenomenon being studied (for example, the number of Germanic names compared with the aggregate of names which are known from reliable evidence to have existed before the year 1000). Even a completely isolated name, if its linguistic attribution is reliable, can have some value in retracing the boundaries or routes of linguistic penetration, or in confirming the survival of linguistic enclaves.

With reference to the pre-Latin suffix *-inco* and the Gothic and Burgundian suffix *-ingôs*, Lot also emphasized the grave danger, which affects whole areas of the study of place-names, of the coincidence of forms in several different languages. This has the most devastating effect when it is a question of nearly related languages; for example the similarity of Old Saxon and Norse makes it difficult, if not impossible, to study with any precision the Saxon settlements in the area of Bayeux and, to a lesser degree, serious confusion can arise between Gothic and Frankish toponymic elements in Aquitaine.[74] Another danger arises in cases where language B, related to language A, arrives in an area where A has already formed the place-names, and proceeds to remodel them according to its own rules, thus making them unrecognizable. For example, in eastern England many English place-names were 'Danicized' more or less superficially between the ninth and the eleventh centuries. This process can even occur several times in the history of one name: the name 'York' represents a Scandinavian form *Jorvik* which was a remodelled version of the O.E. *Eoforwic*, which in turn was a Germanic interpretation of the Celtic name transcribed into Latin as *Eboracum*!

The part played by fashions is fully recognized by students of personal names, and is not without interest for historians: the proliferation of Germanic names in Merovingian Gaul, or of Basque and Iberian names in Gascony in the ninth and tenth centuries, does not indicate direct colonization, but reveals an aspect of civilization which is just as significant, that is to say the prestige enjoyed by a ruling class composed partly of immigrants. But possibly fashions in place-names have been too much neglected. They certainly account for the sudden spread of estate names ending in *-curtis* and *-villa*. Several of these trends enjoyed only a limited popularity, and the place-names they left in their wake were therefore particularly vulnerable. This would probably explain why place-names formed on the basis of a Frankish personal name plus the ending *-iacas* all disappeared from the Pays de Caux under the impact of the Norman invasion. The fashion had doubtless not been accepted by the peasants who lived on in the area after 911, that is to say after the nobility had been replaced by the newcomers.

In France place-name experts have shamefully neglected the study of field names (Fr. *noms cadastraux*, Germ. *Flurnamen*), or microtoponymy, to concentrate on the names of settlement sites. Admittedly the average lifespan of field names is shorter, very few of them going back as far as the year 1000 except where they represent a settlement site which has now disappeared; but they are often very valuable linguistically, and they have made it possible to distinguish many enclaves of the respective minority languages which formerly existed on each side of the linguistic frontier in Belgium and the Rhineland.

In the study of personal names one should take into account not just the basic form of the name in a given period, but also the recurrence of it within a family during the course of several generations. The name Chlodovicus (variously modernized as Clovis or Louis) which Charlemagne gave to one of his sons indicates that the Carolingians were following a Merovingian tradition.

Thus, in reaching conclusions about the density and ethnic origin of settlements, the historian must consider carefully what weight should be attached to the evidence provided by each place-name or personal name, in addition to giving critical study to sources and linguistic evidence. Each case must be taken separately on its own merits. Those rules that can be laid down will be very general and will differ depending on whether the aim is to define a former linguistic area or an area of civilization—two branches of research which far too many writers tend to confuse.

For example, as Lot [no. 322] has succeeded in proving, countless place-names which contain the particle *ville* or *court* with a Germanic personal name as their first or second half have no significance for the history of Frankish settlement or the extent of the Frankish dialect. On the other hand they are extremely useful to the historian of Merovingian civilization, especially in relation to its second stage when the aristocracy grouped round the king turned into a class of great landowners. When trying to trace the history of the settlement only purely Germanic words should be taken into account. Cases where two parts are joined according to the rules of Germanic syntax, or are derived from a root according to Germanic usage, are especially illuminating. Single terms which could have crept into the local Romance dialect and dropped out of it later are to be mistrusted. The presence of an article is often a help in distinguishing them; for example, the place-name 'La Fère' by no means proves that a Frankish-speaking group settled at that precise spot; it only indicates that the institution of the *fara* (see p. 174) was known to people in the neighbourhood who may have spoken Romance for a long time. As this institution is typical of primitive Merovingian society the fact is still of keen interest to the historian, but for an entirely different reason.

Toponymists have long since learned to present their principal conclusions in the form of a map, but the historian must insist on their distinguishing with appropriate symbols the relative value of what they put down on these maps, not only in order of reliability (proven absolutely, probable, or only possible) but also in order of how informative they really are (names which prove colonization, or names which merely indicate influence; names of new settlements or those derived simply from a rechristening).

We must emphasize yet again that the linguistic origin of a name has nothing to do with the historical origin of the settlement; the latter can only be decided through study of the texts (though detailed and relevant texts are rare) or, more usually, through examination of the archaeological evidence. These tell us that dozens of villages in the east of France which have a Germanic name already existed in Gallo-Roman times.

Two subsidiary problems are a question of casuistry as much as of history. At what point does a group become proportionately large enough to impose a name in its own language on a village? Experience of bilingual areas in modern times proves that it is by no means essential for it to constitute a majority; it is enough that it should wield the greater social influence. Secondly, to what extent did the disintegration of the state, and in particular the destruction of the Roman land registers, encourage the enormous change-over of place-names in the early Middle Ages? One suspects that many estate names ending in *-iacum* or *-anum* were only official names which were not much used by the peasants and which disappeared as soon as public authority was no longer there to support them.

As far as archaeological research is concerned, we have already indicated that if it is unable to settle questions of nationality (except where skeletons are found which are obviously of non-Caucasian type), it does on the other hand offer us the most valuable and reliable data on questions of civilization. It is only thanks to archaeology that we can trace the precise limits of each stage in the progress of a new life style, the formation of the Merovingian complex, the areas where Frankish, Burgundian, Alamannic, Gothic or Lombard traits predominated, and so on. This discipline alone allows us to date settlement sites, to trace their distribution and to assess accurately their economic nature. With the perfecting of excavation and laboratory techniques the lessons to be drawn from it are becoming daily more numerous. In short, it is to archaeology that we must look in the years to come for the most substantial re-evaluation of the subject-matter of the present work.

The great majority of archaeological material today comes from chance finds; hence the severely limited value of distribution maps which deal with numbers that are too small. This proportion is rapidly diminishing in favour of organized excavations, which are of infinitely greater value. They alone allow us to tackle general problems methodically. Whereas a burial, particularly if it is an inhumation, attracts the attention of the most ignorant labourer, the traces of a hut built of wood, wattle or daub are only visible to a trained archaeologist. We know a great deal about the Gallo-Roman way of life, at least as far as the upper classes are concerned, but our knowledge of the subjects of the Merovingian kings comes almost exclusively from their tombs. This serious imbalance in our viewpoint will disappear as the results of more and more organized excavations of settlement sites are published.

While awaiting this revolution we must treat with caution works which, following old methods, claim to give a count of 'barbarian burials' without a precise analysis of either the date or the context. Only the broadest and most approximate conclusions can be drawn from them: a good many tombs which have been called 'Merovingian' belong to the eighth, and even the ninth, century, and many so-called 'barbarian warriors' are merely local peasants who owe nothing to the Franks except a few items of dress. The historian must use only those works which are based on critical discussion, excavation reports detailed enough to enable him to check everything he wishes, and material which he has been able to examine personally in museums.

The Barbarians and Rural Life

An assessment of the role of the barbarians in the development of the countryside is beyond the means of research at our disposal, even where historical work is furthest advanced, as in England, northern Gaul or the Rhineland. The more we know, the more the theories elaborated from over-simplified views come to grief. Only a handful of archaeological and legal aspects of the problem can be dealt with here.

Our first obstacle is that we are ignorant of the precise nature of the agrarian economy of the Later Roman Empire. Certain of the large villae were centres of exploitation, but this is not necessarily true of all of them. In many cases the land was probably cultivated by the inhabitants of indigenous hamlets. We know only one thing about crop rotation, and that is thanks to Pliny: the growing of spring cereals was still not common in the Trier area in the first century. It may have become so by the fifth century, however, for there are signs of many innovations in Gaul under the Empire, such as the use of the scythe and even the reaping-machine and the water-mill, and the spread of viticulture throughout the province. Apart from cases of centuriation we know absolutely nothing about how the land was parcelled out or how it was enclosed. It is not even clear which were the areas of concentrated settlement and which of scattered settlement.

The second obstacle is that we know even less about the rural economy after the collapse of the Empire and before the drawing up of the great polyptychs, or estate registers, of the ninth century, and our ignorance about some areas which produced hardly any of these documents, such as the west of France, continues until the eleventh century. In the Merovingian period only the history of land tenure is available to us, and nothing about the exploitation of the land. To date rural archaeology has come up with little more than the ruins of Roman villae and churches, and cemeteries: we know almost nothing about the rural settlements of this period, and nothing at all about agricultural implements. Crop rotation and field patterns are a closed book to us, and the study of field names does not take us back beyond the tenth century.

In these conditions it is futile to attempt to say that later medieval, or even modern, practices date back to the time of the invasions. Notions which have enjoyed a certain popularity for a time, such as that which attributes obligatory triennial crop rotation in regions of strip-farming in open fields to Germanic influence, or biennial crop rotation in irregular enclosures to a survival of Gallo-Roman habits, have no value whatsoever for the historian today. The same must be said of ideas about dwellings (for example the so-called 'Roman' tiled roofs of the south and of Lorraine) and agricultural implements (for example the southern *aratrum* or swing-plough, which is sometimes said to be of Roman origin).

The work of recent historians has shown that 'age-old' customs, or ones said to be 'characteristic of the region', in many cases do not go back for more than a few generations, or are found elsewhere in the most unexpected contexts. It is now known that isolated pockets of biennial crop rotation in the north of France (Alsace and Roumois) started after the end of the Middle Ages, and that triennial crop rotation was only systematically practised in England from the twelfth century on, although it was used from the ninth century onwards in the Paris basin. How, then, can the former be explained as a survival of Roman practice and the latter as an imported Germanic practice? Moreover, methods which were thought to be typically northern have been found as far afield as Sardinia, and even Syria. All this work has not been in vain, but from our point of view its conclusion is negative: 'the unchanging pattern of rural life' is a myth. In reality the rural economy has never ceased to be affected by wide-reaching fluctuations caused by demographic, economic and technological developments. Certain of these fluctuations were no doubt given direction or accelerated by the invasions, but it is impossible for us to distinguish them.[75]

After rejecting all these old theories, what are we left with? To start with, there are some archaeological facts. Many land holdings in England were remodelled at the time of the arrival of the Saxons, although the system which was overthrown was indigenous in nature, and not at all Roman. The archaeologist can also prove that in the most varied regions of Gaul, even very close to the *limes*, the artificial land divisions which had originated in the surveys of the Roman *agrimensores* continued to be respected. It can also be shown that certain settlement sites were inhabited right through the period, and that a good many others were not: in short, each region, perhaps each village and its land, is a separate case. Hundreds more monographs must be written before a synthesis can be attempted, and even that would clear up only a few aspects of the effect of the invasions on rural life.

One must not be led astray as to the impact of the invasions on legal institutions. There can be no conclusive proof except in the case of a very precisely defined institution: thus the reference to the *ius mancianum* on the Albertini tablets could be held to prove the survival of Roman forms of tenure in Vandal Africa. But what are we to deduce from the survival into the Merovingian period of elastic terms like *colonus* or *villa*? The choice of these words to describe the realities of Frankish society implies a certain analogy with the Roman institutions of the same name, but it would be unwise to go beyond that without further information. One can also produce statistics showing that whereas there are many Germanic loan-words in the vocabulary of legal, military and administrative institutions in those areas which continued to be Romance-speaking, there are practically none relating to agricultural or seignorial institutions. But what does this numerical evidence prove about colonization?

One must also be wary of attributing *all* upheavals among rural populations to the invasions. In Spain, for example, there are records of a catastrophic depopulation in the inland regions of the Levant (Carpetania). The Germans had nothing to do with this for we know from chronicles that it was the result of almost continuous epidemics in the sixth and seventh centuries. In short, it seems that the historian cannot be too cautious: even Marc Bloch, at the end of a lifetime of meticulous research, drew conclusions which were not warranted by the evidence [no. 105].

There should also be much more liaison between history and other disciplines, particularly archaeology, the study of place-names and the history of law, at the level of local monographs, before any new attempt is made to present an overall picture.

The Barbarians and the Towns

In attempting to answer the question whether or not the barbarians found a place for themselves in the towns, it is essential to make distinctions between different periods and different peoples.

As a general rule we can accept Tacitus's dictum that *Nullas Germanorum populis urbes habitari satis notum est* (it is well known that German peoples do not live in towns)[76] so long as we do not exaggerate their distaste for urban life. Germania had its *oppida*, vast areas enclosed by an earth, wooden or dry-stone wall, of the same type as those described by Caesar in Gaul, which served as a refuge in times of war, and sometimes as a semi-permanent dwelling-place as well. But there is nothing to indicate that these *oppida* were centres of economic activity, or that they had any status distinguishing them from lowland settlements. None of them served as a pre-urban nucleus for any of the towns of Carolingian Germany; their sites were more suitable for castles than for towns. The peoples outside the former Empire stayed at this primitive stage until the end of the eighth century, when the first of the emporia of Frisia and the Baltic coasts came into being. One can see why the Angles and the Saxons had difficulty in understanding the urban civilization of Britain.

But most of the Germans had come in contact with the Empire along the *limes*, and for military and economic reasons the *limes* was composed of a long string of towns, including Cologne, Mainz, Regensburg, Carnuntum and Aquincum. (Two imperial residences, Trier and Sirmium, were also in the immediate vicinity of the *limes*.) Probably in the fourth century and at the beginning of the fifth century these towns were in the process of losing their prestige: their great monuments were in ruins, their ruling classes had fled, and trade was on the decline. Nevertheless they held a great deal of attraction for the Germans. After a period of initial violence all the Germans showed themselves willing to respect and make use of the urban phenomenon. This early contact with urban life was perhaps more manifest in the case of the Franks: Nijmegen and Utrecht, situated in territory that the Franks had occupied as early as the middle of the fourth century, had kept at least their names. It may have been this familiarity that led to Childeric's choice of Tournai as his seat of government.

The onslaught of 406 was disastrous both for Gaul and for Italy. To be convinced of this we have only to read the famous—and over-literary—letter from St. Jerome to Ageruchia, or to look at the depth of the layers of ash on certain sites such as Strasbourg. The same thing happened in the north of Spain, according to Hydatius. But this invasion did not interrupt urban history to anything like the same extent as that of the third century had done. A few years after the storm had passed on the towns of the West had recovered the rhythm of their life, on the same topographical pattern and under the same administration, which had been more or less restored. Things were patched up, not destroyed for ever. Some of the towns henceforth looked rather like shanty-towns hastily thrown up after a disaster, but the majority continued to be dominated by the two buildings typical of the city during the Later Roman Empire: the *praetorium*, or palace of the governor, and the episcopal basilica.

Since the barbarians who lived in imperial territory sooner or later became federates, the respect which they must have had for the Roman way of life extended naturally to towns. Most of the Germans settled in the country, but their leaders, following the example of the Roman authorities, took up residence in the cities. Each kingdom had an urban residence for its court.[77] This practice was begun by the Visigoths in Bordeaux and Toulouse from 418 onwards (then in Narbonne from 508, in Barcelona from 531 and in Toledo from 551). The Vandal kings established themselves at Carthage in 439, the Burgundians in Geneva about 443 and in Lyons about 470, the Sueves in Braga probably between 430 and 440, and finally the Franks at Tournai before 481 and later in Paris under Clovis. Only the Ostrogoths dared, in 490, to choose an imperial capital, Ravenna, as their capital; the other peoples, possibly because they were afraid of being overwhelmed by the Roman elements of the population, contented themselves with provincial capitals or towns of secondary importance. Trier and Arles were abandoned. Evidently the royal residences set a fashion and what the king did in his town was imitated in other towns by lesser leaders.

Thanks to the remarkable work of L. Blondel relating to Geneva[78] we know the process by which one of the earliest barbarian courts was set up within a Roman town. At the beginning of the fifth century the city was composed of a quadrangular fortified enclosure perched on a hill and dominated by the *praetorium*, the cathedral, and the church of St. Germain, with a vast *suburbium* more or less abandoned to the dead and to their chapels. This arrangement dated back to the third century, and the Burgundian kings respected it. They chose to live in the *praetorium*, taking advantage of its chapel and of the comforts it offered, including baths and a hypocaust, without making any changes for a whole generation. About 500, in the course of a civil war, it was partly destroyed by fire, but was immediately rebuilt on very nearly the same plan, and it was only after the Frankish conquest in 534, when it had outlived its usefulness, that it fell into disrepair. The cathedral likewise survived the fateful year of 443 without incident.

When King Sigismund, who had been converted to Catholicism, rebuilt it, probably between 513 and 517, he consciously copied the great churches of the major imperial cities, constructing beside it a circular mausoleum resembling those of the fourth-century Emperors. Finally, the walls were restored, probably by Gundobad. The settlement of the Burgundians within the town had been an essentially conservative process.

The Burgundian king did not always live in the town. He had at his disposal two large villae, Ambérieu in the Dombes and Carouges on the Arve. The latter has also been excavated by Blondel. It was a Roman villa which had been heavily altered, frame buildings of Germanic type replacing stone constructions; a ditch, probably with a palisade, surrounded it. There the sovereign probably led a life more to his private taste, making use of the palace of Geneva mainly for ceremonial occasions.

Evidence found at Cologne points to the same sort of thing (see p. 129). The Frankish kings on the Rhine respected the immense *praetorium* of the legates of the Roman province of Germania, and very probably lived in it. Wherever possible the same procedure was adopted, and total obliteration of the traditions of urban life is recorded only in Britain. In Italy complete respect for urban civilization was combined with a degree of segregation which had been unheard-of in Roman times. It must be emphasized, however, that even in the barbarian quarters of these towns everything—architecture, plans, and decoration—remained faithful to the Roman tradition. It is impossible to imagine a more expressive gesture of acceptance. In Africa there was no destruction after a few initial incidents. The large-scale reconstruction of the towns in Africa in the sixth and seventh centuries was the work of Byzantine military engineers, who built cramped citadels with materials quarried from the great public buildings. Their work was ten times more efficient in destroying the past than anything the Vandals had done. Finally, in Spain the classical layout of towns was in most cases perfectly respected, except at Toledo, a very small town which had to be rebuilt when it was suddenly promoted to become a large capital city. The enthusiasm with which the barbarians took to the idea of towns is symbolized by the way in which barbarian rulers attempted to achieve immortality by calling cities after themselves. Thus in Africa Hadrumetum (now Sousse) was rechristened Hunericopolis, and in Raetia Chur was called Theodoricopolis for a brief period. About the year 578 Leovigild created the city of Reccopolis, called after his son Reccared, on the Tagus upstream from Toledo.

In spite of the conquerors' respect for urban life their triumph marked the beginnings of a process of decay; but at most one can accuse them of having allowed this to happen, not of having done

anything to bring it about themselves. A quick look at the development
of institutions is enough to convince one of this. When the barbarians
arrived there was hardly any municipal independence except on
paper. The curiae had been put under the guardianship of agents of
the imperial government, the *defensor civitatis* and a financial official,
the *curator*. The role of the *curiales* was often reduced to recording
changes in land tenure in the *gesta municipalia*. The two institutions of
the curia and *defensor* survived for a long time after the invasions. In
Gaul the curia of Le Mans was still functioning in 642, that of Orleans
in 651, and that of Poitiers in 677–8, and the *defensor* was sometimes
still in office in the south and especially in Burgundy until the ninth
or even the tenth century. But these cases of survival are not significant
in concrete terms; in fact the only powers left confronting one another
were the bishops and the military authorities—dukes or counts—and
the latter preferred wherever possible to live in the country rather
than in the city.[79] The spirit of the classical institutions was completely
extinct, as a result of old age more than anything else.

PROBLEMS OF CIVILIZATION

Barbarian Art

The period of the invasions coincides with the triumph of a new set
of aesthetics which reigned for three or four centuries over the ruins
of classical Graeco-Roman art. Obviously the barbarians cannot be
credited with all the innovations. They contributed very little to the
great new trends which changed the face of architecture (such as the
designing of buildings with their internal space rather than their
external appearance in mind, and the concealing of structural materials
under decorative facings) and sculpture (for example, the preference
for very low relief rather than sculpture in the round, and hence for
ornamental motifs rather than representational ones). These trends are
common to both West and East and they either originated in the
imperial art of the Later Roman Empire, or were imported from the
East. We have already shown what resulted from the revival of pre-
Roman indigenous traditions. It only remains to examine the genuinely
barbarian contribution, whether Germanic or Iranian, to define its
limits and to follow its career.

This contribution, without being absolutely confined to them,
involves the applied arts in particular: gold and other metalwork,
to a lesser extent glassmaking and pottery, and probably also textiles,
though about these we know very little. Hence there is a marked
contrast between the so-called 'major arts' and the 'minor arts': by

and large the former were influenced by what was happening in the Mediterranean world, though not without a time-lag and a certain degree of ineptitude, whereas the latter show a great deal of originality and creative energy. The problem is to decide where this new inspiration came from. It is unlikely to have been Germanic, for the only premonitory symptoms of it among the archaeological finds for the first three centuries AD in independent Germany are very unsatisfactory. Can it be attributed to the art of the steppes, and in particular to Persian influence? In fact the latter seems to have played only a very minor part in the movement of the invasions. Perhaps more emphasis should be laid on the revolution in taste that resulted from oriental influences within the Roman world on the eve of the invasions. All three of these approaches have their defenders, although each of them allows for many shades of opinion.[80]

But for a thorough appraisal of the problem one must distinguish several trends within the new direction art was taking. 1) There was an aesthetic revolution whereby more attention was paid to colour and line than to the fullness of form and mass. 2) There was also a new sense of movement, conceived as a perpetually repeated effort filling up every corner of the space within which it was confined until it almost burst free of it, a manifestation of primitive and irrepressible vitality. 3) At the same time an assimilation between the aesthetic and the intrinsic values of the work of art was aimed at: hence the most refined art forms were reserved for gold and silver work. The artist never forgot that he was first and foremost a craftsman: his virtuosity was displayed in strictly technical ways, such as in the use of filigree, enamelling, damascene work and so on, rather than in seeking new forms or expressions. 4) Finally, with rare exceptions, art once again became anonymous. Personal creativity gave way to collective tradition; every work of art was seen as one of a series, and differed only in minor details from similar works.

The revolution in taste on the one hand and the return to anonymity on the other are unquestionably general characteristics of the early Middle Ages, both inside and outside the barbarian kingdoms; no doubt Coptic or Syrian art could furnish equally good examples of these trends. Disagreement turns on the other two points, particularly the second, the animal ornament which took over in jewellery, teeming with life and yet extremely stylized. The study of techniques—particularly those used in cloisonné jewellery—is beginning to throw light on the general picture. Cloisonné jewellery has coloured stones—garnets, almandines, cornelians and so on—or enamels or brightly coloured glass paste, set within fine walls of gold over a cross-hatched ground of gold-foil. It first appeared in southern Russia, then spread quickly towards the west along the routes taken by the Gothic and

Hunnic migrations. The taste for filigree, granulation and damascene work followed the same route.

It seems reasonable to distinguish three phases. The first revival of barbarian art, shortly before 400, coincides with the first barbarian settlements on Roman soil and owes its origin to southern influences transmitted by federates or *laeti*. Then from the middle of the fifth century on oriental influences lead to the widespread adoption of a new form of ornament, based on cloisonné jewellery and the use of coloured stones and on certain simple animal motifs. Finally, towards the end of the sixth century, a new style of cloisonné goldwork and a new form of interlaced animal decoration of extraordinary complexity developed, possibly in Lombard Italy. This last phase owes a great deal to the Romano-Byzantine minor arts, which had meanwhile assimilated numerous features from the art of the Pontic steppes and the east. The adoption of these artistic elements occurred at various different points in the chronological development of barbarian art. It is obvious that we are dealing with a slow process of gestation which is complex at each of its stages and which can never be accounted for simply by borrowings.

Towards the end of this evolution a new style dominated the West, characterized by a unity which is astonishing. There are only regional variations within it: a Nordic and Anglo-Saxon variation, a Franco-Lombard one which was adopted by almost all of the peoples of what had formerly been Germania, with the exception of the Saxons, and a Gothic one which in its last stages was confined to the Iberian peninsula. It is one of the most striking illustrations of the way in which repercussions from the kingdoms which succeeded the Roman Empire were felt throughout the entire Germanic world.

But the prestige of this style was already severely shaken by the revival of Mediterranean influences transmitted by the Church from Italy and Spain, and also from Anglo-Saxon England, a fact which is explained by the circumstances of that country's conversion. Motifs like foliage inhabited by birds, the palmette, and the acanthus leaf quickly regained part of the ground they had lost, while in the Carolingian Empire the minor arts faded into the background as far as broad aesthetic development is concerned.

It must be stressed that the milieux which were least receptive to barbarian art show no evidence of any attachment to authentic Roman tradition. The art which they preferred was not at all classical, for the sources of its inspiration were to be found among the Copts and the Syrians, and in the indigenous world of the eastern Mediterranean, which was at that time enjoying a vigorous renaissance. Transmission was effected either through the orientals who were still to be found in large numbers throughout the West (with the exception of Britain), or through Byzantium. All things considered, its spirit was fairly close to Islamic art, which was partly formed on the same principles: avoidance of the human figure, preference for floral or geometric decoration, and low-relief sculpture. One can understand how Spain, which had been the bastion of this oriental style in its Christian form in the West during the Visigothic period, was able to show such creative vitality, without any perceptible breach with the past, when the style returned to her in its Moorish form after 711.

The Technical Contribution of the Barbarians

We have seen how the barbarian world had produced admirable goldsmiths who were capable of renewing and transforming their art. Historians have long been aware of this contribution, but recently a school of archaeologists inspired by E. Salin and A. France-Lanord has demonstrated that technological superiority extended also to a sphere of vital importance—metallurgy, and in particular the making of weapons.[81] These scholars show that the barbarians acquired or perfected all sorts of metalworking techniques which were remarkable for their ingenuity and efficiency, involving alloying, tempering, forging, welding and so on. They were able to produce a special steel for the cutting edge of their swords or battle-axes which was unequalled until the nineteenth century, and was infinitely superior to that which the imperial arms factories were producing during the Later Roman Empire.

These innovations seem to have owed very little to Roman technology. Some of them were merely continuations of the techniques used by blacksmiths in the proto-historic period, but greatly refined and perfected, while others incorporated oriental techniques. They have been studied in greatest detail in Frankish Gaul. In the same weapon many metals of very different quality were often combined (for example a sword might have a core of soft iron with a tempered steel cutting edge welded to it), forged with infinite patience in a lengthy process involving hammering, welding, twisting and burnishing: the finished product was a real masterpiece of virtuosity. There were swords whose core was made of eight strips of twisted metal wound round one another, doubled back, and then welded together. A cutting edge was welded onto this core, and the whole blade was still only 5mm thick. These techniques produced very beautiful, solid and remarkably flexible weapons. Pattern-welded blades—made up of strips of metal welded together—are three times less likely to become bent in battle than are blades made out of a single piece of metal. This accounts for the affection warriors had for their swords, which is reflected, after a considerable time-lag, in the Norse legends and the *chansons de geste*. Early medieval texts reveal practically nothing of this technical knowledge, doubtless because it was reserved to initiates who had no contact with clerics. The existence of this whole facet of Merovingian civilization would therefore have remained completely unsuspected if laboratory techniques had not recently been applied to archaeology.

This discovery offers ample material for reflection. Opposed to the Gallo-Roman methods of production, which even at that time were modern in their outlook, involving standardization of quality and mass-production, we see the appearance of the medieval concept of the article of practical use which is also a masterpiece, and is always in some way unique. On the other hand, the experimentation of the Frankish smiths is in startling contrast to the meekness with which the scholars of the time bowed to accepted conventions. Was there a possibility of progress in a new direction which remained unfulfilled simply because of the premature revival of the classical tradition among the élite?

Intellectual Life in Barbarian Europe

Although they were the bearers of new ideas in various fields of art and technology, the barbarians did not themselves contribute anything essential to intellectual life. Most of the doctrines to which they showed an attachment—Arianism in particular—had been developed in the Mediterranean world. The only sign of originality in what we know of Gothic literature is the language itself. The mediocre literary attempts of German kings like Sisebut or Chilperic were all well within the lines laid down by Latin education. The only really Germanic contribution to culture, runic script, went unnoticed by everyone except the very Roman Venantius Fortunatus, and served almost no practical purpose. We shall therefore consider only two problems here: to what extent did the invasions contribute to the destruction of classical culture, and did they pave the way for the birth of a Germanic culture at a later date?

Contemporary writers were not aware of any discontinuity except in certain areas, notably Gaul. Nothing of the sort was felt in Italy; until the Byzantine invasion of 534 the *rhetor Urbis Romae* was still employed as an official teacher. Still less was it felt in Spain, where at the beginning of the seventh century Isidore of Seville was still completely steeped in classical tradition, although with enough sense of perspective to realize that in the history of his country a Gothic régime had definitely superseded the Roman one. Moreover he had the detachment to hope that it would prove equally brilliant.[82] One can even suspect the sincerity of Gregory of Tours when he deplores so emphatically the fact that the study of classical literature has died out. No doubt his own language is incorrect and his literary technique is deficient, but what little he preserves of the liberal arts is fairly faithful to classical tradition.[83]

Another form of disruption, just as serious, attracted even less attention. This was the 'intellectual fragmentation of *Romania*' (J. Fontaine) which made each area of the former Western Empire an almost autonomous entity. Like the dialectal disintegration, this intellectual provincialism had set in well before the period of the invasions: as early as the fourth century it had already made considerable progress. In some areas the local culture was wiped out by the catastrophes of the fifth century, but in at least two areas, Africa and Spain, it continued to blossom even after these disasters had ceased. Visigothic Spain remained loyally attached to the last great Spanish authors of the Roman period—Juvencus, Prudentius and especially Orosius—while to all intents and purposes it ignored the work of Cassiodorus and Boethius in Italy, in spite of the long-established links between the Visigoths and the Ostrogoths.[94] This isolationism was confirmed and reinforced by the consolidation of the barbarian kingdoms: when he speaks of Gaul, Isidore of Seville shows not only the ignorance one would expect, but also a little of the contempt and hostility felt by the Goths for the Franks.

As there is no doubt about the continuity of ecclesiastical culture, the efforts of modern historians are concentrated on the question of the survival of a secular culture. In a celebrated article [no. 96] H. Pirenne has dealt with the problem of the education of laymen in Merovingian Gaul. He believed he had found positive evidence to confirm his pet thesis that there was continuity between the classical world and the early Middle Ages up to the time of the Arab conquests. This view has since had to be discounted:[85] public schools on the classical model retreated to the south and died out there at the end of the fifth century, or in the first third of the sixth century at the latest. For aristocrats the only possibility was private tutoring or, later, in the seventh century, an education at court, where the intellectual aspect was not considered particularly important. Only legal training might perhaps still be acquired in a school. Moreover, laymen had neither libraries nor didactic works of secular knowledge at their disposal to expand their horizons, and in any case in a warrior society their interests lay elsewhere.

In Spain the picture is less gloomy. We do not know what became of the schools there, but well into the seventh century counts still had libraries, and technical culture was still widespread enough at the end of the sixth century for the bishop of Mérida to be able to gather a number of *medici* together and organize a free medical service.[86] The Visigothic King Sisebut was a much better scholar than the Merovingian Chilperic. Above all, it was in Visigothic Spain that Isidore of Seville wrote his *Etymologiae* (often also called the *Origines*). Written in the first third of the seventh century, this great work constituted the most conscientious attempt of the early Middle Ages to synthesize for the benefit of succeeding generations the legacy of the scholars of the Later Roman Empire and the patristic period. It was probably of most use to clerics, but by far the greater part of it is devoted to secular knowledge. As J. Fontaine has shown,[87] there was an element of illusion in all this, for the material and social circumstances of a living culture on the classical model had disappeared. But this stubborn loyalty is a manifestation of the fact that until 711 Spain refused to recognize that the classical world had died with the Roman Empire.

In Italy, in this sphere as in others, the classical world survived until the time of Justinian, sufficiently full of self-confidence and vigour for original syntheses still to be made there, particularly by Boethius, for the fine points of scholarship still to be fully appreciated, and for Theodahad to pride himself on being a philosopher-king in the manner of the Antonine Emperors. The Byzantine government after the reconquest was inspired by the best of intentions, and an imperial decree reorganized higher education. As in Spain technical skills survived,[88] and Gregory the Great is proof that at the end of the sixth century Italy was still capable of producing great minds. But the class which was the bearer of this learning had shrunk considerably. Although it had survived in Ravenna and had managed, with great difficulty, to re-establish itself in Rome, everywhere else it was in rout (Venantius Fortunatus fled to Gaul in 565). Even those members of it who had survived physically were scattered and disorganized. Cassiodorus's flight from the world to his Calabrian monastery at Vivarium assumes the character of a symbol when we consider that during the Gothic era he had formed the link between learning and the government. As long as Lombard Italy continued to be an Arian warrior society it remained an intellectual void; by the time it became Catholic it was too late, and it found itself in circumstances very similar to those of Frankish Gaul.

The destruction of classical learning was not the work of the 'great invasions' (an abstract term which is much too general), for it outlived some of them, particularly the Gothic invasions; when this learning disappeared it was less as a result of their direct impact than of the fact that it had been transplanted into a society which had no use for it, and whose human ideals were quite different.

The period of the invasions did not give birth to any Germanic intellectual culture worthy of the name. The scattered efforts in this direction came either before the invasions, with the invention of runes and the work of Ulfila, or after them, with the German authors of the Carolingian period. A time of social and political crisis is obviously not very propitious for the development of thought, but when the culture finally did appear, this colourful period had an irresistible attraction for it: the invasions form the background to almost all of the German epics. The *Hildebrandslied*, which was written down at Fulda roughly between 810 and 820, reflects Theodoric's struggle against Odoacer. All the great works which followed, including *Widsith* in England, the *Edda* and the *Völsungasaga* in Iceland and the *Nibelungenlied* in Germany, drew on memories of the two centuries which separated the struggle between the Goths and the Huns in the Ukraine in 375 from the start of Justinian's reconquest of Italy. It is astonishing to think of the Icelandic scholars who set down the Eddic texts in writing in the twelfth century faithfully transcribing the names for the Carpathians (*Harfadhafjöll*) and the Dnieper (*Danpr*), for Ermanaric (*Jörmunrekr*) and Attila (*Atli*), which they had inherited from 700 years of oral tradition. Although the Anglo-Saxons had had no part in events on the continent, their court bards (*scōp*) nevertheless had to interlard their poems with the same Gothic or Hunnish names.[89] Three or four figures dominate this epic world: two Goths, Ermanaric and Theodoric; Attila the Hun; and possibly a Frank, Theuderic the son of Clovis, who began the conquest of Germany.[90]

Repercussions in Germany

It was a stroke of bad luck for Germanic civilization that the Ostrogoths should have failed to found a lasting kingdom, while the Franks succeeded. Theodoric felt a sense of solidarity with the Germans who had stayed outside the Empire, which is reflected in Cassiodorus's correspondence and in the great sums which poured into the German world as far away as Scandinavia, in the form of soldiers' wages. Clovis and his descendants do not seem to have shared this feeling, for they left their brother-Germans beyond the Rhine to fend for themselves. The Merovingian world took very little interest even in its own German protectorates. This fact is proved in the intellectual sphere by the extraordinary slowness with which the alphabet spread beyond the Rhine. Runic script, which had enjoyed only a limited success on the continent, died out there in the seventh century, but was not replaced by anything else until the ninth century.[91]

This neglect extended, even more scandalously, to religion. Until the Anglo-Saxon mission at the very end of the seventh century the conversion of Germany had been left to a handful of individuals from among the Romance-speaking communities near the linguistic frontier, acting on their own initiative. Their efforts, which were slow and hesitant, had only managed to reconquer the left bank of the Rhine and set up a few bridgeheads in Hesse and in Alamannia.[92] Elsewhere the majority of the ruling classes had probably become Catholic through contact with the court, and a few churches were being built here and there, but there was no ecclesiastical organization and no tradition of religious learning. As soon as it became a question of going beyond the bounds inherited from Rome, the Frankish Church seemed to be seized with a sort of paralysis. (Saxon England continued to feel certain responsibilities towards the Old Saxons on the continent. After its conversion to Christianity these were probably mainly religious in nature, but Bede bears witness to the fact that the Anglo-Saxons also had a sense of ethnic solidarity with the Old Saxons. This may have been one of the factors which prompted the Anglo-Saxon mission to Germany.)

Even in the economic field, Merovingian Gaul hindered the advancement of Germany by not allowing coinage, the principal element essential to any form of development, to cross the Rhine. The extraordinary density of distribution of the Merovingian mints thins out noticeably the nearer one gets to the Rhine, and not a single mint of any size was set up beyond the river. Except in Frisia, which was precisely the region which escaped domination by the Franks, the use of coinage continued to be unknown in Germany beyond the Rhine until the Carolingian period. Until then the people of this area did use precious metals, but weighed on scales rather than struck as coins.[93] Urban civilization was equally non-existent.

All this neglect poses a problem, some of whose social aspects have been ably studied by R. Sprandel [no. 415]. He has shown that in spite of the sixth-century expansion beyond the Rhine, the Roman concept of the frontier of civilization running along the river continued to exist. The new aristocracy, which was formed by the coming together of the Frankish conquerors and the senatorial class, turned its back on the eastern regions. This negative attitude only lost ground when, simultaneously with the rise of the Pippinids in the second half of the seventh century, the centre of gravity of the Frankish kingdom, which had hitherto been in the region of the Seine, the Marne and the Oise, shifted to the north-east.

One gets the impression that the policy of Theudebert and Parthenius, like that of Theodoric on which it was modelled, would have produced a very different situation, had it been pursued. Instead, nothing at all was achieved in the century between the death of Clothar I in 561 and the coming to power of Pippin of Herstal in 679.

INSTITUTIONS

The Legal Framework of Barbarian Society

It is not the aim of this book to study the institutions of barbarian Europe.[94] Nevertheless emphasis must be placed on the fact that the legal institutions were not born of a natural antipathy between the Roman and the German worlds. At the time of the collapse of the Empire, Roman law was no longer a monolithic structure. Recent research has all been directed towards seeking out, behind the façade of classical law which finally triumphed in Justinian's codes, the vulgar law which was practised in the provinces and of which there are occasional glimpses in imperial legislation after the time of Constantine.

It seems to be an established fact that all the Roman codes drawn up under barbarian rule (the *Breviarium Alarici* of 506 for the Visigothic kingdom; the *Lex Romana Burgundionum* of the beginning of the sixth century in the Burgundian kingdom; the *Edictum Theoderici* of the same period in Ostrogothic Italy; and the *Lex Romana Curiensium* of the eighth century in Raetia)[95] were based on this vulgar law, whose increasing popularity in the West the imperial authorities had been powerless to prevent. It also played a large part in the codes created for the barbarians themselves. But a school of legal historians, notably in Spain, thinks that this 'vulgarization' went even further. After the reconquest of Spain, Castilian legal customs contained certain features which were foreign to official Roman law, to the compilations of the Visigothic period and to Muslim law (for example the right of private vengeance, oath-helpers who confirm under oath the good character of the accused, and the *morgengabe*, or gift from the bridegroom to the bride on the morning after the wedding). Where did these features come from? Three hypotheses have been put forward: they were borrowed from Frankish law, they were pre-Roman customs which survived through the medium of a very unclassical vulgar law, or they were produced by the coming together of Roman vulgar law, Gothic customs and Frankish customs.

As for Germanic law, because it was written down in Latin it never comes down to us in a pure form. Its archaic aspects are most apparent in the law of the Franks, the *Lex Salica* 'of 65 clauses' drawn up between 507 and 511, and in that of the Lombards, the *Edictum Rotharii* of 643. In spite of their early date the first code of Visigothic law, the *Codex Eurici*, drawn up some time between 470 and 480, and the Burgundian law code of King Gundobad, of roughly 501–15 (often known by its French name as the *Loi Gombette*), include a massive amount of Roman law. Nothing of the Germanic law of the Ostrogoths or of the Vandals has been preserved. The Alamans and the Bavarians were no longer independent when they drew up their law codes, the *Pactus Alamannorum* and the *Lex Bajuvariorum*; they borrow a great deal from Salic, Gothic or canon law. The other barbarian law codes (the *Lex Ripuarensis*, the *Lex Thuringii* and the *Lex Francorum Chamavii*) are secondary offshoots of Salic law which appeared in the seventh, eighth and ninth centuries respectively. The English laws, which are the only ones to have been written down in a Germanic language (the earliest being the law of Aethelberht of Kent, of the end of the sixth century), form a separate group.

On the basis of the most archaic of these texts it is easy to distinguish a common 'spirit' of barbarian law, characterized by the following traits: the uniquely oral and formalized procedure, the personality of the laws, the role of oath-helpers and ordeals, the rates of monetary compensation (*wergeld*) depending on the gravity of the crime, ties of kinship and so on. There is no question but that these traits formed part of a common Germanic tradition: many of them are found in Scandinavian law, which was set down in writing from the twelfth century onwards far from all possible contact with Roman influence. But doubtless Roman ideas or innovations lurk in more than one corner of barbarian law.

The very idea of codifying laws is revealing: large numbers of both private and official codifications of the law like the Gregorian Code had been compiled by Roman lawyers since the end of the third century. One cannot exclude the possibility that the personality of the laws might have been known, at least tacitly, to Roman vulgar law, in the case of the *laeti* or federates. Certain stipulations in the Salic tables of *wergeld* are so favourable to the king (the *wergeld* was tripled for the king's men, and a high percentage of all compensation devolved to the king) that they must represent modifications which crept in after the consolidation of the Merovingian dynasty. The personality of the laws probably does not indicate ethnic origin as often as has been thought: the clerics, or at any rate the prelates as a body, were thought of as Romans, whatever their descent, and great landowners made wills—an action appropriate to the state of their fortunes, but unknown to Germanic law.

On the other hand Roman ideas reacted on barbarian practice quickly enough for several kingdoms to have abandoned some of these 'fundamental principles'. Thus the Visigothic kingdom, which has left us the most extensive corpus of legislative material, renounced the personality of the laws in favour of the Roman (and modern) idea of territoriality. When and how this came about are questions which are hotly disputed by legal historians.[96] The traditional interpretation is that the Goths lived under the *Codex Eurici*, compiled between 470 and

480 and revised by Leovigild between 570 and 580, and the Romans under the *Breviarium Alarici* of 506. According to this interpretation Recceswinth's *Liber Judiciorum* of 654, which forbade resort to any other law under pain of a fine, created a territorial law, subsequently revised slightly by Erwig in his *Lex Renovata* of 681, and probably also by Egica in 693. But for a long time historians have been wondering whether territoriality was not established in practice as early as the time of Leovigild. In 1941 García Gallo[97] launched a campaign to prove that territoriality came in much earlier—a campaign which ended by adopting very extreme positions. Alvaro d'Ors believes that the *Codex Eurici*, far from representing a very ancient if rather adulterated example of Germanic law, is no more than a compilation of Roman vulgar law, drawn up under the influence of Gallo-Roman jurists and therefore naturally territorial in character.[98] Germanic elements appear, perhaps as a result of Frankish influence, only in the time of Recceswinth; according to his theory the Visigoths would never, in fact, have known the system of the personality of the laws.

It is too early to say how accurate these views will turn out to be, but we may draw the conclusion that it is unwise to infer the existence of the personality of the law in a given country unless documents relating to the application of that law (which are lacking for Spain) establish this directly by reference to the *professio legis*.

Parallel doubts have been expressed by Roels with regard to Burgundian legislation.[99] There is nothing to prove that the *Lex Burgundionum* on the one hand and the *Lex Romana Burgundionum* on the other are two official and parallel texts intended to be applied respectively to the Germanic and the Roman subjects of the Burgundian king. It is quite possible that the so-called *Lex Romana Burgundionum* (a title invented by modern scholars) is only a private compilation,[100] and that the *Lex Burgundionum* is, after all, territorial in nature. In that case it would have to be admitted that Gothic law and Burgundian law were only tailored to fit into a system of personality within the framework of the Frankish kingdom after the conquest of Burgundy by the sons of Clovis, and after the incorporation of Septimania into the kingdom of Pippin the Short. Hence, a true régime of personality would have existed for the first time only in the Merovingian and Lombard worlds, that is to say, in states belonging to the second generation of barbarian kingdoms.

The Structure of the Barbarian States

The first-generation barbarian kingdoms—those founded by East Germanic peoples in the Mediterranean basin—showed very little

H

imagination in the field of politics. They borrowed the mechanism necessary to keep their central and local administration functioning either from Rome, from the government of Ravenna, or from the praetorian prefects, and they kept the fundamental distinction, established by Diocletian, between the civil and military authorities. The kingdoms of the second generation—the Merovingian and Lombard kingdoms in particular—brought many innovations, abandoned whole areas of the classical political structure, and rejected the system of hierarchies and careers laid down under the Tetrarchy.

The Roman system of government operated at three levels, those of the imperial court, of prefects and vicars, and of provincial governors. Only the régimes of Odoacer and Theodoric in Italy kept all of these. Let us look back for a moment to the time of Theodoric, when the correspondence of Cassiodorus allows us to examine the structure of the state much better than in the case of any other barbarian kingdom. What is left of the imperial prerogatives belongs to Theodoric, though the Gothic king by no means insists on all of them. He is still surrounded by the great leaders of the civil service: the *magister officiorum*, the *quaestor palatii* and the *comes sacrarum largitionum*, responsible for the offices of the chancellery, the secretariat and the treasury respectively. All those who hold these posts are Romans, while the Gothic counts are only involved in the private service of the prince and in military affairs. At the intermediate level the praetorian prefects of Italy and of the Gauls are retained, and vicars continue in office in Arles and Rome. At the lowest level the provinces are still in the hands of *consulares*, *correctores* or *praesides*. In short, nothing has changed.

The other kingdoms, having no former capital or prefecture within their jurisdiction, had to be content with simpler structures combining the households of Germanic origin, found everywhere, with administrative units modelled more or less closely on those of the provincial governors, and with a few elements copied from the court at Ravenna or from that of Byzantium. In Toledo the *officium palatinum* combined government, justice, finance and the affairs of the royal household, while the provinces were split up into military commands and put into the hands of dukes. This confusion was already apparent when the seat of Visigothic government was at Toulouse: the *consiliarius* took on the functions which had been restricted to the *quaestor sacri palatii* and to the *magister officiorum* at Ravenna. (A. d'Ors has suggested that the Visigothic king at Toulouse may have annexed to himself the jurisdiction of the prefect at Arles, but this hypothesis has not found general support.) At Lyons the confusion was slightly less (it is known that there was a *quaestor palatii*, and probably also a chancellor and a major-domo), but there too the provincial divisions were forgotten. At Carthage a single *praepositus regni* was set over all the departments of the civil service: the provinces survived as geographic divisions, but they no longer had at their heads an agent from the central government. In the Visigothic and Burgundian kingdoms it was the *comes civitatis*, an official whose post the dying Empire only just had time to institute, who performed the essential administrative duties. Everywhere, in fact, the fundamental resources of the state continued to be provided by the Roman taxation system, the burden of which rested on the Roman inhabitants, through the medium of a government land survey whose registers continued to be kept more or less up to date; the general exemption from taxes which the barbarian estates enjoyed must have diminished the yield as well as increased the burden.

In the second generation kingdoms the memory of the imperial system faded, and civil administration was more or less taken over by court officials or by military institutions. The public resources of the sovereign henceforth played only a secondary role, which was far outweighed by the revenue from the royal estates and by legal profits (though indirect taxation did survive to a much greater extent than direct taxation). Among the Franks nothing was left of the great Roman administrative services; the old land registers were abandoned towards the end of the sixth century (except in Raetia, where they were in use until the eighth century), and not a single administrative division even remotely resembled the former provinces. All local authority was vested in counts and dukes—leaders of military origin. The palace of the Lombard king kept the name of *sacrum palatium* and the rank of *referendarius* (head of the chancellery), possibly thanks to Byzantine influence; but most of the great dignitaries, such as the *marpahiz*, the *stolesaz* and the *scipoz*, were of Germanic origin, while others, like the *vestiarius* and the *cubicularius*, were closely modelled on the hierarchy of the Byzantine exarchate of Ravenna. Direct taxation had practically disappeared, and the provinces, whose boundaries had been altered time and again as the frontiers with Byzantium shifted, yielded to the duchies.

It has only been possible to establish the exact origins and development of the administrative institutions of barbarian Europe in two or three cases.[101] The most important concerns the institution of the counts. The *comes civitatis* appeared in the very last years of the Western Empire; at first he was a dignitary of the imperial entourage or *comitiva*—hence his name—deputed temporarily to some place of prime importance to fill a post of military and civil command there.[102] But the rapid spread of this institution, which was still in an embryonic state in 476, is still unexplained; it implies that the West, in spite of its political break-up, still constituted a recognizable legal unit. Perhaps the Gothic kingdom of Toulouse had a decisive role to play in this diffusion: already in the *Codex Eurici* the existence of counts in the cities was taken for granted. In sixth-century Gaul it was still primarily a southern institution; it only became widespread in the north in the seventh century.[103] In Gothic Italy the use of counts was still only sporadic when Justinian's reconquest temporarily abolished them, but the Lombard kingdom re-established the practice on its own initiative. The Roman ancestry of the rank of duke, whose authority was still essentially military, is even more direct, but among the Goths ducal powers sometimes approximated to those of the provincial governor, an essentially civilian authority.[104] The origin of the equivalences between Latin and Germanic titles, as in *comes* = *grâvo* and *dux* = *herizogo*, ought to be studied. They only became fixed quite late, and even in the Carolingian period *grafio* is often equated to *vicecomes*.

At this point the curious attempt made by Ernest Babut to link the Merovingian administrative hierarchy with the Roman military hierarchy must be mentioned.[105] Babut's proposal is too systematic, but the idea merits detailed critical examination. He suggests that in the middle of the fifth century there was widespread inflation of titles: nearly all the tribunes were promoted to the next rank, becoming counts, and certain counts were made dukes. The fact that these tribune-counts took up residence in the cities would be accounted for by the dislocation of the military *annona*.

The Problem of Hospitalitas

The legal basis for the settlement of the first great barbarian peoples within the Empire was a treaty, or *foedus*, which, on the one hand, laid down that the newcomers would respect the laws of Rome (at least in theory) and, on the other, defined conditions under which the barbarians should be billeted and maintained at the expense of the Romans, in terms inspired by the law relating to military billeting, as set out before the invasions in the Theodosian Code. The clause which had most importance for the history of the settlement was that dealing with *hospitalitas*. This term refers to the assignment of part of a Roman rural estate or group of estates to a small military or family group of barbarians, whose needs with regard to food and shelter must thus be satisfied. Such a system is in theory, as often in fact, largely conservative: it respects the prime rights of the landowners and the boundaries and structure of their estates, as it is only concerned with their yield. It prevents confiscation of property and needless violence: if the barbarian is sensible, he will be interested in the efficient exploitation of the soil in whose fruits he has a share. In theory, any breach of the *foedus* or the departure of the barbarians for another billet restored to the landowner all his prerogatives. As it turned out, the barbarians put down roots, but they were induced to understand, and often to imitate, an agrarian system which was completely new to them. Where it lasted for any length of time, *hospitalitas* was a powerful aid to assimilation.

The texts establish that *hospitalitas* was extended to at least five peoples: the Visigoths, the Burgundians, the Ostrogoths and, briefly, the Alans and the Vandals. Moreover it probably served as a more or less conscious model for other colonists who were not covered by a formal treaty. Unfortunately such information as we have on this vital subject is of poor quality; it is extremely difficult to translate into concrete terms, and the various interpretations proposed by modern historians are highly contradictory.[106] We do not know the details of the clauses contained in the first of the great agreements of *hospitalitas*, that concluded in 418 by the patrician Constantius with the Visigoths of Wallia. The clauses were not identical in all cases; they varied according to the size of the peoples in question and the extent of the regions assigned to them as billets. The Visigoths and Burgundians, who were established in fairly restricted areas, usually received two-thirds of the land, while the Ostrogoths, who had more room in Italy, were content with one-third. In fact the food supplies of many Ostrogoths billeted in the towns, particularly in Ravenna, were provided by the *annona*, and not by the system of *hospitalitas*.

Let us quickly review the principal elements which went to make up *hospitalitas*. As far as the Roman landowners are concerned, only the great estates of the aristocracy were affected—a text of 456 relating to the Burgundians only mentions the senators as being liable for billeting.[107] In some cases, the best-known being that of the Alans in the district of Valence in 440, estates which had been abandoned were the first to be requisitioned. (Presumably the peculiar nature of their nomadic way of life made the Alans better adapted to profit from the *deserta Valentinae urbis* in wandering around with their herds.) Almost always the system affected a limited area only, as the government was more concerned with keeping the barbarian army together than with making sure that the soldiers were evenly and fairly assigned over a large area. A systematic attempt to spread the burden evenly was only found in the best-administered kingdom—Theodoric's Italy, where those landowners who had not handed over a third of their land to the Goths had to deliver a third of their income to a public fund, which was probably used to pay the wages of Goths quartered in towns or along the *limes*. Elsewhere the fact that the great family estates were so scattered was enough to ensure a certain fairness of distribution.

The technical name for the part assigned to the barbarian 'guests' is *sors*, that is to say 'share' or 'lot'. What proportion of the total estate was it? For the Visigoths and the Burgundians it was two-thirds of the land, and the part left to the Romans was therefore referred to as the *tertia*. For the Ostrogoths it was one-third, and here it is the Goths' portion which is called the *tertia*. We do not know what the proportion was for the Alans and the Vandals. The proportion of one-third had a long history behind it; during the Later Roman Empire it was applied to the allowances which the landowners had to give to soldiers or civil servants on official business who were armed with an accommodation voucher, and it had been taken up by Odoacer for the quartering of his troops. The barbarians in Italy were thus treated as if they were soldiers in billets.[108] The proportion of two-thirds in Gaul and in Spain seems to have been an innovation.

These proportions were not applied uniformly to all the parts of an estate. Clause LIV of the *Lex Burgundionum*, which is the most explicit text, indicates that a Burgundian received two-thirds of the land, one-third of the slaves, and half of the forests, the *curtis* (farm buildings) and the orchards. The details of these anomalies are not very clear, but the spirit of the law seems to have been to leave the Roman with more extensive rights on the land cultivated directly by himself and his slaves than on the land held by tenants; as the direct profit from the former must have been larger, the Roman would ultimately have been able to count on about half of his former revenues.

These partitions were organized by Roman officials, and it is in Ostrogothic Italy that we can best see them at work. There the operation was directed by a talented official called Liberius, the praetorian prefect, who, as an agent of Odoacer, had already had experience of a very similar system; under his orders operated the *delegatores* who made the actual partitions by drawing up written documents (called *pittacia*, like the former billeting orders).

The great problem is to know how the partition worked in practice. Did the barbarians in fact receive the third or the two-thirds of the land and cultivate it with their own hands, with the help of the slaves who came to them as part of their *sors*? Or was it in fact only the harvests which were shared out? Did the barbarians take up residence in part of the owner's house, or did they build separate living quarters for themselves? Did the fields of the barbarians form a coherent unit within the estate? It seems that the solutions to these practical problems varied considerably within the general framework of the *foedus*. We have one instance of this relating to living quarters. In 456 a group of Burgundians installed themselves in the house of Sidonius Apollinaris (*Carmina XII*); later on, Burgundians are known to have had their own houses,[109] and the land was divided out equally.[110] Nevertheless neither archaeology nor the study of place-names can reveal to us exactly how a former estate was divided according to the legal proportions in any particular case.

The rights of the barbarian 'guest' over his *sors* only slowly acquired the character of quasi-ownership. Burgundian law made the Roman the sole representative of the estate in legal actions concerning it, and gave him the right of repurchasing the rest of his estate if the barbarian 'guest' left. In Visigothic law the partition and the rights of the guest became sacrosanct at the end of a period of fifty years. A legal fiction which was particularly insisted on in the kingdom of Theodoric regarded the Roman and his guest as associates, *consortes*, and their association as common ownership, *communio praediorum*.

Save in exceptional cases (such as those involving the bringing of new land under cultivation, in Burgundian law), the sources only ever refer to an arrangement made between a single Roman and an individual barbarian. This would imply that among the barbarian settlers there were chieftains who were responsible for their men. It has been suggested that this favoured the establishment of more or less seigneurial links between the barbarian *optimates* and the mass of ordinary soldiers who received land from them; thus two aristocracies, one Roman and the other barbarian, would have found themselves on an almost equal footing.[111]

We know nothing of the psychological aspects of this proximity of the two peoples. In one instance things turned out badly; the nomadic Alans of King Goar, installed by Aetius probably on the Loire in 442, could not come to an understanding with the Gallo-Romans and forcibly ejected the *domini* of the lands that had been assigned to them. The history of the Vandals, who preferred outright confiscation to the system of *hospitalitas*, tells a similar tale. Partition could only succeed among peoples who were already fairly well-disciplined.

The great advantage of *hospitalitas* was that it gave the barbarians the land which was essential for their subsistence, while avoiding violence and laying the burden of the operation upon those best able to bear it. This was a remarkable change of attitude: the system of *hospitalitas* functioned mainly at the expense of the senators, whereas formerly, according to the old imperial laws, they had widely been given preferential treatment in the matter of the billeting of troops; the senator's principal residence, for example, had been exempt. The barbarians found an immediate advantage in this efficient system, for they obtained thereby not only the land, but part of the means of exploiting it. Nevertheless, in the long run the system certainly worked to the advantage of Roman civilization: dispersed in small groups and integrated into the Roman agrarian organization the newcomers were assimilated much more easily.

The most solid bastions of the German way of life, on the other hand, may well have been the more compact colonies established on lands either inherited from the imperial patrimony or confiscated from fleeing landowners. But we must not exaggerate the importance of the agreements of *hospitalitas*. They really concerned only those barbarian kingdoms of the first generation that were set up before the end of the fifth century in the Mediterranean basin. It was in the course of the second generation and in the north of Merovingian Gaul that the most lasting syntheses were formed.

7 Regional Aspects

THE MEDITERRANEAN WORLD

The Invasions and the Disruption of Mediterranean Unity

The Mediterranean brought coherence and unity to the Roman West, not so much strategically or in terms of naval power (the permanent fleets of Misenum and Ravenna still existed in the fifth century, but since the time of Diocletian they had been functioning only on a regional basis, like the oriental fleets), as economically. In the state economy of the Later Roman Empire the shipping routes used by the licensed ship-owners played a vital part. They converged on Italy, and in particular on Rome, which could not survive without the annual shipments of corn from Africa, Sicily and Sardinia. (Egyptian corn, which had been indispensable to Rome, had been diverted to Byzantium since the time of Constantine.) Thus anything which took place in any part of the Mediterranean world, and in the centre especially, had repercussions in the capital of the Empire. Moreover both the inherited estates of the great landowners and the careers of imperial officials embraced the whole of the Mediterranean world. [1]

The barbarian West on the eve of the Islamic conquests, however, showed a striking lack of unity. The grain fleets had disappeared from the seas, and Rome was no longer the great centre it had been. Such trade as survived was mostly carried on directly with the East and, in spite of state supervision of the arrival and departure of vessels, it was promoted by private enterprise. Hardly anyone travelled from one country to another, apart from merchants and professional diplomats, and it was henceforth regarded as an act of treason to own lands in more than one sector of the Mediterranean world at once. Italy, Spain, Africa and Mediterranean Gaul each went their own way. The essential question is whether the invasions can be held responsible for this dislocation. [2]

The first time the barbarians made a serious impact on the Mediterranean world was when Alaric led an expedition into Italy and sacked Rome. This only served to bind the Mediterranean world more closely together, thanks to the movements of refugees. The decline in the population of Rome (the number of *frumentationes* or 'ration books'

219

for corn distribution seems to have fallen from 244,000 to 120,000 between AD 367 and 419[3]) was bound to bring about a diminution in the grain shipments, although they had lost none of their political and economic significance at the time the Vandals took Carthage.

It is to Genseric's credit that he clearly grasped this situation. His aim seems to have been to blackmail Rome by gaining control of her corn supplies. First it was necessary to take over the three principal sources of grain. Genseric had conquered Africa by 439; he gained a foothold in Sicily in the following year and occupied Sardinia around 455. It has been suggested that he would have needed a fleet of war-ships to accomplish his aims. Courtois, who sees Genseric as the founder of a 'corn empire', is of the opinion that requisitioning the ships .of the grain fleet would have given him sufficient for all his needs, but F. Giunta, who sees Genseric as little more than a pirate, considers that as such he would have needed more solid naval support.[4] There are no texts to help us decide who is correct. At any rate as long as Genseric lived the Vandals were able to use their ships to cause the greatest possible inconvenience to the Roman world. From 437 to 477 Vandal pirates were to be found almost all over the Mediterranean. Until roughly 468 there were almost annual raids on the coasts of Italy. In about 474 there were two raids on Epirus and Greece, and a little earlier there had been two raids on Spain, one of which was directed against Galicia on the Atlantic coast, which makes one wonder whether the Vandals had perhaps preserved contacts with their earlier home. Their various activities culminated in the capture of Rome in 455, from which they brought back an immense amount of booty in prisoners and treasure. Under Genseric's successors the Vandal fleet confined itself to defending Vandal territory and to maintaining the links between Africa and the islands across the central Mediterranean. In spite of its Andalusian origins, Genseric's empire did not forge any lasting links between Spain and Africa, nor with Corsica or Sardinia, which were mainly used as places of exile, so one can hardly compare this maritime empire to the thalassocracies which preceded it.

To what extent did the old imperial system survive this terrible crisis? By negotiating with Carthage Odoacer was able to get the importation of grain from Sicily functioning again, and Theodoric continued this *modus vivendi*. The guilds which were responsible for the provisioning of Rome, the *catabolenses* and the *navicularii*, were still functioning in the Ostrogothic period; they brought corn from Apulia, and were requisitioned for transport to Gaul. But it would appear that the shipments from Africa and Sardinia had been dis-continued, and that was the vital factor. African agriculture began to operate in isolation, and Italy had to manage without it; private trade seems to have been more or less broken off. Then the destruction of Rome during the Gothic wars put paid to all hopes of re-establishing the old commercial system; Justinian did nothing to restore the shattered economic and social unity.

Thus the decisive turning-point came slightly before the collapse of the Western Empire. From about 440 to 460 onwards all the countries in the Mediterranean West have to be considered as autonomous entities. Even their reactions to the Byzantine reconquest—which affected all of them to a greater or lesser extent—were entirely different. Some historians have gone so far as to hold Genseric responsible for the eventual destruction of the Empire.[5] This is an exaggeration, but he did bring about the relative isolation in which Spain and Africa found themselves henceforth in relation to Italy and, to a lesser extent, to Gaul. From then on it was only rarely that individuals passed from one country to another.

One result of this fragmentation was that most of the Mediterranean islands were consigned to oblivion. They were of no interest to anyone between the fall of the Vandal kingdom and the start of Saracen piracy around 800. In spite of their being Byzantine or Frankish protectorates in theory, Corsica and Sardinia organized themselves to live as a closed community and turned their backs on the sea—as early as the time of Justinian, the Emperor only held the coastal plains and the mining regions. The Lombard occupation of Italy, and later the Arab occupation of Carthage, broke the last ties which bound them to the outside world. The Sardinian tribes, probably reinforced by African deportees, the *Barbaricini*, achieved real, if unofficial, independence, rather like that of the Moors of Courtois's 'Afrique oubliée'—the Forgotten Africa of the mountains and deserts. Sardinia and Corsica could be considered a sort of 'Forgotten Italy'.

Dalmatia was another casualty. When the Empire split up in the fourth century it had been assigned to the *pars Occidentis*, and had shared the fate of Italy until the fall of the Ostrogoths, so that its security was guaranteed by the dealings the latter had with the hinterland as far as the Danube. After the Byzantine reconquest, however, Dalmatia was to share the disastrous fortunes of the Balkans. By 600 the Slavs were blockading Salona (now known as Split), which was destroyed by the Avars around 614; the inhabitants shut themselves up in the ruins of the fortified palace of Diocletian, and the relics of the martyrs were brought to Rome by Pope John IV (640–2). For a long time this province, which had been the cradle of so many Emperors of the Later Roman Empire, ceased to participate in the life of the West.

Each of the new Mediterranean kingdoms, thrown back on its own resources, was obliged to relinquish part of its territory to the 'indigenous barbarians'. Italy lost her islands to them (with the exception of

Sicily), Spain the Basque Country, and Africa the whole of her western part. It is a familiar story.

A Comparative History of the Germanic Kingdoms in the Mediterranean Regions

It is obvious that at every stage of their history the kingdoms founded by the Goths, the Vandals, and to a lesser extent the Burgundians, were totally different in character from those of Merovingian Gaul, Anglo-Saxon England or Lombard Italy.[6]

Their originality consists firstly in their deep-seated loyalty to the classical system, not only as far as intellectual and political affairs are concerned, but particularly also in the sphere of economics: the monetary economy and long-distance trade, the large estates and the exploitation of slave labour were all preserved just as they had been under the Later Roman Empire. The Romans continued to be represented in this system by their traditional aristocracy, the senatorial class. The same solution was put forward everywhere for the co-existence of barbarians and Romans: a dualist solution favoured by Arianism, whereby the only institutions the two peoples had in common were at the top level, in the persons of the monarch and his immediate followers. The Romans went on living in their cities and often on their own estates, the barbarians in their military establishments. There were two separate ruling classes which did not merge. Wherever this dualism existed a Byzantine reconquest was possible, for even if the barbarian elements were all swept away—and the Vandals and the Ostrogoths disappeared without trace—there was still a Roman organization left to fall back on, which was theoretically standing by, ready to move into action. By way of contrast it is difficult to imagine what would have been left of Gaul if the Franks had been eliminated. The real dividing line between the ancient and the medieval worlds was established only when the classical mechanism had broken down irretrievably. The kingdoms of Euric, Genseric, Theodoric and Gundobad are definitely on one side of this line, while those of Clovis, Reccared and Rothari are on the other.

A comparative study of the barbarian kingdoms could take in other fields, for example that of political relations. First the barbarian West went through a stage of dissension, and distrust of or open hostility towards the Empire, which had its culmination in the time of Genseric; there was bitter rivalry among the various peoples. Then all this changed, not on the deposition of the colourless Romulus Augustulus, but rather with the installation of Theodoric at Ravenna in 493. The barbarian world became organized, and the Ostrogothic state, which was doggedly conservative, became its keystone; links with the Eastern Empire were re-established, and the 'barbarian' world—in the pejorative sense of the word—receded. Such a comparative study offers a rich vein of research.

The Goths and the Sueves

We have already traced the migration of the principal branches of the Gothic group of peoples. However that is not the whole of the story, and much ink has been spilled on questions relating to obscure, if not fictitious, secondary branches. Let us take a quick glance at the issues involved in these purely academic debates.

Before proceeding any further, we must discard the so-called Goths of India, the product of an incorrect interpretation in 1912 of three inscriptions in Buddhist sanctuaries in the region of Poona.[7] A more interesting subject is the little group of Goths in the Crimea.[8] At the time of the Hunnic onslaught at the end of the third century some Goths, instead of fleeing towards the south-west, took refuge in the mountains of the Crimea (Yaïla Dagh). They were Christians from the start, and on the whole lived on good terms with the Byzantines of Chersonesus from the fifth to the fifteenth century. Their little principality miraculously survived the attacks of the steppe tribes and was only wiped out in 1475, by the Ottomans. It is surprising to note that Gothic was still being spoken there in the sixteenth century: an ambassador from the court of Charles V collected sixty-eight words of Gothic from two persons from Perekop about 1560, that is to say a thousand years after the disappearance of East Germanic languages in other regions.

Then there is the group of Goths that entered the Empire in the time of Theodosius and were sent on to Egypt. A papyrus from Antinoë confirms the presence of Arian Goths there who used a bilingual text of the Bible (the Latin text accompanied by Ulfila's Gothic translation). This is the only evidence of this kind left by the countless barbarian garrisons in the Empire.

The Suevic kingdom is undoubtedly one of the most obscure and insignificant of those that resulted from the invasions. The texts which mention it are extremely brief, and were written by people who were not familiar with the court at Braga, so that we know nothing of the historical traditions of the kingdom. The historian R. L. Reynolds [no. 392] has recently drawn on these texts to reconstruct a history of the Suevic kingdom which is radically different from that outlined above. According to him the Suevic migration to Spain was sea-borne, like those of the Anglo-Saxons to England, and of the Heruls and the

Britons that later also landed in Galicia. He asserts that they were not among the peoples who crossed the Rhine in 406, since Jerome only mentions the Quadi. We find this reconstruction unconvincing, but instructive: it illustrates the basic truth that most documents relating to the early Middle Ages supply so few pieces of the puzzle that they can easily be put together in the wrong way.

The Question of the Isolation of the Hispano-Gothic Kingdom

The unique nature of the kingdom of Toledo and the infrequency of its dealings with the outside world are well known. One famous example will suffice to illustrate this: news of Reccared's conversion did not reach the pope until three years after it had taken place, and then it was only by means of an insignificant embassy of three monks who did not even go as far as Rome. However we must not be misled into thinking that Visigothic Spain was entirely cut off. At first, immediately after the defeat at Vouillé, it welcomed Ostrogothic influences, and its distrust of Merovingian and Byzantine policics did not prevent it from absorbing Frankish and oriental influences.

The Ostrogoths provided Spain with two kings, Theudis (531–48) and Theudisclus (548–9), and with the statesmen who set what was left of the political institutions in motion again after 507. But concrete traces of their activity are rare: a few fibulae and buckles of Ostrogothic type of the beginning of the sixth century, and possibly the word *saio*, referring to the man responsible for the execution of royal decisions.

Diplomatic relations with Byzantium, though frowned on by the kings of Toledo, undeniably existed. It was in Byzantium that Catholic exiles like St. Leander and John of Biclar sought refuge, and several economic ideas (like the organization of the *cataplus*, the exchange which controlled foreign commerce) were borrowed from Byzantium, as was the most active of the currents that enlivened Hispano-Gothic art in the seventh century.[9] This could be accounted for either by the long survival of a Byzantine enclave in Baetica, or by commercial contacts.

The contribution of the Franks is more obscure and has been more subject to debate. The civilizations of Visigothic Spain and Merovingian Gaul were very different. The intellectual enthusiasm of the Isidorian era did not extend beyond the Pyrenees, and the books it produced were not available in Gaul until the end of the seventh century, or perhaps even until after 711.[10] The ideology of sacral kingship which had been developed in Spain, at the latest by the time of Wamba (672), was not imitated in Gaul until the time of Pippin the Short. Conversely Visigothic Spain was almost alone among barbarian kingdoms in remaining immune to a fashion as widespread as Germanic animal ornament. But underlying a certain antipathy there is some slight evidence of contact of various kinds. M. Broëns believes he has turned up place-names of Merovingian type (ending in *-curtis* and *-villa*) in Galicia, which he attributes to the Frankish expedition of 542.[11] This is a very bold hypothesis. Zeiss has drawn attention to a set of Frankish grave goods in a cemetery at Pamplona. Most important, in the controversy which still rages about the origin of the non-Roman elements of Castilian common law, one school of thought attributes them to influences from the other side of the Pyrenees (see above, p. 209). Spain may even have had some contact with the Lombards, for Palol Salellas has drawn attention to jewellery of Lombard type in Baetica.

In short, the extreme example of Spain shows that none of the regions of the barbarian West can be seen as an absolutely self-contained unit; even in the case of the most autonomous of them contact with the others was never broken off completely.

GAUL

The First Stages of the Frankish Expansion

The question of the Roman system of defence in the area where the Franks first settled has been revived by recent excavations.[12] The hypothesis of a *limes belgicus* or line of fortifications running across Belgium during the Later Roman Empire not far from the modern linguistic frontier, which was first proposed by G. Kurth, basing his conclusions on place-names, in about 1880, has been reinforced since 1930 by archaeological discoveries. Some of these have been made in other parts of the *limes*: would the Emperors, who seem to have been so anxious to fill in the breaches there, have ignored the yawning gap in the *limes* of the lower Rhine? Other excavations in Belgium itself have revealed the existence of several small forts at strategic points— at the time of writing a total of five. The defenders of the *limes belgicus* hypothesis, once contemptuously dismissed, are now vindicated. Other lines of fortifications are coming to light elsewhere, notably along the coast, where an offshoot of the *litus saxonicum* has been found which will shed much light on the circumstances of the Frankish occupation.[13] However, archaeologists would be wise not to be too hasty in suggesting a link between their finds and the phenomena of linguistic geography.

Our knowledge of the early history of the Franks is so scanty that only too often incautious attempts have been made to supplement it with ideas passed on from one generation of scholars to the next. From time to time one of these ideas is exploded in a sensational manner. This is what happened to the belief that the Salian Franks and the Ripuarian Franks were two separate groups, which was still being propounded as an established fact in 1955 by Charles Verlinden. The critical work of F. Steinbach, E. Ewig and J. Stengers has now shown it to be untenable.[14]

The studies of F. Beyerle on Ripuarian law[15] paved the way for the decisive attack, for they established that instead of being a symmetrical homologue of the *Lex Salica*, the *Lex Ribuaria* was only a secondary variant of it, which was applicable to the Austrasians and was of much later date (it cannot have been drawn up any earlier than 633 and is only known by that name after 803). As for the word 'Ripuarians' itself, contrary to what was formerly believed it does not appear in Jordanes, who speaks only of '*riparioli*' (corps of auxiliaries protecting the bank of a river, probably the Rhône), and it does not figure in the texts of the sixth century, or even of the seventh century. The *Riboarii* appear in history, belatedly, in 726–7, in the *Liber Historiae Francorum*. At that time—and up until the tenth century—the name referred to the inhabitants of the region that includes Cologne, Jülich and Bonn to the west of the Rhine, and the Ruhrgau to the east of it, that is to say approximately the former *civitas Agrippinensium*. It seems likely that the name came from a military command on the banks of the Rhine, more or less modelled on a Roman administrative area. The Ripuarians never constituted a tribe or a branch of the Frankish people. The idea of coherence among the Eastern Franks is itself debatable. One can talk of a *Francia Rinensis* in the geographical sense, as the Cosmographer of Ravenna did, but the only political unit about which anything is known is the kingdom of Cologne.

The Salians, on the other hand, undeniably existed, but it is well-nigh impossible to say who they were. Little of what used to be accepted without question has survived the destructive attack of Stengers. It seems it was only before the emergence of the Merovingian dynasty that the term referred to a political entity; afterwards it was merely a legal term, or a literary equivalent of *Francus*. The autonomy of the Salians can only have been of short duration. We have only two indications of where their homeland could have been, one based on the similarity between the word 'Salians' and the name of the region of Salland on the right bank of the Dutch Rhine, and the other based on Ammianus Marcellinus's assertion that they lived in 'Toxandria', a name which is difficult to interpret. We must not speak of 'Salians', therefore, except when talking about the very earliest stages of the Frankish advance from the Rhine towards the Scheldt. After that it would be wiser to use the more neutral term 'Western Franks'.

The Prestige of the Frankish Warrior

The immense amount of archaeological material available to us allows us to paint an accurate picture of the Frankish warrior of the sixth and seventh centuries. The average Frank was a foot-soldier. His most common offensive weapons were very unusual among the German peoples: a throwing axe and a short sword with a single cutting edge and, less frequently, a spear. He rarely wore a helmet or carried a shield. Only his chieftains fought on horseback, with a long double-edged sword, like so many other barbarians. All over northern and north-eastern Gaul the picture is the same. This warrior was the foundation on which the Frankish kingdom was built, and his tomb is, as it were, the most characteristic fossil of the period. A lot of emphasis has been placed—and rightly so—on the fact that the Frankish conquest marks the triumph of a *Kriegerkultur*, or warrior society, over the mainly civilian population of the Later Roman Empire, a warrior society which is reflected in the row-grave cemeteries which proliferate from the sixth century on.[16]

This description of a Frankish warrior is often overlaid with a veneer of classical words: *francisca* for throwing axe, *framea* for spear, and *scramasax* for sword. In fact these terms are of doubtful origin and although archaeologists remain faithful to them they should be rejected.[17] The Frankish throwing axe with a single cutting edge was only referred to as *francisca*, which means 'Frankish', in Spain, and this word did not pass into Gallic historiography until the eighth century, through the medium of a writer who was copying Isidore of Seville. *Framea* is used in Latin sources with various contradictory meanings: Tacitus uses it to mean a lance and Isidore to mean a sword; Eucher uses it in both senses. The etymology, which must be Germanic, seems to favour the meaning of 'sword with two cutting edges'. The word *scramasax* owes its popularity to Gregory of Tours, who mentions it several times, on one occasion explaining that it is a large knife, but we do not know if it had one cutting edge or two. The only Frankish weapon whose name is known with any certainty is the *angon*, a sort of spear or harpoon with a barbed iron point, but it was rarely used.

This is the traditional portrait, not of one of the Frankish conquerors, but of a soldier in the Merovingian army. The Frank of the invasions is still a shadowy figure, due to the lack of archaeological material of indisputably Frankish origin for the period before Clovis.

The political and military success of the Franks encouraged other peoples in Gaul to equip themselves on the model of the Frankish warrior. Nothing is known about the first stages of this process of imitation, which goes back to the time of Childeric and Clovis. But the spread of Frankish practices over the whole of Gaul can be studied from the time of Clovis's sons; it is an instructive, if arduous, line of research, and one which has not yet been fully explored.

A good example of the complexity of the problem is afforded by Burgundy, which changed its political status in 533–4, when it was incorporated into the Merovingian kingdom. How is this reflected in the archaeological material? The sterling research of Hans Zeiss [no. 232] helps to clarify the position. Before 534 material is scanty, for grave goods are poor. Perhaps this is because Burgundian traditions were close to those of the Goths, like their respective languages, or it may have been that Romano-Christian influences were early and deep-rooted. After 534 there are many more row-grave cemeteries with more elaborate grave goods, that is to say in accordance with the normal 'Merovingian' type. The use of typical weapons, such as the single-edged sword, becomes widespread, once more thanks to Frankish influence. But there is also an increasing number of buckle-plates of a highly original type, with lively decoration, either profane (mainly depicting horses) or biblical (especially representations of the prophet Daniel). We have here a regional innovation which owes nothing to the Frankish world. There is not the slightest proof of any appreciable Frankish immigration, and there is no evidence of any real discontinuity in the principal cemetery, that of Charnay (Saône-et-Loire).

In Aquitaine the problem is just as delicate. The expulsion of a fair number of Arian Goths after the battle of Vouillé is confirmed by historiography; on the other hand not a single text mentions a large-scale influx of Franks. As a result, nineteenth-century archaeologists like Barrière-Flavy [no. 289] attributed all the so-called 'barbarian' tombs they came across to the Goths. Maurice Broëns [no. 184] reacted strongly to this, and with good reason: most of the tombs date from after 507 and show no similarities with the contemporaneous burial-grounds of the Spanish meseta. The majority of the cemeteries in Aquitaine are of characteristically 'Merovingian' type, with the axe and single-edged sword, whereas Gothic tombs never contain weapons; but the grave goods also include purely local elements, notably in the Lauragais, where the inspiration springs from the traditions of the eastern Mediterranean. How is all this to be interpreted? Broëns sees Aquitaine flooded with 150,000 Franks, of whom 50,000 decided to settle there. Apart from the numbers, which are quite unfounded, is this explanation acceptable? Is the situation in Aquitaine really so different from that in Burgundy?

Archaeologists have too often tended to state the problem in terms of conquest and settlement when it ought to be considered in terms of assimilation and civilization, almost of fashion. The real triumph of Rome was to inspire in her subjects the desire to live according to the Roman way of life: the triumph of the Frankish warrior was to have persuaded all those of any consequence in Gaul to adopt *his* way of life, of which the weapons and the grave goods are, for us, the concrete expression.

Some Problems Arising from the Reign of Clovis

The reign of Clovis has always fired the imagination of historians, but the mediocrity of the sources has filled them with despair. Hence the birth (usually followed quickly by the untimely demise) of so many precariously based hypotheses.[18]

The clearest demonstration of our uncertainty is afforded by the still disputed chronology of Clovis's reign. There was relative agreement, in spite of some misgivings, until about 1930; then, in the course of a lively dialogue between L. Levillain [no. 263] and F. Lot[19] on the one hand, and Bruno Krusch[20] and later A. Van de Vyver [no. 268] on the other, the whole question was thrown open again. The hypothesis of Krusch, which was insufficiently supported by the evidence and was really too iconoclastic, need not be taken seriously, but that of Van de Vyver is of very different quality. Although the heat of the controversy has abated somewhat today, the question is nevertheless far from being settled. It would be true to say that we now have two chronological systems which are quite different, and which are equally likely to be correct.

The debate turns on Gregory of Tours's *Hist. Franc.* II, 27, which dates the principal events of Clovis's reign at intervals of five years. The victory over Syagrius in the year V; the victory over the Thuringians in the year X; the victory over the Alamans and the promise of conversion leading up to the baptism in the year XV; the victory over Alaric II also in the year XV. Now it is quite certain that the battle of Vouillé took place, not in the year 496 (or XV) but in 507 (the year XXV–XXVI). Has an error also crept into the information about the victory over the Alamans and about the baptism?

Apart from Gregory we only have two sources of the period which refer to the baptism: a letter from St. Avitus of Vienne, who was almost a contemporary of Clovis's, congratulating him on his conversion, which adds nothing to what Gregory tells us of the event except one precise and unquestionable fact—the day of the baptism, Christmas Day; and a letter from St. Nicetius, bishop of Trier, to the Lombard queen Clotsinde, the grand-daughter of Clovis, written in 567–8, which says that the promise of conversion was made after a visit to

St. Martin of Tours, for which he gives no date. (Before the battle of Vouillé Tours was in Visigothic territory.) Thus our three sources hardly overlap at all: Gregory of Tours is our only authority for linking the baptism and the victory over the Alamans, and for the role of St. Remigius of Reims; Avitus is the only one to give the date as Christmas Day; and Nicetius is the only one who mentions a link with Tours. (Gregory's silence on this point is odd, to say the least!) None of this gives us a definite date, but if one accepts that the journey to Tours did actually take place, it can only have done so at the time of a war between the Franks and the Goths, either the well-known one of 506–7, or another—and this is just possible—in 498. If the baptism is connected with a war against the Alamans it may concern the war of 495–6, attested by Gregory alone, or that of 505–6, which is confirmed by Cassiodorus.

There are, then, two ways of working out a chronological system consistent with most of these facts. One is to stick fairly closely to Gregory, have the date of the baptism as 25 December 497 (Lot), 498 or 499 (Levillain), and accept that Clovis conducted two campaigns in Aquitaine and two against the Alamans. The other method relies more on Cassiodorus, dates the baptism and the sole campaign against the Alamans to 506 (thus rejecting any link between Clovis's conversion and the famous battle of *Tolbiacum*, or Zülpich, fought by the king of Cologne against the Alamans) and leaves ten years blank at the beginning of Clovis's reign, from the year X to the year XX (during which time the war against the Burgundians did unquestionably occur). We owe the latter chronology to Van de Vyver. Both systems, however, have their weaknesses: the necessity for *two* campaigns against both the Visigoths and the Alamans in the first system, and the ten years of silence in the second. How, then, is one to choose between them? One argument which seems to favour the first system is that undoubtedly Clovis's Catholicism helped him in his fight against the Goths in 507, and this would be more understandable if he were a Catholic of eight or ten years' standing than if his conversion had only taken place the previous Christmas. But this assumption does not constitute proof.

Another episode in his reign, known only from Gregory of Tours (*Hist. Franc.* II, 38), has evoked interpretations almost as diverse: the handing over to Clovis of the consular tablets sent by the Emperor Anastasius. The promotion of Clovis to an honorary consulate (there is no question of its having been an actual consulate) is not in itself extraordinary; this distinction had already been conferred on several barbarians, although it is true that they were directly in the service of the Empire. It was probably a diplomatic gesture, congratulating the king on his victory over the Visigoths and seeking his continued support against the Ostrogoths. But what are we to make of the imperial attributes, the purple tunic, the diadem and the title of Augustus, and of Clovis's triumphal ride round Tours, which was so similar to the inaugural procession of the Eastern Emperors? The reactions of historians have been very different. For some of them, notably Fustel de Coulanges, there is a core of truth in the story: Anastasius was anxious to legitimize Clovis's power and to appoint him his representative in the West. For others, in particular for Halphen, the story is pure legend. Every shade of opinion between these two extreme views has its supporters. The most reasonable explanation seems to be that of P. Courcelle [no. 256]: he suggests that in reality Anastasius conferred only the honorary consulate on the Frankish king; the other details are pure showmanship, inspired either by Clovis himself, or by the local clergy of Tours who wanted to celebrate their deliverance from the Goths. In spite of his respect for the imperial prerogatives, Theodoric himself wore the purple and the diadem, and on the Terracina inscription (which was written precisely during the period 507–11) took the title of *semper Augustus*; it is quite clear that in his view these formalities did not imply that he was laying claim to the imperial title or to equality with Anastasius. Moreover no Roman Emperor had been recognized in the north of Gaul since the assassination of Majorian in 461. If one accepts that the people of Tours were responsible for the ceremonial trappings of Clovis's ride, they may well have been intended to encourage the Frankish monarch to adopt a favourable attitude to Rome. If, on the other hand, one believes that Clovis himself was at the bottom of it, then his gesture can be compared, not only to Theodoric's, but also to that of Masties, the petty prince of the mountains of Aurès, in Algeria, who had proclaimed himself *imperator* shortly before.

At all events the episode of Tours had hardly any consequences. There is no other mention of these ambitious titles, and the kingdom of Clovis and his successors continued to be modelled on essentially Germanic lines.

THE ATLANTIC WORLD

Myths and Historical Facts about the Origins of the English

A good deal of our information about the origins of England, whether it comes from Britain itself or from elsewhere, has a markedly epic or mythological flavour. The early stages in the colonization of Kent have been turned into a drama with three principal characters—the British King Vortigern and the Saxons Hengist and Horsa; the origins of the kingdom of Wessex have become the history of Cerdic and Port; and the ultimate defeat of the British is hidden in the heroic story of King Arthur. Far away in the East and writing in the reign of Justinian, the historian Procopius in his *History of the Gothic Wars* has the fortunes of Britain (which he thinks is composed of not one, but two islands, *Brittia* and *Brittania*) inextricably entangled with the poetic legends of the 'Isles of the Blessed' of classical tradition.

Faced with all these texts, the attitude of historians at the beginning of this century was categorical: it was all a hopeless jumble in which crass ignorance and the most extravagant flights of fancy vied for supremacy. The great French medievalist Ferdinand Lot was the supreme exponent of this critical attitude.[21] He denounced the weaknesses of all the sources at our disposal: the bizarre chronology of the Anglo-Saxon Chronicle which noted events at four- or eight-year intervals; the unlikely names of Hengist (stallion) and Horsa (horse), and even of Vortigern (which seems to be merely the Celtic translation of a Latin expression which had wrongly been taken for a personal name); and Port's name, surely derived from a false etymology for Portsmouth. The *Historia Brittonum*, which was responsible for a good many of these myths, including that of Arthur, was 'a romance dating only from the ninth century', and Gildas, the best source, is 'full of appalling blunders'; no wonder Procopius saw the north-west of Europe as nothing but 'a land of chimaeras'.

Since then historians have been cautiously reacting against Lot's hypercritical attitude. They do not deny the obvious mistakes, the etymological origin of some of the legends, or the tendency to personify in a single hero the history of a whole people, but they do give some credence to the chronological and topographical information in the Anglo-Saxon Chronicle. In histories of the origins of the kingdom of Kent like that of J. N. L. Myres, for example, based on archaeological material,[22] or that of K. Jackson, mainly based on linguistic evidence,[23] there is room for Vortigern, Hengist and Horsa, at least as well-chosen symbols. Some scholars, like T. C. Lethbridge and C. F. C. Hawkes,[24] would go even further and restore to these heroic figures the historical reality of which others have deprived them. Cerdic has been less fortunate: his Anglian genealogy, his Celtic name, and his band of Jutes supposedly participating in the foundation of a Saxon kingdom, have earned him universal distrust, especially as archaeology has shown that the alleged area of his landing, near Southampton, remained in British hands for at least fifty years after the date given for his arrival. Arthur appears on the scene too late to have any supporters to vouch for his authenticity,[25] but it is now recognized that his epic represents, as Collingwood was already suggesting in the 1930s, a synthetic, though not over-precise, view of the events which Gildas groups around the figure of Ambrosius Aurelianus. Many valid features have also been discovered in the texts of Procopius: the role given to the Frisians, the Anglo-Saxon methods of fighting (on foot) and of seafaring (by rowing), and the relations between the Angles and the Varini. His two islands of Britain can be explained by there being two main itineraries from Byzantium to north-west Europe, via Gaul and via the Atlantic coast of Spain (for the latter route see below, p. 235), and classical traditions could be responsible for most of his glaring mistakes.[26] At the same time we must not rule out the possibility that some day soon historical research will tip the scales the other way, as it often does, and bring Lot's hypotheses back into comparative favour.

Political and Social Structures in Early England

Until the twentieth century Bede's account of the origins of England, set down at the beginning of the eighth century, was accepted by historians without question. Influenced by what he saw around him, Bede represented early England as made up of homogeneous kingdoms bordering one another, each the result of the immigration of a coherent ethnic group, here the Saxons, there the Angles, there the Jutes. Modern research is getting further and further away from this over-simplified picture.[27] It believes that the relative ethnic unity which existed in the sixth and seventh centuries was not so much the original state of things resulting from the migrations, as the fruit of the geo-graphical partition of British territory among the conquerors and of the military and economic necessities which resulted from it. It would thus be pointless to try to discover the exact continental origin of each of the 'peoples' in Bede's lists, for all of them are the result of regroupings after the migrations.

This new approach has several advantages. It helps to explain the uniformity of Old English right from the period of the earliest literature, in spite of the diversity of origins alleged by Bede. After landing in England, no clan remained in sufficient isolation to preserve its own particular dialect for long; a common language would of necessity have come into being quite quickly. It also sheds some light on the way in which the Old Saxons on the continent—one of the most 'republican' peoples among the Germans—should have become in England the subjects of a number of royal dynasties quite clearly claiming Woden, the god of war, as their founder.[28] Above all, it indicates a similarity between the history of the Anglo-Saxons and that of their nearest Germanic neighbours on the continent, the Franks; as we have always emphatically insisted, all the essential elements of

Frankish civilization in the Merovingian period, including political grouping, were developed *after* the crossing of the Rhine.

We look to archaeology to provide us with many of the insights into the origins of the Anglo-Saxon kingdoms which the texts are unable to reveal. In the last thirty-five years two outstanding excavations have added an enormous amount of information to our stock of knowledge: that of the ship-burial at Sutton Hoo in Suffolk, directed by R. L. S. Bruce-Mitford in 1939, which has brought to life the history of the Wuffingas, the royal dynasty of East Anglia; and that of the palace of Yeavering in Northumberland, directed by B. Hope-Taylor from 1953 to 1957, which has shed much light on the last phase of the pagan era in Bernicia. Thanks to these two excavations we now know a great deal about the artistic and social background to the terse and rudimentary political data of the Anglo-Saxon Chronicle and the royal genealogies.

At Sutton Hoo, nine miles north-east of Ipswich, a great mound concealed a clinker-built ship, 27 metres long by 4.70 metres broad by 1.50 metres deep, designed to be propelled by oars.[29] A funerary chamber which had been constructed amidships contained extraordinarily rich grave goods: Byzantine silverwork from the beginning of the sixth century, cloisonné jewellery, weapons, royal insignia and a small hoard of Merovingian gold coins (gathered together some time between 660 and 670 according to most numismatists, or in approximately 625 according to Lafaurie). Surprisingly, it contained no body. This cenotaph must have been that of either King Redwald, who died about 625, or King Aethelhere, who died in 655; the absence of a body could be explained either by the dead man's conversion to Christianity or by his having died a great distance away. The Sutton Hoo ship-burial shows the coming together of a number of very different traditions—Mediterranean (the metal bowls from Alexandria and Constantinople), Frankish (the coins), Scandinavian, or, to be more exact, Swedish (the idea of a ship-burial itself, and the helmet of Vendel type), and finally British (the hanging-bowl in the Celtic tradition). What better proof that Anglo-Saxon England was not an isolated island lost on the edge of the *oikoumenē*, but one whose aristocracy took part in all the currents of European civilization?

The economic level of Anglo-Saxon society immediately after colonization is a subject of debate among numismatists. To what extent did Britain drift back into a pre-monetary economy between the disappearance of imperial currency at the beginning of the fifth century and the appearance of Merovingian coinage in the second half of the sixth century (and in even greater quantity at the beginning of the seventh century)? Some scholars[30] believe that gold and silver more or less disappeared, but that native communities in the south continued to use copper coinage, in the form of fourth-century types of coins which had almost dropped out of use, or of poor-quality imitations of them (*minimi*). According to this view the monetary tradition was never completely broken, and the surviving Britons were able to pass it on to the Saxons. Others[31] believe that there was complete disruption, and that the hiatus lasted for a long time: the *minimi* are irrelevant, since they were in circulation only until the middle of the fifth century at the latest, and it was only in imitation of continental monarchs that the Anglo-Saxons had the idea of minting coins about the year 670. The problem has not yet been settled, but it must be admitted that the first view is based more on conjecture than on proven facts. It would be difficult to explain how the Britons came to preserve the use of currency in those regions which were taken over by the Saxons, while giving it up in the areas where they retained their freedom. The supporters of 'continuity at all costs' have really gone a bit too far.

Roman Survivals in Celtic Britain

The territories which the Britons managed to hold on to were the least Romanized areas of the island. Except for the survival of Christianity there seems to be every indication that classical traditions rapidly died out there: the language preserved almost no Latin features, economic life reverted to earlier native customs, and society returned to a tribal structure which was totally alien to the classical ideal.

Epigraphy and archaeology now invite us, however, to reconsider the case. There are numerous Latin inscriptions dating from the period after the breach with Rome in the west of Britain.[32] Their style is remarkably conservative: they use consular dates (up to 540 in Penmachno in Wales), and refer to *cives*, a *magistratus*, a *protector* and so on. All this is found in a purely Celtic content (Hiberno-British, to be precise) where inscriptions are usually written in ogam. What are we to make of these Roman features, which sometimes occur right into the seventh century, even later than in Gaul? Was there a direct link between the Mediterranean and the Celtic world?

Narrative sources provide only a very slender indication that there may have been a route from Alexandria to Britain via Spain at the beginning of the seventh century.[33] However, some Byzantine coins of the sixth and seventh centuries have been found in the south of England. For some years now archaeologists have been turning up pottery from the eastern Mediterranean on a dozen sites scattered from Devon and Cornwall and the south of Ireland right up to the Hebrides, and amphorae of the type found in Spain, Sicily and Greece.[34]

Thus a hitherto unsuspected maritime aspect of Roman survival has been revealed, an umbilical cord linking Britain to the Mediterranean, passing through Byzantine Spain (which scholars had believed to be a sort of blind alley).

The Question of Breton

The history of Brittany offers more than one paradox. On the one hand we see the depth of Gallic influences, witnessed by the archaeological evidence and by Caesar's accounts of the strength of the Veneti, and on the other hand we see the paucity of Gallo-Roman finds, particularly in the west of the peninsula, so much so that there has long been uncertainty about the identification of the administrative centres. These circumstances would lead one to believe that the Romanization of the region had been completely superficial, and had abandoned the country areas to Gallic tradition. However, linguists, particularly since Joseph Loth,[35] emphatically insist that as medieval and modern Breton show no trace of Gallic, the Armorican peninsula must have been Latinized along with the rest of Gaul and to much the same extent.

It must be observed here that, firstly, the meagreness of Roman remains applies also to other parts of western France which no one claims to have escaped Latinization; and that, secondly, we are not in a position to estimate with any precision the degree of Latinization of the country districts of the rest of Gaul during the Later Roman Empire; it is quite likely that the Gallic language survived until the beginning of the fifth century in the east of Gaul among the Treveri. Up to that point the fate of Brittany is by no means unusual.

Without embarking on a detailed philological discussion we can point out that linguists have assigned all the Celtic languages to either a continental group (Gallic), or an insular group, divided under two sub-headings: Brythonic, or P-Celtic (Welsh, Cornish and Breton) and Goidelic, or Q-Celtic (Irish and Scots Gaelic). Our knowledge of the insular languages is based on a wealth of reliable material, but our knowledge of Gallic relies solely on a few personal names and place-names and a handful of obscure and laconic inscriptions. The idea that Gallic was a single language is only conjecture; in fact we know practically nothing about the Gallic of the north-west or of the north-east. (Caesar confirms that the Belgae had certain linguistic peculiarities, but we are unable to distinguish them.) This indicates the need for extreme caution in either affirming or denying the possibility of Gallic survivals.

The vigorous resurgence of a Celtic language in Armorica in the fifth century has always seemed to some historians to indicate the existence of a Gallic substratum which was reinvigorated by the immigration from Britain. Until very recently their point of view was almost unanimously rejected as being tinged with romantic fantasy, but now a vigorous reaction, inspired by Canon Falc'hun,[36] is trying to rehabilitate their argument on the basis of linguistic and, in particular, phonetic considerations. According to him the peculiar stress patterns of the dialect of the region of Vannes represent a Gallic survival, as distinct from the Brythonic accentuation of the other Breton dialects. The earliest Breton documents are therefore untrustworthy and misleading because they were produced by clerics, and the ecclesiastical hierarchy at that time was certainly composed of immigrants from Britain who would have transcribed Breton speech into a rationalized form based on Cornish or Welsh. As things stand in this debate at present, history can only bring one verdict: not proven. But at any rate it is encouraging that the question of Breton has been approached from a fresh viewpoint.

Perhaps the current research of J. L. Fleuriot [no. 494], who is preparing a detailed study of the survivals of Latin- and Romance-speaking enclaves in western Brittany to try to discover their geographical extent, will shed some light on the problem. He appears to have established several points, some of which favour Loth's thesis and others of which favour Falc'hun's. It seems highly likely that a living Romance dialect existed in the Middle Ages in eastern Brittany (where the Celtic elements are due to late borrowings, according to Loth, rather than to a surviving substratum, as Falc'hun believes), and here and there in western Brittany, particularly round the towns and over a large part of the coasts of the Vannes region and of Leon. The absence of any traces of Romance in almost the whole of the interior (which must, logically, have been a stronghold of local defence against invaders by sea), would be explained by the survival of a Gallic language. History may benefit a great deal from this battle of linguists.

General Conclusion

In many respects the study of the problems posed by the invasions is, for historians, a long lesson in humility. No other collective phenomenon is so elusive when it comes to seeking the primary causes. In the best-known cases one can gather together precedents, favourable circumstances and accidental occurrences; but none of this can explain the invasion as an inevitable and clear-cut sequence of events. Extending the problem to the ends of the earth, to the north or to the Far East, as was fashionable thirty years ago, hardly adds anything to our ill-stocked arsenal of explanations except new probabilities of error. However if the causes elude us all too often, it is all the more essential for us to understand the effects. In the past only the crude, external aspects of the migratory phenomenon were examined, those of military expeditions and empire-building activities. Nineteenth-century historians soon realized that it was necessary to widen the scope of research by constantly looking at social history, and then at linguistics. The twentieth century has seen the development of the study of place-names and of personal names, and above all of archaeology in all its varied forms. Our field of vision has thus expanded, and each new discipline obliges us to re-examine neighbouring fields of knowledge. As the reader will have seen in the last part of this book, the history of the invasions, perhaps more than that of any other period or phenomenon, is like Penelope's task: theories are woven out of such information as we have, only to be unravelled when fresh evidence comes to light. The knowledge that new revisions, wider and more detailed than previous studies, will soon be forthcoming, has more than once obliged us to suspend our judgment, not through scepticism, but through confidence in the future of historical research: premature dogmatism is one of the worst sins against Clio! Thus illumined and enriched, the history of the invasions in the first millennium AD is singularly instructive. It teaches us that Europe has constantly benefited from all her experiences, even though under duress at times, to create innovating syntheses. This willingness to absorb while modifying, to draw renewed vigour from the ruins, is a recurring motif throughout our account. It is the distinguishing feature of civilization, as distinct from the primitive cultures to which, in spite of appearances, the so-called 'barbarians' of the early Middle Ages do not belong.

Part Three

Sources and Studies

Introduction

The history of the invasions lies at the conjunction of two fields of research: the history of classical Antiquity and that of the Middle Ages. It uses the resources of both. Like the historian of Antiquity the specialist of the migration period makes extensive use of epigraphy, numismatics, monumental archaeology, the study of pottery and so on. As he advances into the Middle Ages he finds that these disciplines provide him with less and less material; thus, once past the seventh century, epigraphy is no longer of any real help. Like the medievalist he uses documents in archives when he can, but before the ninth century these documents are very rare, amounting to little more than the Ravenna papyri and a handful of Merovingian royal charters. Even taking all these disciplines together, the information they provide sheds but little light on the Dark Ages.

It is therefore necessary to turn to rather more hazardous branches of research, such as linguistics, toponymy and anthroponymy. Although they are less familiar to the present-day historian, this is not the place to explain their different methods. I have confined myself to explaining their limitations. While the information they supply is invaluable for cultural history, the data which one can extract from them very rarely fill in the lacunae of political history.

The great weakness of the period under discussion in this book is the absence of a continuous historiographic thread. Some peoples were fortunate enough to have had great chroniclers: the Franks with Gregory of Tours, the Anglo-Saxons with Bede, or the Lombards with Paul the Deacon. But these are only small islands in the middle of the vast ocean of our ignorance. Most facts can only be established through very second-rate documents. Even the most laconic annals or the most shallow lives of saints constitute treasure troves. Often there is not a single written text to throw light on important areas of the history of the invasions, as for instance with the beginnings of the Anglo-Saxon migration to Britain.

The bibliography suffers from these fundamental lacunae. So much work is necessary to establish the smallest fact that any such bibliography tends to become simply a list of short, highly specialized articles. Such detailed research often loses sight of the basic uncertainty of its methods, or of the insecurity of the great theoretical constructions which it helps to build up. One is sometimes astonished to discover after generations of this ant-like toil that the basic facts, received piously from our ancestors, are quite false. The history of the advance of the Ripuarian Franks was discussed for decades before it was discovered that there was no such people as the Ripuarian Franks at the time of the invasions. No doubt other cruel discoveries of this nature will emerge within the study of barbarian law: the question of the personality of the laws, for instance, has been discussed for far too long without first determining whether the laws were in fact always personal in nature. Toponymists, a generation ago, had a similar bitter experience. In general the details are better established than the broad lines of approach.

The history of the invasions is still at the stage of erudition rather than of synthesis. It will remain there for some time to come, because such syntheses demand abilities which are more and more rarely found in the same man. No one should attempt them without being not only a historian but also a linguist, an archaeologist and a jurist, and that sort of scholarship is to be found in only a few exceptional books. Even now too many historians of the crisis of the invasions are only historians and have not learnt from archaeology all the lessons it offers.

This, then, explains the peculiarity of the following bibliography, in which detailed articles form the overwhelming majority of the titles quoted. At the same time I have made an effort to include only those which give material for thought beyond the narrow confines of their subject.

ABBREVIATIONS

AA	Auctores Antiquissimi
CSEL	Corpus Scriptorum Ecclesiasticorum Latinorum
MGH	Monumenta Germaniae Historica
SS	Scriptores
Settimane di studio ...	Centro italiano di studi sull'alto medioevo. Settimane di studio (Spoleto)
CIL	Corpus inscriptionum latinarum

1. Published Sources[1]

I. EPIGRAPHICAL SOURCES

The earliest inscriptions of the barbarian period are included in the various volumes of the *Corpus inscriptionum latinarum*. Some of them are also in:

1 DIEHL, E., *Inscriptiones latinae christianae veteres*, 3 vols. (Berlin, 1924–31)

a The Germans

2 ARNTZ, Helmut, and ZEISS, Hans, *Die einheimischen Runendenkmäler des Festlandes* (Leipzig, 1939)
3 FIEBIGER, O., and SCHMIDT, L., *Inschriftensammlung zur Geschichte der Ostgermanen* (Vienna, 1917; supplements in 1939 and 1944)

b Gaul

4 GOSE, Erich, *Katalog der frühchristlichen Inschriften in Trier* (Berlin, 1958)
5 LE BLANT, Edmond, *Inscriptions chrétiennes de la Gaule antérieures au VIIIe siècle*, 2 vols. (Paris, 1856–65)
6 LE BLANT, Edmond, *Nouveau recueil des inscriptions chrétiennes de la Gaule* (Paris, 1892)

c Spain

7 HÜBNER, Aemilius, *Inscriptiones Hispaniae christianae*, 2 vols. (Berlin, 1871–1900)
8 VIVES, José, *Inscripciones cristianas de la España romana y visigoda* (Barcelona, 1942; 2nd edn. 1969)

d Italy

9 PANAZZA, Gaetano, 'Lapidi e sculture paleocristiane e pre-romaniche di Pavia' in *Arte de primo millenio* (Turin, 1952), 211–296 and 406–410
10 ROSSI, J. B. de, *Inscriptiones christianae urbis Romae septimo saeculo antiquiores*, 2 vols. (Rome, 1857–88)

e Africa

See COURTOIS, *Les Vandales et l'Afrique* [no. 233], appendix II, 365–388

f Great Britain and Ireland

11 HÜBNER, Aemilius, *Inscriptiones Britanniae christianae* (Berlin, 1876)
12 MACALISTER, R. A. S., *Corpus inscriptionum insularum celticarum* (Dublin, 1945–49)

243

J

II. PAPYROLOGICAL SOURCES, ETC.[2]

12 *bis* BONNAL, J.-P., and FÉVRIER, P. A., 'Ostraka de la région de Bir Trouch', *Bull. d'Archéol. algérienne*, ii (1966–67), 239–249

13 COURTOIS, Christian, LESCHI, Louis, PERRAT, Charles, and SAUMAGNE, Charles, *Tablettes Albertini, Actes privés de l'époque vandale* (Paris, 1952)

14 TJÄDER, J. O., *Die nichtliterarischen lateinischen Papyri Italiens, der Zeit 445–700* (Lund, 1955)

III. NARRATIVE SOURCES

The collections of extracts from the narrative sources which relate to particular subjects are put together with the modern works in Section II.

a *Up to the break-up of Western unity*

15 EUGIPPIUS, *Vita Severini*, ed. H. Sauppe, *MGH, AA*, I, 2 (1877) or ed. P. Knöll, *CSEL*, IX, 2 (1886); English translation by L. Bieler, *The Life of St. Severin* (Washington, 1965)

16 *Notitia dignitatum*, ed. O. SEECK (Berlin, 1876; repr. 1962)

17 OROSIUS, *Historiae adversus paganos*, ed. C. Zangmeister, *CSEL*, V (1882); English translation, with introduction and notes, by I. W. Raymond, *Seven Books of History against the Pagans* (New York, 1936) (Columbia Records of Civilization no. 26)

18 'PROSPER TIRO', *Chronicon*, ed. Th. Mommsen, *MGH, AA*, IX (*Chronica minora*, I), 341–485

19 *Ravennatis Anonymi Cosmographia*, ed. J. Schnetz (Leipzig, 1940); German translation by J. Schnetz (Uppsala, 1951)

20 SALVIAN, *De gubernatione Dei*, ed. Pauly, *CSEL*, VIII, 1883; French translation by J.-F. Grégoire and F.-Z. Collombet, 2 vols. (Paris, 1893). English translation by E. M. Sanford, *On the Government of God*, (New York, 1930) (Columbia Records of Civilization no. 12)

b *The barbarian kingdoms*

A general orientation is given by:

21 WATTENBACH, W., and LEVISON, W., *Deutschlands Geschichtsquellen im Mittelalter, Vorzeit und Karolinger. I. Die Vorzeit von den Anfängen bis zur Herrschaft der Karolinger* (by W. LEVISON) (Weimar, 1952); Beiheft : *Die Rechtsquellen* (by R. BUCHNER) (Weimar, 1953)[3]

Gaul

22 FREDEGAR, *Chronicon*, ed. B. Krusch, *MGH, SS. Rer. Merov.*, II (1888), 1–108; English translation of the last book, together with the continuators, by J. M. WALLACE-HADRILL, *The Fourth Book of the Chronicle of Fredegar* (London and Edinburgh, 1960) (Nelson's Medieval Classics)

23 GREGORY OF TOURS, *Historia Francorum*, ed. Omont, Collon and Poupardin (Paris, 1913), or in the *Opera, MGH, SS. Rer. Merov.*, I (2nd edn. 1951); French translation by R. Latouche, 2 vols. (Paris, 1963–65). English translation by L. Thorpe (Harmondsworth, 1974). Selections translated by E. Brehaut (New York, 1916; repr. 1965) (Colombia Records of Civilization no. 2)

24 MARIUS OF AVENCHES, *Chronicon*, ed. Th. Mommsen, *MGH, AA*, XI (*Chronica minora*, II), 225–239

25 SIDONIUS APOLLINARIS, *Opera*, ed. Luetjohann, *MGH, AA*, VIII (1887); French translation by A. Loyen, in course of publication in the *Collection G. Budé*. English translation in the Loeb edition by W. B. Anderson, 2 vols. (London, 1965). Translation of the letters by O. M. Dalton, 2 vols. (Oxford, 1915)

26 VENANTIUS FORTUNATUS, *Opera*, ed. F. Leo and B. Krusch, *MGH, AA*, IV (1881–85)

Spain

27 HYDATIUS, *Chronicon*, ed. Th. Mommsen, *MGH, AA*, XI (*Chronica minora*, II) 1–36

28 ISIDORE OF SEVILLE, *Chronicon*, ed. Th. Mommsen, *MGH, AA*, XI (*Chronica minora*, II), 391–506; *Historia Gothorum*, ed. Mommsen, *ibid.*, 241–303; English translation by Donini and Ford, *History of the Kings of the Goths, Vandals and Sueves* (Leiden, 1966)

29 JOHN OF BICLAR, *Chronicon*, ed. Th. Mommsen, *MGH, AA*, XI (*Chronica minora*, II), 207–220

Italy

30 CASSIODORUS, *Chronicon*, ed. Th. Mommsen, *MGH, AA*, XI (*Chronica minora*, II), 109–161; *Variae*, ed. Mommsen, *ibid.*, XII (1894). Selected translation and summaries by T. Hodgkin, *The Letters of Cassiodorus* (London, 1886)

31 ENNODIUS, *Panegyricus dictus clementissimo regi Theoderico*, ed. Hartel, *CSEL*, VI

32 JORDANES, *Getica*, ed. Th. Mommsen, *MGH, AA*, V, 1 (1882). English translation by C. C. Mierow, *The Gothic History of Jordanes* (Princeton, 1915; repr. Cambridge, 1966)

33 PAUL THE DEACON, *Historia Langobardorum*, ed. Bethmann and Waitz, *MGH, SS. Rer. Langob.*, (1878). English translation by W. D. Foulke, *History of the Langobards* (Philadelphia, 1907)

34 PROCOPIUS, *Bellum Gothicum*, ed. of the Greek text and an Italian translation by Comparetti, 3 vols. (Rome, 1895–98). English translation in the Loeb edition by H. B. Dewing (vols. III to V in the complete edition of Procopius) (London, 1919–28)

Africa

35 FERRANDUS OF CARTHAGE, *Vita Fulgentii*, ed. with a French translation by G. Lapeyre (Paris, 1929)

36 VICTOR OF TUNNUNNA, *Chronicon*, ed. Th. Mommsen, *MGH, AA*, XI (*Chronica minora*, II), 163–206

37 VICTOR VITENSIS, *Historia persecutionis vandalicae*, ed. Petschenig, *CSEL*, VII (1881), or ed. C. Halm, *MGH, AA*, III, 1

Great Britain

38 BEDE, *Historia ecclesiastica gentis anglorum*, ed. C. Plummer, 2 vols. (Oxford, 1896), or ed. B. Colgrave and R. A. B. Mynors, with a translation (Oxford, 1969) (Oxford Medieval Texts)

39 *Anglo-Saxon Chronicle*. The best edition is Earle and Plummer, *Two of the Saxon Chronicles Parallel*, 2 vols. (Oxford, 1892–99; new edition by D. Whitelock, 1952); Version C: ed. by H. A. Rositzke, *The C-text of the Old English Chronicles* (Bochum, 1940); English translation by D. Whitelock, D. C. Douglas, and S. I. Tucker, *The Anglo-Saxon Chronicle* (London, 1961)

40 GILDAS, *De conquestu et excidio Britanniae*, ed. Th. Mommsen, *MGH, AA*, XIII (*Chronica minora*, III), 25–85. English translation by J. A. Giles, in *Six Old English Chronicles* (London, 1848)

41 NENNIUS, *Historia Brittonum*, ed. Th. Mommsen, *MGH, AA*, XIII (*Chronica minora*, III), 111–222, or ed. F. Lot (Paris, 1934). English translation by J. A. Giles in *Six Old English Chronicles* (London, 1848)

IV. DIPLOMATIC SOURCES, ETC.

a Gaul

42 PERTZ, K. A. F., *Diplomata regum Francorum e stirpe merowingica*, *MGH*, in-fol., (Hanover, 1872) (extremely bad)

43 BRÉQUIGNY and PARDESSUS, *Diplomata, chartae et instrumenta aetatis merovingicae*, 2 vols. (Paris, 1843–49)

44 LAUER, Philippe and SAMARAN, Charles, *Les diplômes originaux des Mérovingiens* (Paris, 1908)

45 LOT, Ferdinand, 'Liste des cartulaires et recueils contenant des pièces antérieures à l'an mil', *Archivium Latinitatis Medii Aevi*, xv (1940), 5–24

46 TARDIF, Joseph, *Archives de l'Empire, Monuments historiques, Cartons des rois* (Paris, 1866)

b Italy

47 AGNELLUS, *Liber pontificalis ecclesiae Ravennatis*, ed. O. Holder Egger, *MGH, SS. rer. Langob.* (1878), 265–391

c England

48 BIRCH, W. de Gray, *Cartularium Saxonicum*, 3 vols. (London, 1885–93)

49 KEMBLE, J. M., *Codex diplomaticus aevi saxonici*, 6 vols. (London, 1839–48)

50 HARMER, F. E., *Anglo-Saxon Writs* (Manchester, 1952)

51 ROBERTSON, A. J., *Anglo-Saxon Charters* (Cambridge, 1939; 2nd edn. 1956)

51 *bis* SAWYER, P. H., *Anglo-Saxon Charters. An Annotated List and Bibliography* (London, 1968)

52 WHITELOCK, Dorothy, *Anglo-Saxon Wills* (Cambridge, 1930)

V. HAGIOGRAPHICAL SOURCES

a Collections

53 *Acta sanctorum*, ed. by the Bollandists, 67 vols. (Brussels, from 1643)

54 MABILLON, Jean, *Acta sanctorum ordinis sancti Benedicti*, 9 vols. (Paris, 1678–1702)

55 *Bibliotheca hagiographica latina*, ed. by the Bollandists, 3 vols. (Brussels, 1898–1911)

56 *Passiones vitaeque sanctorum aevi merovingici*, ed. B. Krusch and W. Levison, *MGH, SS. rer. Merov.*, III–VII (1896–1920)

b Criticism

57 AIGRAIN, René, *L'hagiographie, ses sources, ses méthodes, son histoire* (Paris, 1953)

58 DELEHAYE, Hippolyte, *Les légendes hagiographiques* (4th edn. Brussels, 1955). English translation by D. Attwater, *The Legends of the Saints* (London, 1962)

2. Modern Works

I. THE LEGACY OF ANTIQUITY

a Roman society on the eve of its collapse

59 ALTHEIM, Franz, *Niedergang der alten Welt*, 2 vols. (Frankfurt, 1952)

60 BLOCH, Herbert, 'The Pagan Revival in the West at the End of the Fourth Century', in *The Conflict between Paganism and Christianity*, ed. A. Momigliano (Oxford, 1963), 193–218

60 bis BROWN, Peter, *The World of Late Antiquity* (London, 1971)

61 CHÉNON, Émile, 'Étude historique sur le defensor civitatis: III. Le defensor civitatis en Occident après la chute de l'Empire', *Rev. Hist. de Droit*, xiii (1889), 515–537

62 DECLAREUIL, J., 'Des comtes de cités à la fin du Ve siècle', *Rev. Hist. de Droit*, xxxiv (1910), 794–836

63 DEMOUGEOT, Émilienne, *De l'unité à la division de l'Empire romain (395–410)* (Paris, 1951)

64 DILL, Samuel, *Roman Society in the Last Century of the Western Empire* (London, 1898; repr. New York, 1960)

65 HUBAUX, Jean, 'La crise de la 365e année', *L'Antiquité classique*, xvii (1948), 343–354

66 JONES, A. H. M., 'Were Ancient Heresies National or Social Movements in Disguise?', *Journal of Theol. Studies*, x (1959), 280–298

66 bis JONES, A. H. M., *The Later Roman Empire, 284–602. A Social, Economic and Administrative Survey*, 4 vols. (Oxford, 1964). A shortened version has been published: A. H. M. JONES *The Decline of the Ancient World* (London, 1966)

67 LIEBESCHÜTZ, W., 'Did the Pelagian Movement Have Social Aims?', *Historia*, xii (1963), 227–41

68 LOT, Ferdinand, *La fin du monde antique et le début du Moyen Age* (Paris, 1927; 2nd edn. 1951). English translation by P. and M. Leon, *The End of the Ancient World and the Beginnings of the Middle Ages* (London, 1931; 2nd edn. edited by G. Downey, New York, 1961)

69 LOT, Ferdinand, *Nouvelles recherches sur l'impôt foncier et la capitation personelle sous le Bas-Empire* (Paris, 1955)

70 MACMULLEN, Ramsey, *Soldier and Civilian in the Later Roman Empire* (Cambridge, Mass., 1963)

70 bis MACMULLEN, Ramsey, *Enemies of the Roman Order. Treason, Unrest and Alienation in the Empire* (Cambridge, Mass., 1967)

71 MAZZARINO, Santo, *Aspetti sociali del quarto secolo* (Rome, 1951)

72 MAZZARINO, Santo, *The End of the Ancient World* (London, 1966)

72 bis MAZZARINO, Santo, 'Si puó parlare di rivoluzione sociale alla fine del mondo antico?', *Settimane di studio. . .*, ix (1961), 410–425

73 NESSELHAUF, Herbert, *Die spätrömische Verwaltung der gallisch-germanischen Länder* (Berlin, 1938)

73 bis OOST, Stewart Irvin, *Galla Placidia Augusta. A Biographical Essay* (Chicago, 1968)

74   REITTER, Nikolaus, *Der Glaube an die Fortdauer des römischen Reiches während des V. und VI. Jahrhund.* (Münster, 1900)

74 *bis* RÉMONDON, Roger, *La crise de l'Empire romain, de Marc Aurèle à Anastase* (Paris, 1964) ('Nouvelle Clio', no. 11)

75   ROSTOVTZEFF, Michael, *The Social and Economic History of the Roman Empire* (Oxford, 1926; 2nd edn. 1957)

76   SIRAGO, Vito Antonio, *Galla Placidia e la trasformazione politica dell'Occidente* (Louvain, 1961)

77   STEIN, Ernest, *Histoire du Bas-Empire*, 2 vols. (Paris, 1949–59)

78   STROHEKER, K. F., 'Um die Grenze zwischen Antike und abendländischen Mittelalter', *Saeculum*, i (1950), 433–465. Reprinted in [no. 144 *bis*], 275–308

79   SUNDWALL, J., *Abhandlungen zur Geschichte des ausgehenden Römertums* (Helsingfors, 1919)

80   VITTINGHOFF, Friedrich, 'Zur Verfassung der Spätantiken Stadt', *Studien zu den Anfängen des europäischen Städtewesens (Reichenau-Vorträge)* (Constance, 1955–56), 11–39

80 *bis* WES, M. A., *Das Ende des Kaisertums im Westen des römischen Reiches* (The Hague, 1967)

81   WHEELER, Mortimer, *Rome beyond the Imperial Frontiers* (London, 1954)

b Roman culture: survivals and disappearances

82   BARDY, G., 'Les origines des écoles monastiques en Occident', *Sacris Erudiri*, viii (1953), 86–104

83   BONNET, Max, *Le latin de Grégoire de Tours* (Paris, 1890; repr. Hildesheim, 1968)

84   CHADWICK, Nora K., 'Intellectual Contacts between Britain and Gaul in the Fifth Century', *Studies in Early British History* (Cambridge, 1954), 189–263

84 *bis* CHADWICK, Nora K., *Poetry and Letters in Early Christian Gaul* (London, 1955)

85   COURCELLE, Pierre, *Les lettres grecques en Occident de Macrobe à Cassiodore* (Paris, 1943). English translation by H. E. Wedeck, *Late Latin Writers and Their Greek Sources* (Cambridge, Mass., 1969)

86   FONTAINE, Jacques, *Isidore de Séville et la culture classique dans l'Espagne wisigothique*, 2 vols. (Paris, 1959)

87   FONTAINE, Jacques, 'Le problème de la culture dans la latinité chrétienne du IIIe au VIIe siècle', *L'Information littéraire*, ix (1957), 208–215

88   LORCIN, A., 'La vie scolaire dans les monastères d'Irlande aux Ve–VIIe siècles', *Revue du Moyen Age Latin*, i (1945), 221–236

89   LOT, Ferdinand, 'A quelle époque a-t-on cessé de parler latin?', *Bulletin Du Cange*, vi (1931), 97–159

90   LOYEN, André, *Sidoine Apollinaire et l'esprit précieux en Gaule aux derniers jours de l'Empire* (Paris, 1943)

91   LOYEN, André, *Recherches historiques sur les panégyriques de Sidoine Apollinaire* (Paris, 1942)

92   MANITIUS, M., *Geschichte der lateinischen Literatur des Mittelalters*, 3 vols. (Munich, 1911–1931)

93   MARROU, H.-I., *Histoire de l'éducation dans l'Antiquité* (Paris, 1948; 5th edn. 1960). English translation by G. Lamb, *A History of Education in Antiquity* (New York, 1956; repr. 1964)

94   MARROU, H.-I., 'La place du haut Moyen Age dans l'histoire du christianisme', *Settimane di studio . . .*, ix (1961), 595–630

95   MOMIGLIANO, Arnaldo, 'Cassiodorus and the Italian Culture of His Time', *Proceedings of the British Academy*, xli (1955), 218–245

96 PIRENNE, Henri, 'De l'état de l'instruction des laïques à l'époque mérovingienne', *Rev. Belge de Philol. et d'Hist.*, xliii (1934), 164–177

97 RICHÉ, Pierre, *Éducation et culture dans l'Occident barbare (VIe–VIIIe siècles)* (Paris, 1962; 3rd edn. 1973)

98 RICHÉ, Pierre, 'La survivance des écoles publiques en Gaule au Ve siècle', *Moyen Age*, lxiii (1957), 421–436

99 ROGER, Maurice, *L'enseignement des lettres classiques d'Ausone à Alcuin* (Paris, 1905)

100 SCHANZ, Martin, *Geschichte der römischen Literatur, IV*, 2 vols. (Munich, 1914–20)

101 STEVENS, C. E., *Sidonius Apollinaris and his Age* (Oxford, 1933)

102 TARDI, D., *Fortunat, Étude sur un dernier représentant de la poésie latine dans la Gaule mérovingienne* (Paris, 1927)

103 VIELLIARD, Jeanne, *Le latin des diplômes royaux et chartes privés de l'époque mérovingienne* (Paris, 1927)

II. THE INVASIONS: GENERAL WORKS

104 BLOCH, Marc, 'Sur les grandes invasions. Quelques positions de problèmes', *Revue de synthèse*, lx (1940–45), 55–81

105 BLOCH, Marc, 'Les invasions', *Annales d'Histoire sociale* (1945), i, 33–46, and ii, 13–28

106 COURCELLE, Pierre, *Histoire littéraire des grandes invasions germaniques* (Paris, 1948; 3rd edn. Paris, 1964)[4]

107 COURCELLE, Pierre, 'Sur quelques textes littéraires relatifs aux grandes invasions', *Rev. Belge de Philol. et d'Hist.*, xxxi (1953), 23–37

107 bis DEMOUGEOT, Émilienne, 'Variations climatiques et invasions', *Rev. Hist.* ccxxxiii (1965), 1–22

107 ter DEMOUGEOT, Émilienne, *La formation de l'Europe et les invasions barbares. I. Des origines germaniques à l'avènement de Dioclétien* (Paris, 1969)

108 FISCHER, J., *Die Völkerwanderung im Urteil der zeitgenössischen kirchlichen Schriftsteller Galliens* (Heidelberg, 1948)

108 bis HOCHHOLZER, Hans, 'Typologie und Dynamik der Völkerwanderung', *Die Welt als Geschichte*, xix (1959), 129–145

109 LATOUCHE, Robert, *Les grandes invasions et la crise de l'Occident au Ve siècle* (Paris, 1946)

110 LATOUCHE, Robert, 'Aspect démographique de la crise des grandes invasions', *Population*, ii (1947), 681–690

111 LOT, Ferdinand, *Les invasions germaniques. La pénétration mutuelle du monde barbare et du monde romaine* (Paris, 1935; 2nd edn. 1945)

112 LOT, Ferdinand, *Les invasions barbares*, 2 vols. (Paris, 1937)

113 PALANQUE, Jean Rémy, 'Saint Jerome and the Barbarians', in *A Monument to St. Jerome*, ed. F. X. Murphy (New York, 1952), 173–199

114 RICHÉ, Pierre, *Les invasions barbares* (Paris, 1953; 4th edn. 1968). (Collection 'Que sais-je?')

114 bis STROHEKER, Karl Friedrich, *Germanentum und Spätantike* (Zürich and Stuttgart, 1965)

III. THE GERMANS

a General works

115 CAPELLE, Wilhelm, *Das alte Germanien. Die Nachrichten der griechischen und römischen Schriftsteller* (Jena, 1937)

116   CAPELLE, Wilhelm, *Die Germanen der Völkerwanderung, auf Grund der zeitgenössischen Quellen dargestellt* (Stuttgart, 1940)

117   DE VRIES, Jan, *Kelten und Germanen* (Berne and Munich, 1960)

118   DRÖGEREIT, Richard, 'Die Ausbreitung der nordwestdeutschen Küstenvölker über See', *Neues Archiv für Niedersachsen*, xxiii (1951), 229–250

119   FEIST, Sigmund, *Germanen und Kelten in der antiken Überlieferung* (Halle, 1927; 2nd edn. Baden-Baden, 1948)

120   GUTENBRUNNER, Siegfried, *Germanische Frühzeit in den Berichten der Antike* (Halle, 1939)

121   GUTENBRUNNER, S., JANKUHN, H., and LAUR, W., *Völker und Stämme Südost-schleswigs im frühen Mittelalter* (Schleswig, 1952)

122   HOOPS, Johannes, *Reallexicon der germanischen Altertumskunde*, 4 vols. (Strasbourg, 1911–19)

123   KARSTEN, T. E., *Les anciens Germains* (translation by F. Mossé) (Paris, 1931)

124   MELIN, Bengt, *Die Heimat der Kimbern* (Uppsala, 1960)

125   MUCH, R., *Die Germania des Tacitus* (Heidelberg, 1937)

126   REINERTH, Hans, *Vorgeschichte der deutschen Stämme*, 3 vols. (Leipzig and Berlin, 1940)

127   SCHMIDT, Ludwig, *Geschichte der deutschen Stämme bis zum Ausgang der Völkerwanderung*: *I, Die Ostgermanen* (2nd edn. Munich, 1941). *II, Die Westgermanen*, 2 vols. (2nd edn. Munich, 1938–40)

128   SCHÜTTE, Gudmund, *Our Forefathers, the Gothonic Nations*, 2 vols. (Cambridge, 1929–33)

129   SCHWARZ, Ernst, *Goten, Nordgermanen, Angelsachsen. Studien zur Ausgliederung der germanischen Sprachen* (Berne, 1951)

130   SCHWARZ, E., 'Probleme und Aufgaben der germanischen Stammeskunde', *Germanisch-romanische Monatsschrift* (1955), 97–115

131   SCHWARZ, E., *Germanische Stammeskunde* (Heidelberg, 1956)

131 *bis* SCHWARZ, E., *Germanische Stammeskunde zwischen den Wissenschaften* (Constance and Stuttgart, 1967)

132   STEINBACH, Franz, *Studien zur westdeutschen Stammes- und Volkgeschichte* (Jena, 1926)

133   STROHEKER, K. F., 'Die geschichtliche Stellung der ostgermanischen Staaten am Mittelmeer', *Saeculum*, xii (1961), 140–157. Reprinted in [no. 114 *bis*], 101–133

134   SVENNUNG, J., *Scandinavia und Scandia. Lateinisch-nordische Namenstudien* (Uppsala, 1963) (with an English summary)

134 *bis* THOMPSON, E. A., *The Early Germans* (Oxford, 1965)

135   WENSKUS, Reinhart, *Stammesbildung und Verfassung. Das Werden der frühmittelalterlichen Gentes* (Cologne and Graz, 1961)

b Civilization

136   AMIRA, Karl von, *Grundriss des germanischen Rechts* (3rd edn. Strasbourg, 1913; 4th edn. edited by K. A. Eckhardt, Berlin, 1960)

137   BOUDRIOT, Wilhelm, *Die altgermanische Religion in der amtlichen kirchlichen Literatur des Abendlandes vom V. bis XI. Jh.* (Bonn, 1928; repr. 1964)

138   DANNENBAUER, Heinrich, 'Adel, Burg und Herrschaft bei den Germanen', *Historisches Jahrbuch*, lxi (1941), 1–50

139   DANNENBAUER, H., 'Hundertschaft, centena und huntari', *Historisches Jahrbuch*, lxii–lxix (1949), 155–219

140   DE VRIES, Jan, *Altgermanische Religionsgeschichte*, 2 vols. (2nd edn. Berlin, 1956–57)

141   DE VRIES, J., 'Das Königtum bei den Germanen', *Saeculum*, vii (1956), 289–309

142 DUMÉZIL, Georges, *Les dieux des Germains* (Paris, 1959)
143 GIESECKE, Heinz Eberhart, *Die Ostgermanen und der Arianismus* (Leipzig, 1939)
144 GRIERSON, Philip, 'Election and Inheritance in Early Germanic Kingship', *Cambridge Historical Journal*, vii (1941), 1–12
145 GUTENBRUNNER, Siegfried, *Die germanischen Götternamen der antiken Inschriften* (Halle, 1936)
146 KROESCHELL, Karl, 'Die Sippe in germanischen Recht', *Zeitschrift der Savigny-Stiftung für Rechtsgeschichte, Germ. Abt.*, lxxvii (1960), 1–25
147 KUHN, Hans, 'Die Grenzen der germanischen Gefolgschaft., *Zeitschrift der Savigny-Stiftung für Rechtsgeschichte, Germ. Abt.*, lxxiii (1956), 1–83
148 MUSSET, Lucien, and MOSSÉ, Fernand, *Introduction à la runologie* (Paris, 1965)
149 ROSENFELD, Hellmut, 'Buch, Schrift und lateinische Sprachkenntnis bei den Germanen vor der christlichen Mission', *Rheinisches Museum*, xcv (1952), 193–209
150 THOMPSON, E. A., 'Christianity and the Northern Barbarians', in *The Conflict between Paganism and Christianity*, ed. A. Momigliano (Oxford, 1963), 56–78

c *Archaeology*

151 ÅBERG, Nils, *The Occident and the Orient in the Art of the Seventh Century*, 3 vols, (Stockholm, 1943–47)
152 ÅBERG, Nils, *Den historiska relationen mellan folkvandringstid och Vendeltid* (Stockholm, 1953)
153 HOLMQVIST, Wilhelm, *Kunstprobleme der Merowingerzeit* (Stockholm, 1939)
154 HOLMQVIST, W., *Germanic Art during the First Millennium A D.* (Stockholm, 1955)
154 *bis* HUBERT, Jean, PORCHER, Jean, and VOLBACH, W. F., *L'Europe des Invasions* (Paris, 1967) (Collection 'L'Univers des Formes'). English translation by S. Gilbert and J. Emmons, *Europe in the Dark Ages* (London, 1969) ('The Arts of Mankind' series)
155 MARIËN, M. E., *L'Art mérovingien, Musées Royaux d'Art et d'Histoire* (Brussels, 1954)
155 *bis* OTTO, Karl Heinz, *Bibliographie zur archäologischen Germanenforschung. Deutschsprachige Literatur, 1941–1955* (Berlin, 1966)
156 SALIN, Bernhard, *Die altgermanische Thierornamentik* (Berlin and Stockholm, 1904; repr. 1935)
157 TISCHLER, F., 'Der Stand der Sachsenforschung, archäologisch gesehen', *35. Bericht der röm.-germ. Kommission* (1954), 21–215

d *Onomastic studies*

158 FÖRSTEMANN, E., *Altdeutsches Namenbuch* (Bonn, 1900–16)
159 POLENZ, Peter von, *Landschafts- und Bezirchsnamen im frühmittelalterlichen Deutschland* (Marburg, 1961–)
160 SCHÖNFELD, M., *Wörterbuch der altgermanischen Personen- und Völkernamen* (Heidelberg, 1911)
161 SCHWARZ, Ernst, *Deutsche Namenforschung*, 2 vols. (Göttingen, 1950)
162 WOOLF, Henry B., *The Old Germanic Principles of Name-Giving* (Baltimore, 1939)

IV. THE GOTHS

a *General works: origins*

163 *I Goti in Occidente, Settimane di Studio. . .*, iii (1956)

163 *bis* GIUNTA, Francesco, 'I Goti e la Romanità', *Nuove questioni di storia medioevale* (Milan, 1964), 37–56

163 *ter* HACHMANN, R., *Die Goten und Skandinavien* (Berlin, 1970)

164 KLEIN, K. K., 'Frithigern, Athanarich und die Spaltung des Westgotenvolkes am Vorabend des Hunneneinbruchs' *Südostforschung*, xix (1960), 34–51

165 MANSION, J., 'Les origines du christianisme chez les Goths', *Analecta Bollandiana*, xxxii (1914), 5–30

166 OXENSTIERNA, Eric Graf, *Die Urheimat der Goten* (Leipzig and Stockholm, 1948)

167 ROSENFELD, H., 'Ost- und Westgoten', *Die Welt als Geschichte*, xvii (1957), 245–258

168 SCHWARZ, Ernst, 'Die Krimgoten', *Saeculum*, iv (1953), 156–164

169 SCHWARZ, E., 'Die Urheimat der Goten und ihre Wanderung ins Weichselland und nach Südrussland', *Saeculum*, iv (1953), 13–26

169 *bis* SVENNUNG, J., *Jordanes und Scandia. Kritisch-Exegetische Studien* (Stockholm, 1967)

170 THOMPSON, E. A., The Passio S. Sabae and Early Visigothic Society', *Historia*, iv (1955), 331–338

171 THOMPSON, E. A., 'Early Visigothic Christianity', *Latomus*, xxi (1962), 505–519 and 794–810

172 THOMPSON, E. A., 'The Visigoths from Fritigern to Euric', *Historia*, xv (1963), 105–126

172 *bis* THOMPSON, E. A., *The Visigoths in the Time of Ulfila* (Oxford, 1966)

173 VASILIEV, A. A., *The Goths in the Crimea* (Cambridge, Mass., 1936)

173 *bis* WAGNER, Norbert, *Getica. Untersuchungen zum Leben des Jordanes und zur frühen Geschichte der Goten* (Berlin, 1967)

174 WÜST, Walther, 'Goten in Indien?', in F. Altheim, *Geschichte der Hunnen* [no. 509], vol. III, 141–189

b Gothic culture

175 FUCHS, Siegfried, *Kunst der Ostgotenzeit* (Berlin, 1944)

176 LAMBERT, Élie, 'La tradition visigothe en Occident et dans l'art omeiyade d'Espagne', *Annales du Midi*, lxv (1953), 295–300

177 MARCHAND, James W., 'Notes on Gothic Manuscripts', *Journal of English and German Philology*, lvi (1957), 213–224

177 *bis* STUTZ, Elfriede, *Gotische Literaturdenkmäler* (Stuttgart, 1966)

178 MOSSÉ, Fernand, *Manuel de la langue gotique* (2nd edn. Paris, 1956)

179 MOSSÉ, F., 'Bibliographia Gotica', *Mediaeval Studies*, xii (1950), 237–324 and xix (1957), 174–196

179 *bis* PALOL SALELLAS, Pedro de, *Arqueologia paleocristiana y visigoda* (Saragossa, 1954)

179 *ter* PALOL SALELLAS, Pedro de, *Arte hispanica de la epoca visigoda* (Barcelona, 1968) (Text in Spanish, English, French and German)

180 PLATE, Rudolf, *Geschichte der gotischen Literatur* (Berlin, 1931)

181 SCHLUNK, Helmut, 'Arte Visigodo' in *Historia Universal del Arte Hispanico*, II (Madrid, 1947)

c The Visigoths in Aquitaine and Spain

182 ABADAL Y DE VINYALS, Ramon d', *Del reino de Tolosa al reino de Toledo* (Madrid, 1960)

183 BROËNS, Maurice, 'Los Francos y el poblamiento de la peninsula ibérica durante los siglos VI y VII', *Ampurias*, xvii–xviii (1955–56), 59–77

184 BROËNS, M., 'Le peuplement germanique de la Gaule entre la Méditerranée et l'Océan', *Annales du Midi*, lxviii (1956), 17–38

185 CASTRO, Américo, *La realidad historica de España* (Mexico City, 1954)

185 *bis* CLAUDE, Dietrich, *Geschichte der Westgoten* (Stuttgart, 1970)

185 *ter* FONTAINE, Jacques, 'Conversion et culture chez les Wisigoths d'Espagne', *Settimane di studio . . .* , xiv (1966), 87–147

186 GAMILLSCHEG, Ernst, 'Historia lingüística de los Visigodos', *Revista de Filología Española*, xx (1932), 118–150 and 229–260

187 GARCÍA GALLO, Alfonso, 'El carácter germánico de la épica y del derecho en la edad media española', *Anuario de Historia del Derecho Español*, xxv (1955), 583–679

188 GROSSE, Roberto, *Las fuentes de la época visigoda y bizantina* (Barcelona, 1947) (*Fontes Hispaniae Antiquae, IX*)

188 *bis* HILLGARTH, J, N., 'La conversión de los Visigodos: notas criticas', *Analecta Sacra Tarraconensia*, xxxiv (1961), 21–46

188 *ter* HILLGARTH, J. N., 'Coins and Chronicles: Propaganda in Sixth-Century Spain and the Byzantine Background', *Historia*, xv (1966), 483–508

189 LANTIER, Raymond, 'Le cimetière wisigothique d'Estagel', *Gallia*, i (1943), 153–188 and vii (1949), 55–80. Also *Comptes rendus de l'Acad. des Inscriptions et Belles-Lettres* (1947), 226–235 and (1948), 154–163

190 LANTIER, R., 'La céramique wisigothique', *Les invasions barbares et le peuplement de l'Europe* (Paris, 1953), 23–34

191 LOT, Ferdinand, 'La Vita Viviani et la domination visigothique en Aquitaine', *Mélanges F. Fournier* (Paris, 1929), 467–77

192 LOYEN, André, 'Les débuts du royaume wisigoth de Toulouse', *Revue des études latines*, xii (1934), 406–415)

193 MENÉNDEZ PIDAL, Ramon, (ed.) *Historia de España: III. España visigoda* (Madrid, 1940; 2nd edn. 1963)

194 MILES, G. G., *The Coinage of the Visigoths of Spain* (New York, 1952)

195 REINHART, Wilhelm, 'La tradición visigoda en el nacimiento de Castilla', *Estudios dedicados a Menéndez Pidal, I* (Madrid, 1950), 535–554

196 REINHART, W., 'Über die Territorialität der westgotischen Gesetzbücher', *Zeitschrift der Savigny-Stiftung für Rechtsgeschichte, Germ. Abt.*, lxviii (1951), 348–354

197 STROHEKER, K. F., *Eurich, König der Westgoten* (Stuttgart, 1937)

197 *bis* STROHEKER, K. F., 'Leowigild', *Die Welt als Geschichte*, v (1939), 446–485. Reprinted in [no. 114 *bis*], 131–191

198 THOMPSON, E. A., 'The Settlement of the Barbarians in Southern Gaul', *Journal of Roman Studies*, xlvi (1956), 65–75

199 THOMPSON, E. A., 'The Conversion of the Visigoths to Catholicism', *Nottingham Mediaeval Studies*, iv (1960), 4–35

199 *bis* THOMPSON, E. A., 'The Barbarian Kingdoms in Gaul and Spain', *Nottingham Mediaeval Studies*, vii (1963), 3–33

199 *ter* THOMPSON, E. A., *The Goths in Spain* (Oxford, 1969)

199 *quater* WALLACE-HADRILL, J. M., 'Gothia and Romania', in [no. 407 *bis*], 25–48

200 WOHLHAUPTER, Eugen, 'Das germanische Element im altspanischen Recht', *Zeitschrift der Savigny-Stiftung für Rechtsgeschichte, Germ. Abt.*, lxvi (1948), 166–173

201 YVER, Georges, 'Euric, roi des Wisigoths', *Études d'histoire du Moyen Age dédiées à Gabriel Monod* (Paris, 1896), 11–46

202 ZEISS, Hans, *Die Grabfunde aus dem spanischen Westgotenreich* (Berlin and Leipzig, 1934)

203 ZEUMER, Karl, 'Geschichte der westgotischen Gesetzgebung', *Neues Archiv*, xxiii (1898), 419–516 and xxiv (1899), 39–122

204 ZEUMER, K., 'Die Chronologie der Westgotenkönige von Toledo', *Neues Archiv*, xxvii (1901), 411–444

d *Ostrogothic Italy*

205   ÅBERG, Nils, *Die Goten und Langobarden in Italien* (Uppsala, 1923)
206   CECCHELLI, Carlo, 'L'arianesimo e le chiese ariane d'Italia', *Settimane di studio* . . ., vii (1959), 743–774
207   DEGANI, Mario, *Il tesoro romano-barbàrico di Reggio Emilia* (Florence, 1959)
208   ENSSLIN, Wilhelm, *Theoderich der Grosse* (Munich, 1947; 2nd edn. 1959)
209   KRAUS, F. F., *Die Münzen Odovacars und des Ostgotenreiches in Italien* (Halle, 1928)
209 *bis* LAMMA, Paolo, *Teoderico* (Brescia, 1951)
210   MOMMSEN, Theodor, 'Ostgotische Studien', *Neues Archiv*, xiv (1889), 451–544. Reprinted in *Gesammelte Schriften*, VI (1910), 362–484
211   REY, Maurice, 'Théodoric le Grand', *Hommes d'État*, ed. Duff and Galy (Paris, 1936), I, 421–511
212   SCHMIDT, Ludwig, 'Die letzten Ostgoten', *Abhandl. der Preuss. Akad. der Wiss., Phil.-Hist. Klasse*, 1943, no. 10
213   VAN DE VYVER, A., 'Cassiodore et son oeuvre', *Speculum*, vi (1931), 244–292
214   VISMARA, Giulio, 'Romani e Goti di fronte al diritto nel regno ostrogoto', *Settimane di studio* . . ., iii (1955), 409–463
215   WREDE, Ferdinand, *Über die Sprache der Ostgoten in Italien* (Strasbourg, 1891)
216   ZEILLER, Jacques, 'Étude sur l'arianisme en Italie à l'époque ostrogothique et à l'époque lombarde', *Mélanges d'arch. et d'hist. publ. par l'école franç. de Rome*, xxv (1905), 127–146

e *Literary reflections of Gothic greatness*

217   BRADY, Caroline, *The Legends of Ermanaric* (Berkeley, 1948)
218   MENÉNDEZ PIDAL, R., *Floresta de leyendas heroicas españolas. Rodrigo, el último godo*, I (Madrid, 1942)
219   VRIES, Jan de, 'Theoderich der Grosse', *Germanisch-romanische Monatsschrift*, xlii (1961), 319–330
220   ZINK, Georges, *Les légendes héroïques de Dietrich et d'Ermrich dans les littératures germaniques* (Lyons and Paris, 1950)

V. THE BURGUNDIANS

220 *bis* BECK, Marcel, 'Bemerkungen zur Geschichte des ersten Burgundenreiches', *Schweizerische Zeitschrift für Geschichte*, xiii (1963), 433–534
221   BESSON, M., *L'art barbare dans l'ancien diocèse de Lausanne* (Lausanne, 1909)
222   BLONDEL, Louis, 'Le prieuré Saint-Victor, les débuts du christianisme et la royauté burgonde à Genève', *Bull. de la soc. d'hist. et d'archéol. de Genève*, xi (1958), 211–258
223   CHAUME, Maurice, *Les origines du duché de Bourgogne*, 4 vols. (Dijon, 1925)
224   COVILLE, Alfred, *Recherches sur l'histoire de Lyon du Ve au IXe siècle* (Paris, 1928)
225   DUPARC, Pierre, 'La Sapaudia', *Comptes rendus de l'Acad. des Inscriptions et Belles-Lettres* (1958), 371–383
226   JAHN, A., *Geschichte der Burgundionen und Burgundiens bis zum Ende der 1. Dynastie*, 2 vols. (Halle, 1874)
227   KÖHLER, G., 'Die Bekehrung der Burgunden zum Christentum', *Zeitschrift für Kirchengeschichte*, lviii (1938), 227–243
228   LOT, Ferdinand, 'Les limites de la Sapaudia', *Revue savoisienne*, lxvii (1935), 146–156

229 MARTIN, P. E., 'Le problème de la Sapaudia', *Rev. suisse d'histoire*, xviii (1933), 183–205

230 PERRENOT, Th., *La toponymie burgonde* (Paris, 1942)

230 *bis* PERRIN, Odet, *Les Burgondes* (Neuchâtel, 1968)

231 SAUTER, Marc R., and MOESCHLER, Pierre, 'Caractères dentaires mongoloïdes chez les Burgondes de la Suisse occidentale', *Archives des Sciences*, xiii (1960), 387–426

232 ZEISS, Hans, 'Studien zu den Grabfunden aus dem Burgundenreich an der Rhone', *Sitzungsber. der Bayer. Akad. der Wiss., Phil.-Hist. Klasse*, 1938

VI. THE VANDALS

233 COURTOIS, Christian, *Les Vandales et l'Afrique* (Paris, 1955)

234 DIESNER, Hans Joachim, *Das Vandalenreich. Aufstieg und Untergang* (Stuttgart, 1966)

235 FREND, W. H. C., [The Vandals and Africa], *Journal of Roman Studies*, xlvi, (1956), 161–166

236 GAUTIER, Ernest Félix, *Genséric, roi des Vandales* (Paris, 1932)

237 GIUNTA, Federico, *Genserico e la Sicilia* (Palermo, 1958)

238 HEUBERGER, R., 'Vandalische Reichskanzlei und Königsurkunden', *Mitteilungen des Inst. für Österreich. Geschichtsforschung*, xi (1929), 76–113

238 *bis* JULIEN, Charles-André, *Histoire de l'Afrique du Nord*, I (2nd edn. Paris, 1951)

239 LE GALL, Joël, 'L'itinéraire de Genséric', *Rev. de Philologie*, x (1936), 268–273

240 MARTROYE, Félix, *Genséric, la conquête vandale et la destruction de l'Empire d'Occident* (Paris, 1907)

241 MARTROYE, F., *L'Occident à l'époque byzantine : Goths et Vandales* (Paris, 1937)

242 PALLASSE, Maurice, 'Moyen Age vandale en Afrique du Nord. Autour des Tablettes Albertini', *Revue du Moyen Age latin*, x (1954), 161–168

243 SCHMIDT, Ludwig, *Geschichte der Wandalen* (2nd edn. Munich, 1942). French translation, *Histoire des Vandales* (Paris, 1953)

244 WREDE, Ferdinand, *Über die Sprache der Wandalen* (Strasbourg, 1886)

VII. THE LOMBARDS AND LOMBARD ITALY

244 *bis Problemi della civiltà e dell'economia longobarda, scritti . . . raccolti da* A. TAGLIA-FERRI (Milan, 1964)

244 *ter* BERTOLINI, Ottorino, 'La data dell'ingresso dei Longobardi in Italia', *Scritti scelti di storia medioevale* (Livorno, 1968), 19–64

245 BETHMANN, L. and HOLDER-EGGER, O., 'Langobardischen Regesten', *Neues Archiv*, iii (1878), 225–318

246 BLASEL, C., 'Der Übertritt der Langobarden zum Christentum', *Archiv für katholisches Kirchenrecht*, lxxxii (1903), 577–619

247 BOGNETTI, Gian Piero, 'Longobardi e Romani', in *Studi in onore di E. Besta* (Rome, 1939), 353–410. Reprinted in *L'età longobarda* [no. 438a] I, 83–141

248 BOGNETTI, G. P., 'Sul tipo e il grado di civiltà dei Longobardi in Italia' in *Art du Haut Moyen Age dans la région alpine* (Olten, 1954), 41–75. Reprinted in *L'età longobarda* [no. 438a], III, 267–301

249 BRUCKNER, Wilhelm, *Die Sprache der Langobarden* (Strasbourg, 1895 ; reprinted Berlin, 1969)

250 DUCHESNE, Louis, 'Les évêchés d'Italie et l'invasion lombarde', *Mélanges d'arch. et d'hist. publ. par l'école franç. de Rome*, xxiii (1903), 83–116 and xxv (1905), 365–399

251   LÖFSTEDT, Bengt, *Studien über die Sprache der langobardischen Gesetze* (Stockholm, 1961)
252   SCHAFFRAN, E., *Die Kunst der Langobarden* (Jena, 1941)
253   WERNER, Joachim, 'Longobardischer Einfluss in Süddeutschland während des 7. Jh. im Lichte archäologischen Funde', *Atti del I° Congresso di Studi Longobardi* (Spoleto, 1951), 521–524
254   WERNER, J., 'Die Langobarden in Pannonien', *Abhandl. der Bayer. Akad. der Wiss., Phil.-Hist. Klasse*, N.F., no. 55A (1962)

VIII. THE FRANKS

a General works and origins: Clovis

255   BLOCH. Marc, 'La conquête de la Gaule par les rois francs', *Revue historique*, clvii (1927), 161–178
256   COURCELLE, Pierre, 'Le titre d'Auguste décerné à Clovis', *Bull. Soc. Nat. Antiquaires de France* (1948–49), 46–57
257   DE BOONE, W. J., *De Franken van hun eerste optreden tot de dood van Childerik* (Amsterdam, 1954)
258   EWIG, Eugen, 'Die civitas Ubiorum, die Francia Rinensis und das Land Ribuarien', *Rheinische Vierteljahrsblätter*, xix (1954), 1–29
259   HALPHEN, Louis, 'Grégoire de Tours, historien de Clovis', *Mélanges Ferd. Lot* (Paris, 1925), 235–244. Reprinted in HALPHEN, *À travers le Moyen Age* (Paris, 1950), 31–38
260   KURTH, Godefroid, *Clovis*, 2 vols. (Brussels, 1923)
261   KURTH, G., *Études franques*, 2 vols. (Paris and Brussels, 1919)
262   LEVILLAIN, Léon, 'La crise des années 507–508 et les rivalités d'influence en Gaule de 508 à 514', in *Mélanges N. Iorga* (Paris, 1933), 537–567
263   LEVILLAIN, L., 'La conversion et le baptême de Clovis', *Rev. d'hist de l'église de France*, xxi (1935), 161–192
264   LOT, Ferdinand, 'La conquête du pays d'entre Seine et Loire par les Francs. La ligue armoricaine et les destinées du duché du Maine', *Revue historique*, clxiv (1930), 242–253
265   LOT, F., *Naissance de la France* (Paris, 1948)
266   SCHMIDT, Ludwig, 'Aus den Anfängen des salfränkischen Königtums', *Klio*, xxxiv (1942), 306–327
267   STROHEKER, K. F., 'Zur Rolle der Heermeister fränkischer Abstammung im späten 4. Jh.', *Historia*, iv (1955), 314–330. Reprinted in [no. 114 *bis*], 5–29
267 *bis* TESSIER, Georges, *Le baptême de Clovis* (Paris, 1964)
267 *ter* TESSIER, G., 'La conversion de Clovis et la christianisation des Francs', *Settimane di studio . . .*, xiv (1966), 149–189
268   VAN DE VYVER, André, 'La victoire contre les Alamans et la conversion de Clovis', *Rev. Belge de Philol. et d'Hist.*, xv (1936), 859–914; xvi (1937), 35–94; xvii (1938), 793–813
269   VAN DE VYVER, A., 'La chronologie du règne de Clovis d'après la légende et d'après l'histoire', *Moyen Age*, liii (1947), 177–196
270   VERLINDEN, Charles, 'De Franken en Aetius', *Bijdragen tot de Geschiedenis Nederlanden*, i (1946), 1–15
271   VERLINDEN, C., 'Frankish Colonization: a New Approach', *Trans. Royal Hist. Soc.*, 5th ser. iv (1954), 1–17
271 *bis* ZÖLLNER, E., *Geschichte der Franken bis zur Mitte des 6. Jahrhunderts* (Munich, 1970)

b The problems of the linguistic frontier

272 BLOCH, Marc, 'Peuplement et régime agraire', *Rev. de synthèse hist.*, xlii (1926), 93–99

273 DES MAREZ, G., 'Le problème de la colonisation franque et du régime agraire dans la Basse-Belgique', *Mém. Acad. royale de Belgique*, in-4°, 2e sér., ix (1926)

274 DHONDT, Jan, 'Essai sur l'origine de la frontière linguistique', *L'Antiquité classique*, xvi (1947), 261–286 and xxi (1952), 107–122

275 FAIDER-FEYTMANS, Germaine, 'La frontière du Nord de la Gaule sous le Bas-Empire', *Mélanges J. Marouzeau* (Paris, 1948), 161–172

276 GAMILLSCHEG, Ernst, 'Germanische Siedlung in Belgien und Nordfrankreich. Die fränkische Einwanderung und junggermanische Zuwanderung', *Abhandl. der Preuss. Akad. der Wiss., Phil.-Hist. Klasse*, (1937)

277 GYSSELING, Maurits, 'La genèse de la frontière linguistique dans le Nord de la Gaule', *Revue du Nord*, xliv (1962), 5–37

278 HEURGON, J., 'L'hypothèse du limes belgicus, état présent de la question', *Revue du Nord*, xxix (1962), 212–216

279 JUNGANDREAS, Wolfgang, 'Ein romanischer Dialekt an der Mosel zwischen Eifel und Hunsrück', *Zeitschrift für romanischer Philologie*, lxxi (1955), 414–421

280 KURTH, Godefroid, *La frontière linguistique en Belgique et dans le Nord de la France*, 2 vols. (Brussels, 1896–98)

281 PETRI, Franz, *Germanische Volkserbe in Wallonien und Nordfrankreich*, 2 vols. (Bonn, 1937)

282 PETRI, F., 'Zum Stand der Diskussion über die fränkische Landnahme und die Entstehung der germanisch-romanischen Sprachgrenze', *Rheinische Vierteljahrsblätter*, xv–xvi (1950–51), 39–86

283 STENGERS, J., *La formation de la frontière linguistique en Belgique ou de la légitimité de l'hypothèse historique* (Brussels, 1959)

284 VANNERUS, J., 'Le limes et les fortifications gallo-romaines de Belgique. Enquête toponymique', *Mém. Acad. royale de Belgique, Classe des lettres*, (1943)

285 VERLINDEN, Charles, *Les origines de la frontière linguistique en Belgique et la colonisation franque* (Brussels, 1955)

286 WARTBURG, Walther von, *Umfang und Bedeutung der germanischen Siedlung in Nordgallien im 5. und 6. Jh. im Spiegel der Sprache und Ortsnamen* (Berlin, 1950)

c The early medieval archaeology of Gaul

287 ARBMAN, Holger, 'Verroterie cloisonnée et filigrane', *Kungl. humanistika vetenskapssumfundet i Lund. Årsberättelse*, (1949–50), 136–172

288 AUDY, Jean and RIQUET, Raymond, 'La basilique cémétériale de Montferrand (Aude), contribution à l'étude du peuplement des grandes invasions', *Comptes Rendus de l'Acad. des Inscriptions et Belles-Lettres* (1961), 185–204

289 BARRIÈRE-FLAVY, C., *Les arts industriels des peuples barbares de la Gaule*, 3 vols. (Toulouse-Paris, 1901)

290 BLANCHET, Adrien, *Les trésors de monnaies romaines et les incursions germaniques en Gaule* (Paris, 1900)

291 BÖHNER, Kurt, 'Archäologische Beiträge zur Erforschung der Frankenzeit am Niederrhein', *Rheinische Vierteljahrsblätter*, xv–xvi (1950–51), 19–38

292 BUTLER, R. M., 'Late Roman Town Walls in Gaul', *Archaeological Journal*, cxvi (1959), 25–50

293 COCHET, l'abbé, *La Normandie souterraine. Sépultures gauloises, romaines, franques et normandes* (Paris, 1854)

294   Cochet, l'abbé, *Le tombeau de Childéric Ie, roi des Francs, restitué à l'aide de l'archéologie* (Paris, 1859)

295   Dhondt, Jan, De Laet, S. J. and Hombert, P., 'Quelques considérations sur la fin de la domination romaine et les débuts de la colonisation franque en Belgique', *L'Antiquité classique*, xvii (1948), 150–156

296   Faider-Feytmans, G., 'L'aire de dispersion des cimetières mérovingiens en Belgique' in *Études mérovingiennes* (Paris, 1953), 103–109

297   France-Lanord, Albert, 'Un cimetière de lètes à Cortrat (Loiret)', *Revue archéologique*, (1963), i, 15–35

298   France-Lanord, A., and Fleury, Michel, 'Das Grab der Arnegundis in St-Denis', *Germania*, xl (1962), 341–359

299   Hubert, Jean, *L'art pré-roman* (Paris, 1938)

300   Knögel, E., 'Schriftquellen zur Kunstgeschichte der Merovingerzeit', *Bonner Jahrbücher*, cxl–cxli (1936), 1–258

301   Lantier, Ramond, 'Un cimetière du IVe siècle (Vert-la-Gravelle)', *L'Antiquité classique*, xvii (1949), 373–401

302   Lantier, R., and Hubert, J., *Les origines de l'art français* (Paris, 1947)

303   Lindenschmidt, Ludwig, *Handbuch der deutschen Altertumskunde : I. Altertümer der merowingischen Zeit* (Brunswick, 1880–89)

304   Roblin, Michel, 'Cités ou citadelles? Les enceintes romaines du Bas-Empire d'après l'exemple de Paris', *Revue des études anciennes*, liii (1951), 301–311 and lxvii (1965), 368–391

305   Salin, Édouard, 'Sur le peuplement des marches de l'Est apres les grandes invasions', *Comptes Rendus de l'Acad. des Inscriptions et Belles-Lettres* (1945), 498–504

306   Salin, É., *Manuel des fouilles archéologiques : I. Les fouilles de sépultures du Ve au VIIIe siècle* (Paris, 1946)

307   Salin, É., 'Les techniques de la damasquinure en Gaule mérovingienne', *Gallia*, ix (1951), 31–52

308   Salin, É., *La civilisation mérovingienne*, 4 vols. (Paris, 1949–59)

309   Salin, É., and France-Lanord, A., *Le fer à l'époque mérovingienne. Étude technique et archéologique* (Paris, 1943)

310   Werner, Joachim, *Münzdatierte austrasische Grabfunde* (Berlin and Leipzig, 1935)

311   Werner, J., 'Zur Entstehung der Reihengräberzivilisation', *Archaeologia Geographica*, i (1950), 23–32

311 bis Werner, J., 'Frankish Royal Tombs in the Cathedral of Cologne and St. Denis', *Antiquity*, xxxviii (1964), 201–216

312   Wuilleumier, P., Audin, A., and Leroi-Gourhan, A., *L'église et la nécropole Saint-Laurent dans le quartier lyonnais de Choulans* (Lyons, 1949)

313   Zeiss, H., 'Die germanischen Grabfunde des frühen Mittelalters zwischen mittleren Seine und Loiremündung', *31. Bericht der röm.-germ. Kommission*, (1941), 5–174

d Onomastic and linguistic problems in Gaul

314   Dauzat, Albert, *La toponymie française* (Paris, 1939)

315   Dauzat, A., *Les noms de famille de France* (Paris, 1945)

316   Gamillscheg, Ernst, *Romania Germanica. Sprach- und Siedlungsgeschichte der Germanen auf dem Boden des alten Römerreichs*, 3 vols. (Berlin and Leipzig, 1934–35; a partial re-edition, Berlin, 1970)

317   Gröhler, H., *Ursprung und Bedeutung der französischen Ortsnamen* (Heidelberg, 1913)

318 JOHNSON, J., *Étude sur les noms de lieu dans lesquels entrent les éléments court, ville et villiers* (Paris, 1946)

319 LEBEL, Paul, *Les noms de personnes* (Paris, 1946)

320 LEGROS, Élisée, 'Le nord de la Gaule. Linguistique et toponymie', *Bull. Comm. roy. toponymie et dialectologie*, xvi (1942), 161–228

321 LONGNON, Auguste, *Les noms de lieu de la France* (Paris, 1920–29; repr. 1968)

322 LOT, Ferdinand, 'De l'origine et de la signification des noms de lieu en ville et en court', *Romania*, lix (1933), 199–246

322 *bis* LÜDTKE, Helmut, 'Die Entstehung romanischer Schriftsprache', *Vox Romanica*, xxiii (1964), 3–21

322 *ter* NORBERG, Dag, 'A quelle époque a-t-on cessé de parler latin en Gaule?', *Annales (Économies, Sociétés, Civilisations)*, xxi (1966), 346–356

323 ROBLIN, Michel, *Le terroir de Paris aux époques gallo-romaine et franque* (Paris, 1951; new edn. 1970)

324 VINCENT, Auguste, *Toponymie de la France* (Brussels, 1937)

325 WARTBURG, W. von, *Die Entstehung der romanischen Völker* (Halle, 1939). French translation: *Les origines des peuples romans* (Paris, 1941)

IX. THE ANGLO-SAXONS

a *General works: origins*

326 ÅBERG, Nils, *The Anglo-Saxons in England* (Uppsala, 1926)

327 BLAIR, Peter Hunter, *An Introduction to Anglo-Saxon England* (Cambridge, 1956)

328 BLAIR, P. H., 'The Origins of Northumbria', *Archaeologia Aeliana*, 4th ser. xxv (1947), 1–51

329 CHADWICK, H. M., *The Origin of the English Nation* (Cambridge, 1907)

330 CHADWICK, Nora K., *Studies in Early British History* (Cambridge, 1954)

330 *bis* CHADWICK, Nora K., *Celt and Saxon: Studies in the Early British Border* (Cambridge, 1963)

331 CHADWICK HAWKES, Sonia, and DUNNING, G. C., 'Soldiers and Settlers in Britain, 4th to 5th Century', *Medieval Archaeology*, v (1961), 1–70

332 CLARKE, R. Rainbird, *East Anglia* (London, 1960)

333 COLLINGWOOD, R. G. 'The Roman Evacuation of Britain', *Journal of Roman Studies* (1922), 74–89

334 COLLINGWOOD, R. G., and MYRES, J. N. L., *Roman Britain and the English Settlements* (Oxford, 1936)

335 COPLEY, Gordon J., *The Conquest of Wessex in the Sixth Century* (London, 1954)

336 CORDER, Philip, 'The Re-organisation of the Defences of Romano-British Towns in the 4th Century', *Archaeological Journal*, lxii (1955), 20–42

337 CRAWFORD, O. G. S., 'Cerdic's Landing-Place', *Antiquity*, xxvi (1952), 193–200

338 DEMOUGEOT, Émilienne, 'Les invasions germaniques et la rupture des relations entre la Bretagne et la Gaule', *Moyen Age*, lxviii (1962), 1–50

339 DRÖGEREIT, Richard, 'Sachsen und Angelsachsen', *Niedersächsisches Jahrbuch für Landesgeschichte*, xxi (1949), 1–62

339 *bis* EVISON, Vera I., *The Fifth-Century Invasions South of the Thames* (London, 1965)

340 HAWKES, C. F. C., 'The Jutes of Kent' in *Dark-Age Britain* [no. 361], 91–111

341 HODGKIN, R. H., *A History of the Anglo-Saxons*, 2 vols. (3rd edn. Oxford, 1953)

342 HOSKINS, W. G., *The Westward Expansion of Wessex* (Leicester, 1960)

343 JACKSON, Kenneth, *Language and History in Early Britain* (Edinburgh, 1953)

344 JANKUHN, Herbert, 'The Continental Home of the English', *Antiquity*, xxvi (1952), 14–24

K

345   JOLIFFE, J. E. A., *Pre-Feudal England, the Jutes* (Oxford, 1933)

345 bis KIRBY, D. P., 'Vortigern', *Bull. of the Board of Celtic Studies*, xxiii (1968), 37–59

346   LETHBRIDGE, T. C., 'The Anglo-Saxon Settlement in Eastern England. A Reassessment', in *Dark-Age Britain* [no. 361], 112–122

347   LOT, Ferdinand, 'Les migrations saxonnes en Gaule et en Grande-Bretagne', *Revue historique*, cxix (1915), 1–40

348   LOT, F., 'De la valeur historique du "De Excidio. . ." de Gildas', in *Mediaeval Studies in memory of G. S. Loomis* (1927), 229–264

349   LOT, F., *Nennius et l'Historia Brittonum* (Paris, 1934)

350   LOT, F., 'Bretons et Anglais aux Ve et VIe siècles', *Proceedings of the British Academy*, xvi (1930), 327–344

351   MYRES, J. N. L., 'The "Adventus Saxonum" ', *Aspects of Archaeology, Presented to O. G. S. Crawford* (London, 1951), 221–241

352   MYRES, J. N. L., 'Pelagius and the End of Roman Rule in Britain', *Journal of Roman Studies*, 1 (1960), 21–36

353   SAYLES, G., *The Medieval Foundations of England* (London, 1948)

354   SISAM, Kenneth, 'Anglo-Saxon Royal Genealogies', *Proceedings of the British Academy*, xxxix (1953), 287–348

355   STENTON, F. M., *Anglo-Saxon England* (3rd edn. Oxford, 1971)

356   STEVENS, C. E., 'Gildas Sapiens', *English Historical Review*, lvi (1941), 353–373

357   SUTHERLAND, E. H. V., 'Coinage in Britain in the 5th and 6th Centuries', in *Dark-Age Britain* [no. 361], 3–10

358   WHITE, Donald A., *Litus Saxonicum. The British Saxon Shore in Scholarship and History* (Madison, 1961)

359   WHITELOCK, Dorothy, *The Beginnings of English Society* (Harmondsworth, 1952)

360   WILSON, D. M., *The Anglo-Saxons* (London, 1960; 2nd edn. Harmondsworth, 1971)

b *Archaeology*

361   *Dark-Age Britain, Studies Presented to E. T. Leeds*, ed. D. B. Harden (London, 1956)

362   BRUCE-MITFORD, R. L. S., *The Sutton Hoo Ship-Burial: A Handbook* (2nd edn. London, 1972)

363   Fox, Cyril, *Offa's Dyke* (Oxford, 1955)

364   Fox, C., and Aileen, 'Wansdyke Reconsidered', *Archaeological Journal*, cxv (1958), 1–48

365   JESSUP, R. F., *Anglo-Saxon Jewellery* (London, 1950)

366   KENDRICK, T. D., *Anglo-Saxon Art to A.D. 900* (London, 1938; repr. 1972)

367   LEEDS, E. T., *The Archaeology of the Anglo-Saxon Settlements* (Oxford, 1913; repr. 1970)

368   LEEDS, E. T., *Early Anglo-Saxon Art and Archaeology* (Oxford, 1936; repr. 1968)

369   LEEDS, E. T., 'The Distribution of the Angles and Saxons Archaeologically Considered', *Archaeologia*, xci (1945), 1–106

370   MYRES, J. N. L., 'Cremation and Inhumation in Anglo-Saxon Cemeteries', *Antiquity*, xvi (1942), 330–341

371   MYRES, J. N. L., 'Some Parallels to the Anglo-Saxon Pottery of Holland and Belgium in the Migration Period', *L'Antiquité classique*, xvii (1948), 453–472

372   MYRES, J. N. L., *Anglo-Saxon Pottery and the Settlement in England* (Oxford, 1969)

373   THOMPSON, J. D. A., *Inventory of British Coin Hoards* (London, 1956)

373 bis WAINWRIGHT, F. T., *Archaeology and Place-Names and History* (London, 1962)

c Toponymy and linguistics

374 EKWALL, Eilert, *The Concise Oxford Dictionary of English Place-Names* (4th edn. Oxford, 1960)

375 FÖRSTER, Max, *Keltisches Wortgut im Englischen* (Halle, 1921)

376 FÖRSTER, Max, *Der Flussname Themse und seine Sippe* (Munich, 1941)

376 bis GELLING, Margaret, 'Place-Names and Anglo-Saxon Paganism', *Univ. of Birmingham Hist. Journal*, viii (1961), 7–25

377 JACKSON, Kenneth, 'The British Language During the Period of the English Settlement', in *Studies in Early British History* [no. 330], 60–82

378 MAWER, Allen, *The Chief Elements Used in English Place-Names* (Cambridge, 1924)

379 MOSSÉ, Fernand, *Esquisse d'une histoire de la langue anglaise* (Lyons, 1947)

380 SMITH, A. H., *English Place-Name Elements*, 2 vols. (London, 1956)

381 SMITH, A. H., 'Place-Names and the Anglo-Saxon Settlement', *Proceedings of the British Academy* (1956), 67–88

382 STENTON, F. M., 'The Historical Bearing of Place-Name Studies. Anglo-Saxon Heathenism', *Trans. Royal Hist. Soc*, 4th ser. xxiii (1941), 1–24. Reprinted in STENTON *Preparatory to Anglo-Saxon England* (Oxford, 1970), 281–297

X. OTHER GERMANIC PEOPLES

Alamans

382 bis DEMOUGEOT, Émilienne, 'Les martyrs imputés à Chrocus et les invasions alémanniques en Gaule méridionale', *Annales du Midi*, lxxiv (1962), 5–28

382 ter LANGENBECK, Fritz, 'Zwei Ortsnamenprobleme aus der frühmittelalterlichen Elsass', *Beiträge zur Namenforschung*, N.F., i (1966), 2–42

383 SCHWARZ, E., 'Die Herkunft der Alamannen', *Vorträge und Forschungen*, hrsg. von Th. Mayer, i (1954), 37–51

383 bis STROHEKER, Karl Friedrich, 'Alamannen im römischen Reichsdienst', *Germanentum und Antike* [no. 114 bis], 30–53

Bavarians

383 ter BOSL, Karl, *Zur Geschichte der Bayern* (Darmstadt, 1965)

383 quater WERNER, Joachim, 'Die Herkunft der Bajuwaren und der "östlich-merowingische" Reihengräberkreis', *Aus Bayerns Frühzeit, Festschrift für F. Wagner* (Munich, 1963), 229–250

Frisians

384 BOELES, P. C. J. A., *Friesland tot de elfde eeuw* (2nd edn. The Hague, 1951)

Gepids

385 CSALLANY, D., *Archäologische Denkmäler der Gepiden im Mitteldonaubecken* (Budapest, 1961)

386 SEVIN, Heinrich, *Die Gepiden* (Munich, 1955)

Saxons on the continent

387   EHMER, Helmut, *Die sächsischen Siedlungen auf dem französischen Litus Saxonicum* (Halle, 1937)

388   LINTZEL, Martin, *Der sächsische Stammestaat und seine Eroberung durch die Franken* (Berlin, 1933)

389   LOISNE, comte de, 'La colonisation saxonne dans le Boulonnais', *Mém. Soc. Nat. Antiquaires de France* (1906), 139–160

390   SALIN, É., 'Les traces d'industrie et de peuplement saxon ou anglo-saxon en Gaule mérovingienne', *Rev. archéol.*, 6e sér., xxxii (1949), 917–925

391   SLICHER VAN BATH, B. H., 'Dutch Tribal Problems', *Speculum*, xxiv (1949), 319–338

See also TISCHLER [no. 157] and LOT [no. 347]

Sueves

392   REYNOLDS, R. L., 'Reconsideration of the History of the Suevi', *Rev. Belge de Philol. et d'Hist.*, xxxv (1957), 19–47

XI. REGIONAL STUDIES OF THE BARBARIAN WEST

a Gaul

393   BERGENGRUEN, Alexander, *Adel und Grundherrschaft im Merowingerreich* (Wiesbaden, 1958)

394   BODMER, J. P., *Der Krieger der Merowingerzeit und seine Welt* (Zurich, 1957)

395   BOYER, Georges, 'Remarques sur la charte de Nizezius', *Études d'hist. du droit privé offertes à P. Petot* (Paris, 1959), 39–48

396   BUCHNER, Rudolf, *Die Provence in merowingischer Zeit* (Stuttgart, 1933)

397   DE LAET, S. J., DHONDT, Jan, and NENQUIN, J., 'Les Laeti du Namurois et l'origine de la civilisation mérovingienne' in *Études d'hist. et d'archéol. namuroises dédiées à F. Courtoy* (Gembloux, 1952), 149–172

398   DHONDT, Jan, 'L'essor urbain entre Meuse et mer du Nord à l'époque mérovingienne', *Studi in onore di A. Sapori* (Milan, 1957), 57–78

399   EWIG, Eugen, *Die fränkischen Teilungen und Teilreiche*, 511–613 (Wiesbaden, 1952)

400   EWIG, E., 'Volkstum and Volksbewusstsein im Frankreich', *Settimane di studio . . .*, v (1957), 587–648

400 bis   FAVEZ, Charles, 'La Gaule et les Gallo-Romains lors des invasions du Ve siècle d'après Salvien', *Latomus*, xvi (1957), 77–83

400 ter   FAIDER-FEYTMANS. G., *La Belgique à l'époque mérovingienne* (Brussels, 1964)

401   FLEURY, Michel, 'Paris du Bas-Empire au début du XIIIe siècle', in *Paris, croissance d'une capitale* (Paris, 1961), 73–96

401 bis   FOURNIER, Gabriel, *Les Mérovingiens* (Paris, 1966). (Collection 'Que sais-je?')

402   GARAUD, Marcel, 'Le peuplement du Poitou et la conquête franque', *Revue des études anciennes*, lii (1950), 90–102

403   GARAUD, M., 'Note sur la cité de Poitiers à l'époque mérovingienne', *Mélanges L. Halphen* (Paris, 1951), 271–279

404   LATOUCHE, Robert, 'De la Gaule romaine à la Gaule franque, aspects sociaux et économiques de l'évolution', *Settimane di studio . . .*, ix (1961), 379–409

405   LUGGE, Margaret, *Gallia und Francia im Mittelalter* (Bonn, 1960)

406   MAILLÉ, marquise de, *Recherches sur les origines chrétiennes de Bordeaux* (Paris, 1959)
407   PROU, Maurice, *La Gaule mérovingienne* (Paris, 1897)
407 *bis* WALLACE-HADRILL, J. M., *The Long-Haired Kings* (London, 1962)

b *The Rhineland and Germany*

408   *Germania romana*: *I. Römerstädte in Deutschland* (*Gymnasium*, Beihefte, 1) (Heidelberg, 1960)
409   BÖHNER, Kurt, *Die fränkischen Altertümer des Trierer Landes*, 2 vols. (Berlin, 1958)
410   BÜTTNER, Heinrich, 'Das Bistum Worms und der Neckarraum während des Früh- und Hochmittelalters', *Archiv für mittelrheinische Kirchengeschichte*, x (1958), 9–38
411   DEMOUGEOT, Émilienne, 'Note sur l'évacuation des troupes romaines en Alsace au début du Ve siècle', *Revue d'Alsace* (1953), 7–16
411 *bis* DEMOUGEOT, É., 'La Gaule nord-orientale à la veille de la grande invasion germanique de 407', *Revue historique*, ccxxxvi (1966), 17–46
412   EWIG, Eugen, *Trier im Merowingerreich, Civitas, Stadt, Bistum* (Trier, 1954; repr. Aalen, 1971)
413   EWIG, Eugen, 'Civitas, Gau und Territorien in den trierischen Moselländern', *Rheinische Vierteljahrsblätter*, xvii (1952), 120–137
414   FRINGS, Th., *Germania Romana* (Halle, 1932)
415   SPRANDEL, Rolf, *Der merowingische Adel und die Gebiete östlich des Rheins* (Freiburg-im-Br., 1957)

c *Switzerland and Raetia*

416   FRANKEN, M., *Die Alamannen zwischen Iller und Lech* (Berlin, 1944)
417   HEUBERGER, R., 'Das ostgotische Rätien', *Klio*, xxx (1937), 77–109
418   MARTIN, Paul-Edmond, *Études critiques sur la Suisse à l'époque mérovingienne (534–715)* (Paris and Geneva, 1910)
419   MEYER-MARTHALER, Elisabeth, *Rätien im frühen Mittelalter* (Zurich, 1948)
420   SCHMIDT, Ludwig, 'Zur Geschichte Rätiens unter der Herrschaft der Ostgoten', *Zeitschrift für schweizerische Geschichte*, xiv (1934), 451–459
421   SCHMIDT, L., 'Zur Geschichte der alamannischen Besiedlung der Schweiz', *Zeitschrift für schweizerische Geschichte*, xviii (1938), 369–379

d *Spain*

422   DAVID, Pierre, *Études historiques sur la Galice et le Portugal du VIe au XIIe siècle* (Lisbon, 1947)
423   GARVIN, Joseph N., *The Vitas Sanctorum Patrum Emeretensium* (Washington, 1946)
424   GIBERT, Rafael, 'El reino visigodo y el particularismo español', *Settimane di studio . . .*, iii (1955), 537–583
425   MESSMER, Hans, *Hispania-Idee und Gotenmythus* (Zurich, 1960)
425 *bis* SCHÄFERDIEK, K., *Die Kirche in den Reichen der Westgoten und Suewen bis zur Errichtung der westgotischen katholischen Staatskirche* (Berlin, 1967)

e *North Africa*

426   CARCOPINO, Jérôme, 'Un empereur maure inconnu d'après une inscription latine découverte dans l'Aurès', *Revue des études anciennes*, xlvi (1944), 94–120

427   COURTOIS, Christian, *Victor de Vita et son oeuvre* (Algiers, 1954)

428   DEMOUGEOT, Émilienne, 'Le chameau et l'Afrique du Nord romaine', *Annales (Économies, Sociétés, Civilisations)*, xv (1960), 209–247

429   DIESNER, H. J., 'Die Lage der nordafrikanischen Bevölkerung im Zeitpunkt der Vandaleninvasion', *Historia*, xi (1962), 97–111

429 *bis* DIESNER, H. J., *Der Untergang der römischen Herrschaft in Nordafrika* (Weimar, 1964)

430   FREND, W. H. C., *The Donatist Church* (Oxford, 1952; repr. 1971)

431   GAUTIER, E. F., *Le passé de l'Afrique du Nord. Les siècles obscurs* (Paris, 1937; repr. 1964)

432   HEURGON, J., *Le trésor de Ténès* (Paris, 1958)

433   LAPEYRE, G. G., *Saint Fulgence de Ruspe. Un évêque africain sous la domination vandale* (Paris, 1929)

434   LEZINE, A., PICARD, Mme C., PICARD, G.-Ch., 'Observations sur la ruine des thermes d'Antonin à Carthage', *Comptes Rendus de l'Acad. des Inscription et Belles-Lettres* (1956), 425–430

435   ROMANELLI, Pietro, *Storia delle provincie romane dell'Africa* (Rome, 1959)

436   SALAMA, A., 'Deux trésors monétaires du Ve siècle trouvés en Petite-Kabalie', *Bull. Soc. Nat. Antiquaires de France* (1958), 238–240

436 *bis* TENGSTRÖM, E., *Donatisten und Katholiken ; Soziale, wirtschaftliche und politische Aspekte einer nordafrikanischen Kirchenspaltung* (Göteborg, 1964)

437   ZEILLER, Jacques, 'L'arianisme en Afrique avant l'invasion vandale', *Revue historique*, clxxiii (1934), 535–541

f Italy

438   BERTOLINI, O., *Roma di fronte a Bisanzio e ai Longobardi* (*Storia di Roma*, IX) (Rome, 1941)

438 *a* BOGNETTI, GianPiero, *L'età longobarda*, 4 vols. (Milan, 1966–68)

438 *bis* BONFANTE, Giuliano, *Latini e Germani in Italia* (Brescia, 1959; 3rd edn. 1965)

438 *ter* CHASTAGNOL, André, *Le Sénat romain sous le règne d'Odoacre* (Bonn, 1966)

439   HARTMANN, Ludo-Moritz, *Geschichte Italiens im Mittelalter*, I. (2nd edn. Gotha, 1923)

440   HODGKIN, Thomas, *Italy and Her Invaders*, 8 vols. (Oxford, 1880–99)

441   PARIBENI, R., *Da Diocleziano alla caduta del Impero d'Occidente* (*Storia di Roma*, VIII). (Rome, 1941)

442   PEPE, Gabriele, *Il medio evo barbarico d'Italia* (3rd edn. Turin, 1945). French translation, *Le Moyen Age barbare en Italie* (Paris, 1956)

442 *bis* RUGGINI, Lellia, *Economia e società nell' 'Italia annonaria'. Rapporti fra agricoltura e commercio dal IV al VI secolo d. C.* (Milan, 1961)

XII.   PROBLEMS OF CONTINUITY: FROM THE ROMAN EMPIRE TO THE MIDDLE AGES

a General works

443   *Il passaggio dall' Antichità al Medioevo in Occidente, Settimane di studio . . .*, ix (1961)

444   AUBIN, Hermann, *Vom Altertum zum Mittelalter* (Munich, 1949)

444   EWIG, Eugen, 'Résidence et capitale pendant le haut Moyen Age', *Revue historique*, ccxxx (1963), 25–72

b Gaul and the Germanies

446 Böhner, Kurt, 'Die Frage der Kontinuität zwischen Altertum und Mittelalter im Spiegel der fränkischen Funde des Rheinlandes', *Trierer Zeitschrift*, xix (1950), 82–106

447 Garaud, Marcel, 'Le droit romain dans les chartes poitevines du IXe au XIe siècle', in *Mélanges G. Cornil* (Ghent, 1926), 399–424

448 Gaudemet, Jean, 'Survivances romaines dans le droit de la monarchie franque du Ve au Xe siècle', *Tijdschrift voor Rechtsgeschiedenis*, xxiii (1955), 149–206

449 Kurth, Godefroid, 'Les sénateurs en Gaule au VIe siècle', in *Études franques* [no. 261], 97–115

450 Lemarignier, Jean-François, 'Les actes de droit privé de l'abbaye de Saint-Bertin au haut Moyen Age. Survivances et déclin du droit romain dans la pratique franque', *Rev. intern. des droits de l'Antiquité*, v (1950), 35–72

451 Lot, Ferdinand, 'La nomination du comte à l'époque mérovingienne et la novelle 419 de Justinien', *Revue historique de Droit*, 4th ser., iii (1924), 272–286

452 Lot, F., 'Du régime de l'hospitalité', *Rev. Belge de Philol. et d'Hist.*, vii (1928), 975–1011

453 Potrokovits, Harald von, 'Das Fortleben römischer Städte an Rhein und Donau', *Trierer Zeitschrift*, xix (1950), 73–81

454 Rey, Raymond, 'La tradition gallo-romaine dans la civilisation méridionale jusqu'à l'invasion sarrasine', *Pallas*, ii (1954), 155–165

455 Richard, Jean, 'Tribunal et notariat aux temps mérovingiens', *Annales de Bourgogne*, xxxiv (1962), 101–105

456 Stroheker, K. F., *Der senatorische Adel im spätantiken Gallien* (Tübingen, 1948)

457 Tardif, Joseph, 'Les chartes mérovingiennes de Noirmoutier', *Revue historique de droit*, xxii (1898), 763–790

c Switzerland, Raetia, Alamannia

458 Fellmann, Rudolf, 'Neue Forschungen zur Schweiz in spätrömischer Zeit,' *Historia*, iv (1955), 209–219

459 Laur-Belart, R., 'The Late *Limes* from Basel to the Lake of Constance', *Third Congress of Roman Frontier Studies*, ed. E. Birley (Durham, 1952), 55–67

460 Martin, P. E., 'La fin de la domination romaine en Suisse', *Bull. soc. hist. et archéol. de Genève*, xvi (1935), 3–30

460 bis Vetters, Hermann, 'Die Kontinuität von der Antike zum Mittelalter in Ostalpenraum', in *Die Alpen in der europäischen Geschichte des Mittelalters* (Constance and Stuttgart, 1965), 29–48

d Noricum, Pannonia, Dacia

461 Alföldi, Andreas, *Der Untergang der Römerherrschaft in Pannonien*, 2 vols. (Berlin and Leipzig, 1924–26)

462 Iorga, N., *Histoire des Roumains et de la Romanité orientale*, II. (Bucharest, 1937)

463 Janda, Anna, *Die Barschalken. Ein Beitrag zur Sozialgeschichte des Mittelalters* (Vienna, 1926)

464 Kaphahn, Fritz, *Zwischen Antike und Mittelalter. Das Donau-Alpenland im Zeitalter St. Severins* (Munich, 1947)

465 Koller, H., 'Der Donauraum zwischen Linz und Wien im Mittelalter', *Hist. Jahrbuch der Stadt Linz* (1960), 11–53

465 bis Lotter, Friedrich, 'Severinus und die Endzeit römischer Herrschaft an der oberen Donau', *Deutsches Archiv*, xxiv (1968), 309–338

466   Lozovan, Eugen, 'Byzance et la romanité scythique; Romains et Barbares sur le moyen Danube', in F. Altheim, *Geschichte der Hunnen* [no. 509], II, 197–244

467   Schwarz, E., 'Die bairische Landnahme um Regensburg im Spiegel dem Völker- und Ortsnamen', *Beiträge zur Namenforschung*, i (1949), 51–71

468   Zibermayr, Ignaz, *Noricum, Baiern und Österreich. Lorch als Hauptstadt und die Einführung des Christentums* (Horn, 1956)

e Spain

468 *bis* Balil, Alberto, 'Aspectos sociales del Bajo Impero (s. IV–VI). Los senadores hispánicos', *Latomus*, xxiv (1965), 886–904

468 *ter* Fontaine, Jacques, 'Die westgotische lateinische Literatur. Probleme und Perspektiven', *Antike und Abendland*, xii (1966), 63–87

469   Lacarra, José Maria, *Il tramonto della Romanità in Hispania* (Madrid and Rome, 1961)

470   Sánchez-Albornoz, Claudio, *Ruina y extinción del municipio romano* (Buenos Aires, 1943)

471   Sánchez-Albornoz, C., 'El tributum quadrigesimale. Supervivencias fiscales romanas en Galicia', in *Mélanges L. Halphen* (Paris, 1951), 645–658. Reprinted in [no. 472 *bis*], 353–368

472   Sánchez-Albornoz, C., 'Pervivencia y crisis de la tradición jurídica romana en la España goda', *Settimane di studio . . .*, ix (1961), 128–199

472 *bis* Sánchez-Albornoz, C., *Estudios sobre las instituciones medievales españolas* (Mexico City, 1965)

472 *ter* Stroheker, K. F., 'Spanische Senatoren der spätrömischen und westgotischen Zeit', in *Germanentum und Spätantike* [no. 114 *bis*], 54–87

f North Africa

473   Carcopino, Jérôme, 'La fin du Maroc romain', *Mélanges d'archéol. et d'hist. publiés par l'école franç. de Rome*, lvii (1940), 349–448

474   Courtois, C., 'Grégoire VII et l'Afrique du Nord. Remarques sur les communautés chrétiennes d'Afrique au XIe siècle', *Revue historique*, cxlv (1945), 97–122 and 193–226

475   Gagé, Jean, 'Nouveaux aspects de l'Afrique chrétienne', *Annales de l'école des hautes-études de Gand*, 1 (1937), 181–230

476   Ménage, J., *Le christianisme en Afrique. Déclin et extinction* (Paris and Algiers, 1915)

477   Piganiol, André, 'En marge des tablettes Albertini', in *Hommage à L. Febvre*, II (Paris, 1953), 67–70

478   Rössler, Otto, 'Die lateinische Reliktwörter im Berberischen', *Beiträge zur Namenforschung*, xiii (1962), 258–262

479   Seston, William, 'Sur les derniers temps du christianisme en Afrique', *Mélanges d'archéol. et d'hist. publiés par l'école franç. de Rome*, liii (1936), 101–124

g Italy

480   Bognetti, Gian Pietro, 'La continuità delle sedi episcopali e l'azione di Roma nel regno longobardo', *Settimane di studio . . .*, vii (1959), 415–454. Reprinted in [no. 438a], IV, 301–338

481   Bognetti, G. P., 'L'influsso delle istituzioni militari romane sulle istituzioni longobarde del sec. VI e la natura della "fara" ', *Atti del Congresso intern. di diritto romano, Verona 1948*, IV (Milan, 1953), 167–210. Reprinted in [no. 438a], III, 1–46

482 CECCHELLI, Carlo, 'Continuità storica di Roma antica nell'alto medioevo', *Settimane di studio . . .*, vi (1959), 89–149

483 LEICHT, P. S., 'Gli elementi romani nella costituzione longobarda', in *Scritti vari di storia del diritto italiano*, I (Milan, 1943)

483 *bis* LEICHT, P. S., 'Territori longobardi e territori romani', *Atti del I° Congresso di studi longobardi* (Spoleto, 1951), 177–202

484 VACCARI, Pietro, *Ricerche di storia giuridica: I. Il colonato romano e l'invasione longobarda* (Pavia, 1907)

h Britain

484 *a* BARLEY, M. W., and HANSON, R. P. C., (eds.), *Christianity in Britain, 300–700* (Leicester, 1968)

484 *b* RALEGH RADFORD, C. A., 'The Early Church in Strathclyde and Galloway', *Medieval Archaeology*, xi (1967), 105–126

XIII. THE MIGRATIONS OF THE CELTIC PEOPLES

a General works: Great Britain

See particularly JACKSON [no. 343] and [no. 377]

484 *c* CHADWICK, Nora K., *The Celts* (Harmondsworth, 1970)

484 *bis* DILLON, Myles, and CHADWICK, Nora K., *The Celtic Realms* (London, 1967)

485 MARCUS, G. J., 'Factors in Early Celtic Navigation', *Études celtiques*, vi (1953–54), 312–327

486 RALEGH RADFORD, C. A., 'Imported Pottery Found at Tintagel, Cornwall', in *Dark-Age Britain* [no. 361], 59–70

487 RIDGEWAY, Sir W., 'Niall "of the Nine Hostages"', *Journal of Roman Studies*, xiv (1924), 123–136

488 STEVENS, C. E., 'L'Irlande et la Bretagne romaine', *Revue des Études anciennes*, xlii (1940), 671–681

489 VENDRYES, Joseph, 'Pharamond, roi de France, dans la tradition irlandaise', *Mélanges Ferd. Lot* (Paris, 1925), 743–767

490 WAINWRIGHT, F. T., *The Problem of the Picts* (Edinburgh, 1955)

b Armorica

490 *bis* CHADWICK, Nora K., 'The Colonization of Brittany from Celtic Britain', *Proceedings of the British Academy*, li (1965), 235–299

491 COUFFON, René, *Limites des cités gallo-romaines et fondation des évêchés dans la péninsule armoricaine* (Saint-Brieuc, 1943)

492 FALCH'UN, François, 'Le breton, forme moderne du gaulois', *Annales de Bretagne*, lxii (1955), 202–213

493 FALCH'UN, F., *Histoire de la langue bretonne d'après la géographie linguistique*, I (Paris, 1963)

494 FLEURIOT, J. L., 'Recherches sur les enclaves romanes anciennes en territoire bretonnant', *Études celtiques*, viii (1958), 164–178

494 *bis* FLEURIOT, J. L., *Dictionnaire des gloses en vieux-breton* (Paris, 1964)

495 GIOT, P. R., 'Un type de céramique antique inédit de Cornouaille et d'ailleurs', *Annales de Bretagne*, lxii (1955), 164–178

496　LARGILLIÈRE, René, *Les saints et l'organisation chrétienne primitive dans l'Armorique bretonne* (Rennes, 1925)

497　LOTH, Joseph, *L'émigration bretonne en Armorique* (Rennes, 1883)

498　LOTH, J., 'Les langues romane et bretonne en Armorique', *Revue celtique*, xxxvii (1907), 374–403

499　REINACH, Salomon, 'Les Francs et la Bretagne armoricaine', *Revue archéologique* (1928), i, 246–253

c Spain

499 *bis* THOMPSON, E. A., 'Britonia', *Christianity in Britain* [no. 484a], 201–205

500　DAVID, Pierre, 'Étude sur les églises celtiques de Galice', in *Études historiques sur la Galice* [no. 422], 57–63

XIV. THE PEOPLES OF THE STEPPES

a General works

500 *bis* BACHRACH, Bernard S., 'The Alans in Gaul', *Traditio*, xxiii (1967), 476–489

501　DARKÓ, Eugène, 'Le rôle des peuples nomades cavaliers dans la transformation de l'Empire romain', *Byzantion*, xviii (1946–48), 85–97

502　GROUSSET, René, *L'Empire des steppes* (Paris, 1939; repr. 1969)

503　MORAVCSIK, Gyula, *Byzantinoturcica*, 2 vols. (2nd edn. Budapest, 1958)

504　SINOR, Denis, 'Les Barbares', *Diogène*, xviii (1957), 52–68

505　VERNADSKY, George, 'Der sarmatische Hintergrund der germanischen Völkerwanderung', *Saeculum*, ii (1951), 340–392

506　VERNADSKY, G., 'The Eurasian Nomads and Their Impact on Medieval Europe', *Studi medievali*, iv (1963), 401–434

b The Huns

507　ALFÖLDI, Andreas, 'Attila', in *Menschen die Geschichte machten*, I (Vienna, 1930), 229–234

508　ALTHEIM, Franz, *Attila und die Hunnen* (Baden-Baden, 1951). French translation, *Attila et les Huns* (Paris, 1952)

509　ALTHEIM, F., *Geschichte der Hunnen*, 4 vols. (Berlin, 1959–62)

510　ALTHEIM, F., and HAUSSIG, H. W., *Die Hunnen in Osteuropa, Ein Forschungsbericht* (Baden-Baden, 1958)

511　BOOR, H. de, *Das Attila-Bild in Geschichte, Legende und heroischer Dichtung* (Berne, 1932; repr. Darmstadt, 1963)

512　BROWNING, R., 'Where Was Attila's Camp?', *Journal of Hellenic Studies*, lxxiii (1953), 143–145

513　DEMOUGEOT, Émilienne, 'Attila et les Huns', *Mém. de la Soc. d'agric. de la Marne*, lxxiii (1958), 7–42

514　GORDON, C. D., *The Age of Attila. Fifth-Century Byzantium and the Barbarians* (Ann Arbor, 1960; 2nd edn. 1966)

515　HAMBIS, L., 'Le problème des Huns', *Revue historique*, ccxx (1958), 249–270

516　HARMATTA, J., 'Hun Society in the Age of Attila', *Acta Archaeologica* (Budapest) (1952), 277–305

517　HOMEYER, H., *Attila. Der Hunnenkönig von seinen Zeitgenossen dargestellt* (Berlin, 1951)

518　MAENCHEN-HELFEN, O., 'Huns and Hsiung-Nu', *Byzantion*, xvii (1944–45), 222–243

519 Moór, Elemer, 'Zur Herkunft der Hunnen', *Beiträge zur Namenforschung*, xiv (1963), 63–104

519 bis Parducz, M., *Die ethnischen Probleme der Hunnenzeit in Ungarn* (Budapest, 1963) (*Studia Archaeologica*, I)

520 Thompson, E. A., *A History of Attila and the Huns* (Oxford, 1948)

521 Werner, Joachim, *Beiträge zur Archäologie des Attila-Reiches* (Munich, 1956)

c *The Avars*

522 Barišić, F., 'Le siège de Constantinople par les Avares et les Slaves en 626', *Byzantion*, xxiv (1954), 371–395

522 bis Erdélyi, István, *L'art des Avars* (Budapest, 1966)

523 Haussig, H. W., 'Die Quellen über die zentralasiatische Herkunft der europäischen Awaren', *Central Asiatic Journal*, ii (1956), 21–43

524 Kollautz, Arnulf, *Quellenbuch zur Geschichte der Awaren* (Prague, 1944)

525 Kollautz, A., 'Die Awaren', *Saeculum*, v (1954), 129–178

526 Labuda, G., 'Chronologie des guerres de Byzance contre les Avars et les Slaves à la fin du VIc siècle', *Byzantinoslavica*, xi (1950), 166–173

527 Lipták, P., 'Avaren und Magyaren im Donau-Theiss Zwischenstromgebiet', *Acta Archaeologica Hungarica*, viii (1957), 199–268

528 Reinecke, P., 'Die archäologische Hinterlassenschaft des Awaren', *Germania*, xii (1928), 87–98

Additional Bibliography for English Readers

Most of the works cited in the preceding pages are in French and German; even those who read these languages will not find many of them easy to obtain. For this reason a list is here added of those books which are in English and are readily available, which any who wish to read more about the subject may find useful.

Still the best narrative account of the period covered by this book is J. B. Bury, *The Later Roman Empire*, 2 vols. (London, 1923; repr. New York, 1958). A social and economic analysis of the same period is given by A. H. M. Jones, *The Later Roman Empire* [66 *bis*]: see the review of this important book by Peter Brown, in his *Religion and Society in the Age of Augustine* (London, 1972), 46–73. A great deal of very good work on the Later Roman Empire has been done in recent years by English and American scholars: the bibliography of P. Brown, *The World of Late Antiquity* [60 *bis*] is a helpful guide to this recent research. Two works are particularly relevant: W. E. Kaegi, Jr., *Byzantium and the Decline of Rome* (Princeton, 1968) and Lynn White, Jr. (ed.), *The Transformation of the Roman World: Gibbon's Problem after Two Centuries* (Berkeley and Los Angeles, 1966).

J. M. Wallace-Hadrill, *The Barbarian West, 400–1000 A.D.* (London, 3rd edn. 1967) is probably the best introduction to the history of western Europe after the fall of the Western Empire: the third edition has an additional chapter on Visigothic Spain. The forthcoming book by D. A. Bullough, *Europe from the Fifth Century to the Tenth Century* (Longman), will be valuable. There is also the superbly illustrated volume edited by David Talbot Rice, *The Dark Ages* (London, 1965), which contains a number of regional studies by distinguished scholars; the most useful are the chapters on Germanic Italy by Donald Bullough and on Spain by William Culican. The chapters by Lasko and Thomas have been reprinted as books, in expanded versions (see below). It is regrettable that the only Germanic people of the migration period to have been given a volume in the 'Ancient Peoples and Places' series published by Thames and Hudson are the Anglo-Saxons (by D. M. Wilson [no. 360]), though volumes are promised from Donald Bullough on the Lombards and from E. A. Thompson and J. Werner on the Huns. Malcolm Todd, *Everyday Life of the Barbarians: Goths, Franks and Vandals* (London and New York, 1972) has excellent sections on the results of recent archaeological research on early Germanic villages and dwellings in Germany, as well as on other aspects of life among the Germanic peoples.

There are few books in English on the various regions of Europe at this period. The early chapters of Peter Llewellyn, *Rome in the Dark Ages* (London, 1971) are of more general interest than the title might suggest for an understanding of Ostrogothic and Lombard Italy. E. A. Thompson, *The Goths in Spain* [no. 199 *ter*] deals solely with the Gothic contribution to early medieval Spain: Harold Livermore, *The Origins of Spain and Portugal* (London, 1971) takes a broader approach, but is neither so scholarly nor so reliable. For Gaul, C. E. Stevens, *Sidonius Apollinaris and His Age* [no. 101] and Nora K. Chadwick, *Poetry and Letters in Early Christian Gaul* [no. 84 *bis*] are interesting introductions to the fifth century, and Sir Samuel Dill, *Roman Society in Gaul in the Merovingian Age* (London, 1926; repr. 1966) still provides a very readable guide to the sixth. The scholarly and stimulating essays on Frankish

Gaul by J. M. WALLACE-HADRILL have been collected together as *The Long-Haired Kings* [no. 407 *bis*]. Robert LATOUCHE, *From Caesar to Charlemagne* (London, 1968; paperback, 1973) is a narrative history of Roman and Frankish Gaul; Peter LASKO, *The Kingdom of the Franks: North-West Europe before Charlemagne* (London, 1971) is useful only for his accounts of Frankish art.

A great deal of work has naturally been done by English historians and archaeologists on the joint problems of the Anglo-Saxon invasions and the Celtic migrations, and Musset's bibliography, sections IX and XIII, mentions many items. Probably the best two introductions to the first of these two problems are H. R. LOYN, *Anglo-Saxon England and the Norman Conquest* (London, 1962; repr. as paperback, 1970) and D. M. WILSON, *The Anglo-Saxons* [no. 360]. The greatest advances in our understanding are being made by archaeologists, as a glance at any volume of the journal *Medieval Archaeology* will show. For the British aspect see two books by Charles THOMAS: *Britain and Ireland in Early Christian Times, AD 400–800* (London, 1971) and *The Early Christian Archaeology of North Britain* (Oxford, 1971). Much of value can be found in the three volumes edited by N. K. CHADWICK, *Studies in Early British History* (Cambridge, 1954), *Studies in the Early British Church* (Cambridge, 1958) and *Celt and Saxon: Studies in the Early British Border* (Cambridge, 1963). On the Picts see, in addition to WAINWRIGHT [no. 490], HENDERSON, *The Picts* (London, 1967), 'Ancient Peoples and Places' series. For the Atlantic seaboard there is E. G. BOWEN, *Saints, Seaways and Settlements in the Celtic Lands* (Cardiff, 1969) and *The Irish Sea Province in Archaeology and History*, ed. D. Moore (Cardiff, 1970), especially pp. 55–77.

For an introduction to Germanic art and archaeology see Rolf HACHMANN. *The Ancient Civilization of the Germanic Peoples* (London, 1971). The best book on the art of the migration period is HUBERT, PORCHER and VOLBACH, *Europe in the Dark Ages* [no. 154 *bis*], if only for the many very high-quality illustrations, the good bibliography and the sets of architectural plans and maps. George HENDERSON, *Early Medieval* (Harmondsworth, 1972) is a highly original stylistic survey, which treats the whole period from the barbarian invasions to Romanesque as a unity.

EDWARD JAMES

Department of Medieval History
University College, Dublin
May 1973

References

1: The Whirlwind of Invasions

1. This problem is still the subject of violent discussion. A reasonable idea of the dispute can be got from De Vries, *Kelten und Germanen* [no. 117], 55 ff.
2. On this aspect see the excellent little book by Emile Janssens, *Histoire ancienne de la mer du Nord* (2nd edn. Brussels, 1946).
3. *Goten, Nordgermanen, Angelsachsen* [no. 129].
4. Cf. the maps of H. J. Eggers, *Der römische Import im freien Germanien* (Hamburg, 1951), and the convenient summary of the problem by Wheeler, *Rome beyond the Imperial Frontiers* [no. 81].
5. Cf. Musset and Mossé, *Introduction à la runologie* [no. 148].
6. We are using the dates of H. Koethe, 'Zur Geschichte Galliens im 3. Viertel des 3. Jahrhunderts', *32. Bericht des römisch-germanischen Kommission*, 1942 (1950), 199–224.
7. Cf. Jean Gricourt, 'Les événements de 282–292 en Gaule d'après les trésors monétaires', *Revue des études anciennes*, lvi (1954), 366–376.
8. Strabo, VII, 1, 2.
9. This picture, which will be treated in greater detail in a following volume, deliberately avoids certain discussions: the existence of private property or common ownership of land (*Markgenossenschaft*); the origin of the hundred among the various peoples (it seems to be different among the Goths, Franks and Scandinavians); Celtic influences on the origins of the *comitatus*; the respective roles of Roman and Germanic factors in the formation of private armies in the Later Roman Empire, etc.
10. Ammianus Marcellinus, XXXI, 2, 1.
11. Darko, *Rôle* [no. 501].
12. Cf. Sinor, *Barbares* [no. 504] and E. F. Balazs, 'Les invasions barbares', in *Aspects de la Chine* (Paris, 1959), I, 72–76.
13. See Roger Rémondon, *La crise de l'Empire romain de Marc-Aurèle à Anastase* (Nouvelle Clio, no. 11), (Paris, 1964; 2nd edn. 1971).
14. This is a résumé in broad lines of the fairly revolutionary views of D. Van Berchem, *L'armée de Dioclétien et la réforme constantinenne* (Paris, 1952), which has a large following and spares us the necessity of going through the voluminous literature which preceded its appearance.
15. Carcopino ('Un empereur maure' [no. 426]) is wrong to imagine that it has repercussions even as far away as the heart of Roman Africa.

2: The Land Invasions: The First Wave

1. Sirago, *Galla Placidia* [no. 76], 359 and n. 4.
2. Some historians have cast doubt on the matter: Courtois, *Les Vandales* [no. 233], 40–41.
3. Jordanes, *Getica*, IV, 25 and XVII, 94. Cf. Wagner, *Getica* [no. 173 *bis*].
4. See above all Oxenstierna, *Urheimat* [no. 166].
5. Radu Vulpe, *Le vallum de la Moldavie inférieure et le mur d'Athanaric* (The Hague, 1957).

6. The documentary sources have been gathered together and commented on by Courcelle, in *Histoire littéraire* [no. 106], 35–55. Cf. also André Piganiol, *Le sac de Rome* (Paris, 1964).

7. Translators' note : see, in English, E. A. Thompson,' The Settlement of the Barbarians' [no. 198] and Wallace-Hadrill, 'Gothia and Romania' [no. 199 *ter*].

8. This is one of the most interesting ideas of R. de Abadal in *Del reino de Tolosa al reino de Toledo* [no. 182], 61 ff.

9. Cassiodorus, *Variae* [no. 30], III, 43 (ed. Mommsen, p. 100).

10. E. Stein, *Histoire du Bas-Empire* [no. 77], vol. II, 40, n. 1.

11. Fiebiger-Schmidt, *Inschriftensammlung* [no. 3], no. 193.

12. Cassiodorus, *Variae*, XI, XX and XXXI.

13. Jordanes, *Getica* [no. 32], c. 308.

14. Stein, *Histoire du Bas-Empire* [no. 77], vol. II, 127–128.

15. Cf. John L. Teall, 'The Barbarians in Justinian's Army', *Speculum*, xl (1965), 294–322.

16. On the last Ostrogoths see the classic work of Schmidt, 'Die letzten Ostgoten' [no. 212], which is complemented by the papyrological documents, well summarized by Fulvio Crosara in 'Dal V al VIII secolo, sulla tracia dei papiri giuridici d'Italia', *Annali di Storia del Diritto*, iii–iv (1959–60), 349–390, esp. 372–381.

17. The date has been variously interpreted as 406 or 405. We have followed the conclusions of Courtois, *Les Vandales* [no. 233], 38 n. 3.

18. See the text of St. Ambrose, *Expositio in Lucam*, x, 10 and the commentary by Courtois [no. 233], 40.

19. This is the hypothesis of Le Gall, 'L'itinéraire de Genséric' [no. 239], taken up by Courtois, *Les Vandales* [no. 233].

20. Courtois disputes the validity of this assertion by Victor Vitensis, and archaeology supports Courtois. (On the baths at Carthage see [no. 434].)

21. cf. *Vie de Fulgence de Ruspe*, ed. Lapeyre, 11 [no. 35].

22. cf. J.-M. Lacarra, 'Panorama de la historia urbana en la península ibérica desde el siglo V al X', *Settimane di studio* . . ., vi (1958), 920.

23. cf. *Martini episcopi Bracarensis opera omnia*, ed. Barlow (New Haven, 1950).

24. Except for Coville (*Recherches sur l'histoire de Lyon* [no. 224]), who uses 'Burgundions', French historiography prefers the form 'Burgondes', even though it is not well attested; it is used only four or five times in primary sources, and the people were usually called *Burgundiones*. cf. the other doublets, Goti/Gutones and Frisii/Frisones. (On the Burgundians, avoid René Guichard's *Essai sur l'histoire de peuple Burgonde, de Bornholm vers Bourgogne et les Bourguignons* (Paris, 1965), which is untrustworthy.)

25. *Passio s. Sigismundi, MGH, SS. Rer. Merov.*, II, 333. The writer of this text was probably influenced by Jordanes.

26. Ammianus Marcellinus, XVIII, 2, 15. (Loeb English translation Vol. I, 415.)

27. For a résumé of this debate see Altheim, *Geschichte der Hunnen* [no. 509], IV, 193 ff. and the reservations of P. Wackwitz, *Gab es ein Burgunderreich in Worms?* (Worms, 1964).

28. Orosius, *Hist. adv. pag.* [no. 17], VII, xxxii, 13.

29. Coville, *Recherches* [no. 224], 139–152.

30. *Hist. Franc.*, II, xxiv. Gregory was descended from a bishop of Langres who had been a former subject of Gundobad.

31. Marc Sauter, 'Quelques contributions de l'anthropologie à la connaissance du haut Moyen Age', *Mélanges P. E. Martin* (Geneva, 1961), 1–18; and, with P. Moeschler, 'Caractères dentaires' [no. 231].

32. Gregory of Tours gives a good example from the time of Gundobad in the *Liber de virtutibus s. Juliani, MGH, SS. rer. Merov.*, i, 2, 567–568.

3: The Land Invasions: The Second and Third Waves

1. This hypothesis, which was vigorously defended by Werner in 'Zur Entstehung' [no. 311], has been no less warmly attacked by De Laet and Dhondt in 'Les Laeti' [no. 397]. The question remains open. It seems impossible to follow Werner without some reservations: the cemeteries show a clear break about 400, which does not encourage the idea of a direct transmission of civilization. But that this colonization did contribute to the 'barbarization' of Gaul cannot be denied.
2. This is hotly disputed. Cf. Stengers, *La formation de la frontière linguistique* [no. 283].
3. The most intelligent study of these events is still that of Bloch, 'La conquête de la Gaule' [no. 255].
4. The latest study of his reign is that of G. Tessier, *Le baptême de Clovis* [no. 267 *bis*].
5. For the diplomatic preparations see the sound study of Levillain, 'La crise des années 507–508' [no. 262].
6. On the subject of Parthenius, as a general study has not yet appeared, see in the meantime the accounts of A. Nagl, Parthenius no. 21, in Pauly-Wissowa, *Realenzyklopädie*; Stroheker, *Der senatorische Adel* [no. 456], 199; and F. Beyerle, 'Die beiden deutschen Stammersrechte', *Zeitschrift der Savigny-Stiftung für Rechtgeschichte, Germ. Abt.*, lxxiii (1956), 126–128.
7. *MGH, Epp. Merov et Karol. Aevi*, III, 133.
8. Isolated groups of Alamans must have settled in various parts of Burgundy: cf. P. Lebel, 'Noms de lieux dus aux Alamans en Côte-d'Or et en Haute Marne', *XXVIIIe Congrès de l'Assoc. bourguignonne des Soc. sav.*, (1957), 128–130.
9. Concerning the later episodes, see Musset, *Le second assaut contre l'Europe* (Paris, 1965) (Nouvelle Clio, no. 12 *bis*).
10. In the *Origo gentis Langobardorum* of the middle of the seventh century and especially in the *Historia Langobardorum* by Paul Warnefrid, or Paul the Deacon, written at the end of the eighth century; not much attention should be paid to the more prolix Gotha manuscript of the *Historia Langobardorum*, from the beginning of the ninth century.
11. Paul the Deacon, *Hist. Langob.* [no. 33], II, 26.
12. Ewig, 'Résidence et capitale' [no. 445], 36.
13. This interregnum has been variously interpreted. It is generally believed that it saw a return to the Germanic traditions of individualism, reacting against a centralized monarchy. In 'L'influsso' [no. 481] Bognetti wonders if one should not rather consider the opportune intervention of Byzantine gold.
14. Paul the Deacon, *Hist. Langob.*, IV, 24.
15. *ibid.*, IV, 28.
16. *ibid.*, IV, 44.
17. *ibid.*, II, 32. F. Lot, 'Hospitalité' [no. 452], 1005, believes that he was confusing this with the system of *hospitalitas*, whereby the Roman handed over a third of his property to his barbarian guest for his use.
18. Bognetti, 'Longobardi e Romani' [no. 247].

4: The Maritime Migrations

1. We do not accept the revolutionary thesis of Miss V. I. Evison, *The Fifth Century Invasions* [no. 339 *bis*], which states that the area south of the Thames was overrun by a massive army under Frankish direction.
2. On the uneven regional distribution of the villae see J. Alcock, 'Settlement Patterns in Britain', *Antiquity*, xxxvi (1962), 51–54.

3. But Mrs. Chadwick, 'The Colonization' [no. 490 *bis*] thinks that the migration must have begun in the fourth century, perhaps even as early as the end of the third century, due to pressure from the Scots; there is, however, no proof.

4. It is only very hypothetically that Giot, 'Un type de céramique' [no. 495], assigns to the Bretons a type of purplish pottery found along the south-west coast, from Quiberon to Cap Sizun.

5: The Collision of Civilizations

1. The best overall picture is that presented by M. Gysseling, in 'La genèse de la frontière linguistique' [no. 277].

2. The existence of the Eifel enclave is borne out by the Romance vocabulary of a boundary agreement of 721 (ed. W. Levison, *Neues Archiv*, xliii (1922), 383–385).

3. A very good study of the Trier enclave has been made by E. Ewig [no. 412] and especially by Jungandreas, 'Ein romanischer Dialekt' [no. 279].

4. K. Böhner, 'Zur historischen Interpretation des sog. Laetengräber', *Jahrbuch des Römisch-Germanischen Zentralmuseums, Mainz*, x (1963), 139 ff.

5. See A. Dasnoy, 'Quelques ensembles archéologiques du Bas-Empire provenant de la région namuroise', *Annales Soc. archéol. de Namur*, liii (1966), 169–231, on some settlements which were probably military in nature.

6. See W. von Wartburg, *Die Ausgliederung der romanischen Sprachräume* (Berne, 1950). French translation, *La fragmentation linguistique de la Romanité* (Paris, 1967).

7. The estimate of S. Mazzarino for the beginning of the fifth century.

8. A. Coville, 'Les Syagrii', in *Recherches sur l'histoire de Lyon* [no. 224], 3–29, which is complemented by C. Cipolla, *Monumenta Novaliciensia vetustiora*, I, 13 ff. (revised text).

9. Cf. Böhner, *Die fränkischen Altertümer* [no. 409] and Ewig, *Trier im Merowingerreich* [no. 412].

10. Edited by Gose, *Katalog...* [no. 4].

11. Karl Zimmermann, 'Vom Römerkastell Andernach zur mittelalterlichen stadt', *Rheinische Vierteljahrsblätter*, xix (1954), 317–340.

12. Henri Pirenne, 'Le fisc royal de Tournai', *Mélanges F. Lot* (Paris, 1925), 641–648.

13. Fleury, M., 'Paris' [no. 401].

14. Gregory of Tours, *Hist. franc.*, VIII, 31.

15. In any case the land was of very mediocre quality, and the main reason for its being abandoned definitively was that the Frankish kings found that it lent itself well to hunting. Cf Musset, L., 'Les forêts de la Basse Seine', *Revue archéol.* (1950), II, 84–95.

16. See the information on Picardy in R. Agache, F. Vasselle and E. Will, 'Les villas gallo-romaines de la Somme', *Revue du Nord*, xlvii (1965), 541–576; and in R. Agache, *Détection aérienne de vestiges protohistoriques, gallo-romains et médiévaux dans le bassin de la Somme* (Amiens, 1970).

17. Wieruszowski, Helene, 'Die Zusammensetzung des gallischen und fränkischen Episkopats', *Bonner Jahrbücher*, cxxvii (1922), 1–83.

18. Translators' note: the region of Trier may have been a special case: see E. Ewig, 'L'Aquitaine et les pays rhénans au haut Moyen Age', *Cahiers de civilisation médiévale*, i (1958), 37–54.

19. Notably in Salin, *La civilisation mérovingienne* [no. 308], II, 189–192.

20. See for example Heurgon, *Trésor de Ténès* [no. 432].

21. We have borrowed some of these points from R. Lantier, in *Journal des Savants* (1962), 98–99. See also R. Macmullen, 'The Celtic Renaissance', *Historia*, xiv (1965), 93–104 and *Enemies* [no. 70 *bis*], 361–362.

22. Rouche, Michel, 'Le changement de nom des chefs-lieux de cité en Gaule au Bas-Empire', *Mém. Soc. Nat. Antiquaires de France* (1968), 47–64.

23. Bach, Adolf, 'Zur Frankonisierung des deutschen Ortsnamenschatzes', *Rheinische Vierteljahrsblätter*, xix (1954), 30–44.
24. Arnold, W., *Ansiedlungen und Wanderungen deutscher Stämme* (Marburg, 1875).
25. Even though they are still not critical enough the best inventories are to be found in Gamillscheg, *Romania Germanica* [no. 316].
26. This is a résumé of several well-considered pages in J. Fontaine, *Settimane di studio* . . ., ix (1961), 217–221.
27. Bloch, Herbert, 'Ein datierte Ziegelstempel Theoderichs des Grossen', *Mitteilungen des deutschen archäologischen Instituts, Röm. Abt.*, lxvi (1959), 196–203.
28. Fiebiger-Schmidt, *Inschriftensammlung* [no. 3], no. 193.
29. Courcelle, *Les lettres grecques* [no. 85], 258–259.
30. Panazza, 'Lapidi e sculture' [no. 9].
31. Lugge, M., *Gallia und Francia* [no. 405].
32. Cf. the remarkable study by Ewig, 'Volkstum' [no. 400].
33. The contrast has been strongly and justly drawn by Riché, *Education et culture* [no. 97], 220–291.

Conclusion to Part I

1. We support the interpretation of K. F. Stroheker, 'Um die Grenze' [no. 78].

Introduction to Part II

1. Translators' note : cf. A. H. M. Jones *et al.*, *Prosopography of the Later Roman Empire*, I, *A.D. 260–395* (Cambridge, 1971).
2. Courtois, 'L'avènement de Clovis II et les règles d'accession au trône chez les Mérovingiens', *Mélanges L. Halphen* (Paris, 1951), 155–164.
3. The little *Manuel d'épigraphie chrétienne d'après les marbres de la Gaule*, by Edmond Le Blant (Paris, 1869), is out of date and in any case centres on an earlier period. The essay of Paul Deschamps, 'Étude sur la paléographie des inscriptions lapidaires', *Bulletin monumental*, lxxxviii (1929), 5–86, is rather superficial and is biased towards a later period. Both of them, annoyingly, neglect the texts engraved on objects found among grave goods which are so informative about the history of civilization.
4. This is the case, for example, with Barrière-Flavy's monumental compilation [no. 289].
5. 'Les chapiteaux de marbre du VIIe siècle en Gaule, style et évolution', *Cahiers archéologiques*, ii (1947), 69–85; 'Répartition des sarcophages mérovingiens à décor en France', *Études mérovingiennes* (Poitiers, 1952), 117–126; 'Les sarcophages de plâtre à décor trouvés autour de Paris', *Paris et Ile-de-France, Mémoires*, xi (1960), 257–269.
6. H. Zeiss's outline [no. 313] could provide a framework.
7. Of which *L'art pré-roman* [no. 299] is the starting point.
8. *Corpus delle sculture altomedievale*, published by the Centro italiano di studi sull'alto medioevo, of which the first volume (on Lucca) appeared in 1959.
9. A model of practical achievement for a limited area is M. E. Mariën, 'Les vestiges archéologiques de la région de Lesse et Lomme des origines aux Mérovingiens', *Ardennes et Gaume, monographie 4* (Brussels, 1961), as is Patrick Périn, 'Les Ardennes à l'époque mérovingienne', *Études ardennaises*, 1 (1967), 1–46
10. *Histoire littéraire* [no. 106] and 'Sur quelques textes' [no. 107].
11. For the art of the Merovingian period see Knögel, 'Schriftquellen' [no. 300].
12. On the lines of the slightly antiquated essay of the Abbé Tougard, *De l'histoire profane dans les Actes des Bollandistes* (Paris, 1874).

6: General Problems

1. However, see I. Opelt and W. Speyer, 'Barbar', *Jahrbuch für Antike und Christentum*, x (1967), 251–290.
2. cf. Gregory of Tours, *Lib. in gloria martyrum*, 24: *Romanes enim vocant nostrae homines religionis* (for they call the men of our religion 'Romans' [among the Visigoths]).
3. On the word *barbaricarius* see W. G. Sinnigen, 'Barbaricarii, Barbari and the Notitia Dignitatum', *Latomus*, xxii (1963), 806–815.
4. Some concise summaries which have paved the way are: Latouche, *Les grandes invasions* [no. 109], 13–15, and F. Thibault, 'Les impôts directs', *Revue historique de droit*, xxv (1901), 708–709, with a more penetrating glance at the subject in Ewig, 'Volkstum' [no. 400], 609 ff.
5. For this apposite observation we are indebted to Feist, *Germanen und Kelten* [no. 119], 52–54.
6. There are some references to this in Thompson, 'The Conversion' [no. 199], 7.
7. C. Sánchez-Albornoz, *Settimane di Studio . . .*, ix (1961), 437–438; 'El senatus visigodo', *Cuadernos de Historia de España*, vi (1946), up to 45–46; and especially M. Vigil and A. Barbero, 'Sobre los orígines sociales de la Reconquista: Cantabros y Vascones desde fines del imperio romano hasta la invasión musulmana', *Boletin de la Real Academia de la Historia*, clvi (1965), 271–339.
8. This has been studied in a masterly manner by Courtois, *Les Vandales* [no. 233], whose conclusions have been questioned by Frend [no. 235].
9. See Demougeot, 'Le chameau' [no. 428].
10. Cf. Ramsey Macmullen, 'The Celtic Renaissance', *Historia*, xiv (1965), 93–104, which deals mainly with the third century.
11. On the subject of the Frankish officers, cf. Stroheker, 'Zur Rolle der Heermeister' [no. 267].
12. See the bibliographical survey in R. Macmullen, 'Barbarian Enclaves in the Northern Roman Empire', *L'antiquité classique*, xxxii (1963), 552–561. For the Later Roman Empire, cf. Sirago, *Galla Placidia* [no. 76], 499–500.
13. The attack which Maurice Roblin launched on the traditional interpretation in 'Le nom de "Mauretania"', *Bull. Soc. Nat. Antiquaires de France* (1948–49), 171–102, is not very convincing.
14. For example, on reading Longnon, *Les noms de lieu de la France* [no. 321], 127–137. The theories of toponymists would carry more weight if they were backed up by archaeological evidence.
15. In particular see Sirago, *Galla Placidia* [no. 76], 369–398.
16. Courtois, *Les Vandales* [no. 233], 147–8; Ch. Saumagne, 'Les circoncellions d'Afrique', *Annales (Écon., Soc., Civil.)*, vi (1934), 351–364.
17. For an account of the facts see especially *Constance de Lyon: Vie de saint Germain d'Auxerre*, ed. by R. Borius (Paris, 1965). The English translation of Constantius's life of St. Germanus is to be found in Hoare, F. R., *The Western Fathers* (London, 1954). See also the commentaries by W. Levison, 'Bischof Germanus von Auxerre', *Neues Archiv*, xxix (1903), 95–175; Sirago, *Galla Placidia* [no. 76], 380 ff.; Loyen, *Recherches historiques* [no. 91], 45 and 65–6. On the Bacaudae in general see Thompson, E. A., 'Peasant Rebels in Late Roman Gaul and Spain', *Past and Present*, ii (1952), 11–23.
18. See Mazzarino, 'Si puó parlare' [no. 72 *bis*] and Erika Engelmann,' Zur Bewegung der Bagauden im römischen Gallien', *Festschrift H. Sproemberg* (Berlin, 1956), 373–385.

19. Translators' note: see Peter Brown, *Religion and Society in the Age of Augustine* (London, 1972), 184 n.l, for bibliography in English on this problem and for his comments on the work of Myres and Morris.

20. Sirago, *Galla Placidia* [no. 76], 501 ff., has an odd and unconvincing theory about the relations between the *laeti* and the Bacaudae.

21. At least this is the thesis which S. Mazzarino defends so vigorously in 'Si puó parlare' [no. 72 *bis*], 415–416.

22. J. Hubaux, 'La crise' [no. 65].

23. Courcelle, *Histoire littéraire* [no. 106], 55.

24. After R. Thouvenot, 'Salvien et la ruine de l'Empire romain', *Mélanges d'archéol. et d'hist. publ. par l'école franç. de Rome*, xxxviii (1920), 145–163, studied in particular by Courcelle [no. 106], 119–130. By way of contrast see F. Paschoud, *Roma aeterna: Études sur le patriotisme romain dans l'Occident latin à l'époque des Grandes Invasions* (Rome, 1967).

25. On this instructive episode see Chr. Lacombrade, *Synésios de Cyrene, hellène et chrétien* (Paris, 1951), 202.

26. Courcelle, *Histoire littéraire* [no. 106], 189–196.

27. A. Audin, *Rev. archéol. de l'Est*, iv (1953), 61–65 and *Bull. Soc. Nat. Antiquaires de France* (1952–53), 87–88.

28. Gregory of Tours, *Hist. franc.*, V, 17; G. Panazza, 'Lapidi di Pavia' [no. 9], inscr. no. 10.

29. Cf. Wenskus, *Stammesbildung* [no. 135].

30. See the suggestive article of De Vries, 'Königtum' [no. 141].

31. Wenskus [no. 135], 63–78.

32. Schmidt [no. 127], 29–41.

33. Courtois [no. 233], 215–218.

34. E. A. Thompson, 'The Settlement' [no. 198], 66–67.

35. Orosius, *Hist. adv. pag.*, VII, 43, 1.

36. See the beginning of F. Lot, *L'Art militaire et les armées au Moyen Age en Europe et dans le Proche-Orient*, I (Paris, 1946), which is really only a rough outline.

37. On these military problems see *Settimane di studio . . .*, xv (1967), *Ordinamenti militari in Occidente nell'alto medioevo*.

38. *Hist. Langob.*, II, 9.

39. See p. 147. The conclusions of M. Bloch, in 'Les invasions' [no. 105], remain, therefore, largely hypothetical. Cf. what Marius of Avenches says of 569: *Alboenus . . . cum omni exercitu . . . cum mulieribus vel omni populo suo* in fara *Italiam occupavit*. (Alboin occupied Italy with all the army, the women and the whole people 'in fara'.)

40. Especially by Fuchs, *Kunst der Ostgotenzeit* [no. 175]. See also D. P. Dimitrov, 'Les peintures murales du tombeau antique de Silistra', *Cahiers archéologiques*, xii (1962), 35–52.

41. Courtois, *Les Vandales* [no. 233], 229.

42. See E. Doblhofer's fascinating little book *Byzantinische Diplomaten und östliche Barbaren* (Graz, 1955). Translators' note: for a translation of Priskos's account see J. B. Bury, *The Later Roman Empire* (London, 1923), I, 279–288.

43. On this last point R. de Abadal has some penetrating things to say in *Del reino de Tolosa* [no. 182], 30.

44. A list of imperial ambassadors to Carthage can be found in Courtois, *Les Vandales* [no. 233], but he does not supply a commentary.

45. And were condemned in the end for religious reasons: Prosper Tiro, *Chron.*, ann. 437.

46. An incomplete list of the Roman advisers has been drawn up by E. Ewig, 'Résidence et capitale' [no. 445], 30.

47. For Gaul see Adrien Blanchet, *Les enceintes romaines de la Gaule* (Paris, 1907) and Albert Grenier, *Manuel d'archéologie gallo-romaine* (Paris 1931), I, 403–484.
48. Paulinus of Pella, *Eucharisticos*, v. 333–343.
49. Jérôme Carcopino, 'Les *castella* de la plaine de Sétif', *Revue africaine*, lix (1918), 5 ff.
50. Sidonius Apollinaris, *Carmnta* XXII, 101–129.
51. by P. Courcelle in *Settimane di studio . . .*, ix (1961), 644–645.
52. Notably that of Courcelle, *Histoire littéraire* [no. 106].
53. Like the hoard of goldwork found at Ténès: J. Heurgon, *Le trésor de Ténès* [no. 432].
54. The main sources have been collected together by Courcelle, *Histoire littéraire* [no. 106], 40–46, and 'Sur quelques textes' [no. 107], and by Sirago, *Galla Placidia* [no. 76].
55. *MGH, Epist.* I, 319.
56. Though the episode smacks of legend: Paul the Deacon, *Hist. Langob.* [no. 33], IV, 37.
57. Courtois, *Victor de Vita* [no. 427], 58 and 81; R. Louis, in *Saint Germain d'Auxerre et son temps* (Auxerre, 1950), 49 etc.
58. J. Fontaine, *Isidoro do Sévilla* [no. 86], 855–856.
59. There are some epigraphic references in Demougeot, *De l'unité* [no. 63], 525.
60. *CIL.*, IX, 1596.
61. Courcelle, 'Sur quelques textes' [no. 107], 32–34.
62. J. Werner, 'Zu den auf Öland und Gotland gefunden Goldmünzen', *Fornvännen*, xlvi (1949), 257–286.
63. For an account of the booty which did not move out of Africa see Courtois, *Les Vandales* [no. 233], 275. For the booty of the sacks of Rome in 410 and 455 see Courcelle, *Histoire littéraire* [no. 106], 35–40 and 152–154, and Courtois, *Les Vandales*, 194–196.
64. Olympiodorus, *Excerpta, Corpus Scriptorum Historiae Byzantinae* (Bonn), 470, frag. 22.
65. See Paul Allard, 'Une grande fortune romaine au Ve siècle', *Revue des questions historiques*, xli (1907), 5–30.
66. Courcelle, *Histoire littéraire* [no. 106], 69–74.
67. *Hist. adv. pag.*, VII, 43.
68. This fact has been reasonably well demonstrated by Thompson, 'Christianity' [no. 150] and 'Early Visigothic Christianity' [no. 171], 807.
69. One can still benefit from consulting H. von Schubert, *Geschichte der christlichen Kirche im Frühmittelalter* (Tübingen, 1917–21; repr. Hildesheim, 1962), and the shrewd observations of H. I. Marrou in *Nouvelle histoire de l'Église . . .*, I (Paris, 1963), 465–471. The history of German Arianism is being revived thanks to E. A. Thompson [nos. 171, 172 *bis* and 199]. The history of Western Arianism before the arrival of the Germans has been rewritten by Michel Meslin, *Les Ariens d'Occident*, 335–430 (Paris, 1967).
70. *Lex Burgundionum*, xii, 5.
71. To what extent was the prohibition applied in practice by the barbarians? It is certain that the princes always considered themselves exempt from it. For more details see Thompson, 'The Conversion' [no. 199], 32, *The Goths in Spain* [no. 199 *ter*], 58–59, and Courtois, *Les Vandales* [no. 233], 220, who have gathered together epigraphic examples of mixed marriages.
72. Imperial legislation said that heretical churches should be outside the walls. This was not always respected. Nevertheless several Arian churches in Italy were *extra muros* (Aquileia, Milan, Naples). Cf. Cecchelli. 'L'arianesimo' [no. 206].

280   *The Germanic Invasions*

73. 'Ce que nous apprennent sur le peuplement germanique de la France les récents travaux de toponymie', *Comptes Rendus de l'Acad. des Inscriptions et Belles-Lettres* (1945), 289–298, and 'L'anthroponymie française', in *Hommage offert à Ferdinand Lot* (Paris, 1946), 17–37.
74. This is the favourite thesis of Broëns, 'Le peuplement germanique' [no. 184].
75. One can see how the views of historians have changed since 1934, when Roger Dion, contrasting the agricultural systems of the north and the south of France and describing the line which separated the two in the eighteenth century, wrote 'It is like a battle front holding back a powerful German invasion from reaching the south and the west' (*Essai sur la formation du paysage rural français* [Tours, 1934], 150). The author has since modified his views.
76. Tacitus, *Germania*, 16.
77. This problem has been admirably treated at the beginning of Ewig's article 'Résidence et capitale' [no. 445].
78. His numerous articles are summed up in 'Praetorium, palais burgonde et château comtal', *Genava*, xviii (1940), 69–87, and 'Le Prieuré Saint-Victor, les débuts du christianisme et la royauté burgonde à Genève', *Bull de la Soc. d'Hist. et d'Archéol. de Genève*, xi, 3 (1958), 211–258.
79. The basic studies of this subject—which will be dealt with in more depth in another volume—are: Chénon, 'Le defensor civitatis' [no. 61]; Joseph Tardif, 'Les chartes mérovingiennes de Noirmoutier', *Revue historique de droit* (1898), 763–790; Jean Richard, 'Le defensor civitatis et la curie municipale dans la Bourgogne du VIIIe siècle', *Mém. soc. hist. dr. et inst. anc. pays bourguignons*, xxi (1960), 141–145.
80. The debate started off with the great work of the Swedish scholar B. Salin, *Die altgermanische Thierornamentik* [no. 156], which proposed the first acceptable classification of the barbarian styles in the north. The Iranian hypothesis is best set out by the Russian scholar Michael Rostovtzeff, for the first time in his great synthesis *Iranians and Greeks in South Russia* (Oxford, 1922). And, finally, the main supporter of the Roman hypothesis is the Swedish scholar W. Holmqvist, *Germanic Art* [no. 154].
81. Above all see Salin and France-Lanord, *Le fer à l'époque mérovingienne* [no. 309], and by Salin on his own, several less technical works: 'La métallurgie du fer au lendemain des grandes invasions', *Comptes Rendus de l'Acad. des Inscriptions et Belles-Lettres* (1956), 24–29; 'Les techniques de la damasquinure' [no. 307]; *La civilisation mérovingienne* [no. 308]. Translators' note: there is an account of the techniques of sword-making together with a study of literary texts relating to swords in Davidson, H. R. Ellis, *The Sword in Anglo-Saxon England; Its Archaeology and Literature* (Oxford, 1962).
82. See the texts assembled by Fontaine, *Isidore de Séville* [no. 86], 817–818.
83. Riché, *Éducation et culture* [no. 97], 237.
84. These very pertinent observations are from Fontaine, *Isidore* [no. 86], 833 and 843–846.
85. Cf. Riché, *Éducation et culture* [no. 97], 254–291, and his articles 'La survivance des écoles' [no. 98] and 'L'instruction des laïcs en Gaule mérovingienne au VIIe siècle', *Settimane di studio . . .*, v (1958), 873–888, and 'Enseignement du droit en Gaule du VIe au XIe siècle' in *Ius Romanum Medii Aevi*, Pars I, 5b (Milan, 1965).
86. Fontaine, *Isidore* [no. 86], 876, n. 4; *Vitas sanctorum patrum Emeretensium* [no. 423], 192.
87. Fontaine, *Isidore*, 880–881.
88. Riché, *Éducation et culture*, 184–185, has gathered together some significant texts relating to medicine.
89. See Kemp Malone, *Widsith* (2nd edn. Copenhagen, 1962).

90. Some reasonable surveys are to be found in Brady, *The Legends of Ermanaric* [no. 217] and Zink, *Les légendes héroiques* [no. 220].

91. Cf. Musset and Mossé, *Introduction à la runologie* [no. 148] and above all G. Baesecke, *Vor- und Frühgeschichte des deutschen Schrifttums* (Halle, 1940–50).

92. See the map by L. Musset, 'La conversion des Germains', in *Histoire universelle des missions catholiques*, I, (Paris, 1957), 109.

93. Joachim Werner, 'Waage und Geld in der Merowingerzeit', *Sitzungsberichte der Bayer. Akad. der Wiss.*, *Phil.-Hist. Klasse* (1954), I.

94. We shall be taking this up in the volume entitled *Le haut Moyen Age occidental*: *les pouvoirs*.

95. This is not the place to discuss these traditional attributions. Doubts have recently been expressed on the subject of the *Lex Romana Burgundionum* (cf. p. 211) and the *Edictum Theoderici*, which P. Rasi believes was drawn up by Gundobad, the *magister militum*, at Rome, but which A. d'Ors thinks is a text produced by the office of the prefect of the Gauls, which was established in Arles in about 460. (*Estudios visigóticos II. El código de Eurico* [Rome and Madrid, 1960]).

96. Cf. the restatement of the problem of the personality of the barbarian laws in Simeon L. Guterman's essay 'The Principle of the Personality of Law in the Early Middle Ages; a Chapter in the Evolution of Western Legal Institutions and Ideas', *Univ. of Missouri Law Review*, xxi (1966), 259–348.

97. A. Garcia Gallo, 'Nacionalidad y territorialidad del derecho', *Anuario de historia del derecho español*, xiii (1936–41), 168–264; cf. W. Reinhart, 'Über die Territorialität' [no. 196].

98. Alvaro d'Ors, *Estudios visigóticos. II. El código de Eurico* (Rome and Madrid, 1960); cf. by the same author 'La territorialidad del derecho de los Visigodos', *Settimane di studio . . .*, iii (1955), 363–408.

99. Wilfried Roels, *Onderzoek naar het gebruik van de aangehaalde bronnen van Romeins Recht in de Lex Romana Burgundionum* (Antwerp, 1958); see the review by G. Chevrier, *Bibliothèque de l'École des Chartes*, cxviii (1960), 206–209.

100. Which would explain why it 'does not seem effectively to have survived for long after the disappearance of the Burgundian kingdom' (Gaudemet, 'Survivances romaines' [no. 448], 160).

101. Fiscal institutions will be dealt with in the volume entitled *Le haut Moyen Age*: *les pouvoirs*; for an account of the urban institutions, see p. 200).

102. Declareuil, 'Des comtes de cité', [no. 621.

103. Bergengruen, *Adel und Grundherrschaft* [no. 393], 177–178.

104. See especially Rolf Sprandel, 'Dux und comes in der Merowingerzeit', *Zeitschrift der Savigny-Stiftung für Rechtsgeschichte, Germ. Abt.*, lxxiv (1957), 48–84; see also Dietrich Claude, 'Untersuchungen zum frühfränkischen Comitat', *ibid.*, lxxxi (1964), 1–79, and Bergengruen, *Adel und Grundherrschaft* [no. 393], 179–181.

105. E. Babut, 'Recherches sur l'administration mérovingienne', *Revue historique*, cxxxi (1919), 265–266.

106. The most vigorous attempt to clarify the situation has been made by F. Lot, 'Hospitalité' [no. 452], which is complemented by A. D'Ors, *El código de Eurico* (quoted in note 95 above), 173–184.

107. As far as Spain is concerned this fact has been wrongly called in question; but see A. García Gallo, 'Notes sobre el reparto de tierras entre Visigodos y Romanos', *Hispania* i (1941), 40–63; it is by no means certain that after 507 the Visigoths brought the system of *hospitalitas* with them from Gaul into Spain.

108. On the subject of possible prolongations of this proportion into the Lombard period, see p. 93.

109. *Lex Burgundionum*, XXXVII, 7.

110. *ibid.*, LV.

111. Thompson, 'The Visigoths' [no. 172], 119–120.

7: Regional Aspects

1. For the last examples of such pan-Mediterranean careers, see Courcelle, *Les lettres grecques* [no. 85], 299 n. 1.
2. The barbarian reaction to the Mediterranean world has not been studied. Contemporary research, being preoccupied with verifying or disproving Pirenne's thesis, has concentrated very largely on the economic aspect of the problem, and principally in the period from the seventh to the ninth centuries. Some information is to be found in Ensslin, *Theoderich* [no. 208]; Courtois, *Les Vandales* [no. 233], and Courtois, 'Les rapports entre l'Afrique et la Gaule au début du Moyen Age', *Cahiers de Tunisie*, ii (1954), 127–145. See also J. Rouge, 'Quelques aspects de la navigation en Méditerranée au Ve et dans la première moitié du VIe siècle', *Cahiers d'Histoire* (Lyons), vi (1961), 129–154.
3. Sirago, *Galla Placidia* [no. 76], 477.
4. Courtois, *Les Vandales* [no. 233] and Giunta, *Genserico e la Sicilia* [no. 237].
5. J. J. Saunders, 'The Debate on the Fall of Rome', *History*, xlviii (1963), 1–17.
6. The most vigorous attempt to sum up their main characteristics has been made by Stroheker, 'Die geschichtliche Stellung' [no. 133]. We follow him closely.
7. See, most recently, Wüst, 'Goten in Indien?' [no. 174].
8. Vasiliev, *The Goths in the Crimea* [no. 173], and Schwarz, 'Die Krimgoten' [no. 168].
9. See the examples in Zeiss, *Die Grabfunde* [no. 202], 126, and in Pedro de Palol Salellas, 'Hallazgos hispanovisigodos en la provincia de Jaén', *Ampurias*, xvii–xviii (1956), 286–292.
10. The study of the diffusion in Europe of the products of Visigothic culture has hardly started. See the thought-provoking suggestions of Jacques Fontaine, *Isidore de Séville. Traité de la nature* (Bordeaux, 1960), 69–83.
11. Broëns, 'Los Francos y el poblamiento' [no. 183].
12. The state of research up to 1947 is given by Heurgon, 'L'hypothèse du limes belgicus' [no. 278]; see also Faider-Feytmans, 'La frontière du Nord' [no. 275]. The impatience of Verlinden, *Les origines* [no. 285], 36–43 and the sarcasm of Stengers, *La formation* [no. 283], seem unnecessary.
13. J. Mertens, 'Oudenburg et le *litus saxonicum* en Belgique', *Helinium*, ii (1962), 51–62.
14. Ewig, 'Die civitas Ubiorum' [no. 258] and Stengers, *La formation de la frontière* [no. 283].
15. *Zeitschrift der Savigny-Stiftung für Rechtsgeschichte, Germ. Abt.*, (1935), 2; and particularly the preface to the edition of the *Lex Ribuaria* by Beyerle and Buchner (*MGH, Leges*, in-4°, III, 2 [1954]).
16. The idea is strongly expressed—but in a rather dubious context—by Bergengruen, *Adel und Grunherrschaft* [no. 393], 167 ff. The problem is taken up, in a more subtle fashion, by Bodmer, *Der Krieger der Merowingerzeit* [no. 394].
17. See the note by Jean Hubert, *Bibliothèque de l'École des Chartes*, cvi (1945–46), 140–142; for 'francisca', see G. Kurth, *Études franques* [no. 261], I, 42–43; for 'framea', see G. Must, 'The Origin of Framea', *Language*, xxxiv (1958), 364–366.
18. A reasonable idea of the limits of our knowledge can be found in Halphen, 'Grégoire de Tours, historien de Clovis' [no. 259].
19. Lot, 'La victoire sur les Alamans et la conversion de Clovis', *Revue Belge de Philol. et d'Hist.*, xvii (1938), 63–69.
20. B. Krusch, 'Die erste deutsche Kaiserkronung', *Sitzungsberichte der Bayer. Akad.* (1932), 1060.

21. 'Hengist, Horsa, Vortigern et la conquête de la Grande-Bretagne par les Saxons', in *Mélanges Bémont* (Paris, 1913); 'Les migrations saxonnes' [no. 347]; 'Valeur historique du *De excidio*' [no. 348]; 'Bretons et Anglais' [no. 350]; *Nennius* [no. 349].

22. 'Some Parallels' [no. 371], 469 ff.

23. *Language and History* [no. 343], 200 ff.

24. In *Dark-Age Britain* [no. 361], 112–122 and 108–111. For Vortigern, see Kirby, 'Vortigern' [no. 345 *bis*].

25. But even here a reaction is starting: see G. Ashe (ed.), *The Quest for Arthur's Britain* (London, 1968). Translators' note: see also L. Alcock, *Arthur's Britain* (London, 1971; Harmondsworth, 1973), and J. Morris, *The Age of Arthur* (London, 1973).

26. See A. R. Burn, 'Procopius and the Island of Ghosts', *Eng. Hist. Rev.*, lxx (1955), 258–261.

27. The most recent and most vigorous criticism comes from H. R. Loyn, *Anglo-Saxon England and the Norman Conquest* (London, 1962; repr. 1970), 24–26. See also Lethbridge, in *Dark-Age Britain* [no. 361], 116 ff.

28. Cf. K. Sisam, 'Anglo-Saxon Royal Genealogies' [no. 354].

29. Bruce-Mitford, *The Sutton Hoo Ship Burial* [no. 362], has all the essential material. On the date see Lafaurie, *Settimane di studio* . . ., viii (1960), 249.

30. C. V. Sutherland, 'Coinage in Britain in the 5th and 6th Centuries', in *Dark-Age Britain* [no. 361], 3–10.

31. J. P. C. Kent, 'From Roman Britain to Saxon England', in *Anglo-Saxon Coins: Studies Presented to Sir Frank Stenton* (ed. R. H. M. Dolley) (London, 1961), 1–22.

32. Macalister, *Corpus Inscriptionum Insularum Celticarum* [no. 12], and commentary in Jackson, *Language and History* [no. 343], 118–120, and G. Haseloff, *Settimane di studio* . . ., ix (1961), 477–496.

33. For the Life of St. John the Almoner see Grosse, *Las Fuentes* [no. 188], 412–413.

34. Apart from Haseloff (article cited in note 32 above), 480–483, see Ralegh Radford, 'Imported Pottery' [no. 486]; Allen Fox and G. C. Dunning, 'Some Evidence for a Dark Age Trading Site at Bantham', *Antiquaries Journal*, xxxv (1955), 55–67; A. Young, 'A Bronze Age Pin from South Uist', *ibid.*, xxxviii (1958), 92–94. Translators' note: see also C. Thomas, 'Imported Pottery in Dark-Age Western Britain', *Medieval archaeology*, iii (1959), 89–111, and Peacock, D. P. S., and Thomas, C., 'Class "E" Imported Post-Roman Pottery; a Suggested Origin', *Cornish archaeology*, vi (1967), 35–46.

35. Above all *L'émigration bretonne* [no. 497].

36. Falc'hun, 'Le breton, forme moderne du gaulois' [no. 492] and *Histoire de la langue bretonne* [no. 493].

Part III: Sources and Studies

1. See Introduction, Part Two, p. 155

2. The decipherment of the 'Visigothic slates' by Manuel GOMEZ-MORENO, *Documentación goda en pizarra* (Madrid, 1960), is still too uncertain for this work to be placed on the list of sources. See the criticisms of Manuel G. DíAZ Y DíAZ, 'Los documentos hispano-visigóticos sobre pizarra', *Studi medievali*, vii (1966), 75–107

3. More details on the legal sources are given in another volume in the 'Nouvelle Clio' series, *Le haut Moyen Age occidental : les pouvoirs*.

4. All references in the text are to the first edition of 1948.

Index